PHILIP MAZZEI:

Jefferson's "Zealous Whig"

Ink drawing of Philip Mazzei
by Filomena Puglisi
(From an 18th century miniature.)

PHILIP MAZZEI:

Jefferson's "Zealous Whig"

Translated and Edited by
MARGHERITA MARCHIONE

American Institute of Italian Studies
Eight East Sixty-Ninth Street, New York, N.Y. 10021
Printed in the United States of America

Book Design by Emilio Squeglio

Library of Congress Catalog Card Number 75-29945

ISBN 0-916322-01-7 Cloth
ISBN 0-916322-02-5 Paperbound

Marchione, Margherita, translator
Historical and Political Enquiries

Printed with a grant from the
New Jersey American Revolution Bicentennial
Celebration Commission

For Peter Sammartino and Sally, his charming wife

CONTENTS

PHILIP MAZZEI

Historical and Political Enquiries Concerning the United States of North America

THE HERITAGE OF THE PAST
IS THE SEED THAT BRINGS FORTH
THE HARVEST OF THE FUTURE

(Inscribed on the pedestal under the "Female Figure" on the side of the National Archives
building, Washington, D.C.)

PREFACE

by
Giuseppe Prezzolini

Word that Sister Margherita Marchione had agreed to translate a work hitherto unknown to the English language readership, did not come as a surprise; the whole time that I have known Sister, first as a student and later as a scholar, she has been enthusiastically contributing to the development of cultural relations between Italy and the United States. A better occasion could hardly have been offered her than that of translating a work by Filippo Mazzei. I regret that my age and commitments make it impossible for me to delve into the subject; I must be content with wishing Sister much success.

The writings of Eighteenth Century Italian adventurers make pleasurable reading; they are, as a general rule, clear, carefully reasoned and richly informative. In this regard Mazzei compares favorably with his fellow adventurers, Casanova, Cagliostro, Da Ponte and Gorani. His Memoirs continue to make enjoyable and lively reading, and I eagerly await the work Sister Margherita intends to offer the American public: Mazzei's reports from Paris and the letters he exchanged with the King of Poland.

It is to be hoped that the reader will find the following Historical and Political Enquiries Concerning the United States of North America *as entertaining, informative, and replete with brilliant observations as Mazzei's other works.*

As the Bicentennial of the American Revolution is celebrated, few works, I believe, can better take the reader back to that time of great risk and hope than does this one.

ACKNOWLEDGMENTS

I gratefully acknowledge the grant received from the New Jersey Bi-centennial Commission for the printing of this first volume of Philip Maz-zei's *Historical and Political Enquiries Concerning the United States of North America (Recherches historiques et politiques sur les États-Unis de l'Amérique septentrionale)*. Mazzei's Italian manuscript was translated and published in French in 1788; a year later it appeared in German. How-ever, the book was never printed in Italian or English. This edition con-tains all of Volume I except the section written by the Marquis de Con-dorcet: "Lettres d'un Bourgeois de New-Heaven [sic] à un Citoyen de Virginie, sur l'inutilité de partager le pouvoir législatif entre plusieurs corps" (Volume I, pp. 267–371).

As a Bicentennial Project it could not have been published without the additional financial help provided by the friends and organizations who have subsidized it: the Italian Cultural Foundation, the Columbus Citizens Committee, its Ladies Auxiliary, Heritage Bank-North, Morris-town, New Jersey, the Columbian Foundation of Newark, Unico Nation-al-Newark Chapter and District VI of New Jersey, Andrew J. Paradiso, Istituto Italiano di Cultura of New York, Leonardo da Vinci Society, Fort Lee, New Jersey, Tiro A Segno of New York, Italian Welfare League, Betty M. and Leone J. Peters Foundation, Frank Sinatra.

I am especially indebted to Dr. Peter Sammartino, Chancellor of Fairleigh Dickinson University, who first acquainted me with the impor-tance of the first history of the United States written by a foreigner, and to Mr. Vincent Visceglia, president of the Italian Cultural Foundation and chairman of the board of Summit Associates Corporation, who for many years has assisted me in the promotion of all aspects of Italian culture in New Jersey.

I wish to express my sincere appreciation to my dear friend and men-tor, Giuseppe Prezzolini, Professor Emeritus of Columbia University, for his kind words of presentation of this volume, and to Sister Filomena Pu-glisi for the ink drawing of Philip Mazzei.

I am also indebted to the many persons who have generously assisted

me in obtaining materials and information, reading the manuscript and making very valuable suggestions: Dr. and Mrs. Chester K. Frederick, Henri de Bonneval, Reverend Felice Sicheri, Claire Murray, Mario DeVita, S. B. Aiello, Dr. Cyril dos Passos, and Dr. S. Eugene Scalia.

For the many courtesies extended to me, I wish to thank the Reference Department of Fairleigh Dickinson University, Madison Campus, the Library of Congress, the New York Public Library, Columbia University Library, The University of Pennsylvania Library, The American Philosophical Society, The Historical Society of Pennsylvania, Dartmouth College Library, Princeton University Library.

As I acknowledge the gracious assistance of so many friends, I assume full responsibility for any inaccuracies or omissions that may not have been detected. No effort has been made to comment on the historical value of this publication. It is merely hoped that it will serve to help make known Philip Mazzei's contribution to the American Cause.

I have endeavored in this work to follow faithfully the French translation. At times it seemed advisable to correct the spelling of certain names and places; elsewhere, to indicate that this is how it appears in the French edition and, sometimes, to avoid confusion to use only the modern spelling. To render a more readable translation, the capitalization and punctuation have not been adhered to strictly. Brackets have been used whenever an addition to the text has been made. I have tried to be consistent with regard to symbols and format wherever possible. The footnotes in the text, taken from the original, are indicated by asterisks. The translator's notes, which appear at the end of the volume, are enumerated. As far as possible, the English texts of documents quoted have been consulted and only rarely have changes been made. The small Renaissance prints have been reproduced from the original text and are interspersed in order to give the reader a more authentic copy. All the illustrations have been added to help clarify Mazzei's position as a Citizen of Virginia and his influence on our Founding Fathers. Bibliographical references are given as found in the works consulted.

JEFFERSON'S "ZEALOUS WHIG"

The celebration of the Bicentennial should evoke the memory not only of the great Founding Fathers, but also of the numerous unsung heroes of American Democracy. Among these latter there stands Philip Mazzei (1730–1816) whose pen inspired and strengthened the colonists in their struggle for independence. To his dying day he repeatedly proclaimed himself a citizen of Virginia. It was there, under the pen name of "Furioso," that he exhorted the colonists to sever all ties with England. Back in Europe as Virginia's agent he sat down to write his *Historical and Political Enquiries.* . . . Its purpose was not only to give a first-hand account of events but principally to refute errors and misrepresentations circulating in books and newspapers throughout Europe.

Philip Mazzei was born in Poggio a Caiano, a small town near Florence, Italy, on December 25, 1730. He received a degree in surgery and practiced in Florence and Leghorn before going to Smyrna in 1752. But he soon realized that commerce rather than surgery was his calling. So, encouraged by friends, in 1756 he moved to London, where he organized the firm of Martini and Company, importers of cheese, wine and olive oil. In London he made the acquaintance of Thomas Adams and Benjamin Franklin, who urged him to come to America to introduce southern European cultures. Before he sailed for Virginia in 1773, he went back to his native Tuscany for the Grand Duke's permission to export the necessary materials and men. He brought along various agricultural implements and cuttings from vines, trees, and plants—(among these, the so-called Mazzei "corn" and "peas"). He was also able to induce some peasants and a tailor to accompany him. He bought acreage near the present Shadwell Station, about four miles east of

15

Charlottesville, adjoining Jefferson's *Monticello* and synonymously named it *Colle*. (¹)

As is to be expected in a man as versatile and gifted as Mazzei was, his interests and friendships in Italy, England, France, Holland, Poland, America were innumerable. Politically minded, he was among those (²) who were aware of the tensions between Great Britain and the Colonies and lost no time in espousing the cause of the Colonies.

The American Revolution was not the only political upheaval Mazzei witnessed. His involvement with other movements is known—the French Revolution, the Second Partition of Poland, the Industrial Revolution in England. The many documents available to us as well as his correspondence, give ample proof of how highly he was regarded by prominent men from all walks of life— philosophers, merchants, businessmen, politicians, diplomats, noblemen—who sought his friendship and advice. He was, to be sure, not without detractors, who did not, however, go unchallenged, as witness the notes jotted down in pencil by Mr. John Page on the back of a letter he received from Philip Mazzei dated February 11, 1775: "No one but a man lost to all sense of shame, and totally regardless of the truth could call . . . [Mazzei] an hypocrite. Mr. H. [Patrick Henry] himself knows him to be a person of the most unaffected piety and the strictest veracity and honor and most manly openness and candour. I can assure Mr. H. that it is not in his power to hurt . . . [him] in the opinion of the H. of B. [House of Burgesses] and that he is so universally beloved by the people that they would but ill brook such a dismission, as he wishes to

---

(¹) To prevent his mail from being intercepted, he asked the King of Poland to address it to him, not as Mazzei, but as *Baldassar de Colle*: "Je crois qu'il seroit mieux que mes lettres fussent dorénavant adressées à *Mr. Baldassar de Colle, Rue de Regard no. 30 à Paris*. Baldassar est un de mes noms de baptême, et Colle est le nome que j'ai donné, il y a 18 ans, à mon endroit en Virginie." (See Ciampini, *Lettere di Filippo Mazzei alla Corte di Polonia*, p. 256, January 4, 1790).

(²) Another Italian, Vincenzo Martinelli, left England in 1776 and published in Florence his *Istoria del Governo d'Inghilterra e delle Sue Colonie in India e nell'America Settentrionale*. During the Revolutionary War, there were newspapers in Italy such as the "Gazzetta Universale" and the "Notizie del Mondo" that carried articles about the Colonists and their determination to gain

bring out. They know his integrity and abilities and they have felt the good effects of them in his affairs.''

From his letters and memoirs we gather that Mazzei was active not only in his own Albemarle County, but also in Williamsburg and Richmond. Among his letters there is an especially significant one, dated June 29, 1776, and addressed to Patrick Henry, who at the time was at the Virginia Convention in Williamsburg: "In my private capacity I have endeavored to do all in my power for the Public Welfare. . . . I have sent to Mr. John Page a copy of the instructions I had prepared with the justification of the sentiments therein contained and with some reflections upon the English constitution, in which I endeavor to prove its weak basis and heavy errors, and my idea in regard to the nature of the best government which may be easily established by us, who have an opportunity that no People (from what we know from history) ever had before. I have desired Mr. Page to have them corrected and improved, and afterwards published. Would you do me the friendly favor of perusing them, and bestow your advice upon them before they are printed. . . .''

The letter to John Page, lieutenant-governor of Virginia, who was also a member of the Convention, makes it clear that the "instructions" consisted of a plan to create a new government. This letter of June 16, 1776, reveals not only that Mazzei submitted his writings to friends for correction, but also that he wished to remain anonymous: ". . . I would take it as a great favour from you, Sir, and from any of the Gentlemen, if I was to see upon the Newspapers, my sentiments not only put in good English, but even corrected and improved. . . . My composition is Italian with English words. You know that what is elegance in one language is sometimes nonsense in another. . . . As to the other papers, it is entirely owing to a very little remnant of modesty, that I don't desire you to publish that I am the Author of them. I am clear in my principles and I am ready to support them.'',

independence. Regarding Martinelli, Giovanni Schiavo (*Italian-American History*, Vol. I, New York: 1947, p. 480) writes: "more important to us for his dedication than for the data he gathered, for in that dedication to Don Lorenzo Corsini, Grand Prior of Pisa, he refers to 'the difference between England and her American colonies, which now have reached an impasse, the solution of which it is not easy to foresee'.''

During 1774-75, a year before the appearance of Thomas Paine's "Common Sense," Philip Mazzei published a series of newspaper articles under the pseudonym of "Furioso" in Pinkney's "Virginia Gazette." Translated into English by his good friend, Thomas Jefferson, Mazzei's writings sought to change the colonists' attitude toward Great Britain. He himself explains how he and Jefferson agreed "to publish a periodical sheet to be distributed by the gazettes, aiming to show the people the real situation and the necessity to prepare ourselves in order not to be caught by surprise in case of an attack. Since I knew the views of the Cabinet of St. James and particularly its leaders, we agreed that I would do the writing in my language and he would translate it into English."[3] In an article in the "Virginia Gazette" we read: "All men are by nature equally free and independent. Such equality is necessary in order to create a free government. All men must be equal to each other in natural law. Class distinction has always been and will always be an effective obstacle and the reason for it is very clear. . . ."[4]

A disciple, like Jefferson, of the French "philosophes," Mazzei in his *Recherches* repeatedly states that all men are born equally free and independent ("tous les hommes naissent également libres et indépendans"), as does the Virginia Declaration of Rights. Nowhere does he say, with the Declaration of Independence, that all men are created equal. However, in the chapter, "On the Right to Vote and to be a Representative," he adds that when it came to the right to vote and of being elected to office, this indisputable principle was not scrupulously observed. Mazzei recognizes that every citizen has an equal right to the benefits and honors of his country and cannot be deprived of them except for some crime. He considers such a deprivation "an obvious injustice to horrify anyone convinced that *all men are born equally free and independent.*"

In the same chapter Mazzei adds an interesting footnote: "It is with this great truth that the Declaration of our Rights begins. This foundation of American liberty contains all the principles necessary to preserve it. These principles are on the lips and in the hearts

[3] *Memorie della Vita e delle Peregrinazioni del Fiorentino Filippo Mazzei*, edited by Alberto Aquarone, Milano, 1970, p. 214.
[4] *Ibid.*, p. 479. (Fragments of writings published in the "Gazette" at the beginning of the American Revolution by a Citizen of Virginia.)

of all Americans, who have a religious respect for it. It is on this declaration that my hopes rest. As the clouds of old prejudices are dispelled, the pen of one wise and zealous citizen will suffice perhaps to provide an efficacious remedy for the greatest disorder. In the Thirteen States people read, and are avid for instruction. It will be enough to give proof of the transgressions of their representatives for the people to order them to do their duty." Here we see Mazzei's faith in free speech and the power of exposure, for he was aware that politicians were not above being corrupt or corruptible. In another passage his egalitarianism—as to freedom, sex, property—is apparent as he notes that "bias in favor of riches has no other foundation than ancient injustice and is very similar to that which, in various circumstances, exists in favor of the stronger sex. Anyone willing to rid himself of prejudices and become himself again, will not find any satisfactory justification for such discriminations." And as he was conscious of man's injustice to woman, so too was he of the injustice of man to man: slavery. He was for its abolition, but in a gradual way as best designed to benefit the slaves themselves. As a matter of fact, as agent of King Stanislaus in revolutionary Paris, he urged the king, who sympathized with the revolution, to grace with his name the roster of members of the Paris society for the abolition of slavery.

The agricultural undertakings for which Mazzei had come to America were shunted into the background by events of military and political importance. Like Jefferson who had promoted them, he was totally involved in the movement for independence. In fact, when the first danger of a clash between the colonists and the English arose, Mazzei was among those who enlisted. He joined the "Independent Company" of Albemarle as a private, together with Carlo Bellini (a fellow-Tuscan later professor of modern languages at the College of William and Mary) and Thomas Jefferson. As they marched on toward the coast, they were joined by young James Madison and his brother. Mazzei modestly relates that they wanted to make him a lieutenant, but that he declined the honor, saying that as a private he could still perform half the duty of an officer, that is give advice, provided the officers would listen to him. Whether or not the officers listened to him we do not know, but Jefferson did, later, when Mazzei wrote lengthy letters from France replete with advice.

The danger having been averted, Mazzei's company did not see military action and was soon disbanded. He writes that though

he did not go far from home, he was more occupied with political and military affairs than he was with his private enterprises. In his letter of January 11, 1777, to John Page, Mazzei states: "As I am preparing to march to the Continental Camp with as many volunteers as I shall be able to persuade, I must settle everything without delay." While appreciating Mazzei's desire to join the Continental Army, Patrick Henry, who was the governor of Virginia at the time, refused him permission to join the army, saying that he could serve our country better in matters of great importance than as a plain soldier. His pen was needed more than his sword.

Virginia was sorely pressed for money and army supplies. It was decided by Thomas Jefferson, Patrick Henry, George Mason, John Page and others, to send Mazzei as an agent to the Grand Duke of Tuscany, of whose sympathies for the American Cause they had been assured; for, as Jefferson wrote to John Hancock on October 19, 1778, "he possesses first rate abilities, is pretty well acquainted with the European courts, and particularly those above mentioned [Florence and Genoa], is a native of Tuscany with good connections and I have seen certain proofs of the Grand Duke's personal regard for him. He has been a zealous whig from the beginning and I think may be relied on perfectly in point of integrity. He is very sanguine in his expectations of the services he could render us on this occasion and would undertake it on a very moderate appointment."

VIRGINIA'S AGENT

When Mazzei's ship left the Virginia Capes early in 1779, it was seized by an English privateer and he was held prisoner for about three months on Long Island. On his way to Florence he stopped in Paris where he was presented at the king's court as Virginia's agent by his old London friend, Benjamin Franklin, who surely knew of the Grand Duke of Tuscany, if only as the purchaser, through Mazzei, of two specimens of the stove he had invented. And it was in Paris that Mazzei began to champion the American cause abroad not only by word-of-mouth but also by writing letters and articles such as "Why the American States Cannot Be Called Rebels," "The Importance of Commerce With Virginia," "The Justice of the American Cause."

Mazzei was commissioned by Governor Patrick Henry to ask the Grand Duke, Leopold, for a loan and supplies to aid in the war

against England. He was unsuccessful, but his faith in the final success of the American Revolution is seen in his letter of August 26, 1782, to the Grand Duke, which reads: "The ill-considered statements that England will never, at any cost, recognize America's independence, come from persons whose minds are distorted by passion, or who suffer from political shortsightedness, for it is quite clear that such a step, however hard it may be, is inevitable.

". . . America produces everything. By merely shifting the workers who are now engaged in the production of the immense quantities of raw materials that are shipped abroad, she can easily manufacture any article. If it is true that Americans prefer agricultural pursuits to any other, it must be remembered that that is due to force of habit and to the fact that they look upon farming as a more pleasant occupation. Furthermore, there are large tracts of excellent land which are very profitable. This project has been under consideration for some time. The writer was told that he was the first to propose it. The fact is that the writer made the proposal as soon as he received from Dr. Franklin the reply mentioned in his first memorandum. In that reply Dr. Franklin stated that at that time Congress had not even thought of entering into trade relations with European powers. The writer's proposal was submitted to Congress by Mr. Jefferson, whom I have repeatedly mentioned; Dr. Franklin expressed himself as holding the same opinion as the writer."

Others may have held the same opinion, but it was Mazzei's proposal that Jefferson submitted at a time when Congress had not yet entered into trade relations with European powers. Mazzei's letters detail the difficulties he encountered abroad, and also throw light on the character and work of many Americans and Europeans. He received letters from distant friends who gave valuable information in reply to his inquiries and helped the colonists in making important decisions during the war.

Mazzei himself speaks of the nature of his services as Virginia's agent in his report entitled, *A Representation of Mr. Mazzei's Conduct, from the time of his appointment to be Agent of the State in Europe until his return to Virginia*: [5] "He made it a point of confuting with his tongue, and still more with his pen, as long as the war continued, the assertions of the Enemy which might in any way prejudice, directly or indirectly, the American Cause. With

[5] Manuscript is in the New York Public Library.

that view he wrote constantly for the Newspapers of Italy and Holland. The pieces he wrote for Sovereigns, and other people in power, will perhaps show that nothing more could be said to impress them with the Justice of the American Cause, with the certainty of our success, and the advantages to be derived to the nations of Europe from our friendship and Commerce. The Ministers of our good and great Ally, have more than once manifested their approbation of the patriotic Zeal discovered in his writings to them, from the spring of the year 1780, till his return to America.

". . . One of his attentions was to procure, and send over every Intelligence, which might be interesting to America, as well as his conjectures expressed in a manner as to inspire confidence. His numerous connections in Europe, particularly among people in high station and rank, enabled him to become acquainted with secrets of great moment, and with the disposition of many people in power, to procure which he spared no trouble, nor the necessary expense of postage. And to such of them as might be serviceable to Congress he endeavored to convey them by means of Mr. John Adams, and other American patriots in Europe, whenever he could not do it in direct line. . . ."

The recognition given Mazzei by John Adams may be seen in his letter to Thomas Jefferson from Paris dated June 29, 1780: ". . . As far as I have had the opportunity to see and hear, he has been useful to us. He kept good company, and a good deal of it. He talks a great deal, and is a zealous defender of our affairs. His variety of languages, and his knowledge of American affairs, gave him an advantage which he did not neglect." And to Patrick Henry, on June 23, 1783, Adams states: "Mr. Mazzei has uniformly discovered in Europe an attachment and zeal for the American Honor and Interest, which would have become any Native of our Country. I wish upon his return he may find an agreeable Reception."

When Benjamin Franklin received Mazzei's Commission from the State of Virginia, he chose to withhold his credentials. He felt that the States should not have their own agents and that only Congress should be represented abroad. Mazzei was indignant at Franklin's action and did not hesitate to complain to both John Adams and Thomas Jefferson. Yet nothing could destroy Mazzei's love for America. Even his failure to obtain a consulship—a post he never obtained because only natives could be assigned to foreign service—did not lessen his devotion and zeal.

In a letter of May 19, 1780, Mazzei discussed finances, which

were in a state of confusion, with his friend Jefferson: "It is obvious that the European adventurers cannot, during the war, fetch from America but a small proportion of their Capital. My intention has always been to persuade them to leave the greatest part of it in our funds; which would be the means of interesting them in our welfare, and of taking a great deal of paper money out of circulation. The late resolutions of Congress tending to so great, and I hope advantageous, alteration in our finances, put me now entirely at a stand. I am not only unfit to propose anything, but likewise unable to give Satisfaction to any question on the Subject, until you favour me with a clear and thorough information of the whole, which I heartily wish may soon be the Case. I suppose that the States will adopt the plan recommended by Congress, and I wish that the collection of the monthly taxes may prove as easy near the end as I hope it will be at the beginning. It appears to me that the redemption of the currency of individual States becomes unavoidable at the same time; and if I don't mistake, our State is pretty well loaded with it. I hope however that the Sale of our back-lands, and British property will greatly alleviate the heavy burden. The Silence of Congress respecting the money borrowed by them from Individuals at 6 per cent interest, payable in paper-money, induces me to believe they had not as yet agreed on the resolution they should take about it. I expect that our State will follow their Steps in regard to our Loan office."

In 1783 Mazzei returned to Virginia, recalled by Governor Benjamin Harrison. Subsequently, the governor informed him of the decision of the Board in a letter of June 10, 1784: "I have laid your Narrative before the Council together with the several Letters and Certificates you enclosed me to support your demand against the State, and enclose you their advice on the Subject. Mr. Wood the Solicitor has orders to settle the account whenever you shall attend him, on whose report I will forward you a warrant for the balance that shall be due. . . ."

Filled with a sincere longing to remain in America, Mazzei wrote in Italian on June 3, 1785 to his friend Madison: "I am leaving, but my heart remains. . . . America is my Jupiter, Virginia my Venus. When I think over what I felt when I crossed the Potomac, I am ashamed of my weakness. I do not know what will happen when I lose sight of Sandy-Hook. I know well that wherever I shall be and under whatever circumstances I will never relent my efforts towards the welfare of my adopted country."

23

THE CONSTITUTIONAL SOCIETY

In this same letter Mazzei refers to the importance of the role of the Constitutional Society which he had been instrumental in founding and organizing. The members of this group had agreed to discuss problems relative to the welfare of the State before presenting them to the Assembly. John Blair, one of the framers of the Federal Constitution, was elected president. At a meeting on June 15, 1784, the following statement was added to a broadside signed by Mazzei, Madison, Monroe, Randolph, Henry, Page and other important leaders of the period: "The Society being persuaded, that the liberty of a people is most secure when the extent of their rights, and the measures of government concerning them are known, do declare that the purpose of this institution is to communicate by its publications such facts and sentiments, as tend to unfold and explain the one or the other." (6) We also know that Mazzei encouraged Elias Boudinot of New Jersey, Dr. Way of Wilmington and others to join. The original declaration confirms the conviction that Mazzei was a "propagandist" and believed in the power of the written word. It reads:

"We, the underwritten, having associated for the purpose of preserving and handing down to posterity, those pure and sacred

---

(6) The motion for this amendment was made by Mr. Randolph and seconded by Mr. Henry. At this same meeting Mr. Mazzei made the following motion which was seconded by Mr. Corbin:

Resolved, that the title of this institution be "The Constitutional Society".
Resolved, that the President make such notification of this institution as he may think proper.
Resolved, that in case of the necessary absence of the President and Vice-President, this Society may have a right to appoint a President, pro tempore, or Chairman.
As the intention of this Society is to be useful to the Community, and not merely to show a desire of being so
Resolved, that it is expected, that each member should send to the President, every six months, an essay, or problem, on some political thesis of importance, which, it is hoped, will be confined to the subject thereof; and that anyone failing in his duty, be informed by the Secretary that two essays, or problems, shall be expected from him during the next six months; and that any member, on second delinquency herein, shall not thereafter be considered as a member of this Society.

principles of Liberty, which have been derived to us, from the happy event of the late glorious Revolution, and being convinced that the surest mode to secure Republican systems of Government from lapsing into Tyranny, is by giving free and frequent information to the mass of people, both of the nature of them, and of the measures which may be adopted by their several component parts; have determined, and do hereby most solemnly pledge ourselves to each other, by every holy tie and obligation, which free men ought to hold inestimably dear, that every one in his respective station, will keep a watchful eye over the great fundamental rights of the people.

"That we will without reserve, communicate our thoughts to each other, and to the people, on every subject which may either tend to amend our Government, or to preserve it from the innovations of ambition, and the designs of faction.

"To accomplish this desirable object, we do agree to commit to paper our sentiments in plain and intelligible language, on every subject which concerns the General Weal, and transmit the same to the Honorable John Blair Esq. whom we hereby constitute presi-

Resolved, that notice of the meetings of this Society be given in the public papers, at least thirty days previous to the day appointed, and that seven members besides the President, or Vice President, or President pro tempore, be required to constitute a meeting.

Resolved, that candidates to become members of this Society shall be nominated by a member, at a meeting preceding his election or rejection, which shall be determined by ballot, by means of black and white balls, or beans, and that no candidate be admitted a member without the assent of three fourths of the meeting.

Ordered, that a committee be appointed to draw up rules for government and organization of this society.

And a committee was appointed of Mr. Patrick Henry, Mr. Richard Henry Lee, Mr. James Madison, jun., Mr. Philip (correct) Mazzei, Mr. Joseph Jones, Mr. Edmund Randolph, Mr. Alexander White, Mr. John Taylor, and Mr. John Breckenridge.

Ordered, that each member contribute ten shillings to defray the necessary expenses of the institution, and that the Secretary be appointed Treasurer of this Society."

Thus we see that three years before the Constitution was framed, Philip Mazzei served as chief organizer of its forerunner, "The Constitutional Society," whose historic function must have been "as preface to the basic law of the land." (See article by Bess Furman "Signed, Sealed—and Forgotten!" in *Daughters of the American Revolution Magazine*, LXXI, [1937], 1004–1009)

Abbé de Mably. In it Mazzei dwells on the nature of
and on the character of the people of the United
dministration and Education, on Freedom of the Press
. In Volume III, he continues the history of the colo-
es the Quakers, the climate of the United States, and
ith a confutation of the Abbé Raynal's allegations.
ontains a series of essays on the political, financial and
ions in the American Colonies. The chapter on Emi-
ranslation of Franklin's famous *Information to Those
Remove to America*. Other topics discussed are the In-
ry, The Society of the Cincinnati. A Supplement fol-
veral documents including the United States Constitu-
was declared in effect in March, 1789, although it had
in June, 1788. It concludes with the words: "Such
y reflections on the influence of the American Revolu-
t think I have exaggerated its importance, nor that I
arried away by the enthusiasm inspired by the noble
ve contributions this new nation makes to the world."
uable material and documents in these four volumes
historians of the American Revolution. An Italian,
wrote the first *History of the War of American Inde-*
1809, which was later translated into French and Eng-
rinted at least seven times. Carlo Botta mentions the
zzei in his Bibliography. Bernard Faÿ called the *Re-*
n accurate summary of the foundation of the thirteen
a truthful exposition of the economic troubles which
t a break between Great Britain and the Colonies. His
e devoted to the modern United States is very inter-
He showed how the example of the Americans, who
eir ideas of freedom from theory into practice, had
ould help European nations."(7)
did not intend his book to be a philosophical treatise;
opular exposition of the State Governments at work.
on important subjects was supplied by Thomas Jeffer-
dams, James Madison, Benjamin Franklin, and other
e time—men who had either authored the documents
ed their effect.

ionary Spirit in France and in America, New York, 1927, p. 203.

dent of the said society, with powers to congregate the members thereof, either at Richmond or Williamsburg whenever he may suppose that he has a sufficient quantity of materials collected for publication. It is further agreed, that it shall be a rule of the said society, that no publications shall be made till after mature deliberation in the convocation, it shall have been so determined, by at least two thirds of the present members."

Before leaving America on June 17, 1785, Mazzei gave power of attorney to Edmund Randolph, John Blair and James Monroe who were to settle his affairs in Virginia and New York. Later, in Paris he happily met his good friend Jefferson, who had succeeded Franklin as Minister to France.

RECHERCHES . . .

Mazzei's four-volume *Historical and Political Enquiries* . . . was written for the most part in Paris. The printing of it was begun there in 1786. We know that the quotation from Mr. Edmund Burke's petition to His Majesty of September 11, 1775, in Volume I, was sent to him in Paris by John Adams in a letter dated Grosvenor Square, December 29, 1785. After quoting the passage published in the *Remembrancer* concerning the proofs the Colonies had given of their affection for England, Adams then endeavored to encourage Mazzei to continue refuting those who were discrediting the United States abroad: "The 'Mercure de France,' the 'Gazettes de Deux Ponts,' 'D'Avignon,' 'De Bruxelles' which circulate in Paris, and all the gazettes of Germany teem with lies to our disadvantage no less than the English Prints. The strongest motive to them all, is the danger of emigration and as long as men prefer eating to starving, clothes to nakedness, and warm lodgings to the cold air, this danger will not cease, nor the fictions invented against it."

Mr. Faure, a member of the French Parliament, translated most of Mazzei's work into French. The Marquise de Condorcet translated the chapter, "De la société de Cincinnatus"; her husband, "Du général Washington et du marquis de la Fayette, relativement à la société de Cincinnatus (Volume IV, pp. 102–126). Condorcet also wrote a lengthy book review in two parts which appeared in the February 23 and March 1, 1788 issues of the "Mercure de France," concluding: "It is easy to recognize, through the

veil that shrouds the Author [who called hims Virginia"], an illustrious philosopher, worth the elevation of his character, to enlighten rights, and destined through the power of his ence on the happiness of his century and post

There were other reviews such as may spondance Littéraire" by Grimm and Dider "Allgemeine Literatur-Zeitung" of Octobe translation of the *Recherches* appeared in in 1789 with the title *Geschichte und Sta nigten Staaten von Nordamerica—Von ei* In the preface the German publisher wr guished in more than one favorable aspec have been published on the remarkab States against Great Britain. I find in it oughness, less empty declamation, and sions notwithstanding more moderatior pions of the American Revolution."

Mazzei begins the *Recherches* by low-citizens: "The prejudices I fou [state] governments and our present desire to blot them out; but I have wr an apologist. I have spared no effor have tried to indicate the degree of uncertain and, in matters of opini ments as befits a citizen of a free which follows he explains that he the first forms of government in t relationship to Great Britain. I cause of the Revolution. Then I duct of the colonies during a ve period—the space of almost two royal government and the creat

The work did not fail to m raries. Written with a definite thor's personal convictions a cusses chronologically the f teen original colonies. Addit ernment, The Right to Vote Cause of the Revolution. V

tio
gov
Sta
and
nies
con
Volu
socia
grati
Who
dians
lows
tion,
been
have b
tion. I
have b
and im
The
have se
Carlo B
pendenc
lish and
work by
cherches
colonies
brought a
fourth vol
esting.
translated
helped and
Mazze
but only a
Information
son, John
leaders of t
or experienc

(7) *The Revolu*

These patriots were among Mazzei's acquaintances when he was active in Virginia during the Revolution, prior to his going to Europe as Virginia's agent. He was also linked to another friend of Jefferson and hero of the Revolutionary War, Thaddeus Kosciusko, the Polish patriot who had volunteered and brilliantly distinguished himself in the Revolutionary War. He left America, already a free and independent country, to fight for the freedom and independence of his native land. And there he may have met his fellow-American by adoption, Philip Mazzei, who had entered the service of King Stanislaus (elected by the Polish Diet, not hereditary) to ward off diplomatically what Kosciusko tried to do by force of arms: the second partition of Poland. But they failed, as did the king whom they both served and who was admired by still another hero of the American Revolution, Lafayette. In a letter to Mazzei in Warsaw, Lafayette wrote from Metz on April 21, 1792, as follows: "If you are still so fortunate as to be with the King of Poland, I beg you, my dear Mazzei, to pay him the respects of a soldier of liberty, who does not flatter himself into believing that his compliments are pleasing to many kings of Europe, but who likes to express his gratitude as well as his admiration for the leader of the Polish Revolution." Jefferson too was an admirer of the Polish monarch, whose service he unhesitatingly urged Mazzei to enter, when the latter asked him for advice. [8]

As agent and unofficial chargé d'affaires of King Stanislaus in Paris, Mazzei's letters serve to illuminate a critical period of Polish history. Generally in Italian but with the coded parts always in French, this correspondence lends a special color to this period (1788–1793) as Mazzei reports on American affairs and on the French Revolution. Mazzei in his letter to the King, dated Paris, July 8, 1791, gently reprimands him: ". . . Your Majesty is most

[8] "Avendomene il Piattoli fatta la domanda, lo pregai di venir meco a pranzo da Jefferson, temendo che il mettermi a servire un sovrano potesse pregiudicarmi nell'opinione dei miei concittadini; ma Jefferson mi assicurò del contrario, dicendo che il re di Polonia era meglio conosciuto tra noi che in Europa, che era capo d'una repubblica, e non un re dispotico, e che passava per esser il meglio cittadino della sua patria." (See *Memorie della vita e delle peregrinazioni del fiorentino Filippo Mazzei*, p. 310.)

anxious to have little said of you. Your desire is chiefly due to your excessive modesty. In this connection I cannot but think of the reply of my friend Jefferson to the Marquis de La Fayette on the occasion, four years ago, of the unveiling at the Pretorial Palace of a bust of himself which the State of Virginia presented to the city of Paris. On that occasion Mr. La Fayette sincerely regretted all that was being said and written in his honor. Though his modesty led him to regret what was being done in his honor, he did nothing to silence the unkind remarks which are often due to jealousy and envy, and which frequently result in calumny. With apparent seriousness, he replied: 'The only way to avoid such embarrassments is never to do anything worth-while.' Jefferson was right. Good deeds cannot be ignored any more than bad ones; besides, it is not desirable to leave them in obscurity. All that can and should be done to offset the inconveniences that may result from the injurious reports is to be the first to bring the good deeds to public attention with discretion and through the most accredited channels. This is the chief reason why I have always desired to have prompt news concerning my Master and Poland.''

In December, 1791, Mazzei was called by King Stanislaus to Warsaw where he played an important role in trying to improve the finances of Poland, but conditions were so bad that nothing was achieved. Mazzei remained there until July, 1792, when he returned to Italy, establishing his residence in Pisa.

RETURN TO ITALY

Mazzei's correspondence at this time indicates that he was by no means considering retirement. In his letter of December 15, 1804, to his friend Jefferson he inquires about many friends, discusses politics—treaties, commerce, qualifications for certain appointments—and affectionately speaks of his only child, Elizabeth: "My dearly beloved friend, I have never doubted your kindness and your interest in my family. Therefore, I shall tell you that my daughter is both talented and very good-hearted, that she is eager to learn, is quick in understanding many things, is careful in her work, and always asks for explanations. Besides, nature has endowed her with a beautiful body; she is healthy, quite tall for her age; she has a well-proportioned and well-formed body, with a

pleasing countenance. The result is that she is naturally attractive to all. She was born on July 22, 1798."

While living in Pisa, Mazzei was arrested and tried in 1800 for political reasons, one of which was that he had been "one of the most zealous actors in the American Revolution." However, the case was dismissed and Mazzei resumed his letter and pamphlet writing, always hoping to return to his beloved America. His life was a quiet one. He wrote his *Memoirs* which are valuable as source material for the study of American, French, and Polish history. Although completed as early as September 24, 1813, they were published only in 1845–1846 at Lugano, Switzerland, by Marquis Gino Capponi.

Mazzei died at Pisa on March 19, 1816. With insight and accuracy, Mazzei's contemporaries have left us a very interesting verbal portrait in the obituary of the "Aurora" (Philadelphia). After a summary of his career, the article continues: "Mazzei was a distinguished politician. In principles he was a republican and a confessed enemy to tyrants, both of church and of state. His work on America furnishes ample proof of his adherence to the best principles in politics.

"He was possessed of a great ingenuity of character and simplicity of manners. His knowledge of mankind was extensive. He was profoundly adept in the science of human nature. Towards the United States his affections were entirely devoted. His principal consolation in the decline of life was derived from seeing that country flourish, of which he was proud to consider himself an adopted citizen."[9]

On learning from his friend Thomas Appleton of Mazzei's death, Jefferson wrote him on July 18, 1816, from Monticello: "He [Mazzei] had some peculiarities, and who of us has not? But he was of solid worth; honest, able, zealous in sound principles moral and political, constant in friendship, and punctual in all his under-

[9] Reprinted in the Richmond, Virginia, "Argus" on June 26, 1816. Also in Virginia, an article appeared in the "Norfolk Gazette and Publick Ledger" (June 25). It was here that Mazzei was recalled as the person to whom Jefferson had written some twenty years earlier, "the celebrated letter in which Washington and his friends were alluded to." Other newspapers in New York were the "Evening Post" (June 20), the "Columbian" (June 21), the "Commercial Advertiser" (June 24), and "Paulson's Daily Advertiser" (June 25).

takings. He was greatly esteemed in this country, and some one has inserted in our papers an account of his death, with a handsome and just eulogy of him, and a proposition to publish his life in one volume. I have no doubt but that what he has written of himself during the portion of the revolutionary period he has passed with us, would furnish some good material for our history of which there is already a wonderful scarcity. But where this undertaker of his history is to get his materials, I know not, nor who he is."

At the same time Jefferson wrote to Giovanni Carmignani, an Italian professor at the University of Pisa: "I learn this event with great affliction, altho' his advanced age had given reason to apprehend it. An intimacy of forty years has proven to me his great worth, and a friendship which had begun in personal acquaintance, was maintained after separation, without abatement by a constant interchange of letters. His esteem too in this country was very general; his early and zealous cooperation in the establishment of our independence having acquired for him a great degree of favor."

"Posterity is my child," Mazzei had written occasionally in his letters and memoirs. And although he is remembered and revered as friend and patriot, as well as the author of *Recherches*, no one has gathered all his correspondence in order to write a full-length biography.[10] Yet the historical value of Mazzei's connection with our founding fathers was recognized by George Tichnor, the well-known literary historian, who acquired some of his letters. He read them at a meeting of the Massachusetts Historical Society on January 29, 1852, commenting that they were "of considerable historical interest."

Close to Thomas Jefferson, John Adams, Patrick Henry, James Madison, George Washington and other great champions of American Independence, Mazzei himself, in his self-effacing way, promoted the American Cause. It may not be extravagant to say that he must be ranked as one of America's Founding Fathers.

In rendering tribute to Philip Mazzei and his love and devotion for his adopted country, we remember the many immigrants of diverse ethnic backgrounds who, as he did, have made priceless contributions to this new nation conceived in liberty.

---

[10] The work done by R.C. Garlick, H.R. Marraro, and G.E. Schiavo cannot be ignored and is acknowledged as important source material for this study.

principles of Liberty, which have been derived to us, from the happy event of the late glorious Revolution, and being convinced that the surest mode to secure Republican systems of Government from lapsing into Tyranny, is by giving free and frequent information to the mass of people, both of the nature of them, and of the measures which may be adopted by their several component parts; have determined, and do hereby most solemnly pledge ourselves to each other, by every holy tie and obligation, which free men ought to hold inestimably dear, that every one in his respective station, will keep a watchful eye over the great fundamental rights of the people.

"That we will without reserve, communicate our thoughts to each other, and to the people, on every subject which may either tend to amend our Government, or to preserve it from the innovations of ambition, and the designs of faction.

"To accomplish this desirable object, we do agree to commit to paper our sentiments in plain and intelligible language, on every subject which concerns the General Weal, and transmit the same to the Honorable John Blair Esq. whom we hereby constitute presi-

> *Resolved*, that notice of the meetings of this Society be given in the public papers, at least thirty days previous to the day appointed, and that seven members besides the President, or Vice President, or President pro tempore, be required to constitute a meeting.
>
> *Resolved*, that candidates to become members of this Society shall be nominated by a member, at a meeting preceding his election or rejection, which shall be determined by ballot, by means of black and white balls, or beans, and that no candidate be admitted a member without the assent of three fourths of the meeting.
>
> *Ordered*, that a committee be appointed to draw up rules for government and organization of this society.
>
> And a committee was appointed of Mr. Patrick Henry, Mr. Richard Henry Lee, Mr. James Madison, jun., Mr. Philip (correct) Mazzei, Mr. Joseph Jones, Mr. Edmund Randolph, Mr. Alexander White, Mr. John Taylor, and Mr. John Breckenridge.
>
> *Ordered*, that each member contribute ten shillings to defray the necessary expenses of the institution, and that the Secretary be appointed Treasurer of this Society."

Thus we see that three years before the Constitution was framed, Philip Mazzei served as chief organizer of its forerunner, "The Constitutional Society," whose historic function must have been "as preface to the basic law of the land." (See article by Bess Furman "Signed, Sealed—and Forgotten!" in *Daughters of the American Revolution Magazine*, LXXI, [1937], 1004–1009)

dent of the said society, with powers to congregate the members thereof, either at Richmond or Williamsburg whenever he may suppose that he has a sufficient quantity of materials collected for publication. It is further agreed, that it shall be a rule of the said society, that no publications shall be made till after mature deliberation in the convocation, it shall have been so determined, by at least two thirds of the present members."

Before leaving America on June 17, 1785, Mazzei gave power of attorney to Edmund Randolph, John Blair and James Monroe who were to settle his affairs in Virginia and New York. Later, in Paris he happily met his good friend Jefferson, who had succeeded Franklin as Minister to France.

RECHERCHES . . .

Mazzei's four-volume *Historical and Political Enquiries* . . . was written for the most part in Paris. The printing of it was begun there in 1786. We know that the quotation from Mr. Edmund Burke's petition to His Majesty of September 11, 1775, in Volume I, was sent to him in Paris by John Adams in a letter dated Grosvenor Square, December 29, 1785. After quoting the passage published in the *Remembrancer* concerning the proofs the Colonies had given of their affection for England, Adams then endeavored to encourage Mazzei to continue refuting those who were discrediting the United States abroad: "The 'Mercure de France,' the 'Gazettes de Deux Ponts,' 'D'Avignon,' 'De Bruxelles' which circulate in Paris, and all the gazettes of Germany teem with lies to our disadvantage no less than the English Prints. The strongest motive to them all, is the danger of emigration and as long as men prefer eating to starving, clothes to nakedness, and warm lodgings to the cold air, this danger will not cease, nor the fictions invented against it."

Mr. Faure, a member of the French Parliament, translated most of Mazzei's work into French. The Marquise de Condorcet translated the chapter, "De la société de Cincinnatus"; her husband, "Du général Washington et du marquis de la Fayette, relativement à la société de Cincinnatus (Volume IV, pp. 102–126). Condorcet also wrote a lengthy book review in two parts which appeared in the February 23 and March 1, 1788 issues of the "Mercure de France," concluding: "It is easy to recognize, through the

veil that shrouds the Author [who called himself just a "citizen of Virginia"], an illustrious philosopher, worthy for his genius and the elevation of his character, to enlighten men, to defend their rights, and destined through the power of his thought to exert influence on the happiness of his century and posterity."

There were other reviews such as may be found in "Correspondance Littéraire" by Grimm and Diderot in June 1788, and in "Allgemeine Literatur-Zeitung" of October 1, 1788. The German translation of the *Recherches* appeared in two volumes at Leipzig in 1789 with the title *Geschichte und Staatsverfassung der Vereinigten Staaten von Nordamerica—Von einem Virginischen Burger.* In the preface the German publisher writes: "His work is distinguished in more than one favorable aspect from many others which have been published on the remarkable revolt of the Thirteen States against Great Britain. I find in it more method, more thoroughness, less empty declamation, and many more severe expressions notwithstanding more moderation, than in many other champions of the American Revolution."

Mazzei begins the *Recherches* by addressing himself to his fellow-citizens: "The prejudices I found in Europe, regarding our [state] governments and our present situation, inspired in me the desire to blot them out; but I have written as an historian and not as an apologist. I have spared no effort to be accurate and truthful; I have tried to indicate the degree of probability of facts which are uncertain and, in matters of opinion, I have expressed my sentiments as befits a citizen of a free country." In the Introduction which follows he explains that he will give "a brief exposition of the first forms of government in the colonies in order to show their relationship to Great Britain. I shall show you what was the true cause of the Revolution. Then I shall sketch a picture of the conduct of the colonies during a very interesting and singularly critical period—the space of almost two years between the cessation of the royal government and the creation of the republican government."

The work did not fail to make an impression on his contemporaries. Written with a definite purpose, it sets forth clearly the author's personal convictions and sentiments. In Volume I, he discusses chronologically the founding and development of the thirteen original colonies. Additional chapters treat of Law and Government, The Right to Vote and to be a Representative, The True Cause of the Revolution. Volume II consists largely of a confuta-

tion of the Abbé de Mably. In it Mazzei dwells on the nature of government and on the character of the people of the United States, on Administration and Education, on Freedom of the Press and Religion. In Volume III, he continues the history of the colonies, discusses the Quakers, the climate of the United States, and concludes with a confutation of the Abbé Raynal's allegations. Volume IV contains a series of essays on the political, financial and social conditions in the American Colonies. The chapter on Emigration is a translation of Franklin's famous *Information to Those Who Would Remove to America.* Other topics discussed are the Indians, Slavery, The Society of the Cincinnati. A Supplement follows with several documents including the United States Constitution, which was declared in effect in March, 1789, although it had been ratified in June, 1788. It concludes with the words: "Such have been my reflections on the influence of the American Revolution. I do not think I have exaggerated its importance, nor that I have been carried away by the enthusiasm inspired by the noble and impressive contributions this new nation makes to the world."

The valuable material and documents in these four volumes have served historians of the American Revolution. An Italian, Carlo Botta, wrote the first *History of the War of American Independence* in 1809, which was later translated into French and English and reprinted at least seven times. Carlo Botta mentions the work by Mazzei in his Bibliography. Bernard Faÿ called the *Recherches* "an accurate summary of the foundation of the thirteen colonies and a truthful exposition of the economic troubles which brought about a break between Great Britain and the Colonies. His fourth volume devoted to the modern United States is very interesting. . . . He showed how the example of the Americans, who translated their ideas of freedom from theory into practice, had helped and would help European nations."[7]

Mazzei did not intend his book to be a philosophical treatise; but only a popular exposition of the State Governments at work. Information on important subjects was supplied by Thomas Jefferson, John Adams, James Madison, Benjamin Franklin, and other leaders of the time—men who had either authored the documents or experienced their effect.

(7) *The Revolutionary Spirit in France and in America*, New York, 1927, p. 203.

These patriots were among Mazzei's acquaintances when he was active in Virginia during the Revolution, prior to his going to Europe as Virginia's agent. He was also linked to another friend of Jefferson and hero of the Revolutionary War, Thaddeus Kosciusko, the Polish patriot who had volunteered and brilliantly distinguished himself in the Revolutionary War. He left America, already a free and independent country, to fight for the freedom and independence of his native land. And there he may have met his fellow-American by adoption, Philip Mazzei, who had entered the service of King Stanislaus (elected by the Polish Diet, not hereditary) to ward off diplomatically what Kosciusko tried to do by force of arms: the second partition of Poland. But they failed, as did the king whom they both served and who was admired by still another hero of the American Revolution, Lafayette. In a letter to Mazzei in Warsaw, Lafayette wrote from Metz on April 21, 1792, as follows: "If you are still so fortunate as to be with the King of Poland, I beg you, my dear Mazzei, to pay him the respects of a soldier of liberty, who does not flatter himself into believing that his compliments are pleasing to many kings of Europe, but who likes to express his gratitude as well as his admiration for the leader of the Polish Revolution." Jefferson too was an admirer of the Polish monarch, whose service he unhesitatingly urged Mazzei to enter, when the latter asked him for advice. (8)

As agent and unofficial chargé d'affaires of King Stanislaus in Paris, Mazzei's letters serve to illuminate a critical period of Polish history. Generally in Italian but with the coded parts always in French, this correspondence lends a special color to this period (1788–1793) as Mazzei reports on American affairs and on the French Revolution. Mazzei in his letter to the King, dated Paris, July 8, 1791, gently reprimands him: ". . . Your Majesty is most

---

(8) "Avendomene il Piattoli fatta la domanda, lo pregai di venir meco a pranzo da Jefferson, temendo che il mettermi a servire un sovrano potesse pregiudicarmi nell'opinione dei miei concittadini; ma Jefferson mi assicurò del contrario, dicendo che il re di Polonia era meglio conosciuto tra noi che in Europa, che era capo d'una repubblica, e non un re dispotico, e che passava per esser il meglio cittadino della sua patria." (See *Memorie della vita e delle peregrinazioni del fiorentino Filippo Mazzei*, p. 310.)

anxious to have little said of you. Your desire is chiefly due to your excessive modesty. In this connection I cannot but think of the reply of my friend Jefferson to the Marquis de La Fayette on the occasion, four years ago, of the unveiling at the Pretorial Palace of a bust of himself which the State of Virginia presented to the city of Paris. On that occasion Mr. La Fayette sincerely regretted all that was being said and written in his honor. Though his modesty led him to regret what was being done in his honor, he did nothing to silence the unkind remarks which are often due to jealousy and envy, and which frequently result in calumny. With apparent seriousness, he replied: 'The only way to avoid such embarrassments is never to do anything worth-while.' Jefferson was right. Good deeds cannot be ignored any more than bad ones; besides, it is not desirable to leave them in obscurity. All that can and should be done to offset the inconveniences that may result from the injurious reports is to be the first to bring the good deeds to public attention with discretion and through the most accredited channels. This is the chief reason why I have always desired to have prompt news concerning my Master and Poland.''

In December, 1791, Mazzei was called by King Stanislaus to Warsaw where he played an important role in trying to improve the finances of Poland, but conditions were so bad that nothing was achieved. Mazzei remained there until July, 1792, when he returned to Italy, establishing his residence in Pisa.

RETURN TO ITALY

Mazzei's correspondence at this time indicates that he was by no means considering retirement. In his letter of December 15, 1804, to his friend Jefferson he inquires about many friends, discusses politics—treaties, commerce, qualifications for certain appointments—and affectionately speaks of his only child, Elizabeth: "My dearly beloved friend, I have never doubted your kindness and your interest in my family. Therefore, I shall tell you that my daughter is both talented and very good-hearted, that she is eager to learn, is quick in understanding many things, is careful in her work, and always asks for explanations. Besides, nature has endowed her with a beautiful body; she is healthy, quite tall for her age; she has a well-proportioned and well-formed body, with a

CHRONOLOGY

1730: Born at Poggio a Caiano, Tuscany, on December 25.

1736: Attends schools in Prato and Florence.

1747: Is medical student at Santa Maria Nuova Hospital, Florence.

1750: Departs for Leghorn.

1752: Leaves for Smyrna with Dr. Salinas in August.

1756: Arrives in London on March 3.

1757: Returns to Tuscany for brief visit.

1764: Opens a shop in London.

1765: Returns to Italy.

1766: Meets Franklin, Thomas Adams, and other Americans in London.

1771: Presents outline of plan for introducing into the colonies of Great Britain in North America the different cultures of Europe.

1773: Prepares for departure for Virginia.
Leaves Leghorn with Madame Marie Hautefeuille Petronille Martin and her daughter on September 2.
Arrives in November on the frigate "Triumph."

1774: Marries Madame Martin.
Is elected a vestryman of St. Ann's Parish, to care for poor. Publishes articles in Pinkney's "Virginia Gazette."
Presents a Proposal for forming a company or partnership for the purpose of raising and making wine, oil, agruminous plants, and silk.

1775: Joins the "Independent Company" of Albemarle as a private.

1778: Is proposed by Jefferson as Virginia's Agent in Europe.

1779: Signs oath of allegiance to Virginia on April 21.
Is taken prisoner by an English privateer on June 20, and forced to live in New York for three months.
Sails with his family for Cork, Ireland and reaches Nantes, France in November.

1780: Goes to Italy from Paris in June.

1782: Leaves Florence in November for Holland.
Arrives in Amsterdam in December.

1783: Visits The Hague, Leyden, Rotterdam, Brussels, Lille and returns
to Paris in May.
Goes to Lyons, Montpellier, and Toulouse.
Arrives at Hampton, Virginia in November.
1784: Is paid by Virginia for his services to the State.
Is instrumental in organizing "The Constitutional Society."
1785: Sails from New York on June 17 and arrives in Paris on July 22.
1786: Goes to Holland in January and returns to Paris in March.
1788: Publishes four volumes of *Recherches* . . . in Paris.
Becomes agent in Paris of King Stanislaus of Poland.
1789: His *Recherches* . . . appear in German.
Is one of the founders of the "Club of 1789" and its secretary of
foreign correspondence.
1791: Leaves Paris for Warsaw.
Is granted citizenship by the Polish Diet.
1792: Participates at the celebration of the first anniversary of the granting of the Polish constitution in Warsaw.
Goes to Vienna and then to Pisa, Italy.
1796: Marries Antonia Antoni.
1798: His only child Elisabeth is born on July 23.
1802: Leaves for St. Petersburg on April 12, and arrives on June 14.
Remains three months in Russia.
Returns to Pisa.
1805: Goes to Florence and Rome in July, at the request of Jefferson, to
engage two Italian sculptors to work in Washington, D.C.
1813: Completes his *Memoirs* on September 24.
1814: Writes his last letter to Jefferson.
Executes his last will on December 3.
1816: Dies in Pisa on March 19.

Garden and old Church of Buonistallo. *(Courtesy, Comune di Poggio a Caiano)*

Philip Mazzei's Baptismal Certificate, December 25, 1730, Poggio a Caiano. *(Courtesy, Comune di Poggio a Caiano)*

Letter of Philip Mazzei, Surrey Street, London, England, dated October 6, 1772, and addressed to Thomas Adams at Richmond on James River, in Virginia. *(Courtesy, Virginia Historical Society)*

Dear Sir,   Surry Str.t 6. October 1772.

    Translation of a paragraph of a letter from Bro=
thers Maggei dated Leghorn 14. Sept. 1772.

"As to wheat we may tell you, that at present it is
"here a very good Article, & is supposed it will conti-
"nue to be so; the wheat of Philadelphia would
"sell now 21. livres per bag, & that of Maryland
"19 ½ . You may encourage your friends to send some
"cargoes here, & if you take a share in them you
"will certainly do right, because in Tuscany the
"harvest has failed. Think of it seriously, & go
"about it without Loss of time, as orders have been
"sent from hence for speculation. We don't know if they
"will be executed or not, but let it be as it may, it
"must always turn to a good account. If any body
"pleases to direct them to us we will do all our endea=
"vours for their interest, & they may draw, if they chuse, for part
"of the value."

I send you this by the New-york packet, & shall send
the copy by every ship that goes to America. I shall
set out next week, but will leave the copies; it is
of to great consequence. According to the prices you
told me, there would be a proffit at 14. livres per bag.
It is scarse every where, & the profit is certain at all
events. Pray, send 3 or four cargoes of it directly, &
let you & I have as much concern in them as possible.
You see by the above that we may have money ad=
vanced by my relations if we chuse. Consider, my
dear Sir, that this is the most favourable opportunity
it could happen to answer all our purposes. I have
no time at present to write about other subjects. I
am,   Your most affectione.
most dear Sir,   Humble St. Ph. Maggei.

Most dear Sir,

Florence 12. April 1773:

You must ^have^ known of Mr. Griffin before the receiving of this
in what unhappy situation he left me with Mrs. Martini &
her daughter. I find myself still abbandon'd by my friends in Lon=
don. Dr. Fothergill said to me that his opinion was ^that^ the plan
could not be executed ^with so small a sum^ & declined advancing a farthing towards
it, till the subscription is full. Mr. Brown, who found then
Dr. Fothergill's behaviour very odd, now makes use of the same
excuse, & has refused to accept my draft of Mr. Neave's order
for his £.100. subscription. This is not all; he never wrote me
a sillable since I left London, never answer'd my letters, left
me entirely in the dark, nor even gave me notice of £.50.
he recd. of Count Bruehl long ago. What do you think, my
dear friend, of Mr. Brown, & the Doctor? I say that this world
is a strange Theatre, & Mankind the worse set of animals,
that performs upon it. The Dr. a few days before the above
conversation had agreed to advance the £.100; & was the
first to propose that the Plan should be executed in proportion
to the present subscription, & increased as the new subscri=
bers came in. Mr. Chamier paid £.50. in my hands before I
left London, & has now accepted my draft for the other 50.
Mr. Neave has desired me to draw upon him ^now^ for 50, & for
the other monets from Virginia. I have been obliged to leave
many hundreds to ^be^ received by Mr. Johnson, Mr. Neave's favorite
clerk & friend, & he has not yet been able to receive £.30.
However in spite of my miserable situation I have not lost my
courage. I had 2. conferences with the GrandDuke, & have obtained
what I hope will give you pleasure in the next page.

First page of a three-page letter of Philip Mazzei, Florence, Italy, dated April 12, 1773, and addressed to Thomas Adams in which Mazzei comments on his financial plight and his efforts to obtain certain concessions from officials in Italy prior to coming to Virginia. (Courtesy, *Virginia Historical Society*)

Most Dear Friend,   Florence 6. August 1773.

I hope that my last of the 25.ᵈ July may have induced you to engage all your best friends in sending wheat to Leghorn, & that you will take as good share in each cargo yourself. I must not tell you that there is a good prospect of doing well; there is a certainty, the prospect is of doing exceedingly well. But you must, my dear friend, spare no trouble in procuring that it may be of the very best, & well cleaned. Mr. Celesia, who mr. Griffin knows to be a very sensible gentleman & well conversant in this Article, writes me from Genoa, that the Philadelphia is from 4. to 8. ⅌ cent heavier than the Virginia Wheat. This proceeds that at Philadelphia as well as at New York they take more pains in cleaning it. Two are the good qualities that are requisite in wheat, & which will make it sell at more advantage. It must be heavy & make white bread. Yours will be equal at least to any other if you spare no trouble in cleaning it, especially from a great quantity of wild things that are like little onions. The cleaner it is the most heavier it must be. This is the year in which you must establish in the mediterraneum the good opinion of the Virginia Wheat, besides the great profit that will enjoy every one that will be concerned in it. I cannot prescribe the sum I would be concerned in

First, fourth and fifth pages of a letter about business matters from Philip Mazzei to Thomas Adams, dated August 6, 1773. *(Courtesy, Virginia Historical Society)*

agree 2 to sail immediately for our blessed Land, where in the most humble state I hope to enjoy that
happines, which I should not find out of it in the
most elevate situation in life. If this should fail,
I dont Know whether it would be more prudent
for me to go to you upon the first ship that comes with fish about the beginning of November,
as I wrote to you in my last, or to expect the
arrival of the wheat. Was I certain that you
would take my advice, I think I should stay, but
the uncertainty of it 2 the desire of being
with you make me incline to sail by the first
opportunity whatsoever. I would have gone
to any other Port in the Mediterraneum before
now to seake for a passage, but it would have
costed me too great an expence without a
certainty. I have told you my present situation, 2 in
my last I gave you a hint of disappointments 2 misfortunes that have reduced me very low, but I
would not have you be in the least uneasiness
for me. I hope you will beleave that I speake
from my hart. Know then, my dear friend, that
I want no courage, that I want nothing else but
to be in Virginia, that I could not bear the idea
of being obliged to any body for my subsistance, 2
that nobody will be happyer than I shall if even

I should be left without a farthing as long I shall be able to get my bread in any hono=rable way whatsoever. I wrote to you some time ago that I have obtain'd some privileges from the Grand-Duke, especially that of exporting from His Estates at all times any quantity & quali=ty of cuttings, seeds, plants, & trees to America, which will easely produce the wellfare of Vir=ginia if you lose no time about it, as I hope to prove to you by word, & will not attempt to do it by letter. I mention'd to His Royal Highness the corrispondence that may be continual on account of the wheat trade, which he likes very well. Tuscany has not grown this year wheat for 4 months; nothwistanding a great quantity of it has been exported to Genoa & France at such price, that if you had here now 10 or 12 cargoes of it you would get at least 30 ⅌ cent profit. The Pope has made it hanging matter this year the expor=tation of a half bushel of it from his estates. We usually were supplied from Barbary & Egypt; & now on account of the intestine war in Egypt they send there wheat from Barbary. I will end by telling you, that Leghorn will be a very good market for you till the new Crop, & that you may send 20; or 30. cargoes as well as one. Take my advice, present my compliments to your Brother, Mr. Griffin, & Mr. Dooley, & beleave me for ever, most dear Friend,   Your sincere & Affect. Servant Ph. Mazzei

Title page of bound volume containing Mazzei's defense of Baretti. *(Courtesy, British Museum, London)*

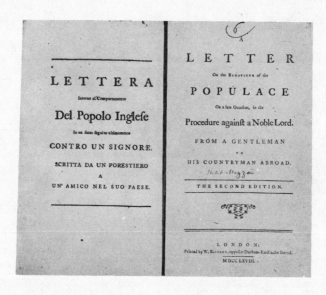

Title page of the second edition of one of Mazzei's early pamphlets, on which Mazzei had written his name in ink. *(Courtesy, Library of Congress)*

THURSDAY, December 4, 1774.   THE   NUMBER

VIRGINIA GAZETTE.

OPEN TO ALL PARTIES, BUT INFLUENCED BY NONE.

WILLIAMSBURG: PRINTED BY   JOHN PINKNEY,
FOR THE BENEFIT OF   CLEMENTINA RIND'S CHILDREN.

All Persons may be supplied with this GAZETTE at 12 s. 6 d. a Year. ADVERTISEMENTS, of a moderate Length, are inserted for 3 s. the first Week,
and 2 s. each Time after; long ones in Proportion.——PRINTING WORK, of every Kind, executed with Care and Dispatch.

WILLIAMSBURG, *December* 2.

The Lucy, Driver, from Salem, and the Triumph
Frigate, Rogers, from Leghorn, are arrived in James
river; in the latter, we hear, many gentlemen came
paffengers, in order to fettle and cultivate V I N E S
in this colony.

Announcement of Mazzei's arrival in America which appeared in the December 2, 1773, issue of the "Virginia Gazette." *(Courtesy, Colonial Williamsburg Foundation, Williamsburg, Va.)*

THE ship TRIUMPH will certainly fail for *London* in fix weeks,
agreeable to charter, and will take in tobacco, on liberty of con-
fignment, at 8 l. fterling per ton. Any perfon inclinable to ship tobacco
in her will be pleafed to fend their orders to Mr. *James Donald* at *Man-
chefter*, to Mr. *Charles Duncan* at *Blandford*, to captain *Rogers* at *Bermuda Hundred*, or to the fubfcriber at *Curle's*, who will be extremely
obliged by the affiftance of his friends.

    3   PHILIP MAZZEI.

"The Triumph" Mazzei's chartered ship announced in the "Virginia Gazette," July 28,
1774. *(Courtesy, Colonial Williamsburg Foundation, Williamsburg, Va.)*

43

Mazzei's home, "Colle," Charlottesville, Virginia, as it appeared in 1933. *(Courtesy, Richard C. Garlick)*

Sirs,   Richmond 7. December 1773.

I had the honour to deliver to the Academies
of Turin & Bologna in Italy & to the Grand Duke
of Tuscany the first volume of the Transactions of
the American Philosophical Society, which Dr. Franklin
gave me for that purpose in London. Inclosed you will
find the answers from Bologna & Florence, & the copy
of that from Turin as the original of it is in one of
the 4. volumes I had from that Accademy for the
American Society. The said 4. volumes I shall take
the first opportunity to forward to you as soon as you
will please to let me know by what channel I am to
send them. I have likewise 5. pamphlets written by
Mr. Fontana, who has written many more, & every
one containing some discoveries, but he could not find
the others at that time & has promised to send them
by the first opportunity. I shall reside in Virginia, &

45

as I have engaged to forward to you whatever may be hereafter committed to my care from that part of the World, so I shall esteem it a particular honour at all times to be employed by the American Philosophical Society in the like service. I am with profound respect,

Your most Obedient
& most Humble Servant
Philip Mazzei

Philip Mazzei
Richmond Dec 1773

Advising that he had from
Dr Franklin remitted the 1st
Vol to the Societies of
　　Bologna ✓
　　Turin ✓
　　Florence
& had the 4 Vol of the
　　Turin Transactions

Mazzei's letter to the American Philosophical Society, from Richmond, December 7, 1773. *(Courtesy, American Philosophical Society)*

Caro Amico   Virginia 10. Febb. 1774.

La scarsezza di tempo non mi permette di scriver molto.
Vi scrissi ai 25. Xbre per la via di Londra, e in conseguenza spero che sarete pronto a partire. Il Latore è il
Cap.no che condusse me, e condurrà voi. Vi mando l'inclusa aperta, affinchè la leggiate, e potrete poi consegnarla
così, o sigillarla, secondo il vostro genio. Portate con voi
qualche mazzo di minchiate, e qualche schioppo da andare a caccia. Sopra una dozzina di violini dai 3 agli 8.
ruspi l'uno ci sarebbe da guadagnar bene. Per il papag-
gio di tutti voi altri ò dato ordine al Sig.r Bettoia a
Livorno che provveda il necessario. Se avete denaro cam-
biatelo a Livorno, e portate tutte pezze colonnarie di
Spagna. Nell'antecedente dei 25. Xbre vi rammentavo di
portar le canzonette a 2. voci, della musica nuova e di
gusto p circa 50. ruspi, un assortimento di semi d'ogni
sorta d'ortaggio e fiori, e 4. o 6. paia di piccioni grossi
ma grossissimi, da far razza; e vi dicevo come vi con-
fermo che Mr. Jefferson vi aspetta a braccia aperte.
Le mie nuove dalla partenza fino a questo tempo le à il
Bellini, che à ordine di leggervele. Addio.

                              Vostro Amico vero
                              Filippo Mazzei.

NUMBER

THE VIRGINIA GAZETTE.

THURSDAY, DECEMBER 1, 1774.

OPEN TO ALL PARTIES, BUT INFLUENCED BY NONE.

WILLIAMSBURG: PRINTED BY JOHN PINKNEY, FOR THE BENEFIT OF CLEMENTINA RIND's CHILDREN,

All Persons may be supplied with this GAZETTE at 12s. 6d. a Year. ADVERTISEMENTS, of a moderate Length, are inserted for 3s. the first Week, and 1s. each Time after; long ones in Proportion.——PRINTING WORK, of every Kind, executed with Care and Dispatch.

NANSEMOND, November 19, 1774.

To Mr. PINKNEY.

SIR,

THIS county committee being informed that Mr. Anthony Warwick had lately imported into this county, from on board the ship Ross, captain Boyd, from Britain, a chest of East India tea, and that Mr. Michael Wallace, in the said ship, had imported half a chest, and the same was landed at Milner's warehouse, in this county, the said Warwick and Wallace being called on, came before the committee this day, and, on an enquiry, we find the facts to be, that the said ship Ross arrived in Elizabeth river, in the county of Norfolk, with the said tea on board, that application being made to the said Warwick and Wallace (then at Norfolk) by some of the committee of that county to have the tea landed there, they objected thereto, and said, by the bills of lading the tea was to be landed at Milner's, in Nansemond, that they insisted it should be delivered there, and that they would then inform the committee of Nansemond, and deliver it up to them.

As the character of a man who has accepted so odious an office as that in which we at present see general GAGE will naturally be extremely misrepresented and disguised, the following ESSAY towards it, by a person who has long known him, cannot be unacceptable to the public: it shall be given with the strictest regard to candour and truth.

GENERAL GAGE had the misfortune to be born of a family, almost time out of mind, the appertenance of a court; from them he imbibed strong prepossessions, not only in favour of the sacredness and infallibility of kings, but of ministers; from them he was taught to think but lightly of the rights of the people at large, and to consider their complaints rather as indecorums than objects of concern and deference. He received the rudiments of education at one of the public schools, where, unhappily, the history, transactions, laws, and constitution of our own country, are totally neglected, some acquaintance with which is certainly of more importance than the being able to scan the flattering versifiers of

*L'ingannare, il mentir, la frode, il furto,
E la rapina di pietà vestita,
Crescer col danno e precipizio altrui,
E far a sè di l'altrui biasmo onore,
Son le virtù di quella corte infida,*

is the exact description of the court of Great Britain.

There is no doubt but that all the tricks of this court have been played off upon general Gage, the craft of Mansfield, the plausibility of North, and the same cajoleries of the cabinet (which duped Chatham, and ensnared poor Yorke to his destruction) have been employed to seduce him into the odious office he at present holds. A man of a bad character would not, they thought, have answered their purposes so well, as a fair reputation in the agent frequently sanctifies the iniquity of the principal. The awkward and ridiculous figure he makes demonstrates that he has not a single attribute for the works of villainy. Had we been blessed with upright, able ministers, a Sully, a Pitt, or a Panin, it is more than probable that general Gage would have been a favourite, and there is less doubt that he would have executed their

pians or rectitude with credit, ability, and fuccefs.

NEW YORK. *November 14.*

HIS majefty has been pleafed to appoint colonel Guy Johnfon fuperintendant of Indian affairs, in the northern diftrict of North America, in the room of fir William Johnfon, deceafed.

His excellency general Gage has ordered the victualling office to be immediately removed from this city to Bofton.

The camp at Bofton, under the command of that excellency general Gage, was to break up as laft Wednefday; when the laft troops from this place, and thofe from Quebec, were then to difembark from the tranfports, and all march into quarters in one day.

We have not the leaft reafon to imagine that the packets will be ordered from this port for Bofton, at leaft, the poft mafters general, nor the agents for the packets here, have no fuch accounts.

NEW YORK, *committee chamber, November 7, 1774.*

"WHEREAS at the late continental congrefs, held at Philadelphia, it was refolved that a committee be chofen in every county, city, and town, by thofe who are qualified to vote for reprefentatives in the legiflature, whofe bufinefs it fhall be attentively to obferve the conduct of all perfons touching the affociation entered into by the members of the faid congrefs, in the name and on the behalf of themfelves and their refpective conftituents, and when it fhall be made to appear to the fatiffaction of the majority of any fuch committee, that any perfon within the limits of their appointment has violated the faid affociation, that fuch majority do forthwith caufe the truth of the cafe to be publifhed in the gazette; to the end that all fuch foes to the rights of Britifh America may be publicly known, and univerfally contemned, as the enemies of American liberty, and that thenceforth the parties to the faid affociation will refpectively break off all dealings with him or her."

Which faid refolve of the committee being this day taken into confideration by the committee of correfpondence of this city of New York, they do hereby recommend to the freeholders and freemen of the faid city to affemble together at the ufual places of election, in their feveral wards, at 10 o'clock in the forenoon, on Friday the 18th day of this inftant November, then and there to elect and appoint eight fit perfons in each refpective ward to be a committee of infpection for the purpofe expreffed in the faid refolve of the congrefs.

By order of the committee.

ISAAC LOW, Ch.

...purpofes age. From thence he was removed to a French academy, where what is taught is more calculated to give air and fafhion to a man of the world than to qualify him for the office and duty of a citizen; it confifts in little attainements (undoubtedly becoming a gentleman) but it neither infpires fentiment nor beftows the knowledge neceffary to an Englifhman and member of a free community. He came into the army early, but here, too, he was unlucky. Inftead of taking his poft in the line as a common officer, he was attached to the perfon of a court general, a general fo totally deftitute of every quality of a-foldier that it is univerfally allowed had he not been a courtier he never could have arrived beyond the degree of a recruiting ferjant. In fuch a fchool as this no enlarged, generous, political fentiments, could poffibly be gleaned, whereas the common officers of marching regiments, uncontaminated by attendance on the perfons of court minions, have frequently a very liberal way of thinking on this great fubject.

General Gage is not a man of brilliant parts, but has what the world calls a plain, good underftanding; that fort of underftanding which, had he given it fair play, by keeping good company, was capable of being dilated to a refpectable fize. By keeping good company, I mean, converfing with fenfible men and fenfible books; but by neglecting thefe points, he has, perhaps, reduced it below its natural ftandard; for wit, like other things, from want of proper exercife and ftimulation, is apt to contract and grow blunt. I have now been fo extremely free refpecting this gentleman's connections and education, that I may expect fome credit with regard to his perfonal virtues, and the natural qualities of his heart, and here I am afraid I fhall want language to do him juftice. As a friend, he is warm, earneft, zealous, and fteady; as a companion, he is eafy, focial, unaffected, and complaifant; as a hufband and father, he is gentle, indulgent, and affectionate; as a gentleman, he is punctilious, veracious, and well bred; and as a man, he is juft, charitable, and benevolent.

When we confider, therefore, general Gage in his public and private capacity, a contrariety of paffions fills our breafts, the effects of which are difagreeable beyond defcription; indignation, compaffion, contempt, and refpect, alternately reign. In contemplating the office, abftract of the man, we execrate and defpife him; in contemplating the man, abftract of the office, we love and reverence him. Thus have an unhappy education, unhappy connections, but above all, the arts of a moft corrupt and wicked court, metamorphofed a man, intended by nature to be one of the ornaments of the human race, into the object of every virtuous citizen's deteftation.

It appears to this committee that the tea was landed at Milner's a few days after taken from the fhip, but does not appear that any information was then made to the faid committee by either of them, agreeable to their promife. A few days after that, the tea arrived at Milner's. The faid Warwick and Wallace attended at a meeting of the merchants in Williamfburg, where one of the committee of Nanfemond demanded of Mr. Warwick if he had imported any tea in that fhip, and where it was: He readily anfwered that he had imported a cheft of ten, with other goods, defigned for a ftore in Carolina, and and that it was faft to that ftore in his abfence, but was willing that the fame fhould be brought back and delivered up to the committee of Nanfemond, and that they might do with it as they pleafed, and did give orders accordingly to bring back the faid tea. Mr. Wallace then declared that he had imported half a cheft of tea in the faid fhip, and that it was then in his ftore at Milner's, ready to be delivered to the committee. The faid Warwick and Wallace have this day, before the faid committee, promifed, on their honour, to keep the tea fafe, ready to be delivered up to the committee when required, and that none of it fhall be fold or ufed until the affociation fhall be diffolved, and they both have this day voluntarily figned the affociation agreed to by the general congrefs, and declared they were well pleafed therewith, and that they would ftrictly adhere thereto, and feemed forry their intentions fhould be mifconftrued, as they never did intend to fecret the faid tea.

By order of the committee.

JOHN GREGORY, clerk of the committee.

Mr. PINKNEY,

OPEN TO ALL PARTIES *is your motto: Encouraged by it, I have enclofed you a piece addreffed to the perfon who figns himfelf* A CUSTOMER *in the paper of the 10th* inftant, *which I beg may appear in your next gazette.*

An ANSWER *to* NONSENSE.

WHAT could poffefs you, ftupid dunce,
To write in rhyme and profe at once?
In rhyme you halt; in profe you lie,
Which one may fee with half an eye;
But left you fhou'd deny th' affertion,
I'll prove it, juft for my diverfion:
The prieft, for fix months, had but half,
Inftead the whole, you fenfelefs calf?
Infpect the veftry book, and fee
Who tells a lie, fir, you, or me?
But fee the frothy coxcomb fret,
And cry, judge, judge, oh! judge the feet,
For what? Anfwer, I pray thee, true:

THURSDAY, December 1, 1774.   THE   NUMBER

VIRGINIA GAZETTE.

OPEN TO **ALL PARTIES,**   BUT INFLUENCED BY **NONE.**

WILLIAMSBURG: PRINTED BY   J O H N   P I N K N E Y,
FOR THE BENEFIT OF   CLEMENTINA RIND's CHILDREN.

All Persons may be supplied with this GAZETTE at 12 s. 6 d. a Year. ADVERTISEMENTS, of a moderate Length, are inserted for 3 s. the first Week, and 2 s. each Time after; long ones in Proportion.——PRINTING WORK, of every Kind, executed with Care and Dispatch.

* *L'ingannare, il mentir, la frode, il furto,*
E la rapina di pieta vestita,
Crescer col danno e precipizio altrui,
E far a se de l'atrui biasmo onore,
Son la virtu' di quilla corte infida,

Pinkney's VIRGINIA GAZETTE, Williamsburg, December 1, 1774. The article on General Gage ending with verses in Italian seems to be the work of Philip Mazzei. *(Courtesy, Virginia State Library)*

Frammenti di scritti pubblicati nelle gazzette al principio della rivoluzione americana da un cittadino di Virginia.

Per ottenere il nostro intento bisogna, miei cari concittadini, ragionar su i diritti naturali dell'uomo e sulle basi di un governo libero. Questa discussione ci dimostrerà chiaramente, che il britanno non è mai stato tale nel suo maggior grado di perfizione, e che il nostro non era altro che una cattiva copia di quello, con tali altri svantaggi che lo rendevano poco al di sopra dello stato di schiavitù.

Dopo esamineremo come il governo devesi formare per essere imparziale e durevole.

Questa materia è stata tanto amplamente trattata da vari scrittori di vaglia, ch'io non ambisco ad altro merito che a quello di trattarla in uno stil familiare e semplice; onde possiamo facilmente intenderci.

Gli scrittori di stile sublime mi perdoneranno; essi non àn bisogno che alcuno scriva per loro. Io scrivo per quelli, che dotati di buon senso non ànno avuto il vantaggio d'un educazione studiosa, e bramo di adattare il mio stile alla lor capacità. So bene che lo stile sublime à spesso attratto il consenso degli uomini, pur troppo disposti ad ammirare quel che non comprendono; ma è finalmente venuto il tempo di cambiar costume; il dover nostro è di procurar di comprendere per giudicar da noi stessi.

Tutti gli uomini sono per natura egualmente liberi e indipendenti. Quest'eguaglianza è necessaria per costituire un governo libero. Bisogna che ognuno sia uguale all'altro nel diritto naturale. La distinzione dei ranghi n'è sempre stata, come sempre ne sarà un efficace ostacolo, e la ragione è chiarissima. Quando in una nazione avete più classi d'uomini, bisogna che diate ad ognuna la sua porzione nel governo; altrimenti una classe tiranneggierebbe l'altre. Ma le porzioni non possono farsi perfettamente uguali; e quando ancor si potesse, il giro delle cose umane dimostra che non si manterrebbero in equilibrio; e per poco che una preponderi la macchina deve cadere.

Per questa ragione tutte le antiche repubbliche ebbero corta vita. Quando furono stabilite gli abitanti eran divisi per classi, e sempre in contesa, ogni classe procurando di aver maggior porzione dell'altre nel governo; cosicchè i legislatori doveron cedere ai pregiudizi dei costumi, alle opposte pretensioni dei partiti, e il meglio che poteron fare fu un misto grottesco di libertà e di tirannia.

Le loro imperfezioni costituzionali diedero origine a molti disordini, che sono stati ultimamente descritti con i più orribili colori da persone male intenzionate per indisporre il buon popolo di questo continente contro i governi repubblicani; ed alcuni uomini di buona fede ancora ànno fatto lo stesso perchè la loro inattenzione ai veri buoni principii di governo non à permesso loro di discernere, che le repubbliche

Beginning of article by Mazzei translated into English by Thomas Jefferson and published, it is said, in the *Virginia Gazette*. (*Memorie*, Vol. II)

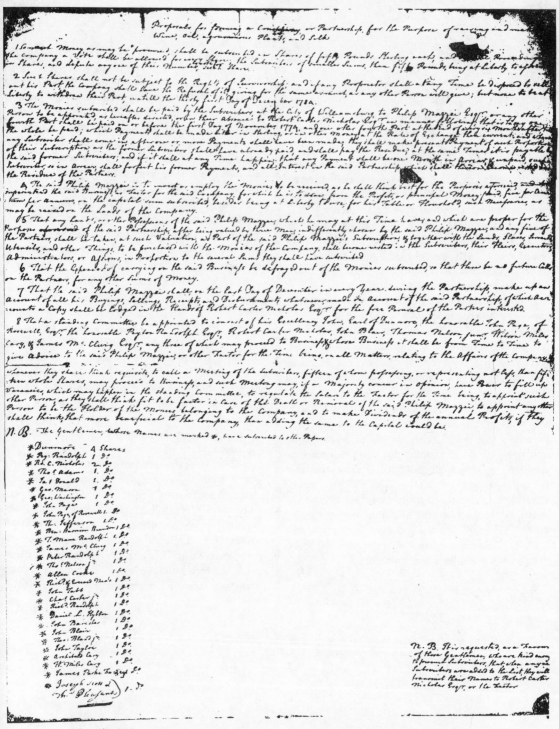

Mazzei's Proposals for forming a Company or Partnership for the Purpose of raising and making Wine, Oil, agruminous Plants, and Silk. [November, 1774] *(Courtesy, Virginia Historical Society)*

Mazzei's letter to John Page, dated February 11, 1775, on which Mr. Page jotted down notes in pencil defending his friend Mazzei. (*Courtesy, New York Public Library*)

1706–1790

A reissue (London, 1824) of the original engraving by Rider, after a painting by Elmer.

Dear Sir,   Philad.ª Dec. 27. 1775

    It was with great Pleasure I learnt from Mr Jefferson, that you were settled in America, and from the Letter you forward'd me with, that you like the Country, and have reason to expect Success in your laudable and meritorious Endeavours to introduce new Products. I heartily wish you all the Success you can desire, in that, and in every other Undertaking that may conduce to your comfortable Establishment in your present Situation.

    I know not how it has happened that you did not receive an Answer to your Letter from the Secretaries of our Society. I suppose they must have written, & that it has miscarried. — If you have not yet sent the Books which the Academy of Turin have done us the Honour to present us with, we must, I fear, wait for more quiet Times before we can have the Pleasure of receiving them, the Communication being now very difficult.

: A. Mazzei.   I

Benjamin Franklin's letter of welcome to Mazzei, dated December 27, 1775. (*Courtesy, Dartmouth College*)

I can hardly suspect Mr Walpole of the Treachery against you which you mention, especially as he was then expecting to have Lands of his own in America, wherein the Productions you were about to introduce must have been beneficial. I rather suspect a Person whom you may remember was frequently with him, I mean Martinelli. — I rejoice that you escap'd the Snares that were laid for you, and I think all America is oblig'd to the Great Duke for his Benevolence towards it, in the Protection he afforded you, and his Encouragement of your Undertaking.

We have experienc'd here that Silk may be produc'd to great Advantage. While in London I had some Trunks full sent me from hence three Years successively, and it sold by Auction for about 19/6 the Small Pound, which was not much below the Silk from Italy.

The Congress have not yet extended their Views much towards foreign Powers, and particularly not to those of Italy, who are so distant. They are nevertheless oblig'd by your kind Offers of your Service which perhaps in a Year or two more may become useful to them. I am myself much pleas'd that you have sent a Translation of our Declaration to the Great Duke; because having a high Esteem for the Character of

56

of that Prince, and of the whole Imperial Family, from the Accounts given me of them by my Friend Dr Ingenhausz and yourself, I should be happy to find that we stood well in the Opinion of that Court.

Mr Fromond of Milan, with whom I had the Pleasure of being acquainted in London, spoke to me of a Plant much used in Italy, and which he thought would be useful to us in America. He promis'd at my Request to send me some of the Seeds, which he has accordingly done. I have unfortunately forgotten the Uses, and know nothing of the Culture. In both those Particulars, I must beg Information and Advice from you. It is called Ravizzoni. I send Specimens of the Seeds inclos'd.

I received from the same M. Fromond Four Copies of a Translation of some of my Pieces into the fine Language of your Country. I beg your Acceptance of one of them, and of my best Wishes for your Health & Prosperity. With great Esteem & Regard, I have the Honour to be, Dear Sir,

Your most obedient
and most humble
Servant

B Franklin

Agricultural communication of Philip Mazzei to the Georgofili Academy of Florence, dated February 7, 1776, Virginia. (*Courtesy, Centro Studi Ricerche di Museologia Agraria*)

First two pages of the letter Mazzei sent to Colonel Page with his "instructions." *(Courtesy, Library of Congress)*

Dear Sir,   Colle January 11th 1777.

Inclosed I send you &c. If mr. Gstave should think,
that it could be of some service to him the having it upon the
News-papers, he has my consent. Should he not be satisfied
with what I have said, I wish you will make him sensible, that
truth is the only guide of all my actions, & that I cannot
be influenced by his present professions, or his former indiscreet
behaviour. He would be glad to have one of our people, & offered to give 25. pounds a year for him. I could not give him
any encouragment, as I am (unfortunately) an agent, & not the
only proprietor; but as our Company was instituted on the
view of public more than private benefit, I am willing to let
him have 2. of them, if you only agree with me in opinion.
I think mr. Gstave is is in a great want of an assistant able
to manage the vines in his absence, & that it may be proper to have
some of them cultivated in a method something different from
what is practised in his native place. I have a young
man very capable, who has a younger cousin of his, whom
he would have along with him, if he should go from me.
It may be mr. Gstave's interest to have them both, if he
has proper ground to raise garden-stuff for the Williamsburg
market, as the elder is likewise a very good gardner. In such a case
it would be necessary for mr. Gstave to give such a security for
the payment of the money, as to save me from censure, some
of our gentlemen being very ready to bestow such favours on me.
The money ought to be paid to you, & I would let you know
what part of it you should let those people have to buy
cloaths &c. for themselves. It is highly necessary, that our peo

Mazzei's letter to John Page, January 11, 1777. (Courtesy, New York Public Library)

ple should be ignorant of such an agreement for many reasons
not necessary to explain. They should not know, that Mr. Estes
deposites in your hands more money, than what I shall let
them they are to receive themselves. And they are to be told
that their salary shall encrease if they behave well. &c.

I must have an answer by the return of the Post. As I
am preparing to march to the Continental Camp, with as many
volunteers as I shall be able to persuade, I must settle every
thing without delay. As Mr. Jefferson (the bearer of this
to Fredericksburg) is in a hurry to set out, I am obliged
to have the part of the inclosed copied by a friend,
while I am blundering in this— My respects to Mrs. Page,
the Governor & Mr. Blair, & any body else whom in your conscience you think intitle to them. I wont mentioned Mr. Madison,
Dr. McClurg, & some worthy Clergymen, because by mentioning
&c.: should this paper ever be lost, every one not mentioned
would think me the greatest &c. &c. I am,

   Dear Sir

     Your most Obt. H. Servt.
      Th. Muffee

  He will go, & I cannot stop him.

Letter from George Washington to Mazzei, dated July 1, 1779. (*Courtesy, Library of Congress*)

1732–1799

From an engraving, after the original portrait, painted at Mount Vernon in 1772, by Charles Wilson Peale.

1743–1826

From a steel engraving in Appleton's Cyclopaedia of American Biography. Original was painted for John Adams in 1786 by Matthew Brown.

Sir,   Paris, April 21.st 1780.

The first time I spoke, according to my Instructions, to D.r Franklin on the purport of my mission, he observed that so many people had come to Europe from every State on that kind of business, that they had ruined our credit, & made the money-men shy of us. I said that Virginia should not partake of the blame on my account, as I would not let them know my business, unless I was pretty well sure of success. Having since taken the opportunity of mentioning the subject several times to him, he never failed giving some marks of disapprobation & displeasure. About 3 weeks past (that is to say about a month since I had first mentioned the matter to him) his reflections induced me to observe, that while Congress called on the several States to supply their men in the Continental Army with things, which must be got from Europe, it became a necessity for them to seek for credit & money; that the persons sent by the States on that errand may perhaps have not proceeded with all the Discretion required in such cases; but as to the dishonour & discredit, which you think, says I, that they have brought upon us by spreading such an idea of american poverty, I must beg leave to differ from you, Sir, since all Europe knows that we want a great many things from hence: that we have no species: & that we cannot, during the war, remit enough of our produce to pay the debts. The only 2 points to gain are, I continued, the persuading them of the solidity & resources of the States, & that we are firmly determined to keep our Independence.; & then mentioned the

His Excell.y Th.s Jefferson Gov.r of Virginia.

Letter of Philip Mazzei to Thomas Jefferson, Governor of Virginia, dated April 21, 1780.
(Courtesy, The Historical Society of Pennsylvania)

reasons I have to expect that I shall be believed, particularly in Florence & at Geneva. We have tried in Geneva, he said, without effect. As I had informed him of my views there from the beginning, his desiring so long to acquaint me with that unlucky trial made a sudden & disagreeable impression on my spirits for a double reason. But that was nothing in comparison to what I have felt to Day. He had at last signified to me that the 6 p. cent was offered. But, sir, says I, at the very first conversation on the subject I informed you that I was impowered to give only 5; had I known this at that time I could have given notice of it to Marquis la Fayette, & the Assembly would have been informed of it in the spring — session. "I don't think of it", said he, with a true philosophical indifference, "it never came into my head.") I have lost no time, Sir, to come & write you the intelligence, with which I have been most disagreeably surprised this Day; knowing that there is at present a vessel ready to sail, & I heartily wish that you may receive one of the 4 copies before the Assembly rises. you will, I hope, excuse my blundering more than usual, as I am really discontented. In coming from the Doctor, who lives 3 miles out of Town, I was a thinking what to do. I have resolved to proceed on my journey as soon as I can raise money, & to go & lay a foundation for executing the orders I may receive hereafter. It is requisite to observe, that however great my success may be in infusing notions of our solidity & resources, & a desire of entering into our views, I cannot with any degree of prudence mention the terms expressed in my Instructions, as Dr. Franklin's offer is certainly known every where; the experiment having been tried by the medium of public Bankers. The offering less than it has already been offered, would be ridiculous & perhaps injurious to the credit of Congress. If the state should not like the terms, I might act for Congress & probably succeed, at

though others have failed. I intend to mention it to the Doctor, & if I should meet with more philosophy than zeal, I have a mind to explain the whole matter to Mr. John Adams (if he offers me an opening to do it) & avail myself of his advice & assistance. The established character of his great abilities & patriotism all over the Continent would sufficiently warrant my step, besides what I know of him from the late Governor, & still more from yourself. I hope soon to entertain you with some favourable accounts of European affairs & I have the honour to be most respectfully,

Sir,

your Excellency's most Obedient & most humble Servant
Philip Mazzei

BIBLIOGRAPHY

1. American Philosophical Society, Philadelphia, Pennsylvania.
   The whole collection comprises 194 items: Correspondence from Filippo Mazzei to Giovanni Valentino Mattia Fabbroni (from 1773 to
   1816); also one letter to the American Philosophical Society from
   Mazzei, December 7, 1773; two letters from Bettina Mazzei to G.
   Fabbroni; one letter from G.A. Carmignani to F. Mazzei, November
   20, 1811; one letter from G. Fabbroni, November 1, 1809; one letter
   from B. Franklin—Passy, Sunday; one letter from La Rochefoucauld, May 30, 1783; five letters to G. Fabbroni with references to Mazzei; seventeen letters from Signora Petronille Mazzei to
   G. Fabbroni (1780–82).

2. Colonial Williamsburg, Williamsburg, Virginia.
   "Virginia Gazette"—December 2, 1773, July 28, 1774, December 1,
   1774, May 24, 1776.

3. Columbia University Library, New York
   Correspondence of Philip Mazzei to Gouverneur Morris, May 7,
   1785; Scipione Piattoli, July 3, 1803; Thomas Jefferson, February 13,
   1811.

4. Dartmouth College Library, Hanover, New Hampshire.
   Correspondence, Jefferson to Mazzei, April 4, 1780–July 9, 1811; 15
   items. Mazzei to Jefferson, October 5, 1815; Notes by Mazzei on letter from Jefferson, dated April 5, 1790; Franklin to Mazzei, December 27, 1775; Mazzei to John Blair, May 12, 1785.

5. Historical Society of Pennsylvania, Philadelphia, Pennsylvania.
Letter dated April 16, 1784, from Patrick Henry to the Governor of Virginia, supporting Mazzei's claims for payment of expenses incurred.
Dreer Collection Statesmen of Europe: Correspondence to Mr. Short, June 6, 1792; Governor Thomas Jefferson, April 21, 1780; Governor Benjamin Harrison, September 6, 1782, December 3, 1783, May 21, 1784; to Philip Mazzei from James Madison, Jr. Endorsement of conduct as agent of Va. Same of J. Page, D. Diggers and D. Jameson, April 25, 1783.
Society Collection: Correspondence to Benjamin Harrison, September 6, 1782; Dr. Franklin et al., November 2, 1782.
American Miscellaneous Collection: Correspondence to John Ridgely, October 20, 1807.

6. Library of Congress, Washington, D.C.
Miscellaneous Manuscripts Collection: Correspondence to and from Mazzei, June 28, 1773–July 18, 1817; 42 items. Principal correspondents include John Adams, Jefferson, Lafayette, James Monroe, Edmund Randolph, and John Blair. This group also includes Mazzei's copy of David Humphreys' *Poem Addressed to the Army of the United States of America* (New-Haven, Paris, 1785), inscribed to him by the author.
Peter Force Papers, Series VIII-D: Thirty-eight items in one volume; extracts and copies of letters, August 19, 1780–January 4, 1782; copies of three essays [1780–82] "Ragioni per cui non può darsi agli stati Americani la taccia di ribelli. Scritto al Principio del 1781"; "Riflessioni tendenti a prognosticar l'evento della presente guerra. Scritte nel mese d'Aprile del 1781," and "Istoria del principio, progresso, e fine del denaro di Carta degli Stati Uniti Americani, scritta in Gennaio 1782"; two copies of proposals for forming a company or partnership for the purpose of raising and making wine, oil, agruminous plants, and silk, 1774.
Thomas Jefferson Papers: Correspondence, December 27, 1782–April 5, 1818; 32 items (last 3 items pertain to Mazzei's estate). Microfilm editions of the Jefferson Papers are available to scholars in the Princeton University Library, the Columbia University Libraries, and the New York Public Library.
James Madison Papers: Correspondence, June 13, 1779–December 15, 1804; 31 items. The Madison Papers microfilm is available in the Princeton University Library, and Seton Hall University.
James Monroe Papers: Two Mazzei items dated October 3, 1785, and April 24, 1796; The Monroe microfilm is available at Seton Hall, and the Teaneck campus of Fairleigh Dickinson University.

George Washington Papers: Two Mazzei items dated January 27 and July 1, 1779; The Washington Papers microfilm is available in the Princeton University Library; Seton Hall University, South Orange; and the Teaneck campus of Fairleigh Dickinson University.

7. Massachusetts Historical Society, Boston, Massachusetts
   Sixteen items: Correspondence with Jefferson, Rieux, Vernon, Randolph, Page, Appleton; Also in Jefferson to William Pennock, Patrick Gibson; in Appleton to Jefferson, Randolph to Jefferson; in Pickering to Madison. Pledge of annual subscription of the Reverend Charles Clay for conducting services of the "Calvinistical Reformed Church" in Charlottesville, February 1777; Power of attorney to James Monroe, May 2, 1786; Account with Mazzei, of George Nicholas, 1785–86 (April 27, 1785).

8. New York Public Library, New York
   Twenty-eight items: Correspondence to Jefferson, November 27, 1779–April 8, 1781 (sixteen letters); seven letters to John Page, February 11, 1775–May 8, 1785; one letter to Benjamin Harrison, April 26, 1782; Extract from the official French Gazzette of Janary 25, 1780; Narrative of Mazzei's capture and imprisonment by the British; Memoranda showing how Mazzei forwarded his dispatches to Jefferson; Representation of Mr. Mázzei's Conduct, from the time of his appointment to be Agent of the State [of Virginia] until his return to Virginia.

9. The College of William and Mary, Williamsburg, Virginia
   In the Tucker-Coleman Papers there is a 13 page manuscript entitled "Observations on the Law of Virginia to regulate navigation" on which George Tucker has written "by Mr. Mazzei" and it is dated 1784.

10. University of North Carolina, Chapel Hill, North Carolina.
    Broadside on the Society of the Constitution

11. University of Pennsylvania Library, Philadelphia, Pennsylvania
    German translation of Mazzei's *Recherches*, 1789.

12. Virginia Historical Society, Richmond, Virginia
    Six items: Correspondence to Thomas Adams, October 6, 1772–June 10, 1780 (five letters); Proposal for forming a Company or Partnership for the Purpose of raising and making Wine, Oil, agruminous Plants and Silk, November 1774.

13. Virginia State Library, Richmond, Virginia
In the collection of Executive papers there are seven letters: six to Governor Jefferson, February 8, 1780–May 20, 1780; one to Governor Benjamin Harrison, June 10, 1784. These have been printed in the Calendar of *Virginia State Papers*. Resolution of the Virginia Council Journal, 1783–1785; (Pinkney) Virginia Gazette, December 1, 1774; List of Virginians who renounced allegiance to George III on April 21, 1779. Item 3026, photocopy of broadside of *The Constitutional Society*. See Ray P. Hummel, Jr., *Southeastern Broadsides before 1877*, Richmond: Virginia State Library, 1971.

14. France
Archives des Affaires Etrangères à Paris: Polonia Nr. 315, 316, 317, 318, 319, 320.
Biblioteca Polacca a Parigi: a) Nr. 37—Copie delle lettere di Stanislaw August Poniatowski a Filippo Mazzei dal 4.IX.1788 al 10.VIII.1791; b) Nr 32 (cartella 43)—lettere del cancelliere Jacek Malachowski a Filippo Mazzei (originali), 11 let. dal 29.IX.1790 al 13.IV.1791.
Bibliothèques et Archives Municipales, Mantes-Sur-Seine. Riflessioni tendenti a prognosticar l'evento della presente guerra, scritte nel mese d'aprile 1781 da Filippo Mazzei—24 p. Ragioni per cui non puo darsi agli Stati Americani la taccia di ribelli, scritte al principio del 1781—du même—16 pages. Storia del principio, progresso e fine del denaro di carta degli Stati Uniti Americani, scritta al principio del 1782—du même—16 pages. Lettre de Filippo Mazzei sur le meme sujet. (Observations d'un ami des Americains sur le gouvernement de la Virginié.)
Aix-en-Provence Library. Twenty-eight pages of rough draft of document pertaining to the contents of proposed propaganda news, in French and Italian; Letters from Filippo Mazzei, Amsterdam, November 28, 1782, in Italian.

15. Italy
Biblioteca Nazionale Centrale di Firenze—(Miscellaneous Materials) Nuovo Fondo Capponi: Lettere e scritti di Filippo Mazzei alla corte di Polonia degli anni 1788–1792. Autografo del Mazzei: "Narrativa della mia missione in Europa fino al mio ritorno in Virginia." Particolari, 32, 194: F. Mazzei a P. Paoli, Pisa (3 gennaio 1793).
Archivio di Stato di Pisa *Carte Manzi*, b. IV *Rapporti di Polizia*, b. 24 Lettere a Francesco Maria Gianni.
Archivio Maruzzi di Campiglia Marittima (Livorno).
Centro Studi Ricerche di Museologia Agraria has manuscripts from

the Georgofili Academy in Florence dated February 7, 1776 (Accademia Economico-Agraria dei Georgofili, Logge degli Uffizi, Firenze).
Comune di Poggio a Caiano—Baptismal and Death Certificates.

16. Poland
Archivio Centrale degli Atti Antichi di Varsavia: a) raccolta dei Popiel—numeri: 39, 58, 87, 90, 165, 184, 185, 186, 187, 218, 221, 222, 393, 405, 406, 418 e 422; b) Archivio Reale Polacco, segnato K. III—numeri: 43, 204, 278.
Ossolineum, Wroclaw: Raccolte di Aleksander Czolowski nr. 975/I—Parlamento dei Quattro Anni. Corrispondenza segreta del re Stanislaw August con Mazzei, suo agente diplomatico a Parigi, dall'anno 1789 all'anno 1791, fogli 1–17.
Dubois de Jancigny (Letter to Mazzei, 11.I.1791) MS in Archives générales d'actes anciens, Archívum Glówne Akt Dawnych, ul. Diuga, 24, Warsaw, Popiel Collection, cote, 207.
Mazzei, Filippo. Letters and reports to King Stanislaus-Auguste from Warsaw, Vienna, Pisa. Lucques and letters of Stanislaus-Auguste to Mazzei (1792–93). MS in Archives of Poniatowski at Jablonna near Warsaw, belonging to Count Maurice Potocki.

17. England—British Museum. See General Catalogue of Printed Books, New York, Readex Microprint Corp., 1967, V. 17, p. 85.

18. Switzerland
Geneva Library—Vail mss. Letter from Benjamin Franklin to Philip Mazzei, March 1783.

NEWSPAPERS

"*Argus,*" June 26, 1916, Richmond, Virginia.
"*Aurora,*" June and July 1916, Philadelphia, Pennsylvania.
"*Journal de Paris,*" 10 maggio 1788.
"*Mercure de France,*" février 1788.
"*Notizie del mondo,*" Firenze.
"*Gazette de Leyde,*" Holland.
"*Virginia Gazette,*" Williamsburg, Virginia. (Purdue and Dixie) July 28, 1774; (Purdue) May 24, 1776; (Rind) December 2, 1773; (Pinkney) December 1, 1774.

ARTICLES, PAMPHLETS, BOOKS

Adams, C.F. *The Works of John Adams.* Boston: Little, Brown, and Company, 1852. 10 vols.

Albemarle County Deed-book, Number 7, Albemarle County Court House, Charlottesville, Virginia.

Appleton's Cyclopaedia of American Biography, Edited by J.G. Wilson and J. Fiske. New York: D. Appleton and Co., 1894. 6 vols.

Badini, C.F. *Il vero carattere di Giuseppe Baretti, pubblicato per amor della virtù calunniata: per disinganno degl'Inglesi: e in difesa degl'Italiani.* (Introduction by Philip Mazzei.) Venezia-London, 1770.

Baldwin, S. "The authorship of the Quatre lettres d'un bourgeois de New-Heaven." New Haven: Tuttle, Morehouse & Taylor, 1900, 263–281.

Ballagh, J.C. *The Letters of Richard Henry Lee.* New York: The Macmillan Co., 1911. 2 vols.

Barbera, P., "La Polonia e l'Italia." *Lettura*, Milano, July 1, 1917.

————. "A proposito di uno storico italiano degli Stati Uniti." *Rassegna Nazionale*, Firenze, February 1, 1918, 2nd ser., XL, 218–20.

————. "Un Fiorentino Cittadino Americano." *Marzocco*, Firenze, August 1, 1920, 3.

Bernardy, A.A., "Contributo alla formazione degli Stati Uniti di America." *Il giornale di Politica e Letteratura*, Roma, XVIII, 1–2. Bernari, C. "Filippo Mazzei, un toscano fra due rivoluzioni." *Letteratura*, July–October 1965, 3–15.

Berti, G. *Russia e stati italiani nel Risorgimento.* Torino: Einaudi, 1957, 231.

Bigelow, J. *The Works of Benjamin Franklin.* New York: G.P. Putnam's Sons, 1904. 12 vols.

Bollettino Storico Pistoiese: XIX (1917); XXVIII (1926); XXXII (1930); XXXVII (1935); XLIV (1942).

Borneman, R. "Franzoni and Andrei: Italian Sculptors in Baltimore, 1806." *The William and Mary Quarterly*, 1953, 108–111.

Bozzolato, G. *Polonia e Russia alla fine del XVIII secolo. (Un avventuriero onorato: Scipione Piattoli).* Padova: Marsilio, 1964.

Branchi, E.C. "Memoirs of the Life and Voyages of Doctor Philip Mazzei." (Translation) *William and Mary College Quarterly Historical Magazine*, Williamsburg, 2nd ser., 1929, IX, 161–74, 247–64; 1930, X, 1–18.

Brant, I. *James Madison.* Indianapolis: Bobbs-Merrill Co., 1941–61. 6 vols.

Brissot de Warville, J. *Résponse à une critique des lettres d'un cultivateur americain des Quakers.* Paris, 1788, 27.

_____. *Examen critique des voyages dans l'Amérique septentrionale de M. le marquis de Chatellus.* London: 1786. 143.

_____. *New Travels in the United States of America.* London: J.S. Jordan, 1792, 483.

Brodie, F.M. *Thomas Jefferson An Intimate History.* New York: Norton, 1974, 594.

Camajani, G.G. "Filippo Mazzei illustre figlio di Poggio a Caiano." *Toscani nel Mondo,* Firenze: Associazione Internazionale Toscani nel mondo, April 1975, 3–5.

Catalog of Manuscripts. Massachusetts Historical Society, Boston: G.K. Hall, 1969. 7 vols.

Chinard, G. *Thomas Jefferson, The Apostle of Americanism.* Boston: Little, Brown, and Company, 1920, 548.

Ciampini, R. *Un osservatore italiano della rivoluzione francese. Lettere inedite di Filippo Mazzei al re Stanislao Augusto di Polonia.* Firenze: Rinascimento del Libro, 1934.

_____. *Lettere di Filippo Mazzei alla Corte di Polonia (1788–1792).* Vol. I: July 1788–March 1790. Bologna: Zanichelli, 1937.

Condorcet, Marquis de. *Déclaration des droits traduite de l'Anglois, avec l'original à coté.* (Translation by Mazzei.) London-Paris, 1789.

Cordasco, F.-La Gumina, S., *Italians in the United States.* New York, 1972.

Coxe, T. *Strictures upon the letter imputed to Mr. Jefferson, addressed to Mr. Mazzei.* Lancaster: Dickson, June, 1800.

Croce, B. "Aneddoti di storia civile e letteraria, III: Appunti da libri rari del Settecento." *La Critica,* XXI, 1927, 329–334.

Curtis, C.D. *The King's Chevalier, A biography of Lewis Littlepage,* Indianapolis–New York, 1961.

_____. *Szambelan Jego Królewskiej Mósci* (Il Ciambellano di Sua Maestà). Traduzione di T. Tatarkiewicz, epilogo di Z. Libizowska. Warszawa, 1967.

D'Ancona, A. *Scipione Piattoli e la Polonia.* Firenze: Barbèra, 1915.

Dembinski, B. *Rosja a Rewolucja Francuska* (La Russia e la Rivoluzione Francese). Krakow, 1896.

_____. Stanislas-Auguste et ses relations intellectuelles avec l'étranger. *La Pologne au VII Congrès international des sciences historiques.* Warsaw 1933, 408–429.

Diaz, F. *Francesco Maria Gianni. Dalla burocrazia alla politica sotto Pietro Leopoldo di Toscana.* Milano-Napoli: Ricciardi, 1966, 404.

Dictionary of National Biography. Edited by S. Lee. New York: Macmillan and Co.–London: Smith, Elder and Company, 1894. Vol. 37.

Durham, L.C., "The Constitutional Society and Philip Mazzei." *Richmond Times Dispatch,* (Sunday Magazine Section), 1938.

Enciclopedia Italiana. Edizioni istituto Giovanni Treccani. Milano–Roma: MCMXXXIV–XI. Vol. 22.

Fabre, J.*Stanislas-Auguste Poniatowski et l'Europe des lumières. Étude de cosmopolitisme.* Paris: Les Belles Lettres, 1952, 350–351, 507–522, 673–679.

Faÿ, B.*The Revolutionary Spirit in France and in America.* New York, 1927.

_____. *Bibliographie critique des ouvrages français relatifs aux États-Unis.* Paris: Librairie Ancienne Edouard Champion, 1925, 108.

Feldman, J. *Na przelomie stosunkow polsko-francuskich 1774–1787. Vergennes wobec Polski.* (Alla svolta dei rapporti polacco-francesi 1774–1784. Vergennes di fronte alla Polonia). Krakow, 1935.

Fisher, S.G. *The Struggle for American Independence.* Philadelphia: J.P. Lippincott Company, 1908. 2 vols.

Francovich, C. "La rivoluzione americana e il progetto di costituzione del granduca Pietro Leopoldo." *Rassegna storica del Risorgimento,* XLI, 1954, 371–377.

Franklin, B. *The Papers of Benjamin Franklin.* Compiled by L.W. Labaree. New Haven and London: Yale University Press, 1970.

_____. *The Writings of Benjamin Franklin.* Edited by A.H. Smith. New York: Macmillan, 1905–07, 10 vols.

Furman, B., "Signed, Sealed—and Forgotten!," *Daughters of the American Revolution Magazine,* 1937, LXXI, 1004–1009.

Garlick, R.C. *Philip Mazzei—Friend of Jefferson. His Life and Letters.* Baltimore, 1933.

_____. *Italy and the Italians in Washington's Time.* New York: Italian Publishers, 1933.

CONTENTS.—Philip Mazzei, by R.C. Garlick, Jr.—Washington and the Italians, by A.F. Guidi—American travellers in Italy at the beginning of the 18th century, by Giuseppe Prezzolini.—Francesco Vigo, savior of the midwest, by Bruno Roselli.—Lorenzo da Ponte, by Luigi Russo.

Gerbi, A. "Filippo Mazzei: L'esperienza contro le utopie e i vituperi." *La disputa del Nuovo Mondo. Storia di una polemica, 1700–1900.* Milano-Napoli: Ricciardi, 1955, 290.

Giannini, T.C. *Giorgio Washington.* Contains an unpublished letter from George Washington to Mazzei. Bologna, 1933.

Giovannetti, A. *L'America degli italiani.* Modena: Edizioni Paoline, 1975.

Goggio, E. "Italy and the American War of Independence." *Romanic Review,* vol. 19, 1929, 25–34.

_____. *Italians in American History.* New York: Italian Historical Society, 1930.

Guidi, A.F. *Relazioni culturali fra Italia e Stati Uniti d'America.* Padova: Cedam, 1940, 21.

Hamilton, J.C. *Life of Alexander Hamilton.* Boston, 1879.

Harrison, Benjamin, Letter Book of. Archives of the Virginia State Library, Richmond.

_____. Executive Papers of. Archives of the Virginia State Library, Richmond.

Henry, P. *Life, Correspondence and Speeches.* Edited by W.W. Henry. Vols. I and II.

Hunt, G. *Life of James Madison.* New York: Doubleday, Page and Company, 1902, 402.

Jefferson, Thomas, Executive Papers of. Archives of the Virginia State Library, Richmond.

_____. *Memoir, Correspondence and Miscellanies from the Papers of.* Edited by T.J. Randolph. Charlottesville, Va., 1829. 4 vols.

_____. *Notes on the State of Virginia.* Edited by P.L. Ford. Brooklyn: Historical Printing Club, 1894, 235.

_____. *Observations sur la Virginie.* Traduites de l'Anglois par M. l'abbé Morellet. Paris: Barrois, 1786, 390.

_____. *Writings.* Edited by H.A. Washington. New York, 1853, vols. IV and VII.

_____. *Writings.* Edited by P.L. Ford. New York, 1894, vols. III, IV, V, VII, VIII, IX, X.

_____. *Writings.* Monticello Edition. Washington, 1905, vols. V, VI, VII, IX, XVI, XIX.

_____. *Writings.* Edited by A.E. Bergh. Washington, 1907.

_____. *The Papers of Thomas Jefferson.* Compiled by J.P. Boyd. Princeton: Princeton University Press, 1948.

_____. *The Papers of Thomas Jefferson.* Compiled by Elizabeth J. Sherwood and Ida T. Hopper. Princeton: Princeton University Press, 1954–1973, vol. 1–18.*** (See references to Mazzei at end of Bibliography.)

Journals of the House of Burgesses of Virginia, 1773–1776. Edited by J.P. Kennedy. Richmond, 1905.

La Piana, A., *La cultura americana e l'Italia.* Torino: Einaudi, 1938.

Latrobe, B.H. *The Journal of Latrobe.* New York, 1905.

Lesnodorski, B. *Polscy Jakobini. Karta z dziejów insurekcji 1794* (I Giacobini Polacchi. Una pagina della storia dell'insurrezione del 1794). Warszawa, 1960.

Lo Gatto, A.F., *The Italians in America 1492–1972. A Chronology and Fact Book.* New York, 1972.

Lossing, B. J. *Washington and the American Republic.* New York, 1870.

Lukaszewicz, W. *Filippo Mazzei 1730–1816. Profilo biografico.*

"Kwartalnik Historyczny", Kraków, 1948, fasc. 3–4, 301–335.

———. *Filippo Mazzei, Giuseppe Mazzini, saggi sui rapporti italo-polacchi.* Wroclaw: Zaklad Narodowy im. Ossolińskich, 1970, 30.

Madison, J. *Writings.* Edited by G. Hunt. Vols. II, V, VI.

———. *Letters and Other Writings.* Congressional ed. Washington, 1865.

———. *Letters and Other Writings.* Edited by R. Washington. Charlottesville, 1901.

MacDonald, W. *Documentary Source Book of American History.* New York, 1918.

Malone, D. *Jefferson the Virginian.* Boston: Little, Brown and Co., 1948.

———. *Jefferson and the Rights of Man.* Boston: Little Brown and Co., 1951.

———. *Jefferson and the Ordeal of Liberty.* Boston, Little, Brown and Co., 1962, 267.

Manghi, D.A. *Filippo Mazzei.* Pisa: Tip. Sociale Beato Giordano, 1926.

———. "La grande giornata italo-americana," *Messaggero Toscano,* July 4, 1918.

Manuscript Sources for Research on the American Revolution. Washington: Library of Congress, 1975.

Marraro, H.R. "Philip Mazzei, Virginia's Agent in Europe." *Bulletin of the New York Public Library,* March and April, 1934.

———. "The Four Versions of Jefferson's Letter to Mazzei." *The William and Mary College Quarterly Historical Magazine,* Williamsburg, Va., January 1942, 2nd Ser., XXII, 18–29.

———. "Mazzei's Correspondence with the Grand Duke of Tuscany during His American Mission." *William and Mary Quarterly,* Williamsburg, Va., July 1942, XXII, 275–301; October 1942, XXII, 361–380.

———. "Unpublished Correspondence of Jefferson and Adams to Mazzei." *The Virginia Magazine of History and Biography,* Richmond, Va., April 1943, LI, 113–133.

———. "Jefferson Letters Concerning the Settlement of Mazzei's Virginia Estate." *The Mississippi Valley Historical Review,* Iowa City, Iowa, September 1943, XXX, 235–242.

———. "Unpublished Mazzei Correspondence during His American Mission to Europe 1780–1783." *William and Mary College Quarterly Historical Magazine,* Williamsburg, Va., July 1943, XXIII, 309–327; October 1943, XXIII, 418–434.

———. "Philip Mazzei and His Polish Friends." *Bulletin of the Polish Institute of Arts and Sciences in America,* New York, April 1944, II, 757–822.

———. "Unpublished Mazzei Letters to Jefferson." *The William and Mary Quarterly,* Williamsburg, Va., October 1944, 3rd ser., I, 374–396; January 1945, 3rd ser., II, 71–100.

_____. "Notes and Documents. Philip Mazzei on American Political, So-
cial, and Economic Problems." *The Journal of Southern History*,
1949, XV, n. 3, 354–378.

_____. "The Settlement of Philip Mazzei's Virginia Estate." *Virginia
Magazine of History and Biography*, Richmond, July 1955, v. 63,
no. 3, 306–331.

Massei, F. "Due autografi inediti di Vittorio Alfieri." Roma: *Nuova Antologia*, 1921.

_____. "Un dimenticato: Giuseppe Timpanari." *Rassegna nazionale*,
October 16, 1920, 284–297.

Massara, G., *Viaggiatori italiani in America (1860–1970)*. Roma: Edizioni
di Storia e Letteratura, 1975.

*Materialy i badania do dziejów powstań oraz ruchów spolecznych i naro-
dowych w Polsce. Insurekcje* (Materiali e studi sulla storia delle in-
surrezioni e dei movimenti sociali e nazionali in Polonia. Insurre-
zioni), vol. I, red. Adam Szelagowski, Warszawa, 1928, 200–238.

Mazzei, Filippo. "Introduction" in *Il Vero carattere di Giuseppe Baretti*
by C.F. Badini. Venezia (London, 1770), British Museum, 11429b.

_____. Recherches Historiques et Politiques sur les États-Unis de l'Amé-
rique Septentrionale . . . Paris: chez Froullé, 1788, 4 v., xvi, 383;
259; 292; 366.

_____. *Geschichte und Staatsverfassung der Vereinigten Staaten von
Nordamerika* . . . Leipzig, 1789, 4 v.

_____. Translation of *Declaration des droits* by the Marquis de Condor-
cet. London [Paris], 1789.

_____. Memorie della Vita e delle Peregrinazioni del Fiorentino Filippo
Mazzei. Lugano, 1845–1846. 2 vols.

_____. "Mazzei's Memoirs" translated by E. C. Branchi. *The Columbi-
an Monthly*, May and July, 1928. *William and Mary Quarterly*,
July–October, 1929, January, 1920.

_____. *Memoirs of the life and peregrinations of the Florentine, Philip
Mazzei, 1730–1816*. Translated by Howard R. Marraro. New York:
Columbia Unversity Press, 1942, 447, and Millwood, N. Y.: Kraus
Press, 1973.

_____. *Memorie della vita e delle peregrinazioni del fiorentino Filippo
Mazzei*. Edited by Alberto Aquarone. Milano: Marzorati, 1970,
561. 2 vols.

_____. *Libro mastro di due mondi, memorie di Filippo Mazzei*. Roma:
Documento, Libraio Editore, 1944.

_____. *A letter on the Behaviour of the Populace on a Late Occasion, in
the Procedure against a Noble Lord. From a Gentleman to His
Countryman Abroad*. (Italian and English) [Political Pamphlets,
XXV, no. 6, Library of Congress. The name of the author, Philip
Mazzei, appears in ink below the title.] London: Bingley, 1768.

————. "Ragioni per cui non si può dare agli Stati Americani la taccia di Ribelli." 1781.

————. "Riflessioni tendenti a prognosticare l'evento della presente guerra." 1781.

————. "Istoria del principio, progresso e fine del denaro di carta . . ." 1782.

————. "Osservazioni sulla proposta legge per regolare in Virginia la navigazione dei bastimenti marittimi." 1784.

————. "Riflessioni su i mali provenienti dalla Questua e su i mezzi di evitargli." Pisa, 1799.

————. "Riflessioni sulla Natura della Moneta e del Cambio." Pisa, 1803.

————. "La Giustizia della Causa Americana."

————. "La Probabilità d'un Felice Evento."

————. "L'Importanza di Procurarsi il Commercio colla Virginia."

————. "Riflessioni d'un amico della verità sulla pace di Formio."

————. "Frammenti di scritti pubblicati nelle gazzette al principio della rivoluzione americana da un cittadino di Virginia."

————. Testamento del "Cittadino degli Stati Uniti" Filippo Mazzei, conservato nell'Archivio privato Maruzzi di Campiglia Marittima, Livorno. Bollettino storico pisano. XXXVI–XXXVIII, 1968, 270–272.

McIlwaine, H.R. (editor). *Official Letters of the Governors of the State of Virginia.* Richmond, 1926. 3 vols.

Merriam, E.A. *A History of American Political Theories.* New York, 1910.

Micocci, A.A. "Philip Mazzei and the Constitution." *Romanica,* Philadelphia, May, 1936.

Mira, G. "Un italiano del Settecento collaboratore dell'indipendenza americana: Filippo Mazzei." *Nuova Antologia,* vol. 276, 1917, 223–237.

Monroe, J. *Writings.* Edited by S. M. Hamilton. New York, 1898.

New York. *The Colonial Laws of New York from the Year 1664 to the Revolution,* vol. 1, Albany: J. B. Lyon, 1896.

Pace, A. "The American Philosophical Society and Italy." *Proceedings of the American Philosophical Society,* vol. 90, 1946, 387–421.

————. "Benjamin Franklin and Italy." *The American Philosophical Society,* Philadelphia, 1958, 105. In the Appendix (pp. 385–388) there are 4 unpublished letters of Mazzei to Franklin and one of Franklin to Mazzei.

Padover, S. K. *A Jefferson Profile as Revealed in His Letters.* New York: The John Day Co., 1956.

Palmer, W.P. *Calendar of Virginia State Papers,* vol. I. Richmond, 1875.

Palmieri, E. "Il genio politico di Filippo Mazzei." *Il Progresso Italo-Americano,* New York, July 5, 1939.

Papers of the Continental Congress, 1774–1789 (Correspondence of American Diplomats in Paris). Washington: National Archives.

Parton, J. *Life of Thomas Jefferson.* Boston–New York: Houghton, Mifflin and Co., 1902, 764.

Pei, M. *Our National Heritage.* Boston–New York: Houghton, Mifflin and Co., 1965.

Pisano, L.F., *The Italians in America.* New York: Exposition Press, 1957, 293.

Racca, V. "Filippo Mazzei e la rivoluzione Nord-Americana." *Nuova Antologia,* September–December 1949, 72–83.

Randall, H.S. *The Life of Thomas Jefferson.* New York, 1858. 3 vols.

Records of the Governor and Company of the Massachusetts Bay in New England. Massachusetts. v. 1, 1628–1641. Boston: W. White. 1853.

Riedesel, Madame de. *Letters and Memoirs.* New York, 1827.

Rolle, A. *The Immigrant Upraised.* Oklahoma City, University of Oklahoma, 1968.

Rostworowski, E. *Ostatni król Rzeczypospolitej. Geneza i upadek Konstytcji 3 Maja* (L'ultimo re della Repubblica. Genesi e fallimento della Costituzione del 3 Maggio). Warszawa, 1966.

Rowland, K.M. *The Life of George Mason.* New York, 1892.

Rymszyna, M. *Gabinet Stanislawa Augusta* (Il Gabinetto di Stanislaw August). Warszawa, 1962.

Schiavo, G.E. *The Italians in America Before the Civil War.* New York-Chicago: The Vigo press, 1934, 160.

_____. *Philip Mazzei, one of America's founding fathers* (a chapter from *Four centuries of Italian-American History* . .). New York: Vigo Press, 1951, 129–182.

Sparks, J. *Correspondence of the American Revolution.* Boston, 1853. 4 vols.

Tognetti, Burigana, S. *Tra riformismo illuminato e dispotismo napoleonico. Esperienze del "cittadino americano" Filippo Mazzei con appendice di documenti e testi.* Roma: Edizioni di storia e letteratura, 1965, 127.

Visconti, D. *Le origini degli Stati Uniti d'America e l'Italia.* Roma, 1940, 68.

Wandruszka, A. *Leopold II.* Wien-Munchen: Verlag Herold, 1965. 2 vols. *Pietro Leopoldo: Un grande riformatore,* Firenze: Vallecchi, 1968.

Washington, George. *Diaries.* Edited by J.C. Fitzpatrick. New York, 1925. 4 vols.

Wharton, F. *The Revolutionary Diplomatic Correspondence of the United States,* Washington, 1889. 6 vols.

Woods, E. *Albemarle County in Virginia.* Charlottesville, 1901.

Zimmern, H. "Story of Mazzei." *New England Magazine,* Boston, October, 1902, XXVII, 198–211.

funds sent from Va., **11**:354

handwriting, **11**:575

illness, **14**:344, 383

John Adams' report on, **3**:469–70

letter to Congress mentioned, **5**:585
letter from, cited, **7**:117
letters from, to Adams quoted, **8**:475n–476n
letters sent by, **7**:538; **8**:73, 207, 219, 381, 405, 409, 417, 421, 428, 444, 460, 574; **9**:445
letter to, cited, **11**:394
letter to, from Celesia cited, **10**:429
letters to, from Madison: cited, **14**:4n;
letter to, from Page: cited, **15**:195
loss of money, **8**:296

Madison's comments on, **7**:122
Madison tries to sell his books, **13**:499
Mari's letter of credit for, **9**:123
memoranda regarding persons and affairs in Paris, **7**:386–91
messages to friends in France, **15**:613–15
misfortunes of, **13**:166
mission in Europe for Va., **6**:115
money sent by Edmund Randolph, **11**:85

observation on nightingales, **11**:372

payment of expenses, **8**:475, 510, 538

Penet's comments on, **3**:384
plan of operations by French land and naval forces, **3**:382
plan to go to Annapolis, **7**:121
portrait of Castruccio Castracani obtained for TJ, **17**:422.
portraits of Columbus, Vespucci,

Cortez, and Magellan: arrangements for copies in Florence, **15**:xxxvi
proposal for company to produce wine, oil, etc., **1**:156–9

quoted in *Mercure de France*, **12**:667

Recherches Historiques et Politiques sur les États Unis d'Amérique, **9**:72n; **10**:10n; **11**:43
recommended as U.S. commercial agent abroad, **2**:210–11, 224–5
R.H. Lee's comments on, **2**:215–216
remittance promised, **11**:249
reports archaeological discovery in Siberia, **7**:123
requests for commission, **4**:51
return to America, **7**:30–2
rough draft of Declaration of Independence sent to, **1**:415n

settles near Monticello, **1**:159n
sends copy of Va. act for religious freedom to Celesia, **10**:412
signature to Va. oath of allegiance, **2**:129
shortage of funds, **11**:297
Smith's opinion of, **12**:620
subscription to support of clergyman, **2**:7
sued by wife, **7**:555n
suggested as U.S. agent to Duke of Tuscany, **2**:28n

TJ asks to have commission and instructions sent to, **3**:376
TJ's diary on affairs of, **16**:308–9
TJ's patience tried by, **17**:22, 23n
TJ referred to for information, **8**:118

Va. property: Derieux offers to buy, **17**:234–6, 400–1; sale of, authorized, **18**:308; TJ advises sale of, **16**:307–9
visit to Netherlands, **9**:636
visit to "Rosewell," **8**:117

81

Whereas by a late act of General assembly freedom of Religious opinion and worship is restored to all, and it is left to the members of each religious society to employ such teachers as they think fit for their own spiritual comfort and instruction, and to maintain the same by their free and voluntary contributions. We the subscribers, professing the most Catholic affection for other religious societies who happen to differ from us in points of conscience, yet desirous of encouraging and supporting the Calvinistical Reformed church, and of deriving to ourselves, through the ministry of it's teachers, the benefits of Gospel knolege and religious improvement; and at the same time of supporting those, who having been at considerable expence in qualifying themselves by regular education for explaining the holy scriptures, have dedicated their time and labour to the service of the said church; and moreover, approving highly the political conduct of the revd Charles Clay, who, early rejecting the tyrant and tyranny of Britain, proved his religion genuine by it's harmony with the liberties of mankind, and, conforming his public prayers to the spirit and the injured rights of his country, ever addressed the God of battles for victory to our arms, while others impiously prayed that our enemies might vanquish and overcome us: do hereby oblige ourselves our heirs executors and administrators to pay to the said Charles Clay of Albemarle his exrs. or adminrs. the several sums affixed to our respective names on the 25th day of December next, and also to make the like annual paiment on the 25th day of December in every year following until we shall withdraw the same

or until the legislature shall make other provision for the support of the said Clergy. In Consideration whereof we expect that the said Charles Clay shall perform divine service and preach a sermon in the town of Charlottesville on every 4th Saturday till the end of the next session of general Assembly and after that on every 4th. Sunday or oftener if a regular rotation with the other churches which shall have put themselves under his cure will admit a more frequent attendance.

And we further mutually agree with each other that we will meet at Charlottesville on the 1st. day of March in the present year and on in every year following as long as we continue our subscriptions and there make choice by ballot of three Wardens to collect our said subscriptions to take care of such books and vestments as shall be purchased for the use of our church to call meetings of our Congregation when necessary and to transact such other business relating to our said Congregation as we shall hereafter confide to them.

February. 1777.

Th: Jefferson, six pounds.
Philip Mazzei sixteen shillings & eight pence
Randolph Jefferson two pounds ten shillings

Jo: Jouet 1.10.
Nicholas Lewis 2.0.0
Rich: Henderson 2.0.0

Peter Marks Twenty five shillings
Richard Gaines ten shillings
Lewis Craddock ten shillings

Benjamin Calvert 10/.
Richard Moore 10/.
James ___ 10—
___ Bryan ___
Thos. Garth Fifteen shillings
James Minor Twenty shillings
William Tandy Twenty shillings.

Pledge signed by Thomas Jefferson, Philip Mazzei, and others, to support the Reverend Charles Clay, Minister of the Calvinistical Reformed Church. *(Courtesy, Massachusetts Historical Society)*

Dear Sir   Williamsburg Apr. 4. 1780.

The Fier Rodrigue being to sail within about three weeks, I think it a safe opportunity of writing to you, and of sending you according to your desire the two bundles of papers indorsed "fogli da estrarne principj di governo libero" &c. and "pamphlets, newspapers, fogli stampati," which with this letter will be addressed to the care of Penet & co. of Nantz. — I have heard nothing certain of you since your departure except by letter from Gen.l Phillips in N. York that you had been taken, carried into that place, and per-mitted to take your passage for England. — all the progress has been made in complying with your memorandums which my situation would admit. some of your accounts (of the smaller kind) have been denied; others are paid, and some still to be paid. I have put into the hands of mr Blair & into the loan office for you since your departure as follows,

  1779. July 1. £ 261-10-6

   Sep. 27. £ 609.

  1780. Mar. 16. <u>£ 384-18</u>
       £ 1255. 8-6

being all I have received for you. I wrote to mr Phripp to press a final settlement. his death however has prevented it. I shall renew my endeavors with his executors when known to me. Generals Phillips and Riedesel with their families were permitted to go to N. York on parole last September. Maj.r Irving succeeded at Colle & still continues. there is reason to beleive a part of those troops will be exchanged; but whether the lot will fall on the Major is unknown. your vines & trees at Colle

Jefferson's unsigned letter to Mazzei from Williamsburg, dated April 4, 1780, in which he gives him news of the war. (Courtesy, Dartmouth College)

have suffered extremely from their horses, cattle & carelessness. I sent my people there this spring under the direction of Anthony, and had the young trees in your nursery transplanted. but I think you need not count on the possibility of preserving any thing of that kind under present circumstances. there have been applications to purchase it; which will await your orders. Madame de Riedesel was at the Barclay springs when the permission came for her to go to New York. she of course went from thence. I expect she had with her the other books you had lent her, as none but Candide were returned. Giovannini went with them as far as the state of New-York, but not being permitted to go in, he returned, & is now in my service, as is also Anthony. Giovanni also lives with us, working for himself. Anthony is still desirous of returning, & I shall endeavor to procure him a passage. Pellegrino took his departure in some vessel, was taken, carried into N. York, & is now in Philadelphia, from which place he wrote me this information, desiring to get back to this country. — I have not yet sent on Fontana's works to Philadelphia, expecting the plates from you. should I be able to remit some tobacco to France to enable you to comply with my commissions to you I will give you notice of it: tho' should any merchant undertake to fulfill them as mentioned in the paper I shall be glad of it, settling the price in tobacco; in doing which the worth of tobacco must be estimated from the European market, making proper deductions for risk and transportation: for with us there is no such thing as settled prices. I wish not to receive any of the people I wrote for these two years.

85

I would also have the Encyclopedie, Buffon, & Belidor omitted. all the other things, adding a pair of stays, are ten times more desireable than when you were here. indeed you can form no conception how much our wants of European commodities are increased tho' the superiority of the French & Spanish fleets in Europe, and their equality here have reduced the risk of capture to be very moderate. hearing of mr Bettoia's captivity & distress in New York, I wrote to him making a tender of any services I could render him. but I have since heard he had left that place before my letter could have got there.

The seat of government is removed from this place to Richmond. I take my final departure hence within four or five days. the principal military events since you left us are the evacuation of Rhode-island by the enemy; the surprize of Stoney point (a post about 30 miles above N. york) by our general Wayne attended with the capture of upwards of 1000 prisoners; the defeat of the joint forces of Count d'Estaing & our Genl Lincoln before Savanna with the loss of about five hundred killed on the side of the allies; the reduction of the English posts on the Missisipi by the Spaniards and about a thousand prisoners taken in them; and a late expedition of the enemy from N. York against Charlestown. about 7000 men, commanded by Clinton & Cornwallis left N. York for the invasion of South Carolina. what number arrived safely we know not. they experienced in their passage a month of continual tempest, so dreadful as to bear full comparison with the hur-

ricanes of the West Indies. we learn certainly that they were obliged to throw all their horse over board. they are now on James's island, which is separated from Charlestown by a water of a mile & a half broad. Gen. Lincoln, ~~????~~ defends the town (which is rendered amazingly strong) with about 5000 men, of whom 2000 only are regulars. the Virginia & North ~~????~~ lines of regulars under generals Woodford, Scott, & Hogan, are on their march thither; part of them probably there by this time. they will add 3500 excellent souldiers to Lincoln's strength. no blow had been struck on the 5th of the last month, which is our latest intelligence. that is likely to be the only active scene in the ensuing campaign. we have had all over N. America a winter so severe as to exceed every thing conceivable in our respective climates. in this state our rivers were blocked up to their mouths with ice for six weeks. people walked over York river at the town of York, which was never before done, since the discovery of this country. regiments of horse with their attendant waggons marched in order over Patowmack at Howe's ferry, & James river at Warwick.

Not knowing how far this letter may travel post, I do not overburthen you with paper or words. the handwriting & matter will make known to you the writer, without his signature, who therefore bids you Adieu!

Permettete, che prostrato avanti la R. A. V. col massimo rispetto, in questa memoria scritta in forma di lettera, vi esponga certe cose, che spero dover esser di vostra soddisfazione, che il mio dovere mi obbliga a comunicarvi, e la prudente e necessaria politica m'impone di non comunicare ad altri:

Prima però bisogna, ch'io mi rifaccia da lontano, e scriva una specie di giornale per narrare certi aneddoti, che a prima vista parranno stranieri alla materia, ma che devono servir di base fondamentale a V. A. R. per concepir la naturalezza di certe conseguenze, che altrimenti potrebbero aver l'apparenza d'improbabilità.

Siccome speravo, che si potesse aprir colla Virginia una corrispondenza vantaggiosa pe gli Stati di V. A. R., conforme ebbi l'onor di dirvi, amato Principe, prima di partire per quel paese, arrivato là mi feci un dovere di rappresentare nel miglior aspetto possibile la libertà concessami dell'estrazione di cose; la coltivazion delle quali era là sommamente bramata, come pure di persone adatte all'opera manuale nella coltivazione delle medesime.

Non mi ricordo, se prima di partire io mi prendessi la libertà di comunicare a V. A. R. certe espressioni contenute in una lettera pervenutami in Firenze dal Sig: Tommaso Adams di Virginia, delle quali segue la traduzion letterale: "Io vi consiglio, e vi scongiuro a non perder tempo a venir da noi; "qua tutti vi conoscono, tutti vi aspettano a braccia aperte, e tutti son pronti a "secondare la lodevole intrapresa, alla quale vi siete accinto." Avevo conosciuto questo degno mio Amico in Londra, e in 14 mesi ch'ei vi si trattenne, si fece quasi vita insieme. Egli è uno dei migliori uomini del Mondo, à gran senso comune, e possiede sufficienti cognizioni, benchè non sia profonde [nelle] scienze. È amato sommamente, e bastantemente stimato. In quel Paese le buone qualità di cuore godono la prima considerazione, quelle della mente la seconda, e a queste ogni altro riguardo cede. Parlando della Nazione in generale, non intendo dir che non vi siano eccezioni, ma non son molte, nè molto nocive; poichè l'opinion pubblica le tiene in freno.

Il Sig: Adams aveva ottenuto in mio favore prima del mio arrivo 5000 acri di terra in luoghi da me indicatigli come propj per le accennate coltivazioni, e mi aveva fatto conoscere in modo, che in un giro di circa 800 miglia che feci per la Virginia, non trovai persona, che appena sentito il mio nome non mi facesse comprendere ch'io non gli ero ignoto. Ciò è facilissimo

Mazzei's report to Leopold, the Grand Duke of Tuscany, dated May, 1781. (Courtesy, Biblioteca Nazionale di Firenze)

o seguire in quel Paese, perchè i 2 Rappresentanti di ogni Contea nell'Assemblea Generale dello Stato, quando ritornano a casa danno piena soddisfazione
alla curiosità dei loro elettori, talchè presto si sa nei luoghi anche più remoti tutto quello segue di qualche rilievo. Da quel che ò d[etto] si può dedurre
che le mie parole dovevano esigere qualche considerazione. In fatti il nome di V. A. R. era volentieri e generalmente ripetuto con segni di rispetto
e gratitudine. È da considerarsi che non ignoravano le leggi che in varj
Stati dell'Europa proibiscono l'estrazione, che V. A. R. mi aveva benissima-
mente concessa.

Ma quel che molto contribuì alla mia veduta, fu il trovarsi Governatore
Mylord Dunmore, e il Viaggiatore Gen[eral] Lee. Ambidue parlavano di V. A. R.
in modo, che doveva aggiunger credito a quel che diceva io stesso. V. A. R.
sa, che il Gen[eral] Lee, malgrado la sua singolarità ed eccessiva stravaganza,
è uomo di gran talento, che à molto veduto e multissimo letto, e che non manca
d'eloquenza. Lord Dunmore non à le dette qualità, ma era creduto uomo di b[uone]
viscere, e fù molto amato, prima che il Governo inglese l'obbligasse ad ope-
rare in modo, che lo rese detestabile. Parlava spesso di Vienna, e delle accoglien-
ze statogli fatte a quella Corte; si doleva di non esser restato al servizio della Casa
d'Austria come ne aveva avuta intenzione; e dicendo le ottime qualità di tutta
la famiglia Imperiale, si esprimeva superiormente quando parlava di V. A. R.
Potrei ripetere molti suoi detti, che lo proverebbero evidentemente; ma spero che
il mio carattere sia bastantemente noto a V. A. R. [...] non esser sospetto di parzia-
lità, nè di esagerazione. Oltre di che, avendo dovuto fuggir di Virginia, è divenuto
mio acerrimo nemico.

Il Gen[eral] Lee poi dipingeva da bravo pittore tutte le vostre virtù, e alle[...]
faceva giustamente risplendere l'amabile gentilezza dell'animo vostro, e rileva-
va accidentemente la saviezza dei vostri regolamenti, e la vostra indefessa attenzione al pubblico bene. Conturoche i suoi difetti fossero alquanto conosciuti, egli era
stimato pe' suoi talenti; viaggiava continovamente; andava pe tutto, e pe tutto
parlava molto, il che lusingava il suo genio e incontrava quello dei Virginiani,
ai gli generalmente piace più l'ascoltare che il parlare. Nei tempi delle
Adunanze generali ai pranzi pubblici si beveva alla salute del Granduca di
Toscana con gran piacere di tutta la compagnia.

Io ò giudicato proprio di farvi questo racconto, Amatissimo Principe,
affinchè non vi sentiate ripugnanza a credere, che io non [...] dicendo, che
non posso esprimervi a qual segno voi siete stimato e amato in quel Paese. Questi
sentimenti si son poi diffusi in tutti gli Stati Uniti, per i motivi che dirò a suo
luogo. Credono in Virginia, che V. A. R. abbia molta propensione [per] loro, e veramente i loro sentimenti [per] V. A. R. suppongono la corrispondenza. È pro-
babile che io abbia dato motivo a questa loro credenza, come è certo che ò pro-

cerato di confermarla, specialmente dopo la rivoluzione, perchè ò preve= duto le buone conseguenze che necessariamente ne devono derivare alla pace. Avevo già persuasi alcuni miei Amici fin dal principio a mandare i loro figli a educarsi a Pisa, e prima di partire fui asicurato, che subito che sarà libera la navigazione ci verranno i giovanetti di quasi tutte le princi= pali famiglie di Virginia. I vantaggi che da ciò ne ricaverebbero la manifattu= ra della Toscana e il commercio generale sarebbero immensi per ragioni chiare e certe, ma troppo lunghe a descriversi.

Nel mese di Marzo 1775, spandosi molto accreditata la voce in Virginia, che il Governo d'Inghilterra avrebbe mandato dei commissarj ȧ trattare un'accomo= damento con soddisfazione delle Colonie; io che con pochi altri ero di opinione di= versa, ~~consonare~~ supposi (conforme significai a V. A. R.) che questo fosse un colpo di politica del Gabinetto inglese ȧ addormentarci, e feci quanto potei ȧ tenere gli animi svegliati. Pochi giorni dopo Lord Dunmore convocò l'Assem= blea ȧ il Mese di maggio, e significò, che aveva ordine di far proposizioni, sarebbero state di universal soddisfazione. In quel frattempo io ricevei 2 ri= sposte da Londra, una dal Conte di Bruhl Inviato di Sassonia, e l'altra dal Sig. Antonio Chamier, secondo nel Dipartimento di guerra, ma in sostanza il primo (poichè maneggiava tutti gli affari), dalle quali appariva chiaramente che non vi era speranza d'accomodamento. L'ordinanza dei Deputati d'ordine del Popolo essendo terminata, la comunicai al Sig. Tommaso Jefferson mio intimo Ami= co e vicino, presentemente Governator di Virginia, e che allora era ȧ andare al Congresso. Si convenne di quel che ci parve proprio di proporre, e ~~ȧ~~ ne scrissi anche al D.r Franklin (paremente Membro del Congresso) che fu dell'istessa nostra opinione. Ma nel Congresso ancora vi era un numero troppo grande di per= sone, che tuttavia speravano un accomodamento, il che produceva un ritardo pernicioso nei preparativi da farsi ȧ propria difesa. In fatti vollero mandare una 2.da supplica concepita in tali termini, che Jefferson nel mandarmene la copia mi scrisse: "Voi vi maraviglierete della nostra viltà, ma è stato necessario "di sottometterci per evitar la divisione tra noi. Il solo nostro conforto sarà d'aver "la mandata in buona compagnia." La compagnia fu la Dichiarazione di vo= lersi Difendere, non ottenendo giustizia. In occasione della D.a Dichiarazione, che ebbi l'onore di spedir subito colle mie riflessioni a V. A. R., il D.r Franklin, che doveva rispondermi relativamente alle proposizioni portate al Congresso da Mr. Jefferson mi scrisse, come segue: "I Sig.ri Al Congresso non anno ancora estese le "loro vedute a formare Alleanze, nè a provvedere ai loro bisogni da paesi "molto remoti. Essi vi restan per altro molto obbligati della vostra offerta "e dei lumi che avete comunicati, i quali tra un'anno o due potranno esser "loro (secondo la mia opinione) molto utili. Vi ringrazio io med.o di cuore

"per la traduzione della nostra Dichiarazione che avete mandata al Granduca " perché, avendo la più alta opinione di quel Principe e di tutta la Famiglia " Imperiale, ... le relazioni avutene da voi medesimo, e dal mio buon'Amico " il D.r Ingenhousz, vorrei che noi stassimo bene a quella Corte."

Nella guerra, che presentemente sostengono i 13 Stati Uniti la Virginia contribuisce ... tanto in uomini che in denaro, e in altro. La Virginia è lo Stato più antico, più vasto, più ricco, più abbondante d'uomini grandi; e la sua popolazione e i suoi prodotti crescono e son per crescere infinitamente più che negli altri. È seguito dal famoso Giovanni Adams di Massachussetts, che ora è in Olanda, che nel Congresso i Deputati degli altri Stati ànno sempre avuta una gran deferenza al voto della Deputazion di Virginia. Non è dunque da maravigliarsi, che ... mezzo della Deputazion di Virginia, e specialmente di Mr. Jefferson, che fu presto conosciuto ... uno dei più degni e più savi uomini d'America, e ... mezzo del D.r Franklin V.A.R. fosse presto conosciuto, amato, e stimato ... in tutti gli Stati.

Alcuni dei principali cittadini di Virginia ... capacità e zelo, confidando molto, come tuttavia confidano nella propensione di V.A.R. a favor loro e credendo ch'io potessi esser utile alla causa Americana qui e in altri luoghi ancora, cominciarono a far sentire il lor desiderio, ch'io fossi mandato in Europa dal Congresso. Fu scritto, conforme ebbi l'onor di dire a V.A.R. nella prima udienza, al sig.r Riccardo Lee, allora capo della Deputazion di Virginia, il quale fece uso di alcune delle notizie comunicategli ... ottenere i suoi fini, tacque le più importanti d'onde nacque l'imprudenza di dare il carattere pubblico a Mr. Izard, ed usò fino la sfacciata indiscretezza di non consegnare al sopra detto sig.r Gio: Adams una lettera inclusagli da Jefferson, perché da quella che Jefferson scrisse a lui comprese che era dell'istesso tenore. Dissi pure a V.A.R. che gl'intrighi dei fratti Lee furon conosciuti, e che furono tutti coperti dagl'impieghi tanto in Europa che in America.

Non avendo il Congresso giudicato proprio di mandare Agenti in Europa, che tenessero celato il lor carattere, lo Stato di Virginia determinò di mandar me ... i suoi affari propri. Quando ero ... partire nel mese di Giugno del 79, ritornando dal Congresso il menzionato Amico mio sig.r Tommaso Adams mi disse, che tra 2, o 3 mane sarei stato ricercato dal Congresso, ed essendo egli stato il più attivo promotore delle commissioni che dovevano darmisi, mostrò gran dispiacere di quel che era seguito. L'imbarco era pronto; partii immediatamente, fui preso prigioniero ... tradimento del cap.no, e gettai in mare le credenziali e le istruzioni, conforme ebbi l'onor di dire a V.A.R. narrandole la lunga serie delle mie avventure fino al mio arrivo in Italia.

Ero stato qualche tempo in Italia quando conobbi, che alcune commissioni non erano eseguibili dentro i limiti prescrittimi, e specialmente la più importante. Bisognerò scrivere nuove Credenziali e Istruzioni, e siccome il Governo, che non à altro potere che l'Esecutivo, deve, prima di far cambiamenti, essere autorizzato dall'Assemblea Legislativa, possono indugiar molto a venire, considerando che, oltre i soliti ostacoli, ci è ora quello d'esser la Virginia divenuta il Teatro della guerra.

La mancanza delle Credenziali per altro fa presentemente comodo, poiché, se mai V. A. R. non credesse di dover anche accedere a veruna cosa, non ostante tutte le più circospette precauzioni, la repugnanza non comparirebbe, e le circostanze potrebbero cambiare prima che giunga la necessità di spiegarmi.

Il Sig.r Giovanni Adams, Ministro Plenipotenziario degli Stati Uniti all'Aja, e in cui tutta l'America confida, avendomi ultimamente scritto d'Amsterdam per affari riguardanti il Congresso, gli risposi, che sebbene non vo anche ricevuta le nuove Credenziali, non mi pareva di dover intraprendere di servir'il Congresso senza il consenso del Governo di Virginia, nel che la mia principal veduta fu di prender tempo.

Non credo ora opportuno di tediar più lungamente V. A. R. col parlar d'affari non eseguibili presentemente, il che per altro farò dopo il mio ritorno da Livorno e Pisa, fra 2 o 3 mane, se mi permetterete di continovare. Intanto supplicando la Vostra Benignità a voler degnarsi di leggere con qualche attenzione i 2 annessi fogli, io eseguisco alcune delle incombenze datemi, che sono il procurar di dimostrarvi la giustizia della Causa Americana, in primo luogo, e in secondo la probabilità di un felice evento.

In un altro foglio, se vi degnerete di riceverlo, dimostrerò l'importanza di procurarsi il commercio colla Virginia, che sarebbe tutto attivo, per supplire al quale non à anche la Toscana lavoranti abbastanza. Io procuro intanto coll'aiuto di mercanti e di manifattori, d'informarmi di tutto quello che si fa; di suggerire quel che si potrebbe fare; e di disporre le cose in modo da non perder tempo ad eseguire, subito che le circostanze lo permettano.

Siccome la cosa che anno più a cuore gli Americani, è la buona opinione, e più d'ogni altra valutano la vostra e quella dell'Augustissimo vostro Fratello, io vorrei tralle grazie maggiori che mi à favorito, ed è di favorirmi la vostra somma Bontà, quella di ottenere che per mezzo vostro fosse tolto dall'Imperatore il foglio che à per titolo = Ragioni, per cui non può darsi agli Stati Americani la taccia di ribelli.

Non mi scuserò, Amat.mo Principessa, sulla franchezza del dire, e la natura lezza dello stile, perché mi è parso di vedere, che vi piace la verità nuda,

senza frangia, e senza orpello. Il mio rispetto per la vostra Persona e per le vostre grandi e singolari virtù, non può esser maggiore; ma esista nel cuore, come esisterebbe nei fatti avendone l'opportunità, e non nell'insignificante pomposità di parole e di frasi.

À Monsieur

Monsieur Mazzei Député
des États de Virginie hôtel
des Colonies.

Rue des Prouvaires

3.

Paris. 30. Mai. 1783.

Je verrai ce Soir Mr. Haüy, Monsieur, pour causer avec lui sur les moïens de le Satisfaire, et je vous prie d'être bien persuadé que votre interêt pour lui sera pour moi un grand motif de lui rendre Service. Nous avons perdu avant hier Mr. le Duc d'Estissac mon Oncle, affligé moi même je suis encore entièrement occupé de Soigner Sa famille affligée; c'est ce qui m'empêchera de pouvoir vous chercher ou vous recevoir d'ici à mon départ fixé à après demain; je vous prie de recevoir par écrit mes Souhaits pour votre heureux retour dans la patrie que vous vous êtes choisie; et l'expression Sincere de tous les Sentimens avec lesquels j'ai l'honneur d'être, Monsieur, Votre très humble et très obéissant Serviteur,

Le Duc de la Rochefoucauld.

Mr. Mazzei,

Rochefoucauld's letter to Mazzei, May 30, 1783. *(Courtesy, American Philosophical Society)*

16°

Filippo Mazzei presenta i suoi umilissimi ossequj al Duca de la Rochefoucauld, e si prende la libertà di trascrivergli qui sotto una reflessione, che egli à aggiunta a quelle che già scrisse sul presente Governo di Virginia, delle quali S. E. volle degnarsi di prender copia.

"Il diritto di Suffragio e di Rappresentanza è riservato ai soli possidenti, mentre gli obblighi del Cittadin son comuni a tutti gli abitanti. Questa è una grande offesa alla giustizia, che deve senza riguardo alcuno essere imparziale in tutto; ma se l'equità dovesse influire, insegnerebbe di esentare i poveri dagli aggravj piuttosto che dai diritti."

Montesquieu nel suo spirito delle Leggi pare che abbia voluto fare l'elogio della Costituzione Inglese, piuttosto che l'analisi; per il che il Mazzei à creduto di doverlo spesso confutare nei suoi scritti sul Governo, che furono pubblicati nelle gazzette di Virginia. La sopraddetta osservazione è diametralmente opposta agli aristocratici sentimenti di quel celebre Scrittore.

Il Mazzei si prende parimente la libertà d'inviare al Sig.r Duca ciò che Mr. De Marmontel à scritto in conseguenza delle sopraddette reflessioni, supplicandolo di prendersi l'incomodo di rimandarglielo quando ne avrà fatto quell'uso che giudicherà proprio.

30. Maggio 1783.

In questo momento riceve il Mazzei l'obbligantis= simo biglietto che il Sig.r Duca gli à fatto l'onore di

Letter of May 30, 1783, addressed to De La Rochefoucauld. Mazzei speaks of his writings on Government which were published in the *Virginia Gazettes*. (Courtesy, *Bibliothèque Municipale, Mantes-La-Jolie*)

scrivergli. Egli partecipa vivamente della sua presente afflizione, gli rende infinite grazie delle sue gentilezze che desidera di poter giungere a meritare, e desidera non meno che gli faccia la giustizia di credere, che non avrebbe ardito di raccomandargli M.r Haüy, se non avesse conosciuto nel Sig.r Duca ciò che gli vien confermato dal gentilissimo suo biglietto, cioè un'animo non solo propenso, ma bramoso di giovare alle persone meritevoli.

Sir,   Roswell, 3. December 1783.

        I take the liberty to inform your Excellen-
cy & the other Gentlemen of the Council of my
arrival in Virginia; & that I shall do myself
the honour to present my respects to your
Excell.^y in person, as soon as it will be in my
power to proceed to Richmond. In the mean
time I am most respectfully,

    Sir,

                        your Excelly.^s most humble
                        & most Obedient Servant
                                Philip Mazzei

His Excelly.^y Ben: Harrison Esqre Govr of Virginia

Letter of Philip Mazzei to Benjamin Harrison, Governor of Virginia, dated December 3, 1783. *(Courtesy, The Historical Society of Pennsylvania)*

A Representation of Mr Mazzei's conduct, from the time of his appointment to be Agent of the State in Europe untill his return to Virginia.

The eighth of January, one thousand, seven hundred and seventy nine, the Governor and Council, in pursuance of a resolution of the General Assembly, appointed Mr Mazzei to go to Europe, and to be Agent there, for the purpose of obtaining a loan of Gold and Silver (not exceeding the sum of nine hundred thousand pounds Sterling), of purchasing *goods* in Italy, for the use of the armies; and of procuring by all means in his power, ———— to be of Service to the American Cause.

Mr Mazzei, proud of the Trust his Country had honour'd him with, desired to be of as little charge to it as possible, during the time of his service — The Governor having asked him, if one Thousand pounds sterling would suffice to bear his expences for twelve months, he answered that such a Sum would not be too great for the first Year, considering the extraordinary expences of travelling; that in case he should stay any length of time in one place, even less would do; and that, according to his opinion, prudence and wisdom required that at all times, and more especially in the present critical time, the American ministers and agents in Europe should on every occasion exhibit a decent Republican oeconomy. The Governor then asked him, what might satisfy him, as a compensation for the loss of his time, and the neglect of his affairs; to which he answered, that nothing could satisfy him, but the good will of his fellow Citizens, if he should be so happy as to return with success, and that he wished for nothing more.

The following Narration will prove whether he has forfeited their confidence; or if he is intitled to their approbation, from the whole of his conduct, *especially* when one considers the essential services he could have rendered his Country at the most critical times, if he had not been constantly kept in a State of uncertainty, and without the

I have ... made a paper entitled "A representation
of Mr. Mazzei's conduct from the time of his appointment
to be agent of the State in Europe untill his return to Vir...
and believe the proceedings of the Executive Board which
I was a Member of it to be therein correctly stated, & as...
having been present at the conversation between Governour
Henry & Mr. Mazzei relative to an allowance of £ 10...
per annum for his expences I can say nothing as to that ...
I recollect only that that sum was mentioned at the B...
as a salary not exceeding the dignity of the business on which
he was to be sent, & that the prevailing idea was that the salary
should be left unfixed till his return to Virginia when he sh...
to receive a decent reward over and above the sum which
he should have necessarily expended in supporting the rank ...
promoting the object of his Commission.

April 25th 1783.   Copy   J. Madison Jr

2 I have also received the abovementioned Representat...
& think it contains a true state of facts as far as relate...
Circumstances which could come under my observation while...
Member of the Executive: & I have the same idea of a
compensation to be allowed Mr. Mazzei for his services as ...
find expressed by Mr. Madison in his Certificate above writt...

Rosewell May the 1st 1784   Copy   John Page

Testimonials by J. Madison, Jr. and John Page. (*Courtesy, Biblioteca Nazionale di Firenze*)

Having perused Mr. Mazzei's Representation contained in a written paper communicated to me by him respecting his Conduct as an Agent from this State, to sollicit a Loan of Money in Europe, agreable to a Resolution of the General Assembly, I am of opinion, as far as my memory serves me, that all the facts stated in the two or three first pages of the said Representation are just & true, and I do well remember, that nothing more than a general agreement was or could be made with Mr. Mazzei respecting any allowance for Expences or reward for his Services, at the time he was employed by the Executive, for the purpose aforesaid: This general agreement, as well as I can recollect at this time, was "that the Executive expected they were to furnish Mr. Mazzei their Agent, from time to time, whilst upon this public business with as much money or credit as would be necessary to defray his Expences (as a Gentleman) during the time he should be employed in the service of the State and that a reward for his Services, loss of time &c should be the Subject of consideration upon Mr. Mazzei's return to this Country or when the purpose of his Agency was ended"

Copy / Dudley Digges

I was not present when Mr. Mazzei's appointment as Agent was made by the Governor & Council — an unfortunate circumstance prevented my attendance for several weeks

Testimonial by Dudley Digges. (*Courtesy, Biblioteca Nazionale di Firenze*)

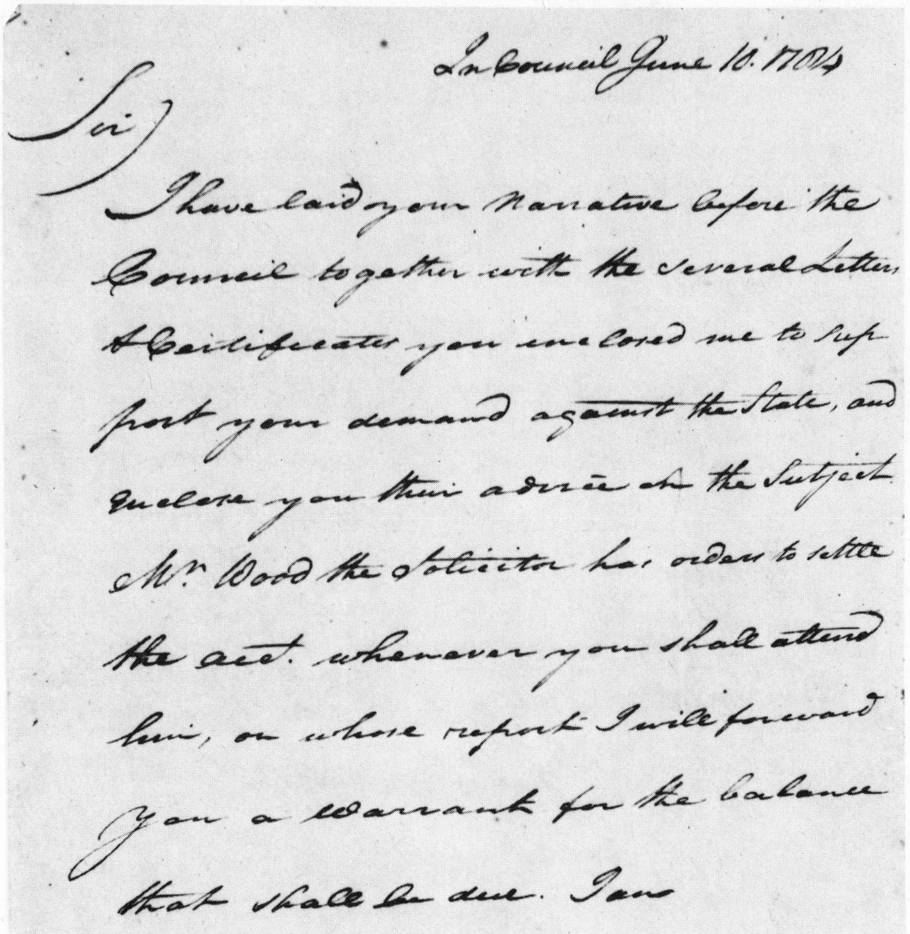

In Council June 10. 1784

Sir)

I have laid your Narative before the
Council together with the several Letters
& Certificates you enclosed me to support your demand against the State, and
enclose you their advice on the Subject
Mr. Dood the Solicitor has orders to settle
the acct. whenever you shall attend
him, on whose report I will forward
you a warrant for the balance
that shall be due. I am

Sir
Your most obedt. &
most humble Servant

Benj Harrison

Mr. Mazzei

Letter from Benjamin Harrison, Governor of Virginia. (*Courtesy, Biblioteca Nazionale di Firenze*)

In Council June 10th 1784

His Excellency having laid before the board the narrative of Mr. Philip Mazzei and other papers relative to his conduct whilst Agent for this State in Europe for the purpose of borrowing a Sum of money;

The Board taking the same under their consideration, advise that Mr. Mazzei should receive at the rate of Six hundred Louis dor $ Annum from the 8th January one thousand seven hundred & seventy nine being the time of his appointment to the 8th of April eighty three as a compensation for his Services & to defray his expences; And the Board reflecting on the patriotic exertions of Mr. Mazzei in favor of this ~~State~~ Country in his aforesaid appointment, are of Opinion that he has conducted himself therein with activity, assiduity & zeal, and that the ill success which has attended that business is by no means imputable to him but to certain coincident circumstances, and that his conduct merits the approbation of the ~~Executive~~ Board, of which this advice is to be considered as a testimonial

Copy

Resolution passed by the Board of Trade of Virginia, June 10, 1784: "And the Board reflecting on the patriotic exertions of Mr. Mazzei in favor of this Country in the aforesaid appointment are of opinion that he has conducted himself therein with activity, assiduity and zeal, and that the ill sweep which has attended that business is by no means imputable to him but to certain coincident circumstances, and that his conduct merits the approbation of the Board of which this advice is to be considered as a testimonial." *(Courtesy, Biblioteca Nazionale di Firenze)*

THURSDAY, December 4, 1776.   THE   NUMBER

VIRGINIA  GAZETTE

OPEN TO **ALL PARTIES,** BUT INFLUENCED BY **NONE**

WILLIAMSBURG: PRINTED BY FOR THE BENEFIT OF   J O H N   P I N K N E
CLEMENTINA RIND's CHILDREN.

All Persons may be supplied with this GAZETTE at 12/. 6 d. a Year. ADVERTISEMENTS, of a moderate Length, are inserted for 3/. the first We and 1/. each Time after; long ones in Proportion.——PRINTING WORK, of every Kind, executed with Care and Dispatch.

MIDAS, a remarkable large jack ass, imported last fall from *Malta,* by *Philip Mazzei,* esq; stands at my plantation in *Prince George* county, and covers at two dollars the leap, 40 s. the season, and 3 l. to ensure.---It may not be amiss to inform the publick, that, from the difficulty of obtaining and the expense attending the importation of an ass of this kind, his price for covering is necessarily much higher than any one of the common breed, but it will be amply compensated by the size and strength of the mules he gets.

THEODORICK BLAND, jun.

Notice in the "Virginia Gazette," May 24, 1776, about one of the jackasses Mazzei imported for breeding purposes. *(Courtesy, Colonial Williamsburg Foundation, Williamsburg, Va.)*

A Monsieur
Monsieur Mazzei chez Son Ex=
cellence Monsieur Jefferson
Grille de Chaillot
a Paris

John Banister 22. X.bre 1785.
réponse   6. Feb. 1786

I John Banister of the County of Dinwiddie in Virginia, do engage with Philip Mazzei esq.r that if the said Mazzei will import, or thro' the means of any other Person cause to be imported a good large and Serviceable He ass of the Breed of the Island of Malta, and deliver, or cause him to be delivered to me, that I will maintain him in the best manner as a Stud, that all the expences attending the ass shall be defrayed by me after he shall have been landed in this State, that I will endeavour to make the most of him, and will divide the Same in equal Parts with the said Mazzei, allowing each to the other for all the Mares which either may put to the said ass — And the said Mazzei shall be at liberty after the expiration of two covering Seasons to reassume to himself the sole & absolute Property in the said ass, and not sooner, and also further agree, and oblige myself to pay all charges that may accrue upon the removal of the ass from the Place of his landing to my house, if the Place of landing is within the State, and that I will not take more or less for his Services to Mares than ten Spanish milled dollars, by the Season & so in proportion — It is also to be understood that it shall be optional in me to return the ass to the said Mazzei

First and last pages of an agreement dated September 17, 1784 and addressed to: "Monsieur Mazzei chez Son Excellence Monsieur Jefferson, Grille de Challiot à Paris," from John Banister. (*Courtesy, Biblioteca Nazionale di Firenze*)

from the Services of the &c, but am not to be accountable for bad debts should any such happen, the Cost of all Suits should such proceeding be found necessary, to be borne equally by both Parties.

Test ——

Dun: Rose

John Banister
Sepr 17. 1784

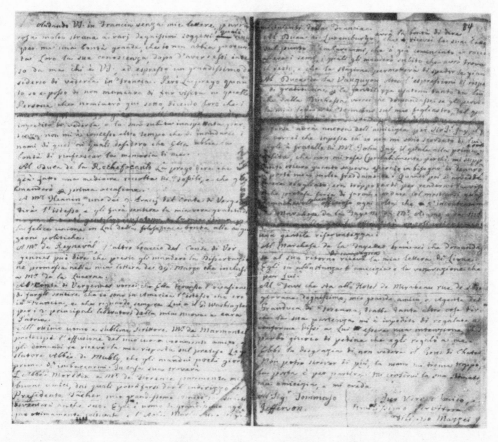

Portion of Mazzei's memorandum to Jefferson. *(Courtesy, Library of Congress.)*

1736–1799

From a painting by Sully.

Last two pages of a three-page letter, dated April 16, 1784, in which Patrick Henry supports Mazzei's claims for payment of the expenses incurred while in the service of Virginia and quotes a letter from John Adams praising Mazzei's work in France. *(Courtesy, Historical Society of Pennsylvania)*

WE, the underwritten, having associated for the purpose of preserving and handing down to posterity, those pure and sacred principles of Liberty, which have been derived to us, from the happy event of the late glorious Revolution, and being convinced, that the surest mode to secure Republican systems of Government from lapsing into Tyranny, is by giving free and frequent information to the mass of people, both of the nature of them, and of the measures which may be adopted by their several component parts; have determined, and do hereby most solemnly pledge ourselves to each other, by every holy tie and obligation, which free men ought to hold inestimably dear, that every one in his respective station, will keep a watchful eye over the great fundamental rights of the people.

That we will without reserve, communicate our thoughts to each other, and to the people, on every subject which may either tend to amend our Government, or to preserve it from the innovations of ambition, and the designs of faction.

To accomplish this desirable object, we do agree to commit to paper our sentiments, in plain and intelligible language, on every subject which concerns the General Weal; and transmit the same to the Honorable John Blair Esq; whom we hereby constitute president of the said society, with powers to congregate the members thereof, either at Richmond or Williamsburg whenever he may suppose that he has a sufficient quantity of materials collected for publication. It is farther agreed, that it shall be a rule of the said society, that no publications shall be made till after mature deliberation in the convocation, it shall have been so determined, by at least two thirds of the present members.

JOHN BLAIR,
JAMES MADISON,
ROBERT ANDREWS,
JAMES M°CLURG,
JOHN PAGE,
JAMES INNES,
MANN PAGE,
JAMES MADISON, Jun.
PATRICK HENRY,
THOMAS LOMAX,
EDMUND RANDOLPH,
WILLIAM SHROT,
WILLIAM FLEMING,
JOHN BRECKINRIDGE,
ARCHIBALD STEUART,
JOSEPH JONES,
WILLIAM NELSON, Jun.
B. RANDOLPH,
JAMES MARSHALL,
RICARD HENRY LEE,
WILLIAM LEE,
LUDWELL LEE,
WILLIAM GRAYSON,
FRANCIS CORBIN,
PHILIP MAZZEI,
WILSON C. NICHOLAS,
JOHN NICHOLAS,
JOHN TAYLOR,
J. BROWN,
RICHARD B. LEE,
SPENCER ROANE,
ALEXANDER WHITE,
JAMES MONROE,
ARTHUR LEE.

At a meeting held on the 15th of June, 1784.

Resolved, that the following declaration be added to the paper originally signed by the members, viz.

" The Society being persuaded, that the liberty of a people is most secure when " the extent of their rights, and the measures of government concerning them are " known, do declare that the purpose of this institution is to communicate by fit " publications such facts and sentiments, as tend to unfold and explain the one or " the other."

Broadside announcing the organizaton of The Constitutional Society. (*Courtesy, Virginia State Library*)

ON the eleventh day of June, one thousand seven hundred and eighty-four, the following gentlemen, to wit, Mr. William Fleming, Mr. Patrick Henry, Mr. James Madison, jun. Mr. Edmund Randolph, Mr. Joseph Jones, Mr. William Lee, Mr. Phillip Mazzei, Mr. Mann Page, Mr. Archibald Steuart, Mr. John Breckenridge, and Mr. William Nelson, assembled in the City of Richmond, and on consideration that Mr. John Page, the Reverend Mr. Madison, and the Reverend Mr. Andrews were out of the State, determined that the members present, forming a majority of those who were within the State, might constitutionally hold a meeting of this Society.

Mr. Henry by the unanimous request of the meeting took the chair.

Mr. Mazzei reminded the Society of the necessity of chusing a President, and recommended Mr. John Blair whose talents and virtue point him out as a proper person to fill that office, and the said Mr. Blair was thereupon unanimously elected President of this Society.

Mr. Randolph recommended Mr. William Fleming as a person in every respect qualified to act as Vice-President of this Society, whereupon the said Mr. Fleming was unanimously elected Vice-President of the same.

Ordered, that Mr. Nelson be appointed Secretary to this Society.

Ordered, that a committee be appointed to draw up rules for the organization of this Society.

And a committee was appointed of Mr. Henry, Mr. Richard Henry Lee, Mr. Madison, Mr. Mazzei, Mr. Jones, and Mr. Randolph.

And then the Society adjourned till Tuesday next precisely at 6 o'clock, P. M.

At a meeting held on Tuesday the 15th day of June, 1784, present sixteen members, Mr. Fleming the Vice-President took the chair.

ON a motion made by Mr. Randolph, and seconded by Mr. Henry, to add, by way of amendment to the paper which was originally signed by the members of this Society, a declaration in the following words, viz:

" The Society being persuaded, that the liberty of a people is most secure when the extent
" of their rights and the measures of government concerning them are known, do declare that

" the purpose of this institution is to communicate by fit publications such facts and sentiments, " as tend to unfold and explain the one or the other,"

It passed in the affirmative.

On a motion made by Mr. Mazzei and seconded by Mr. Corbin,

Resolved, that the title of this institution be " The Constitutional Society."

Resolved, that the President make such notification of this institution as he may think proper.

Resolved, that in case of the necessary absence of the President and Vice-President, this Society have a right to appoint a President, pro tempore, or Chairman.

As the intention of this Society is to be useful to the community, and not merely to shew a desire of being so.

Resolved, that it is expected, that each member should send to the President, every six months, an essay, or problem, on some political thesis of importance, which, it is hoped will be confined to the subject thereof; and that any one failing in this duty, be informed by the Secretary that two essays, or problems, will be expected from him during the next six months; and that any member, on a second delinquency herein, shall not thereafter be considered as a member of this Society.

Resolved, that notice of the meetings of this Society be given in the public papers, at least thirty days previous to the day appointed, and that seven members besides the President, or Vice-President, or President pro tempore, be required to constitute a meeting.

Resolved, that candidates to become members of this Society shall be nominated by a member, at a meeting preceeding his election or rejection, which shall be determined by ballot, by means of black and white balls, or beans, and that no candidate be admitted a member without the assent of three fourths of the meeting.

Ordered, that a committee be appointed to draw up rules for the government and organization of this Society.

And a committee was appointed of Mr. Patrick Henry, Mr. Richard Henry Lee, Mr. James Madison, jun. Mr. Philip Mazzei, Mr. Joseph Jones, Mr. Edmund Randolph, Mr. Alexander White, Mr. John Taylor, and Mr. John Breckenridge.

In the early part of my stay in Virginia, I had occasion to speak with Jefferson of the heavy damages caused in Italy by the embanking of rivers and, above all, in Tuscany, after the Count de Richecourt, chief of the regency, permitted the deforestation of the mountains, beyond the limits fixed by law during the time of the republic, and which Leopold extended indefinitely, not foreseeing the heavy damage that would result: that is, a lack (since the water, not being kept back, cannot filter down and form them) of rich water sources, which are so useful; frequent floods, followed by droughts, both of which make navigation difficult, dangerous, and sometimes impossible; the raising of the river's bed, owing to the depositing of fine soil (since the water carries away the best); and the necessity of continually raising the river embankments, which in several places can barely stand. The time does not seem far off when the water, asserting its rights, will seek a new and more convenient bed, with heavy damages to the landowners. The descendants of those who cut down the woods and who enjoyed the benefit of two or three good crops, will find stones where once was soil and woods.

Jefferson agreed that the adoption of a law against deforestation would be an excellent thing; but not before its importance had been realized, because to interfere with a landowner's right of doing as he pleases with his own property is too repugnant to the principles of liberty. But when the heads of families realize that it would avoid dire consequences for their descendants, they themselves will ask for the law.

Our government, even though set up in a hurry and during turbulent times, was preferable to any other, be it ancient or modern. Nevertheless, it was soon recognized that it permitted of improvement. However, it was agreed to wait until everyone could attend to it.

Upon my return from Europe, while Jefferson was in Boston, about to sail to replace Franklin, some members of the Assembly proposed to revise the Constitution, while others feared that by jumping out of the frying pan they would fall into the fire. I proposed the formation of an organization, with the title of Constitutional Society, to discuss privately all that was to be publicly discussed and enacted by the Assembly.

They wished to make me president; I refused, foreseeing that after reporting to the government on my mission, I would have to return to Europe. I nominated Mr. John Blair, who was unanimously elected by a voice vote.

The several meetings, held at the president's home in Williamsburg, were a source of satisfaction to me. As the narration of my life has come now to the time when I was a guest at Mr. Mann Page's home on the Rappahannock River, whence I wrote the President a long letter, I remember having a rough draft of this letter and, having looked for and found it, I am now enclosing it herewith.

Since in the note with which you persuaded me to write the story of my life, you rendered me justice by saying that *never have I forsaken in spirit my beloved and adopted country*, I am pleased to have found the said rough draft, which may, if need be, justify your opinion. You will also see by it that, before leaving, I had already written my reflections on the navigation of the four principal rivers of the state, which reflections I did not wish published before the public had been sufficiently enlightened, by means of the education which, through the press, it was to receive from our society.

I will translate my letter for you and enclose the translation with the original, to spare you the trouble, should you want to read it to someone who does not know the English language.

Footnote from Mazzei's Memoirs, p. 285.

113

Mazzei's courtyard, Pisa. *(Courtesy, Columbia University)*

Two views of the Mazzei house at Pisa. *(Courtesy, Library of Congress)*

MEMORIE

DELLA

VITA

E DELLE

PEREGRINAZIONI

DEL FIORENTINO

FILIPPO MAZZEI

CON DOCUMENTI STORICI SULLE SUE MISSIONI POLITICHE
COME AGENTE DEGLI STATI-UNITI D'AMERICA, E DEL RE STANISLAO
DI POLONIA.

VOLUME PRIMO.

LUGANO

TIPOGRAFIA DELLA SVIZZERA ITALIANA

1845

Title page of *Memorie*, Vol. I, as first published at Lugano, Switzerland. *(Courtesy, Columbia University)*

Letter of Mr Philip Mazzei to Mr John Blair, President of the Constitution Society.

Dear Sir, — In my preceding I mentioned that I would write to you on the subject of our Society. When I reflect on the great benefit the Community may derive from such an institution I can't help wishing most heartily the component members

would seriously set down determined to fulfill their engagements. A great deal is yet wanting to bring our government to that degree of perfection necessary to protect effectually the interest and honour of our country, and to transmit freedom to our distant posterity.

The very gentlemen who last year opposed in the House of Delegates the calling of a convention for the purpose of amending it, agreed that there are in it many imperfections, and I heard several among them declare that they only oppose it for fear of having a worse one. The same apprehension I had myself, and am still of opinion that it would be a beginning at the wrong end if such a thing is attempted before the People at large are sufficiently acquainted with the danger attending (attending?) their imperfections, and the only way to avoid them. This once done they would turn themselves to those men, who are willing and able to perform the grand work.

= The People in general will cheerfully go right, if you show the way to them. The present great misfortune proceeds from their being easily misled by the ignorance and malice of a few, because the good and sensible among us, who (according to my observation) are in a much greater proportion than in any other civilized nation I know, will not make use of their tongue and pen for the improvement of the minds of their fellow-citizens. However in a truly free country, where the national happiness and prosperity of every individual stand on an equal footing, it seems that the illiterate part of mankind are to expect from those, who have had the advantage of a learned education, instruction and good advice, as children from their parents. Our Society was instituted for that laudable purpose only. We have promised it to each other, to our citizens at large, and the world. There is no excuse for us if we should be

Copy of Mazzei's letter to John Blair in which he discusses the benefits of The Constitutional Society, dated May 12, 1785. (In *Memorie*, Vol. II)

deficient. Sensible of the importance of the object, we did not rest satisfied on the propensity, which every honest heart feels for the good of the community: we have pledged our honor to use our utmost exertions to promote it. — The People, I am confident, when they see a number of respectable gentlemen (among whom some of the first characters in the Country) purposely employed in instructing them (in which undertaking they can have no particular interest, besides the noble satisfaction of exerting their talents in support of liberty) will not only rejoice, and be thankful to them, but they will also in all matters, not easily understood, pay regard to their opinion in preference to that of certain persons, who now too easily and too often succeed to mislead them — There

prosperity of the community, which will afford the cunning and self-interested favorable opportunities to deceive a number of good men, because their disagreable consequences will easily and soon be seen and felt, while their good effects (though so far superior as to bear no proportion with the inconveniencies) cannot be conceived, or rather foreseen but by a few, on account of their being remoter and the results of a variety of causes. Such, for example, is the propriety of one or two Ports only in our State for exports and imports. — A worthy member of our Society made me promise to send him my notions in writing on this subject, before I leave the Country: but I would not chuse to have them published, until the Society have, by fit publications, established their character, and prepared the People rather to look for them to accept their instructions. — Permit me, Sir, earnestly to beg of you that you will be pleased, at the first meeting, to point out the duty, and the necessity of being active, and engage to give yourself a good example. For my part, I am now going out of this my dear adopted country. Should I return, I don't conceive that the present imperfections of our Government could produce any material bad consequences during my life, and I have no children: but the honest part of the inhabitants of the Globe are my brethern, posterity my children, and were I to go, and spend the remainder of my days in China I would always with pleasure

contribute to the forming of an asylum for mankind from oppression. My insufficiency shall not excuse me. I know that my duty will be accomplished, so long as I perform my engagement to the best in my power, and so far you may depend upon. — I wish likewise that you will be pleased to propose at the next meeting the admission of foreign honorary members, which if agreed to, I would be glad to receive in New York a full information of the manner of receiving them, and their duty, as I intend (provided the society will give me leave) to make the offer to the Duke de la Rochefoucauld in Paris, to marquis Beccaria in Milan, to Mr Fontana in Florence and Mr Spallanzani in Bologna, besides such others, to whom the society should direct that I should do the same. — In expectation of your commands, I have the honor to be with great regard and esteem, Sir,   Yours &c Philip Mazzei.

  Mansfield 12. May 1785.

P. S. — Mr Mann Page intends to be at the next meeting, and to propose Mr John Minor, who has declared to me, that, if he has the honor of being received a member of our society, he will never be deficient in his duty as such. In case Mr Page, by some unforeseen accident, should be prevented attending, I beg you will be so good as to propose him yourself, signifying at the same time, that I have known Mr Minor ever since I returned from Europe both in the college and out of it, and that he has always appeared to me to be an ingenious, learned and worthy young gentleman —

Sig. Giovanni Blair presidente della società costituzionale.

Caro signore!

Nella mia precedente dissi, che vi avrei scritto sul soggetto della nostra società. Quando rifletto agli immensi vantaggi che la nazione può ricevere da una tale istituzione, io non posso astenermi dal desiderare ardentissimamente, che i membri che la compongono si determinino seriamente a soddisfare al loro impegno. Manca tuttavia molto per condurre il nostro governo a quel grado di perfezione, che deve efficacemente proteggere l'interesse e l'onor della nostra patria, e trasmetter la libertà ai nostri più remoti posteri. Quei medesimi che si opposero l'anno scorso alla convocazion d'una convenzione per correggerlo, convennero che vi son molte imperfezioni, e che vi si opposero unicamente per timore di peggiorare. L'istesso timore avevo io stesso, e son tuttavia d'opinione, che sarebbe mal fatto il principiare prima che il popolo sia bastantemente informato del pericolo che sovrasta mediante l'accennate imperfezioni, e del solo mezzo di rimediarvi. Fatto questo il popolo s'indirizzerebbe subito a quei soggetti che son disposti ad eseguire e capaci di perfezionare la grande intrapresa.

Il popolo andrà per la strada retta, mentre gli sia indicata. La presente gran disgrazia procede dall'esser facilmente traviato dall'ignoranza o malizia di pochi, perché i buoni e sensati (che qui sono in molto maggior proporzione, che in ogni altra civilizzata nazione a me nota) non vogliono far uso della lingua e della penna per illuminare quei loro concittadini, che non hanno potuto avere una studiosa educazione. Per altro, in un paese veramente libero, dove la prosperità e felicità nazionale stanno sull'istesse basi per tutti, pare che quella porzione d'abitanti, che non ha potuto avere una studiosa educazione, debba aver diritto all'istruzione, e ai consigli di quelli che l'ànno avuta, come i figli dai loro padri.

La nostra società fu istituita per questo solo oggetto; l'abbiamo promesso uno all'altro, ai nostri concittadini, e al mondo. Non vi può essere scusa per noi, se manchiamo. Sensibili dell'importanza dell'oggetto non ci contentammo della propensità che ogni cuore onesto risente per il pubblico bene; impegnammo il nostro onore a far tutti gli sforzi possibili per produrlo.

Quando il popolo vedrà un numero di rispettabili concittadini (tra i quali alcuni dei più gran caratteri esistenti nella nostra patria) impiegarsi unicamente per istruirlo (nella quale intrapresa non possono avere altro interesse, che la nobile soddisfazione di far uso dei propri talenti per sostener la libertà) non solo ne sarà consolato e grato, ma, su tutti i soggetti non facili a comprendersi, preferirà la loro opinione a quella di certi soggetti, che hanno finora ottenuto bene spesso l'intento di traviarlo.

Translation by Mazzei of his letter to John Blair in which he discusses the benefits of The Constitutional Society, dated May 12, 1785. (In *Memorie*, Vol. II)

Vi saranno sempre in ogni paese alcuni regolamenti necessari alla prosperità pubblica che forniramo ai furbi egoisti i mezzi d'ingannare un buon numero di bene intenzionati concittadini, perchè gl'inevitabili inconvenienti d'ogni cambiamento sono immediatamente veduti e sentiti, mentre i buoni effetti che devon resultarne (quantunque superiori senza proporzione agli inconvenienti) non possono esser preveduti che da pochi, perchè sono generalmente remoti, e il resultato d'una varietà di cause. Tale, per esempio, è la proprietà d'uno, o due soli porti nel nostro Stato per l'esportazioni, ed importazioni.

Un degno membro della nostra società m'indusse a promettergli di mandargli le mie nozioni su questo soggetto prima della mia partenza, ma non vorrei che fossero pubblicate prima che la società avesse stabilito il suo carattere per mezzo dei fogli pubblici, e avvezzato il popolo a desiderare, piuttosto che a ricevere le loro istruzioni.

Permettetemi di pregarvi quanto so e posso di mettere in veduta alla prima adunanza la necessità e il dovere di essere attivi e di darne voi stesso l'esempio. Io m'allontano adesso da questa patria adottiva, e ritornandoci, come spero, non credo che le attuali imperfezioni del nostro governo possan produrre i temuti inconvenienti, mia vita durante; ma i posteri sono miei figli, e foss'io per andare a vivere e morire nella China, contribuirei sempre con piacere alla formazione d'un asilo per l'uman genere oppresso. Non vor-

rei che la mia insufficienza mi servisse di scusa. So che avrei fatto il mio dovere, adempiendo alle mie promesse, e di questo potete starne sicuro.

Desidero che alla prima adunanza, proponghiate l'ammissione di membri onorari forestieri, e, se viene accordata, gradirei d'averne notizia prima di partire da New York, poichè ò intenzione (mentre la società me l'accordi) di farne la proposizione al duca de la Rochefoucauld in Parigi, al marchese Beccaria in Milano, al signor Fontana in Firenze, al sig. Spallanzani in Bologna, e a tutti quelli che la società mi ordinasse di far l'istesso. — Ho l'onore di essere con gran rispetto e stima, vostro ecc. ecc.

Mansfield, 12 maggio 1785.

P. S. Il sig. Mann Page à intenzione di venire alla prima adunanza, e di proporre il sig. Giovanni Minor, il quale mi à assicurato che se ottiene l'onore d'esser ricevuto membro della nostra società, non mancherà mai al suo dovere come tale. In caso che da qualche inaspettato accidente non fosse permesso al sig. Page di venire, vi prego di proporlo voi stesso dicendo ai nostri soci che l'ò conosciuto quando era nel collegio, come dopo che ne fu escito, e che sempre ò avuto luogo di crederlo un ingegnoso, erudito e degno giovanotto.

First two pages of an eight-page letter from John Adams to Mazzei. (Courtesy, Library of Congress)

John Adams

1735–1826

From an original painting by Copley.

Sir,   Mansfield, 7 May 1785.

As the inclosed letters from our most worthy
friends Col. Banister & Mr. Th.' Adams, may contain
some thing more than an introduction for me to the honor
of your acquaintance, I have thought proper not to carry
them away with me to France, Holland, & Italy, in all which
places the execution of your commands would afford me at any time
a sincerily great satisfaction. I expect to be in Philadelphia
about the 20.th & in New-York about the end of this, to embark
for Lorient in the Packet of next month. Your absence
from Williamsburg, much longer than I had been made
to expect, having deprived me 'till now of the honor of your
commands, I shall call at the Post & Stage Offices in Philadelphia & New-York, in hope of finding them directed to me at
one of the said places. I propose to take the liberty of paying
my respects in person to Mr. Robert Morris & to desire the
honor of his commands to Europe, though I had never an opportunity of being introduced to him. There I shall probably mention your kind offer to make me known both in Philadelphia & New-York, in which I have been unfortunately
disappointed. I have the honor to be with great regard &
esteem,
      Sir,   your most Obed.t Humble Serv.t
                                        Philip Mazzei.

Mazzei's letter to Gouverneur Morris from Mansfield, dated May 7, 1785. (Courtesy, Columbia University)

Beginning and end of a letter to Mazzei from Edmund Randolph, first attorney general of the United States. (*Courtesy, Library of Congress*)

Letter to Mazzei from John Blair, signer of the Constitution and justice of the United States Supreme Court. (*Courtesy, Library of Congress*)

Last two pages of Mazzei's power of attorney to James Monroe witnessed by Jefferson and William Short, Paris, May 5, 1786. *(Courtesy, Massachusetts Historical Society)*

Dear Sir   Marseilles Apr. 4. 1787.

I have had the pleasure of finding your friend Soria. alive
and one of the most considerable merchants here. I delivered
him your letter and he has shewn me all the attentions which
the state of his mind would permit. a few days before my
arrival his only son had eloped with jewels & money to
the value of 40,000 livres, and I believe is not yet heard of.
he speaks of you with friendship, and will be happy to see
you on your way southwardly. he has promised to make
me acquainted with a well informed gardener whom
I expect to find among the most precious of my ac-
-quaintances. from men of that class I have derived the
most satisfactory information in the course of my journey,
& have sought their acquaintance with as much industry
as I have avoided that of others who would have made me
waste my time on good dinners & good society. for these
objects one need not leave Paris – I find here several
interesting articles of culture: the best figs, the best grape
for drying, a smaller one for the same purpose without
a seed, from Smyrna, Olives, capers, Pistachio nuts, almonds.
all these articles may succeed on, or Southward of the Chesapeak.
from hence my inclination would lead me no further East-
-ward: as I am to see little more than a rocky coast.
but I am encouraged here with the hopes of finding some
-thing useful in the rice fields of Piedmont, which are

                                                    said

Mr. Marree

said to be but a little way beyond the Alps. it will probably be the middle of June before I get back to Paris. in the mean time I wish to observe to you that if this absence, longer than you had calculated on, should render an earlier pe- cuniary supply necessary, lodge a line for me at Aix, poste restante, where I shall find it about the last of this month, and I shall with great pleasure do what may be needful for you. be so good as to present me res- pectfully to the Maison de la Rochefoucault, and accept yourself very sincere assurances of esteem and regard from Dear Sir

Your affectionate friend & humble sert.

(signed)   Th. Jefferson

HISTORICAL
AND
POLITICAL ENQUIRIES
on
THE UNITED STATES

of

NORTH AMERICA,

In which are treated the establishment of the thirteen Colonies; their accords and their differences with Great Britain; their governments before and after the Revolution, etc.

By a Citizen of Virginia

[Philip Mazzei]

FIRST PART

Written at Colle, [Virginia]

Available in Paris,
at Froullé Bookstore, quai des Augustins,
corner of Rue Pavée
1788

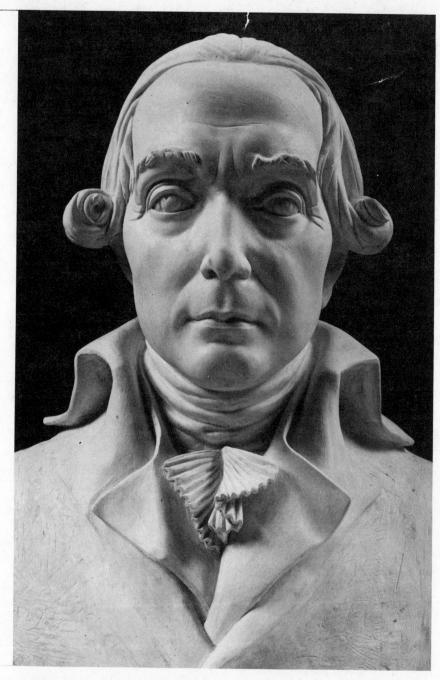

Filippo Mazzei—Bust by the sculptor Moschi. *(Courtesy, Comune di Poggio a Caiano)*

TO THE PEOPLE

OF

THE UNITED STATES OF AMERICA

My dear fellow-citizens,

The prejudices I found in Europe concerning our [state] governments and present situation inspired in me the desire to dispel them; but I have written as an historian and not as an apologist. I have spared no pain to be accurate and truthful. In the case of uncertain facts, I have endeavored to indicate the different degrees of probability. In matters of opinion, I have expressed my feeling as becomes a citizen of a free country.

My observations concerning our [state] governments were based upon the several written constitutions. To analyze them more thoroughly one would have to live in each of our states long enough to get to know what [the constitutions] leave unsaid as well as the laws enacted and all that has to do with their enforcement. It is a task that not a single one of us can accomplish, unless he, following the example set by certain European writers, be willing to criticize and express opinions groundlessly.

The defects to be corrected in our [state] governments demand your entire attention. But as your zeal compares them with

the degree of perfection of which they are capable, your peace of mind requires that you note how much greater have always been and are still the defects rampant in other [governments]. Man's first care should be that which is most neglected: the pursuit of happiness. Nature makes us only too prone to grieve over the ills we are subject to; philosophy invites us to be mindful of those we are exempt from.

It happens only too frequently to anyone that has not traveled to imagine that elsewhere the defects he sees at home are not met with. Soon enough experience would convince you that in spite of what still remains for you to do, you have great sources of comfort in what you have already accomplished. Observe the advances of philosophy, and realize that you have the power to profit by them.

The interest the cause of liberty inspires in the friends of human kind has moved one of the greatest men (1) of the century to outline a plan of legislation he deemed best designed to preserve it. His plan is contained in four letters he kindly addressed to me and which I have placed toward the end of Part I in view of the analogousness of the subject matter. Although I cannot wholly agree with him as regards suffrage and representation, I think his letters offer many profound views which may be of great benefit.

Further on you will find some reflections of mine, dictated by my desire to see our [state] governments improved, which I thought proper to submit for your consideration, confident of your indulgence on this score as on all others.

FOREWORD

This work was written for the most part, and the printing begun, in 1786; consequently, it became necessary to add a Supplement in order to inform the reader of the later occurrence of some important events, and these details will enable you to better understand that the principal aim of the author is to give you accurate information on all that concerns the United States of America. Thus, you will be able to consider these states separately or together from the clearest possible point of view, to correct yourself the infinite errors diffused through ignorance or political misunderstandings, and be in a position to form probable conjectures of your own.

It must be understood that by the word *people* in this work, I mean the entire nation, except in certain cases when I must distinguish from the body of citizens the small number of those who are elected to conduct state affairs. Thus every time I speak of the relationship between the nation and the administrators, the latter are not included in the meaning of the word *people*. But when I say *the people of Virginia, the people of Pennsylvania, etc.*, the reader should interpret it as all the inhabitants of the state of which I speak and, I say interchangeably *the citizens, the inhabitants* or *the people of the United States*.

INTRODUCTION

As the American Revolution has attracted the attention of Europe, many writers have hastened to deal with such an interesting subject and, not to be outstripped, each has rushed his work into publication before it was possible to acquire sufficient source material and before taking the time or care to procure all possible information.

Some, in telling the story of the Revolution, have given us a novel. It has already been said that, if in the book by Mr. [Hilliard] d'Auberteuil (²) the English general were called *Hector* and the American general *Achilles*, it could be called the history of the Trojan War.

Recently there appeared a three-volume work with this pompous title: "The impartial history of the military and political events of the last war in the four parts of the world." It is a collection of erroneous reports and geographical blunders. It would take too long to list all those who have written with the same levity. I shall limit myself to speak of those writers whose fame might give credence to their errors.

The Abbé Raynal (³) does not seem to have shown with respect to us the accuracy of which he boasts. One might suggest that he believed too readily anything that would give him occasion to make his eloquence shine, and the knowing reader, while admiring the warm and energetic style with which the Abbé Raynal so frequently repeats his invocations to truth, regrets that he did not know it better.

The Abbé de Mably (⁴), inspired, as he asserts, by this zeal and desire to be helpful, wrote his observations on the government and the laws of the United States in a period of his life little suited to scrupulous research of recent material. Therefore

one cannot be surprised that his observations are generally based on inaccurate information.

If ignorance is to be preferred to error, one must agree that the actual state of opinion in Europe concerning America is worse than before the Revolution. The observations of the Abbé de Mably have contributed in a special way to accredit numerous fantasies which continue to circulate on the Continent at the expense of the United States.

The large number of books he had written before, and his zeal in proclaiming their usefulness for humanity, had already established his reputation in the world. What gave him greater credibility was the fact that from the beginning of the American Revolution he had shown much enthusiasm in its favor and had visited in Paris some of the more illustrious citizens of the United States. That is not all. For several months before his observations were published, one could read in several newspapers that Congress had asked the Abbé de Mably to prepare a plan for a constitution. A letter I received from one of the more famous writers of our century convinced me that this ridiculous idea was beginning to gain credence. This letter, dated June 3, 1783, begins thus: "I am being asked, Sir, and the question comes from afar and from important persons, if it is true that the greatest republic on earth, that of the United States of North America, has asked the Abbé de Mably for advice on the fundamental laws of the government it must choose.

"If I were to rely only on appearances and my own opinion, I would answer that a country that has given itself a form of government worthy of serving as a model, and laws whose wisdom and equity are a reproach to the most progressive of nations, does not need to look elsewhere for illumination, etc."

After informing me of his opinion of de Mably, my correspondent went on: "I therefore beg you, Sir, to tell me what could have given origin to this audacity and what is the vague and insignificant courtesy which the Abbé de Mably could take as a request from your republic for him to clarify your laws."

I answered that since 1776, the States had already formed their respective governments; that Congress intervened only in the affairs of the Confederation without having the right to legislate; that it never occurred to any of the thirteen United States to have recourse to foreigners; neither would they have asked their

own citizens, who were absent, nor would they consult them in any way on how to establish or better their government or formulate a code of laws; that the Abbé de Mably, whom I had met by chance, had agreed with me that the rumor regarding this was false. Yet it was useless to try to convince him not to leave the public in error or at least write to the journalist who had diffused this falsehood; furthermore, I took the liberty of calling his attention to the fact that his silence would give credence to a lie or at least make one suspect that he was not beyond contributing to it. During my second voyage from America to France, I succeeded in obtaining the Abbé de Mably's book. It was clear that, after announcing that he had read "with all possible attention the different constitutions which the United States of America had chosen", he spoke of them in an unfaithful and confused manner.

His principles of government, often in opposition to true republican principles, have made him criticize some points whereby we have given liberty the best possible basis, and sometimes approve other points where we have not had as much circumspection as we should have had.

Since in his first letter he praises us with ardor for certain merits which he attributes to us, and since on all occasions he professes an interest in our glory and our prosperity that rises to enthusiasm, we believed he was predisposed in our favor. This helped to increase faith in assertions of his which tended to spread distorted ideas about our affairs both with regard to their present and their future state.

If his book—coming from a country where it is permissible to say and to write all the evil imaginable against the United States—had not appeared, it is probable that reports of alleged disorder and even anarchy in the United States and many other lies and exaggerations reported in the English newspapers, would not have been believed. But how can one doubt when such a writer, who pretends to take the greatest interest in our destiny* represents us as having the most disastrous position a body politic can be in? It is for this reason that the errors of the

---

*The one who translated his observations into English called us the *special friends of the Abbé de Mably.*

Abbé de Mably have had more repercussions than those of the Abbé Raynal and therefore require a more formal and more extensive refutation. I shall pass over in silence those writers who are less known and particularly those whose pen we know is under the influence of politics or of vengeance.

My principal purpose is to give the most accurate and clear idea of the situation in the thirteen United States, and, above all, of their governments. This is possible because I can avail myself of historical facts that can cast light on the subject we shall examine.

I shall begin with a brief exposition of the first forms of government in the colonies in order to show their relationship to Great Britain. I shall show you what was the true cause of the Revolution. Then I shall sketch a picture of the conduct of the colonies during a very interesting and singularly critical period—the space of almost two years between the cessation of the royal government and the creation of the republican government. After that, I shall speak of the formation of different governments; I shall try to give a suitable idea of their nature and of their spirit; and, after placing in evidence the errors that were committed by renowned writers speaking of our republics and of the parts of North America where they were established, I shall conclude with some observations relative to my subject.

I hope that these reflections on the government of the United States, inserted in this work, will not displease anyone. Every man should be interested in the formation of a good government, in whatever part of the globe this government might be situated, and should contribute as much as he can to its establishment.

The reader should not be surprised at the length of these refutations because we do not want to content ourselves solely with proving that the two authors against whom they are directed deserve little trust. Rather we have seized the occasion to discuss, to clarify, to give details which will render the subject matter more interesting and the refutations less dull. At the same time, these discussions can serve to refute the misinterpretations of still other writers.

ON THE COLONIES
which gave birth to the

THIRTEEN UNITED STATES
OF AMERICA

A complete history of the establishment of the colonies, to which the American Republic owes its origin, would be of little interest to those who have no reason to want to know all the details. There are many things that should be preserved only in public archives. We believe, therefore, that giving a clear, sure and accurate idea of the beginnings and the progress of their foundation will be sufficient. What is most important to know is the character of those who laid the foundations and their relationship with Great Britain. One should not confuse those founders whose aim was solely to make a fortune with those who sought only the advantage of enjoying freedom. Acquaintance with the true temperament of the first immigrants will help the reader not to be surprised by the conduct of their successors under different circumstances. A brief exposition of the facts will convince him that recently Europe has not been informed about America and the people who inhabit it except by fiction writers and gazetteers.

The famous discovery of Columbus, the voyages of Amerigo Vespucci, those of the Venetian Cabots who established themselves in Bristol, and various other expeditions organized by the English and the French, do not fall within the scope of this work. The colonies are its only subject.

THE FOUNDING OF
VIRGINIA

The English who gave birth to the colonies in North America were simple adventurers who ventured forth at their own expense and risk. Consequently, the country of which they became proprietors, whether they bought it from the inhabitants commonly called Indians or Savages, or whether they conquered it from them, should belong to them as sovereigns in the true sense of the word without needing the approval of others. But Sir Walter Raleigh, head of the first expedition, apparently to avoid any claims England might make in the future against his rights or those of his successors, made an agreement with Queen Elizabeth and obtained a charter on March 25, 1584.

This charter guaranteed in perpetuity to Sir Raleigh and to his successors the absolute dominion of the territory of which he would take possession with full and complete authority to form a legislative body and establish a government similar, as far as it was possible, to the English government. This territory must be united to England, *through the bonds of an alliance and of perfect friendship.* Such are the exact expressions in the charter. Assuredly these determine neither the qualities of the rulers, on the one hand, nor those of the subjects, on the other.

Sir Raleigh immediately sponsored a trip with two ships and took possession of all the land that is situated between the twenty-fifth degree of latitude and the Gulf of Saint Lawrence, and because the Queen had no desire for marriage, he called it *Virginia* in her honor. He visited Roanoke Island, situated near the thirty-sixth degree of latitude, between the sandy banks and the stretch of water which was called, about one hundred years later, *Albemarle Sound.* But it does not seem that he left anyone on the island or on the mainland.

The following year he sent several ships under the command of Sir Richard Grenville, who left one hundred and eight persons on that island, governed by a certain Ralph Lane. Because of imprudence, many died of hunger, and the following year the others returned to England with the famous Admiral [Francis] Drake, who passed through this area after the end of his expedition to the Spanish islands.

Around the same time, Sir Raleigh left England with one ship, and two weeks later Sir Grenville took the same route with three ships. Sir Raleigh arrived at Cape Hatteras, whence, hearing no news of the one hundred and eight persons of whom we have spoken, he returned to England. Grenville landed on the island, but failed to discover the fate of the group. He left fifty other men there with enough provisions for two years. All of them were killed by the natives.

There are those who claim that Raleigh never went there in person. Whether or not that is true, the important facts remain the same.

In the summer of 1587, three other ships arrived there, with several families and provisions on board. Raleigh appointed a certain John White governor and gave him twelve assistants, and ordered him to settle on Chesapeake Bay, which probably he was unable to enter. This political body was designated: *The Governor and the Assistants of the City of Raleigh in Virginia.*

The following year, White went to England for new recruits and the necessary supplies for the newly founded colony. Raleigh equipped a fleet which, as it was ready to set sail, the Queen ordered not to leave but join the Royal fleet against the enormous Spanish fleet which was later, in large part, shipwrecked along the coasts of England.

Two years later White finally left. His crossing was long and difficult, and he arrived during the month of August 1590 at Cape Hatteras where a furious wind forced him to cut the cables and to pull out again on the high seas. He was obliged to return to England without seeing his poor people, the one hundred fifteen persons he had earlier left on the island and of whom no one ever heard again.

Another cause of White's delay was Sir Raleigh's financial failure. He had already, since 1587, begun to feel the effects of

the enormous expenses which his expeditions required, and the Queen's order which had prevented the departure of his fleet was probably what led to his complete failure. He had spent more than forty thousand pounds sterling, without ever receiving the least help from the government: on the contrary, it had done him much damage, interrupting his operations on various occasions. On the 7th of March 1589*, Raleigh granted to [Sir] Thomas Smith and others, in consideration of the money they had furnished to continue the expedition, "the freedom of commerce in his new land, with the privilege of not paying taxes for seven years, with the exception of the fifth part of the gold and silver of the mines which they might discover." He made an agreement with them and with the other assistants who were in Virginia: "that he confirmed the document of incorporation which he had given them in 1587, with all the prerogatives, jurisdictions, rights and privileges which the Queen had accorded to him**."

Clarity and accuracy are not found often in the documents of this period and that is why this grant has occasioned among writers a very great diversity of opinions. In the charter which Raleigh had obtained, the Queen had reserved for herself one fifth of the gold and silver, as also did Raleigh in the document he made in favor of Smith and his associates, from which it would seem that his reservation referred to the Queen and not Raleigh. The document of incorporation which he promised to confirm with all the concessions mentioned above, that is, all the *prerogatives, jurisdictions,* etc., seems to be a complete renunciation of all his rights. On the other hand, Raleigh, while speaking of freedom of commerce *in his new land,* appears to make for himself a large reserve, although the only specified reserve is the

*Some writers and printers have followed the old style for the dates occurring before the reform of the calendar; others have reconciled them with the new computation, and many have not been very accurate. It is therefore probable that some dates between the first of January and the 25th of March, may be wrong by one year. We ask the reader to take this into consideration.

**The Abbé Raynal says, and his assertion is completely correct: "The company that was established, under the attractiveness of its magnificent promises, obtained from the government in 1584, the absolute power to dispose of all the discoveries that would be made." Vol. 8, p. 309.

Queen's. Colonel Richard Bland, in his dissertation full of sentiment and erudition on the rights of the colonies, printed in Virginia in 1766, says that Raleigh renounced his rights, and he
does not speak of any exception. Some authors state that after the
year 1590, Raleigh made five other expeditions, the last of which
was in 1602. This would prove that he was always interested. At
any rate, Raleigh, having been put in prison at the beginning of
the reign of James I and having remained there for fifteen years,
banned by a sentence which condemned him to death, could not
have been further involved in this enterprise*. It is also equally
certain that if the five expeditions had taken place, the persons
who were sent must have experienced the same sad destiny as
those left by White, since no one has ever had the least knowledge up to this period of what happened to them. James I, caring
little about the rights of his subjects and interested in his own
claims, gave Virginia to two companies, with a new charter dated April 10, 1606.

Some have claimed that Raleigh lost his right in 1603, as a
result of the sentence about which we have spoken, as if an English tribunal could have the power to exercise its authority on a
country situated outside the jurisdiction of England. Moreover,
the grant was made to Smith and his associates in 1589, and
therefore how could a sentence given fourteen years later be detrimental, even if the lands had been situated in this kingdom?

There are some writers who see the charter of 1606 as a confirmation on the part of James I, in favor of the company that had
contracted with Raleigh. Others assert that he made an agreement with new adventurers. Most likely Thomas Smith and his
associates, or his successors, together with other persons con-

*Raleigh was locked up in London Tower, accused of having conspired
against the King, and was condemned to be beheaded, without any proof of
having committed the crime. The King commuted the sentence but did not absolve him. After fifteen years of prison, that is, in 1618, he allowed him to
leave, but he still refused to absolve him. He gave him the command of twelve
ships, with which to take possession in Guinea of a very rich gold mine, and at
the end of this expedition, which failed, he had him beheaded by virtue of the
old sentence. Hume (⁵), whom many persons believe to be a courtier, considered him, in the sixth volume of his history, as one sacrificed to the resentment
of the Spaniards, whom the King did not want to displease, because at that
time he strongly desired to obtain a Spanish princess for his eldest son.

tributing to this enterprise, did not attempt to argue over the rights of Raleigh with a vain, capricious King, drunk with kingly power.

The charter was, as I have explained, granted to two companies. The first was called the *London Company*: its territory, according to the charter, extended from the thirty-fourth degree of latitude up to the forty-first. As for the other, which was called the *Plymouth Company*, we shall speak of it later.

The London Company made great efforts to establish a colony. It sent Captain Newport with a rather considerable number of emigrants, among whom were some Polish and Dutch people. Newport arrived in the first days of May 1607 between the two capes through which one passes into Chesapeake Bay and veering to the right, he penetrated about fifty miles up the Pawhatan River. He landed on a peninsula, and when he departed for England, he left about two hundred persons there.

Captain John Smith, called the *Voyager*, setting sail for Roanoke, where White, as we said, had left one hundred fifteen persons, found himself between two capes and called the northern one *Cape Charles*, and the southern *Cape Henry*, in honor of the King's sons. The Pawhatan River was named *James River* in honor of the King, and the peninsula on which the new inhabitants settled and fortified themselves, was called for the same reason *Jamestown**.

Colonel Bland reports that, after many attempts, the company was discouraged because of the heavy expenses, just as Sir Raleigh had been; that with his new associates he strengthened his company and that they obtained a new charter. It is certain that the one made in 1606, in which the first principals mentioned were Sir Thomas Gates and Sir George Somers, was annulled by another of May 23, 1609, in which the principal

---

*One hundred seventy-four years later, on August 2, 1781, at this same place which, within two or three years, had become an island, landed the French troops commanded by the Marquis de Saint-Simon. They were transported there by a powerful fleet, to whose help the Americans principally owe the taking of all the English army under the command of Cornwallis, and the return of peace in Virginia. I do not mean to say that the fleet took part in the attack, since the geographical location would not permit it, but it prevented Cornwallis from escaping, and from receiving help.

named was the Count of Salisbury. One no longer finds this title, *The Company,* etc., but *The Treasurer and The Company.* James reserved for himself the fifth part of the gold and silver, as Queen Elizabeth had done, and their successors nearly always did the same thing.

According to the historical account of this Smith, who remained nineteen years in America and was for some time governor of Virginia, in 1609 nine ships arrived with five hundred persons under the command of Gates, Somers and Captain Newport. The fleet was dispersed by a strong wind. Gates and Somers, having found refuge in Bermuda with one hundred fifty persons, constructed two small ships of cedar, with which on May 10, 1610, they set sail for Virginia, where they arrived on the 20th. Finally, some time later, they all re-embarked, and they would have abandoned the country completely if, on coming down the river, they had not encountered Lord Delaware with three ships bringing them all necessary supplies. I omit here a long list of anecdotes, and I shall say that Smith's report is full of dangerous, sad, fatal adventures, so much so that the thing that seems most marvelous is the persistence of these first adventurers, speculators and emigrants.

For some time, the Company was content to send to Virginia some administrators, and a quantity of poor wretches. If it had continued this same method, perhaps a colony would never have been established. The speculators had formed a false idea of this country. Instead of envisioning it as a very advantageous refuge to enjoy freedom, they imagined it as a possible source of great wealth. Their views were based on commerce and on the hope of finding mines of precious metal; perhaps they feared competition, and they wanted to preserve their monopoly. As the Indians had nothing but furs to give in exchange, and as the Europeans were in the service of the Company, commerce could reimburse only a very small part of the expenses. Fortunately for us the precious metals were never found, and all Americans, sincerely loving their country, must desire this happy soil be not defiled by human nature.

The speculators finally felt that, since they had not gone there to settle, they could not derive any benefit except by selling or renting lands. To encourage the emigrants, it was necessary at first to give them lands with conditions little different from gra-

tuitous grants. The lands were rented on condition of paying a modest portion of their produce. It seems, according to the registers of the company, that in 1667 no more than fifty-four persons remained in its service; that for their annual payment those who rented the lands carried into the storehouses four hundred bags of Indian corn and tobacco was sold from 18 deniers to three sterling coins per pound.

This change of administration made many lovers of liberty resolve to establish themselves there, and the arbitrary principles of James I contributed not a little to their decision. In 1619, eleven ships transported one thousand two hundred sixteen persons, men, women and children, who settled on the shores of the James and Yorck [sic] Rivers.

The government of the Company was neither stable, nor in keeping with the ideas and character of the colonists. There was in Virginia at the head of the government, sometimes a president, sometimes a treasurer, sometimes a governor, and the power was exercised less according to fixed rules than according to the temperament of the one to whom it was entrusted. There were many noblemen and gentlemen among the associates, as is shown by the book published in 1620 by *order of the treasurer and of the council*. The treasurer was at that time the Count of Southampton. A society of noblemen, gentlemen and merchants, whose only aim was gain, could not govern in a satisfactory manner for those who had emigrated only for love of liberty. They regarded themselves the masters of the country, and they recognized no limits. Therefore, when they realized they were a large enough number, the colonists began to assemble and to deliberate. The result of their meetings was that they chose representatives to defend their rights. The right to vote was exercised by all landholders without exception.

On July 24, 1621, the company decided that in the future, a legislative body would be established in Virginia to be called *General Assembly*, consisting of a governor, 12 councilors and some representatives of the people; that the councilors and the representatives should make the laws and that the governor should have the power to approve or reject them; that the laws would go into effect only after being ratified by the Company; and that as soon as the government of the colony was formed and well established, the ordinances of the company would no

147

longer be valid for the colony without the consent of the General Assembly. The governor and the councilors were chosen by the Company, which could also depose them at will.

One must not be surprised at the sudden and considerable change in the conduct of the colony's affairs since the representatives of the people had assembled only a few months before and had resolved to act. As for sovereign power, the colonists began to make serious distinctions between the rights of the natives and the claims of the Europeans. The lands which the company gave under certain conditions to the colonists, for the most part had been bought from the Indians; others had been obtained by peace treaties concluded after some wars, or rather some raids and skirmishes. But the colonists believed they could buy directly from the legitimate proprietors with more justice and more benefits for all. The Company acted, however, with prudence in granting what it could not withhold, and a voluntary act preserved its sovereignty. If the ministers of George III had acted with the same moderation, American liberty would not exist.

The sovereignty of the Company was not long-lived. James I, who never lacked pretexts to justify using force to circumvent the law, stripped the company completely of its rights to the one hundred thousand pounds sterling which they had spent to establish the colony without ever receiving the least help from the English government.

The stockholders, living as they did under the arbitrary government of this King, were forced to yield. On the other hand, this did not affect the colonists. They were only interested in their own rights and furthermore they were not very pleased with the government of the Company. James did not neglect to take advantage of this circumstance, on which he based his claims to appropriate the Company. The new form of government which the King proposed to them not being to their liking, it was rejected, and they declared themselves satisfied only after all the rights existing before the extinction of the Company were reconfirmed for them.

All of which goes to show clearly that James I became King of Virginia, as he was of England, without either land depending in any way upon the other.

The colonists liked the royal government, so much so that at

the beginning of the differences which arose between Parliament and the King when the renewal of the charter of the Company by decree of Parliament came into question, the General Assembly opposed it strongly with a solemn protest on the first of April 1642 and denounced as an enemy of the country, with confiscation of all goods, anyone who attempted to make any change in the government. As a result, Charles I assured the colony that there would be no innovations. The sovereignty of the Company offended the pride of the colonists and the admission of Parliament's authority would have destroyed freedom.

After Charles I was beheaded, the usurper Cromwell, having become English tyrant under the important title of Protector of the Republic, was obliged to send a fleet of warships against the colony, which wanted to recognize as head of its government the oldest son of the deceased King. Finally, it was necessary to yield to force. But this was done only after both sides stipulated the articles of capitulation, following the style of warring nations.

Here are the most important [articles]:

1. Virginia and its inhabitants were under the dominion of the Republic of England, not as a conquered nation, but as all states that surrender voluntarily, and they enjoy the same privileges and exemptions as the free people of England.

2. The General Assembly will meet as before, and direct the affairs of the colony.

3. Virginia will have the possession of and the privilege of extending the territory designated by the old boundaries and specified in the charters of previous kings.

4. The inhabitants of Virginia will have everywhere, and with all nations, the same freedom of commerce as the English.

5. Virginia will be exempt from taxes, ordinances, impositions of all kinds; and without the approval of the General Assembly, no onus can be imposed, nor fortresses or castles built, nor foot soldiers kept there.

The representatives of Parliament signed the capitulation in Virginia on March 12, 1651, and it was subsequently confirmed by Cromwell in England. At the return of Charles II, Parliament annulled all that had been done by Cromwell. Therefore, if a solemnly made act could be annulled by only one of the two parties, Virginia ought to have remained, according to the historical

149

facts we have reported, absolutely independent of England. If, on the contrary, the capitulation retained its validity, the dependency expressed in the first article remains, but on the conditions under which it was stipulated: that is, that the Virginians enjoy all the rights and all the privileges of the English people; that they have commerce with all nations freely; that they possess the territory designated by the old boundaries; that they will administer their own affairs as before; that they will not be taxed except with the approval of their own assembly; that in Virginia there will be no foot soldiers, no fortresses built, etc.

During the month of January 1659, the Virginians unanimously proclaimed Charles II, then a refugee in Holland, King of England, Scotland, France, Ireland and Virginia, and recalled to the government Sir William Barklay [Berkeley], who had already been governor at the time of [Charles'] father. This act of independence merits our attention. Charles II was therefore King in Virginia, some time before he was assured of being returned to the throne of England.

During his reign, which was not favorable to liberty, as shown by the act of Parliament of the year 1650—of which we will have occasion to speak later on—England claimed to have a monopoly on the commerce of the colonies*. There was much debate. There was much writing to demonstrate there would be reciprocal advantages, especially because of the protection to the commerce of the colonists England would give with its fleets.

Notwithstanding the protests, the right of controlling commerce was exercised and this pretended right opened the way for several acts of Parliament during the same reign, one of which established a duty on things that were transported from one colony to another. The Virginians opposed this strongly. They sent representatives to England, instructing them to show that the right to impose taxes belonged to the General Assembly. The representatives returned with an ordinance of Charles II, dated April 19, 1676, in which it was declared that taxes could not be imposed on the inhabitants and proprietors of the colony, except with the consent of the General Assembly, with the exception of

*At this time, several other colonies had been established, to which we shall refer later.

150

the taxes that Parliament would place on products sent from the colony to England.

The General Assembly was for Virginia what Parliament was for Great Britain, and according to law the colony did not depend on England any more than Hanover actually depended on it. All the laws were made in the name of the King and of the Assembly of the colony, with the following formula: *By the order of his most excellent Majesty the King, and with the consent of the General Assembly, etc.*

THE FOUNDING OF
MASSACHUSETTS

The territory of the second company, called the Plymouth Company, extended, according to the charter of 1606, from the thirty-eighth degree of latitude to the forty-fifth. The thirty-ninth degree, the fortieth and the forty-first could therefore belong to one or the other of the two companies. The charter granted possession to the first occupant and decreed that between the two settlements there must be a distance of one hundred miles. The documents of this period are, in general, written in a way which would furnish material for a dispute among lawyers.

Among the most ardent members of this company were Ferdinando Gorges, governor of Plymouth, and Sir John Popham, principal judge. In 1607 some of the associates made an expedition, settled in a place named Sagadahoc, near the forty-fourth degree of latitude, and made plans for a large settlement. During the winter, which was very severe, many of them died, among others George Popham, their president. Some of the principal promoters of the enterprise died in England, among whom were John Popham, brother of the president, and Sir John Gilbert, brother of the admiral. All events caused those who still lived at Sagadahoc to return home the following year, and thus the project was abandoned.

The project was inspired by the description of this territory given by Captain Bartholomew Gosnold, one of the associates of Raleigh, who, in 1602 wishing to go to Virginia by a more direct route, had instead landed there by chance, giving the name of *Cape Cod** to a promontory near which he had caught a large

Cod-Fish in English, is *morue* in French.

153

number of codfish. He landed on the small neighboring islands and built a small fort as the beginning of a settlement, but he could not convince any of his people to remain. He called [the islands] Elizabeth Islands, in honor of the Queen. On one he saw, as one still can, a very large quantity of wild vineyards, and he gave it the more particular name of *Martha's Vineyard.*

After Gosnold's voyage, other adventurers went there, mainly from Bristol. Business was extremely good, both because of the abundance of fish and the excellent furs which the Indians sold them in exchange for things of very little value. A certain Captain Hunt, a man without honor, cleverly attracted about twenty Indians aboard his ship and sold them to the Spanish at Malaga in the Mediterranean, in exchange for African Moors*. The memory of this wickedness was probably one of the reasons (if not perhaps the only one) why the Indians of these territories were implacable enemies of the English and their descendants, and, in general, preferred to ally themselves with the French.

In 1603, Henry IV, King of France, gave to a person named de Monts, letters patent granting him all the land within the fortieth and forty-sixth degrees of latitude, under the name of Acadia.

After the stockholders in the Plymouth Company had made various costly and useless attempts to colonize, the French and the English continued to fish along the coast and to barter with the Indians. But neither of the two nations seemed disposed to establish a colony, which would have required large initial expenses and much time before it could become productive. Some historians claim that the aforementioned Ferdinando Gorges, and Captain [John] Mason each lost twenty thousand pounds sterling there. Perhaps no settlement would have taken a stable and permanent form, at least for a long time, if religious persecutions had not caused many Englishmen to think of emigrating.

The Anglican church, which, with episcopal pomp, had inherited religious intolerance, persecuted the Puritans, the Presbyterians and, in a sense, all those who did not want to conform to its rules and who for this reason were called *nonconformists.*

*Douglas [William, *A summary, historical and political of the first planting, progressive improvements, and present state of the British settlements in North America*, Boston, 1747-52], Vol. 1, p. 264.

A group of the persecuted, who from 1606 on had taken refuge in Holland, decided in 1617 to go to America in order to be able to preserve more easily the purity of their doctrine. The Dutch tried in vain to convince them to establish themselves on the shores of the Hudson River, where Dutch sovereignty had been obtained by Captain Hudson, who had acquired it with the customary ceremony of civilized nations, which consists in setting foot on territory, giving it a name and claiming possession. Religious zeal persuaded these faithful that the customs of the Dutch were not severe enough and, moreover, their sympathy for their old compatriots had not been extinguished. Consequently, they petitioned the London Company for a part of the land where they could live separately. The request was granted, and several of the principal members of the company petitioned James the First to grant them complete freedom of religion; but this casuistic King refused. Douglas* states that the King gave his consent, but he is mistaken. His conscience permitted him only to promise that he would not bother them.

Because such a promise did not seem to provide sufficient assurance, they no longer wished to emigrate. Finally, two years later, hoping that distance would free them from the persecution of the episcopal courts of justice, they returned to their first idea. Almost half of the companions of the famous Robinson headed for Southampton and embarked on two ships which the bad weather forced several times to return to port. One remained with a group of the emigrants. The other set out to sea and arrived at Cape Cod on November 11, 1620.

Hutchinson** states that Robinson's companions possessed only those rights that they had received from nature. The emigrants themselves had known, before sailing, that the lands which the London Company had granted them were within the boundaries of the Plymouth Company. These settlers, discouraged and reduced to a state of languor, had little by little disappeared. Many of its members were long dead and those left were disheartened. There was no question about it. This new

*Douglas, *Ibid.*, Vol. 1, p. 369.

**Hutchinson [Richard, *The War in New-England*, London, 1677], Vol. 2, p. 455.

emigration kindled hope, especially in those who had had considerable losses. Ferdinando Gorges ([6]) and Captain Mason were among those most active in obtaining a new charter. It was granted to them on November 3, 1620, and at the same time Robinson's companions had already reached the coast of America. While the latter were en route, it was rumored, probably among those who possessed the least that, as soon as they reached land, everyone would be equal and that each would be able to do just as he pleased. This situation convinced the more prudent that in order to prevent the deadly effects of anarchy, which threatened, it was necessary to prepare the following decree to be signed by everyone before setting foot on land.

"In The Name of God, Amen. We, whose names are underwritten, the Loyal Subjects of our formidable Sovereign Lord King James, by the Grace of God King of England, Scotland, France and Ireland, Defender of the Faith, etc. Having undertaken for the Glory of God and Advancement of the Christian Faith and the Honour of our King and Country, a Voyage to plant the First Colony in the Northern Parts of Virginia, do by these present solemnly and mutually in the presence of God and one another, unite in a Civil Body Politick, for our better Ordering and Preservation, and Furtherance of the Ends aforesaid; And by Virtue hereof to enact, constitute, and frame such just and equal Laws, Ordinances, Acts, Constitutions and Offices, from time to time, as shall be thought most meet and convenient for the general Good of the Colony, unto which we promise all due Submission and Obedience. In Witness whereof we have hereto subscribed our names at Cape Cod the eleventh of November, in the 18th year of the Reign of our Sovereign Lord King James of England, France, and Ireland, and Scotland, the fifty-fourth. Anno Domini, 1620. Signed, John Carver, William Bradford, Edward Winslow, etc."

This document was signed on board probably by all those who were of an age to sign. In all there were forty-one, of whom I have named the first three; I have omitted the rest as superfluous. The sandy and barren land which they reached obliged them to take their ship along the coast until they could find a place suitable for cultivation. There they stopped and called it New Plymouth. Some historians claim that the name had already been given by Captain Smith who, during one of his fre-

quent voyages, had landed in the same place. Their right to the territory was very uncertain until 1624, when they finally obtained the approval of the New Plymouth Company. It is true that they had already bought it from the Indian tribes who were the owners*; but this fact did not protect them from the claims of those who were empowered to grant approval. Because the Indians sold large tracts of land at a very small price, the Europeans who based their rights on discoveries or on charters or patents, claimed for themselves the exclusive right to buy them in order to have a monopoly. Since this patent was very vague, they obtained another in 1629, and this one, according to Douglas,** was equally obscure, so much so that in 1641 the English commissioners delegated by the court to resolve a difference between them and the Colony of Rhode Island on the subject of boundaries, were not able to understand it.

The Colony of New Plymouth made no great progress. In 1624, it consisted of no more than one hundred eighty inhabitants, men, women and children. It continued to govern itself however with its own laws until the year 1692 when it was incorporated into Massachusetts.

The charter of November 3, 1620, of which we have spoken above, was granted to forty persons. Among the associates the best known were Ferdinando Gorges, Captain John Mason, the Duke of Lenox, the Marquises of Buckingham and of Hamilton, the Earls of Arundel and of Warwick and Sir Francis George. The new company was named *The Council of Plymouth for the affairs of New England.* The name of New England had been already given to the northern part of Virginia by Captain Smith whom we have mentioned several times.

The lack of order in the conduct of business and ignorance of the location of these territories had this effect: that often the same lands granted by the Council of Plymouth, were sold or given to several persons, and very often it happened that the lands given by one grant extended over those given by another.

*Douglas, *op. cit.*, Vol. I, p. 370, says that they bought it from Massasoit, Sachem of the Pakanokat, who was delighted with their alliance, being then at war with the numerous Narraganset tribes.

**Ibid., Vol. I, p. 395.

157

This gave rise to many cases more than fifty years later, which would have arisen at that time if the inhabitants had been more numerous, or if it had been more difficult to obtain land. In the first years, emigration was very slight. There were several settlements in different places, but until 1628 none of importance. In that year, when members of Parliament were sent to the tower of London and other prisons for having spoken out freely against the abuses of the Anglican Church, the anti-episcopal sects lost all hope of reform within the church. There was a large number of persons who resolved to go to serve God in America, above all the Puritans. Ferdinando Gorges reports in his history of New England that in a short time the competition for emigration grew to such a point that the King issued a special ordinance forbidding all persons to depart without permission. The same historian adds: "Thus what I predicted a long time ago—when with money I could scarcely find anyone who wanted to remain—has now been accomplished."

The charter of the Council of Plymouth contained the right to grant the lands but not to govern them. During the same year 1628, they obtained another charter for this purpose, and the Company of the proprietors elected a governor (Matthew Cradock), a vice-governor (Thomas Goffe), eighteen assistants and a secretary. They elected for Governor in America a certain Mr. John Endicott, who was entirely subordinate to the government resident in England. All these companies had one and the same object, love of profit. The hope of finding mines of precious metal had disappeared. It seemed that now the sale of lands and business became their principal or their only purpose.

The following year, a number of rich persons, of whom some were of distinguished rank, discontented with the arbitrary government of England, for both temporal and spiritual reasons, told the Company they would go to America on condition that a charter would follow them. The Company which had not yet derived any profits and was not optimistic in this regard, willingly consented. It was stipulated that those proprietors who remained in England would participate for the first seven years in the profits from the sale of lands and commerce, and that the administration of business would be entrusted to ten persons, of whom five would reside in America and five in England. At any rate, this agreement referred only to financial matters. The right

to govern themselves and the other privileges belonged solely to the colonists. The five persons who remained in England were M. Cradock, N. Wright, J. Eaton, T. Goffe, and J. Joung [sic]. The five who sailed to America were J. Winthrop, Sir Richard Saltonstall, J. Johnson, J. Dudley and J. Revel.

The desire to emigrate was very strong, but one could not emigrate without great difficulty, and many of those who were most enthusiastic about the project did not have the courage to execute it. The largest number arrived only during the course of the following year, that is, in 1630, an unforgettable era because of the misfortunes they experienced.

During this time agriculture was limited to some vegetables and Indian corn but in a very small quantity. There were few farmers among the early emigrants and the land was all wooded. At first they busied themselves building homes and providing themselves with the necessities for bearing the rigor of the seasons and defending themselves against Indian attacks. They had begun bringing in some maize from Virginia, but the largest portion of foodstuffs came from England and, mail being neither certain nor regular, there were frequent shortages.

Whatever the cause, in 1630 the famine was so great that many people died from sicknesses which usually manifest themselves when food is scarce, inedible and of bad quality. Among the latest emigrants, a good portion were accustomed to living in the midst not only of necessities but luxuries, and this group was less able to resist calamity. Many were obliged to eat snails, mussels and other shellfish and, in place of bread, eat roots of plants called *ground nutts* [sic] (which are very inferior to potatoes) and even acorns. Hutchinson reports that one inhabitant went to the home of the Governor to present his complaints, then retraced his footsteps, having learned that even in the home of the Governor himself the last loaf of bread had been placed in the oven. Among the victims who succumbed to the misfortunes and calamities of this year, Hubbard ([7]) cites Lady Arabella Johnson daughter of the Earl of Lincoln, whose death he relates in a most touching manner. Her husband, a much esteemed man, unable to bear the sorrow that this loss caused him, survived her by only two months.

The spirit of emigration did not die as a result, but only waned a little. The arbitrary government of the court and of the

church more than ever caused it to revive. The settlements increased prodigiously, the larger ones on the Gulf of Massachusetts, a name that the Colony took later on.

During the first years, the Governor and his assistants exercised legislative and executive power. But the people who aspired to civil, as well as religious, liberty, began to assemble in different districts and deliberate. Finally, in the year 1634, they elected their representatives. Until then, and only after the government became established in America, the people had enjoyed the right to vote for the election of those who governed, without representatives. At the General Assembly for the elections of this year, twenty-four representatives of the free men of the Colony suddenly presented themselves to the great surprise of the magistrates, and the people, before proceeding to any election, stipulated:

"That none, but the General Court*, hath power to make and establish laws, nor to elect and appoint officers, as Governor, Deputy Governor, Assistants, Treasurer, Secretary, Captains, Lieutenants, Ensigns, or any of similar importance, or to remove such upon misdemeanor, or to determine duties and power of said officers.

"That none, but the General Court, hath power to raise monies, to impose taxes, or to dispose of lands, namely to give and confirm properties."

The election of the magistrates having been accomplished, the people agreed on the following:

"That the General Court shall meet four times yearly, summoned by the governor, and not to be dissolved without the consent of the majority of its members.

"That equally the freemen of each plantation can choose two or three persons, before each General Court, to confer and to prepare the business they shall judge proper to submit for consideration at the next court; that the persons who shall hereafter be deputed by the freemen of several plantations to deal in their behalf with the affairs of the commonwealth shall have the full power and vote of all the said freemen, for making and enforcing laws, granting lands, etc., and dealing with all other affairs of the

*The legislative body of the State of Massachusetts is still called *General Court.*

160

commonwealth in their behalf, except the elections of magistrates and other officers, wherein each freeman is to give his own vote personally."

Such was the second constitution that the people of America gave themselves. The Colonies of Rhode Island, Connecticut and New Hampshire derived their origin from Massachusetts and followed its example.

Emigration was constantly increasing. In 1633, the Council considered whether it would be necessary to prohibit it absolutely and, in 1637, emigration was forbidden by an ordinance of the King. This produced the effect of all prohibitions: the desire only became stronger and much larger groups hastened to America. There are only two ways to keep men in a country: either make them happy or put them in chains. Several writers claim that before 1640, two hundred ninety-eight ships were seen leaving the old England for the new, transporting about four thousand families, which formed a nucleus of twenty-one thousand two hundred persons, men and women and children. Hutchinson says that in 1639, fishing began to flourish, that already the country was supplying more food than was needed, that much of it was sent to the islands [West Indies], that payment was made in products from the islands, as well as in gold and silver, and that part of the profits was forwarded to England to pay for manufactured goods which they were obliged to order continually.

The laws of the early settlers were in conformity with the austerity of their religion and customs. Several of these laws reflect a reprehensible severity which some writers have very much exaggerated without rendering justice to those which deserve to be praised. As a result of a law concerning slavery (rejected by these early legislators, *as contrary to the natural laws of man and detrimental to society*) a Negro, who had been forced to leave Africa and was sold in the State of Massachusetts, was, through the special intervention of the General Court in 1645 taken from the colonist who had bought him and sent back to his country*.

---

*Memoirs of the State of Massachusetts.

THE FOUNDING OF
RHODE ISLAND

The Colony of Rhode Island owes its origin to that of Massachusetts, or rather to the intolerance, in matters of religion, that the new inhabitants had brought with them from England. The persecutions they had suffered, instead of producing moderation in them, seemed to excite in their hearts the desire for vengeance. Sects multiplied daily. The same arguments employed to support one extreme produced others. The Puritan sect divided and subdivided itself ad infinitum. The Brounistes [sic], the Independents, the Antinomians, the Muggletonians, the Separatists, and many others, were so many schisms of the same sect. The very ones who professed the dominant religion were not in accord on all points of their beliefs. Each church, which ·they called *Congregation*, differed from others in some thing.

To promote unity and even uniformity (as far as the particular bigotry of each congregation permitted) they began to hold synods, according to the custom of the Presbyterians, whose name, however, they did not adopt. They took the general denomination of Congregationalists. In the history of the early days of the Colony, no mention is made of the Presbyterians, and the Anglicans established themselves there only toward the end of the reign of Charles II. The Anabaptists appeared after the year 1640, animated by the same spirit of fanaticism that had caused their destruction in Germany. Their behavior caused different laws to be enacted in 1644 and 1646, against those "who disturbed the peace of the churches, who insulted the magistrates, who opposed baptism of children or disapproved of it and would purposely leave the church during the ceremony, and who did not recognize the authority of the magistrates." The Quakers appeared in 1654. At first they showed themselves to be

more violent and more fanatical even than the Anabaptists and it was necessary to enact still more rigorous laws against them. The Catholics did not have the courage to appear there until the period of our glorious Revolution, which changed the mode of thinking on that subject, as on other points essential to human happiness.

In 1635, two years before the synod began, one Roger Williams, minister of the Salem church, a very good man according to historians, was excommunicated because of his *Antinomian, Familistic Brounist and other equally fanatical principles.* He was banished by the legislative power of the Colony of Massachusetts, *as a disturber of the peace, of the church and of the community.* Williams went to settle at Seaconck [sic], having obtained lands from the Indian Chief Massasoit, whom we have already mentioned. The magistrates of the small Colony of New Plymouth compelled him to withdraw since Seaconck was within the limits of their charter. They did not claim that Massasoit did not have the right to sell but that Williams was chased out because of heresy. Moreover the governments of the Colonies prohibited individuals from buying lands from the Indians without the consent of the public authority in order to avoid fraud in the contracts, to prevent an individual from buying too much property to the detriment of the community, and to make public the deed of sale as soon as possible because often it happened that the same lands were claimed by more than one tribe. The motives of the Colonies differed from those of the proprietary companies, or rather of the possessors of patents, who reserved for themselves the exclusive right to buy the lands from the Indians in order to have a monopoly. Williams transferred, with the small number of those who followed him, to the opposite shore of the Patuket [Pawtucket] River, obtained from the Chief of Narraganset various tracts of land and called the place *Providence.* During the year 1640, around forty persons assembled and formed a kind of government.

During the first synod that was held at New-Town [Newton] on the Bay of Massachusetts in 1637, the religious opinions of various sectarians were condemned. It seems that the Congregationalists adopted the expression of the Anglicans, who, perhaps contemptuously, designated by the generic name of *Sectarian* all those whose principles in matters of religion differed from

theirs. Having been so maltreated after that, these people retreated with their friends and their sympathizers to the island of Aquateneck, now called Rhode Island, and bought it from the Indians on March 24, 1638. They established a committee of eighteen from their number, and formed a kind of government which changed several times during the space of two years. In 1640 they agreed that a committee entrusted with public administration should consist of a Governor, a Vice-Governor and four assistants. This lasted until the year 1662.

During the course of the year 1642, eleven persons bought from the Indians a place called Schowamet and changed this name to Warwich [sic], in honor of the Earl of Warwich, who had the charter for a very large stretch of land in this region and who had never used it. A patent of the Duke of Hamilton reaffirmed the grant of all the territory, which actually took in the state of Rhode Island and a part of Massachusetts and Connecticut. The Duke having neglected his rights, his descendants tried more than once to reassert them, but the inhabitants proved that the conditions had not been fulfilled. Almost all the members of the Plymouth Company who had charters for the entire province experienced the same fate. One of the reasons used against the presumed rights of Hamilton was that the lands had not been bought from the Indians. It seems, according to what historians say in this regard, that in the opinion of the colonists the right of proprietorship had to have as a basis a cession by the natives of the country. The founders of Warwich soon merged with those of Providence.

In 1643 Williams went to England as a representative of the Colony which he himself had founded and obtained from the Earl of Warwich, parliamentary governor and admiral of all the English plantations*, a kind of charter, which asserted "that the incorporated plantations of Providence on the Bay of Narra-

---

*The Colonies were often, during the early days, called Plantations, a name which Providence continued to use, even after it was incorporated in Rhode Island. One must not be surprised that Williams had recourse to the Earl of Warwich rather than the King, since the war between Parliament and the King was only beginning. Religion kept the Colonies of New England on the side of Parliament, just as it kept Virginia and Maryland on the side of the King.

ganset in New England could have such form of government that the majority of free men judged convenient to their situation, and could make laws they believed best for them and were in conformity with those of England wherever nature and the location would allow them."

These small Colonies, which now form the State of Rhode Island, were incorporated, by virtue of a charter of Charles II dated July 8, 1662, under the name of the Colony of *Rhode Island, and Plantation of Providence.* The first assembly was held at New-Port on March 1, 1663, and among other things, it proclaimed that all Christians, with the exception of Catholics, would enjoy the same privileges with regard to the rights of citizens, and that all the purchases of lands from the Indians without the consent of the Assembly would be annulled and the buyers subject to *taxation.*

THE FOUNDING OF
CONNECTICUT

Similarly the Colony of Connecticut owes its origin to Massachusetts, for the same reasons as Rhode Island, and its establishment goes back to the same period. During the summer of 1636, numerous persons, discontented for religious reasons, abandoned, together with their ministers, Newtown, Dorchester, Watertown, and Rocksbury [sic], and went to settle on the shores of the Connecticut River, where they founded Hartford, Watersfield, Windsor, Springfield, etc. Those who found themselves outside the boundaries of Massachusetts assembled at Hartford, agreed on the manner in which they would be governed and elected magistrates. The following year some emigrants from England did the same thing at New-Heaven [sic], which they founded on the shore opposite Long Island. The two small colonies of Hartford and New-Heaven continued to govern themselves separately, up to the period when they were merged under the name of the *Colony of Connecticut*, by virtue of the charter of Charles II, of April 23, 1662.

THE FOUNDING OF
NEW HAMPSHIRE

Among the large number of charters that Captain Mason, of whom I have spoken several times, obtained at different times from the Plymouth Council, and which were the source of infinite lawsuits, was one from the year 1629 which granted him the whole State of New Hampshire, just as it is at present, and a part of the territory of the adjacent colonies. Another, in his name as well as that of Ferdinando Gorges, extended over a part of the country granted by the preceding one. On August 19, 1635, Charles I favored Mason with a charter for the same land alluded to in the charter of 1627 and gave him also the right to govern and to confer honors. (The Mason Family was always in great favor among the Stuarts.) In 1639, Gorges obtained from the same King another charter, which granted him full rights of jurisdiction and which included a part of the territory granted to Mason four years before. Finally, the right of jurisdiction over all the territory mentioned in the two charters, one of which Charles had given to Mason, the other to Gorges, he himself had already conferred on the Plymouth Council by the charter of 1628 which, as I have said, was taken to America by the founders of the Colony of Massachusetts.

In 1629, many inhabitants along the shores of the Bay of Massachusetts, desiring to settle on the land which now forms the State of New Hampshire, following the example of the founders of New Plymouth, summoned the Indians who owned the property. The acquisition was remarkable because of the solemn ceremonies observed on both sides, and even more so because of the lawsuits which have lasted about a century among

the buyers, their heirs and successors, and the heirs and successors of Gorges and Mason.

The Indians sold the land to John Wheelwright, Augustine Story, or Storer, Thomas Wight, William Went-Worth [sic], and Thomas Levet. The latter reserved for themselves hunting and fishing rights, compelled the buyers, by contract, to pay an annual tribute of a woolen suit, and stipulated the condition that a colony be founded within the space of ten years. This was called the *Wheelwright Purchase*, probably because he cooperated more than the others, and because he was named first in the document.

It must be observed that, besides the difference between the rights of those who bought from legitimate owners and the claims of Mason, the charter of 1629, by which the Plymouth Council granted, as I have said, this land to Mason, is of a later date than Wheelwright's purchase.

In 1638 this Wheelwright, a dedicated minister of the Gospel and brother of the famous religious zealot, Anne Hutchinson, was exiled with his followers by the government of Massachusetts, on a matter of a dispute over the principles of the Antinomians. Just as the time prescribed for Wheelwright and his companions to found the Colony was about to expire, they went there, formed a body politic among themselves, and for some time governed themselves separately. Soon there were actually four settlements, each of which governed itself by its particular rules.

Mason died in 1635. Francis Norton, in charge of his widow's affairs and executor of the will, since the heir was a minor, directed an establishment which Mason had set up with various aims. But the widow, either for lack of funds or for fear of ruining herself and her child, wrote to Norton that it was beyond her means to pay the people who had been hired by her husband— and to whom he owed much in arrears—and that consequently she declared each one of them free to take care of himself as best he could. After that the furniture was sold and divided among the creditors. There were among other things, says Belknay [sic], (⁸) compiler of the history of New Hampshire, one hundred head of cattle, both bulls and cows, which Norton sold in Boston at twenty-five pounds sterling each, which shows how rare livestock was at that time—even though those were of ex-

traordinary size. These animals were a breed that Mason had imported from Denmark; those of Rhode Island, the largest I have seen in any part of the world, are probably of this breed.

The inhabitants of this small settlement of which I have just spoken, doubting that they could defend themselves in case of an invasion and feeling affection for the government of Massachusetts, asked to be taken under its protection and its jurisdiction. The decree of union was signed on April 14, 1741, bestowing, under the title of proprietors, to those who had charters, the proprietorship of a considerable tract of land. It seemed either that the inhabitants really wanted to recognize the validity of some of the charters of Gorges and of Mason or that they respected the expenditures which the latter had made.

As for the labyrinth of lawsuits, which I have said were caused by these charters, it must be recalled in general that, at the time of Cromwell, the Masons received only what seemed just and equitable to the inhabitants, and that when the Stuarts returned to the throne, the Masons obtained sufficient protection to subject the colonists to vexation and ruin.

Finally in 1679 Charles II, using various specious pretexts, separated the government of New Hampshire from that of Massachusetts and appropriated it. The apparent reason was that he wanted to free the inhabitants from oppression although they begged to remain under the government of Massachusetts. The governors and the other ministers of the King had orders to protect the Masons, which gave them the means to commit extortion and other injustices, the popular assembly not being strong enough to protect and uphold their rights.

THE FOUNDING OF
MARYLAND

Lord Baltimore and William Penn, founders of the Colonies of Maryland and of Pennsylvania, were the first to take advantage of the charters which the Kings of England granted. Among those who went from England to America for reasons of religion, Sir George Calvert, Secretary of State, who was later Lord Baltimore, became famous. Toward the end of the reign of James I he went to Virginia with persons of various sects, who were encouraged to leave their country for the same reason. Being a zealous Catholic, he was badly received by the Virginians who were no less zealous in favor of the Anglican religion. He returned therefore to England to ask Charles I for a charter granting a tract of land north of the Patowmac [Potomac] River, which the Virginians had not yet reached with their settlements. It was promised to him, but, since he died shortly afterward, it was granted to his son. In this charter, dated the 10th of June, 1632—because of the superficial knowledge of the geography of the country and negligence then so common—the boundaries of the territory were indicated in a manner that would provoke, after a long period of time, interminable lawsuits between the heirs of Baltimore and the Penn family.

The Virginians protested against the division of what they called their territory but they could not prevent it. Lord Baltimore called his land Maryland, in honor of Marie, the wife of Charles I. As governor he sent Leonard Calvert, his brother, with Jeremy Hawley and Thomas Cornwallis, equerries, his assistants, etc., and, it seems, they held equal power with him in the administration of affairs. They departed from Cowes, a port on the Isle of Wight, on November 22, 1632, touched the Barbados and Saint Christopher, arrived in Virginia on February 24, 1633

and at the Potomac River on the following March 3rd. They were about two hundred, most of them from very distinguished Catholic families, who brought with them the means to settle comfortably. In spite of this, historians say that during the first two years there Lord Baltimore spent about forty thousand pounds sterling. Since he was rich and devout, it is probable that he exercised his generosity in favor of those of his religion who asked his help. After surveying the country near the river, they settled with the consent of the Indians, in one of their villages called *Yamaco*, a name that they changed to *Saint Mary*.

During the English civil wars, Lord Baltimore was deprived of his jurisdiction by Cromwell; and Charles II gave it back to him on the Restoration. Later James II, his brother and his successor, in whose soul the doctrine of royal power was as important as religious zeal, took it away again although the Baltimore family was very devout in the Catholic religion which was so dear to him. Finally Baltimore regained it in the reign of William, on the condition that he engage a Protestant governor.

The kings always took care to insert in the charters some clause whereby they reserved their sovereign rights. For example, Baltimore's charter strengthened the obligation to bring each year to the castle of Windsor the tribute of two Indian arrows, for as long as the request would be made. The population made rapid progress in Maryland for good reasons. Virginia supplied foodstuffs to the new settlers, up until the time when they could obtain from their own land the quantity they needed. The frontiers on the side of the Indians were very limited; therefore it was not difficult for the inhabitants of Maryland to maintain peace with them. The settlements of other European nations did not cause them to withdraw, with the exception of a small colony of Swedes who occupied some lands on the Delaware Bay, and whose number was too small to be of danger to their neighbors. The Christian religion, without the exception of any sect, enjoyed freedom of worship. The Catholics could not be persecuted, the landholder and the majority of the inhabitants being of that religion. On the other hand, the nature of the circumstances did not permit them to be intolerant.

The greatest benefit which those who had charters derived from the lands was a very moderate perpetual tax, which they levied on sales and on donations. This fee was called *quit-rent*.

In Maryland the proprietor fixed it at two penny sterling for each hundred acres*. Later he increased it to four pennies. Toward the year 1740 he wanted to raise it to ten pennies, but he did not succeed. If the kings had speculated better, they could have received considerable revenue from the quit-rent. They had reserved it for themselves in Virginia, but Charles II transferred a part to some noblemen, giving them a license for the territory situated between the Rappahanock River and the Potomac River. The representatives from Virginia opposed it in London, but those who had obtained the license made some concessions to the Colony, and by this means obtained its consent**.

---

*The acre is an English word, or rather a word which was brought to England by the Saxons or Normans, and which is still used in Normandy. It contains forty-three thousand five hundred sixty English square feet.

**The quit-rent of Virginia was an income of the Prince of Wales, which gave occasion, in the early period of the Revolution, to two members of the Assembly to reveal their scrupulous judgment at the expense of their knowledge of public law: for when the question of suspending the payment came up, these men, whose love for the cause of the country surpassed all others, opposed it with extreme fervor, one of them affirming that *we are at war with the father, and not with a poor small child*. The property of Northern-Neck, the name of the territory situated between the Rappahanock River and the Potomac River, after passing through several hands, belonged to Lord Fairfax, who lived and died there in 1781, at a very advanced age. He never became enmeshed in the affairs of the Revolution, and the quit-rent was paid to him until his death.

THE FOUNDING OF
NEW YORK

Before speaking of the founding of Pennsylvania, it is well to say something about the settlement of New York and that of New Jersey which preceded it.

The territory situated between the colonies of the London Company and those of the Plymouth Company, which the charter of 1606 had granted to both, was abandoned by both the one and the other. The Swedes and the Finns were the first, who, in small numbers, repaired to this area and settled on the Delaware Bay. A little later, a few Dutchmen settled near the mouth of the Hudson River, called thus by Captain Henry Hudson, an Englishman who, having discovered it in 1608, gave it his name.

The history of these beginnings is unquestionably the most confused and the most obscure of all the colonies. Little explanation for this can be found and the memoirs left us were written much later by persons of little education and perhaps not sufficiently impartial. From all that can be gathered it seems that before the year 1618 there were also some Englishmen in the neighborhood of the Hudson River; that, between that handful of Dutchmen and Englishmen there continually broke out quarrels leading to fisticuffs, and that victory belonged first to one group, then to the other; that the Dutchmen finally established a kind of government; that James I complained, and the Commonwealth answered him that it was the private business of the Amsterdam Company; that Sir Samuel Argol, Governor of Virginia for the London Company, conquered them in 1618; that James sent a certain Edward Langdon to govern, and that he called the territory New Albion; that the Dutch settlers placed themselves under the care of its government; and that in 1620 James permitted the Dutch to board the ships being sent to Brazil in order to get provisions and to obtain some wood.

According to some writers, during the English civil wars the Dutch took possession of the land which now forms a large part of the States of New York, New Jersey and Delaware, and a small portion of the State of Pennsylvania. They called it New Netherlands, or New Belgium, establishing several settlements and built a city on the end of the continent, between Long Island and the Hudson River, to which they gave the name of New Amsterdam, giving the name of North River to the Hudson River, which still retains the two names. They erected on the Delaware River a fort which they called Casimir, now New-Castle in the State of Delaware. They called Zoïd River (the south river) the Delaware River. This river has preserved, together with the bay, the only name given to either one in 1610, in honor of Lord Delaware who landed there by chance, seeking Virginia of which the Company had made him governor or president.

Other writers claim that, as early as 1623, the Dutch actually settled there and appointed a governor with the title of Director General of New Belgium. This is not without foundation, because during this time the English emigrants were going to Virginia and New England. The Dutch, by means of the ships which were being sent to Brazil—and which touched on this coast en route, as per agreement—could very easily have settled there. James I was not disposed to make a test of strength outside of his country. Vanity, royal prerogative and theology kept him completely occupied.

Being simple farmers, the Swedes and the Finns who occupied principally the territory that now forms the State of Delaware, sought for their security, as several writers say, the protection of the Dutch who were richer and more numerous. In 1655 Jean Kizeing, the Swedish governor, made a formal grant of the lands to Peter Stuyvesant, Dutch governor. Smith ([9]), in his history of New-York, says that the Dutch suppressed them by force.

Having resolved to make a conquest, Charles II began by allotting the proprietorship and sovereignty to the Duke of York, his brother, who later became James II, and granted him a charter to this effect on March 12, 1664. A fleet with military troops forced New Amsterdam to surrender, and all the other settlements followed its example. The name of New Amsterdam was replaced by that of New York, which was also given to the whole territory. As the boundaries were uncertain, the new ruler tried

to extend them as far as he could. On June 24 of the same year, 1664, he granted to Lord Berkeley of Straton and to Sir George Carteret the area which now forms the State of New Jersey.

The Dutch ceded to Charles II all New Belgium with the Treaty of Breda in 1667. They took it back during the war that Charles declared against them in 1672 and later ceded it in 1674, with the Treaty of Westminster, without ever recovering it again. To avoid any future difficulties, on the following June 29, Charles gave his brother a new charter on that land which had had a change of rule since the first cession.

Although the government of New York was administered by persons who were appointed by a prince who favored despotism, there reigned there a kind of civil and religious liberty which probably owed its existence to the fact that the inhabitants were a mixture of different nations, although for the most part Dutch. The character of the people deserves some attention. The Episcopalians, inclined in general to favor the monarchy, organized only after much time. The first Anglican church, Trinity Church, dates only from the year 1696. As for the Catholics, very few went there, although the proprietor and, consequently, the governors were very zealous partisans of this religion, which was finally prohibited after the abdication of James. This is evident from one of the first laws of the Colony prior to the Code which began to be formulated in April 1691. I shall refer to seven of them so as to give the reader an idea of the relationship of the Colony to Great Britain, and of the precepts prevalent at that time. As for the rest, they would not be of sufficient interest to you.

I. The kings of England alone are invested with the right to rule this colony, and that none can exercise any authority whatsoever in this province, if they have not received it directly from the king, by a decree signed with his great seal of the realm of England.

II. The legislative power and the supreme authority (under the control of the king) resides in the governor, in the council and in the representatives of the people in general assembly; the exercise and administration of the government belongs to the governor, and to the council, with the consent of at least five counselors, to rule according to the laws of the province, and for any defect therein, according to the laws of England.

III. The laws shall be in force as long as they shall not be abolished by the king, or that the term will not have expired.

IV. Each man must be judged by his peers, and all verdicts shall be made by twelve men of the neighborhood. In all criminal offenses, anyone presumed guilty must be denounced as such in court by the grand jury, and then judged by twelve jurors.

V. In all cases, except for the crime of treason and other crimes for which the laws of England do not permit the giving of bail, bails must be permitted, provided they are sufficient.

VI. No tax or imposition can be made except by the general assembly.

VII. Every church or Christian sect, which is not dangerous to the peace of the province, must be received, with the exception of the Catholic Church.

It remains only for me to observe that the assembly of the people, under the government of the Duke of York, was not convoked before the year 1683. Perhaps it would never have been convoked, if the experience of nine years had not demonstrated the absurdity of wanting to establish an absolute government in this region. The inhabitants had already begun to emigrate, and it was feared either that the territory would be depopulated or that the people would finally choose their own representatives, just as had happened in Virginia and New England.

THE FOUNDING OF
NEW JERSEY

We have already said that the Duke of York, on June 24, 1664, ceded a part of the territory that his brother had given him to Lord Berkeley of Straton and to Sir George Carteret, and that this part was called New Jersey. Philip Carteret, brother of George, was the governor until the year 1672. During the course of 1670 quit-rent was established. The inhabitants stood on their own rights—refusing to pay it—because they had bought the lands directly from the Indians. In 1672, they rebelled and nominated another governor. Philip Carteret went to England where the war against Holland kept him until 1674. That year he returned to Jersey and all was peaceful.

Lord Berkeley ceded his rights to others who agreed with Lord Carteret to divide the property. The same year, the Duke of York gave a new charter to George Carteret. The eastern part of the territory was ceded to him by the heirs of Lord Berkeley, who in turn received from him cession of the western part. This division, which was confirmed by a decision of the General Assembly, was the reason why, for some time, it was called "the two Jerseys."

Sir Edmond Andros, Vice-Governor of the Province of New York, of which the Duke [of York] had retained the title of Governor until his succession to the throne, took possession arbitrarily of the government of western Jersey, to the detriment of the successors of Lord Berkeley. In 1680, he acted in the same way with regard to eastern Jersey and had Carteret taken as a prisoner to New York. A short time afterward, the eastern part was restored to Carteret, and the western to the successors of Lord Berkeley, and Andros was called back by his government.

These restitutions and this recall have caused some writers

to say that Andros acted in this way on his own initiative. But this is nothing more than hypothesis. We need only be aware of the duplicity and arbitrary instincts of James II to judge differently, and his later conduct does not leave, in this regard, any doubt. When he ascended the throne, he made Andros governor of New England, gave him New York and at the same time subjected the two Jerseys to his government, after taking from the proprietors and appropriating them as though they were his incontestable patrimony.

After the abdication of James, the proprietors regained possession from King William. Various sales of this territory, the divisions and subdivisions, the rights which, from time to time, some persons claimed because they had bought them from the Indians, and the weakness of the government, whose leaders could not agree, caused the proprietors, in 1702, to cede all rights of jurisdiction to the Crown. They obtained, in exchange, a kind of charter, which prescribed for all future governors certain regulations whereby to protect their land. It was forbidden, for example, to agree to any tax which the Assembly would place on the vacant lands, and to buy lands from the Indians without the consent of the proprietors. The latter were obliged to see to it that the owners cultivated what they owned. In 1683 the two Assemblies, one for East and the other for West Jersey, had forbidden, under threat of severe penalties, any purchases without the consent of these proprietors. It sufficed therefore that the governors could not give their consent to the revocation of these laws. During the year 1703, the two Jerseys were reunited under one government over which the governor of New York presided and, thirty-three years later, the government of New Jersey was entirely separated from that of New York.

THE FOUNDING OF
PENNSYLVANIA AND DELAWARE

William Penn, founder of the Colony of Pennsylvania, obtained for this territory, on the 4th of March 1681, a charter from Charles II, who reserved for himself, according to custom, a fifth part of the gold and silver of the mines and an annual tribute of two buckskins delivered at Windsor Castle. Of the large number of conditions which this charter contains, here are those which I deem most important:

The province shall be called Pennsylvania.

William Penn, his deputies and lieutenants, with the approbation of the majority of freemen, or of their assembled representatives, shall make laws for the raising of money for public utilities, form courts, appoint judges, etc.

Laws shall be consonant with reason and not repugnant or contrary to those of England and the King shall reserve to the Crown the right to investigate private business and to judge it in case of appeals.

In all cases where the positive law of the province is silent, the laws of England shall be followed.

A duplicate of all laws, so made and published as aforesaid, shall, within five years after the making thereof, be transmitted and delivered to the Privy Council. If within the space of six months after they are received, they are declared contrary to the lawful prerogative of the crown, or contrary to the faith and allegiance due to the legal government of England, they shall be adjudged void.

The proprietors can impose such taxes on merchandise which the assembly shall determine.

They shall have an agent in London, to be answerable to the Crown for any alleged misdemeanor, and in the case where they

shall be condemned by the courts and do not satisfy the conditions within the space of one year to defray the damages in his Majesty's courts, the government will be resumed and retained till payment has been made without any prejudice however in any respect to the landholders or inhabitants, who are not to be affected or molested thereby.

They can transfer proprietorship.

The ownership of lands already occupied by Christians shall be reserved for them.

The King will place neither taxes, nor revenues on this province without the approval of the proprietor, or of the assembly, or without a decree of the English Parliament, etc.

It seems, according to this last article, that the King, foreseeing that his will would be supported by the proprietor, or by an act of the English Parliament, could levy a burden of taxes and impositions on the colony without the consent of the Assembly.

But this move, totally destructive of the freedom of the colony, is found to be contradicted several times in the same charter by terms which have the opposite meaning. As a self-contradictory agreement, it could not bind the contracting parties, that is to say, the King and Penn. Not only did it disregard the other colonies, but it could not take into account the inhabitants of Pennsylvania whose predecessors had made their particular agreements with Penn either before leaving England, or after their departure, as we shall see.

On July 11th of the same year, the proprietor and those who had resolved to emigrate with him, agreed:

That before the distribution of lands to the purchasers, they shall take what would be necessary for roads;

That all business with the Indians would be performed in public market;

That all differences between the settlers and the Indians shall be judged by six settlers and six Indians;

That for every five acres, there be one acre of trees, in order to preserve the oak and the mulberry trees for the construction of ships and the production of silk;

That no one would leave the province without notification in the marketplace three weeks in advance.

On April 25, 1682, a new, very extensive document to assure the liberty and the privileges of the people was signed by both

parties. This document, called the Charter of William Penn, stipulates among other things:

That the government shall reside in the general assembly of the province which shall consist of the governor and representatives of freemen, to make laws, levy taxes, establish courts and duties, etc.

That the number of representatives shall not exceed in the beginning two hundred persons, and never five hundred; that there be seventy-two councilors to draw up the laws and propose them for the approbation of the general assembly, which shall exercise the executive and judicial power and other functions such as the inspection of the treasury, of all public places, etc.

It regulates the method of electing the representatives of the people and the councilors, the time of the assembly, the elections of magistrates, the manner of administering justice, etc.

It suggests that in the first year, the assembly will be composed of all the freemen, and that it will then be composed of their representatives.

It ends by declaring that no article can be changed without the consent of the governor and of six-sevenths of the freemen meeting in the provincial council and in the general assembly.

On the 5th of May of the same year, an addition was made containing a certain number of articles, among which the following three deserve to be mentioned, namely:

"That all men making their residence in the province, who pay taxes to the government, shall be considered as freemen and shall enjoy the right of electing and being elected to any position that there be;

"That whoever recognizes Almighty God shall not be disturbed in his religious beliefs in matters of faith or culture, nor forced to kneel or to frequent any minister;

"That the first day of each week shall be a day of rest.*"

These contracts between Penn and the emigrants were made and signed by both parties before leaving their country. Therefore, when they came to America the first thoughts Penn had

---

*This agreement made between the Quakers and Penn, whom Abbé Raynal assures us to have been a Quaker, deserves to be compared with what he says of the Quakers (op. cit., Vol. 9, p. 12): "The temples were to their eyes only. . . . The Sunday rest was only *useless leisure*."

were to make plans for Philadelphia and to change, as much as he could to his own advantage, the articles on which they had been in agreement.

Since here we are describing a man whom some writers have rendered so famous, and whose character has been falsely interpreted rather than exaggerated, it is well to place the reader in a position to judge it after knowing the facts.

It is a remarkable fact, or rather one that seems incomprehensible, that the London court would give such a charter to William Penn, precisely at the time when it proposed to take back all the charters from the colonies already established and from the communities of its own kingdom.

An examination of the circumstances will end our surprise.

We know how much the Duke of York ardently desired to re-establish the Catholic religion. Penn was his intimate confidant and continued to be even when the Duke ascended the throne. According to the general opinion of well-informed persons, the idea of beginning with universal tolerance was suggested to him by Penn, as the easiest means to arrive at his purpose. As for the religious principles of Penn, opinions have been very divided. Some have believed him to be a Quaker, others a Jesuit. What is certain is that his conduct was absolutely Jesuitical and did not resemble that of the Quakers, except on points where Quakers resemble the Jesuits.

The motive that led Penn to agree, before his departure from London, to a government favorable to the people, was the hope of increasing the number of followers. Consequently he printed and published this system of government under the following title: "The Frame of the Government of the Province of Pennsylvania, in America; together with certain laws agreed upon in England, by the governor and divers freemen of the aforesaid province. To be further explained and confirmed *there* by the first provincial council, *if they see meet.*"*

The author of these historical notes on the constitution of Pennsylvania, says in this regard:

*This book [*An Historical Review of the Constitution and Government of Pennsylvania*], printed in London in 1759, under the direction of Dr. [Benjamin] Franklin, contains a complete collection of facts taken from authentic memoirs.

"At the head of this Frame, or system, is a short preliminary discourse, part of which serves to give us a more lively idea of Mr. Penn's preaching in Grace-Church Street [sic], than we derive from Raphael's Cartoon of Paul preaching at Athens; as a man of conscience he sets out; as a man of reason he proceeds; and as a man of the world he offers the most plausible conditions to *all*, to the end that he might gain *some*."*

The discontent between Penn and his followers began with the request he made for quit-rent. They opposed it, regarding a tax on lands they had bought as hard and unjust. Penn was very persuasive. He made of himself two distinct persons: one was the proprietor and the other, the governor. The proprietor sold the lands, and the governor must be maintained by the community. The author of the work which I have just quoted says that Penn combined the astuteness of the serpent with the innocence of the dove. The governor, said Penn, needed a legislative body. He made them believe that in paying the quit-rent, they would be exempt from taxation. These considerations, accompanied by an external adaptability to circumstances, resulted in the obligation to pay the quit-rent. This did not stop the imposition of taxation but the proprietor himself never wanted to contribute his share. This alleged father of his people, whose humanity, justice and generosity have been so celebrated, this man so marvelous that in order to describe his sublime and almost divine character the Abbé Raynal asks permission *to use the language of the fable,* fought all his life against his people to exempt his own goods from the just share of his obligations and to transmit his claim, as arbitrary as it was unjust, to his descendants who, after his example, always refused to agree to have their goods taxed, even during the time of the greatest calamities.

The conditions which Penn before leaving England believed he must grant, produced their effect and, after attracting the largest number of people possible**, he tried, once he ar-

*Ibid., p. 12.

**The Abbé Raynal has judged fit to say (*op. cit.,* Vol. 9, p. 15), that all the Quakers wanted to follow him, and that he, "inspired by a prophetic light, at first only wanted to lead two thousand."

rived in America, to find a pretext to change the system of government.

As was said in the chapter on New York, New Belgium took in a small part of Pennsylvania. Consequently, the Duke of York, in his position as head of New Belgium, in order to protect Penn from all difficulties, granted him all the territory to the west of New Jersey. The three counties, then called the *territory*, which now form the small State of Delaware, and which had already for some time been inhabited by Europeans, were thus included in the grant. Penn claimed that besides this the King had accorded him jurisdiction with a charter—but this document has not been seen by anyone—and in 1704 the representatives of the people of Pennsylvania, who had several other reasons for discontent with Penn, made him realize that they doubted the existence of such a title. The author of the historical review of the constitution of Pennsylvania, after speaking of the imposition of the quit-rent, adds: "Penn, having in this instance experienced the weight of his credit and the power of his persuasion, no sooner landed, then he formed a double scheme to unite the province with the territory, though it does not appear he was properly authorized to do so, and to substitute another frame of government for the former, which, having answered the great purpose of being an inducement here at home [in England] for collecting subjects, he was now inclined to render somewhat more favorable to himself in point of government."*

In uniting the new province and the territory under one sole government, it became necessary to change several of the agreements made in London. Penn convoked at Chester the freemen of both places in the month of December 1682, and proposed the union. The province opposed it and did not want any change in the charter. The proprietor, with his usual astuteness, tried to prove that the union would be of very great advantage, that the changes made in the charter would not detract from the first agreement; finally, he managed to obtain the union and make them accept a new system of government without even observing the formalities required by law. This simplified, for the future, the means of obtaining new changes and we shall see that this was, in practice, his intention.

*Benjamin Franklin, *op. cit.*, p. 18.

188

At the second assembly which took place in Philadelphia in the spring of 1683, Penn proposed a third system of government, more in conformity with his views, which he also succeeded in having adopted. This last one kept a little of the first and the second, and in several points it differed essentially from both of them.

About two years later a confrontation occurred between him and Lord Baltimore concerning boundaries. Penn with pleasure seized upon this pretext to go to London, leaving the colony at a time when it seemed least excusable in the eyes of those with whom he had promised to pass the rest of his life. James had ascended the throne and already begun to prepare his artillery. It was natural that Penn should desire to go to London in order to be near him. Actually he served him with much zeal, although on certain occasions with little honor, especially in the stubborn dispute that this monarch had with the Fellows of Magdalen College.

The situation in which Penn left things in America, and the instructions which he later sent to his lieutenants, kept discord constantly alive. What contributed even more to the discord was probably his reservation of the right to approve or reject the laws made in his absence, so that the consent of the commissioners and of the vice-governor was null unless confirmed by him. He had left the government in the hands of five commissioners. In 1686, he ordered them to change the form of government again. The strong opposition that he encountered led him to believe that a single person would have less difficulty in succeeding. Consequently, he sent a certain John Blackwell in the capacity of vice-governor, who seized the opportunity to sow dissension among the representatives and the councilors. After many useless attempts, he failed, under false pretexts, to attend the Assembly which was held in the month of May 1689; for this reason public affairs were at a standstill. The representatives, tired of waiting in vain, made two declarations; in one they exposed the conduct of the vice-governor and in the other they prohibited the requirement of certain taxes which they ordinarily had to pay him.

Finally, Blackwell appeared. He told them some very strange things, among others the following:

"The honorable proprietor, for reasons known to himself,

hath given me positive instructions to let all the laws lapse, except the fundamental, and to call together the legislative body to pass such of them as would be fitting for the future, which it is my full intention to do.

"The honorable proprietor would, by his patent from the King, authorized by himself, his heirs, etc. with consent of the freemen, make and, under his seal, publish necessary laws for the good of the people, which had never been done under all requisite forms whilst he himself was here. I very much doubt whether what were passed or would hereafter be passed, would have that due sanction or stability which laws require, etc."

He concluded by showing himself disposed to do nothing about it.

The reasons known to him, that is, to the proprietor, which he did not deign to communicate to us, are a little in the style of Asiatic sovereigns. If the laws had not been made in the required form while the proprietor was on hand, and if this neglect was sufficient to render null even those which would be made later, what opinion should one have of similar legislation? The most favorable conclusion, since there was no other reason for his non-appearance, is to assume his discourse sincere. Furthermore how can this negligence which the proprietor's lieutenant believed could nullify what would be done in the future, be in accord with the declaration quoted by us that he made earlier, that is to establish laws which were to be allowed to lapse or others that would be fitting.

This matter would take too long to discuss fully. If the reader finds some ambiguity in the passages that have been placed before his eyes, then he should have recourse to the text and read all of it. The part quoted will seem like geometric reasoning in comparison to the rest of it. The representatives replied, and they combined clarity and good sense with astonishing moderation. Blackwell later resorted to other expediencies as miserable as the first, but always without success. The same conduct, on both sides, lasted for considerable time, that is, moderation and firmness on the part of the representatives, duplicity and deceit on the part of the proprietor. If friendship is the result of rapport between characters, one must not be surprised that the friendship that existed between James II and William Penn was indissoluble.

190

Finally James abdicated the throne. The new sovereigns did not favor Penn. In 1693, they took over the government of Pennsylvania, but three years later it was given back to him. No one knows why.

At the first meeting of the assembly that took place after the return of the proprietor, the representatives complained to their vice-governor that they had not been convoked according to the statutes. To give the government more stability and establish clearer and less complicated statutes, the representatives proposed a well-thought-out form of government, which in the end would be a new constitution. The vice-governor gave his consent in 1697, but it had no effect, because the proprietor did not judge it proper to ratify it.

At the end of 1699, the proprietor himself went to America for the second time and, at the first assembly that took place in the Spring of 1700, he again proposed the system of government of 1683 which was accepted with all the formalities; at the same time he promised to present another system more agreeable to the two parties. However, for some time he only occupied himself with his own interests. He convoked the assembly sometimes at New-Castle, capital of the territory, sometimes at Philadelphia, and employed all the shrewdness of which he was capable to persuade the inhabitants of each of the two colonies to accept his views.

The last assembly which he himself convoked took place in the month of September, 1701. At the opening, he apologized for convoking it one month before the established date, adding that the enemies of the colony in England had taken advantage of his absence to harm him, a fact which obliged him to depart immediately.

His talk was full of expressions of affection and interest. He gave them to understand that it was with infinite regret that he found himself forced to leave them. He spoke of his abiding love of a tranquil and retired life. He said that nothing could lessen (except the submission that he owed to the providence of God) his affection for the country nor change his resolution to return with his family to settle there permanently; and after various other expressions of affection and sympathy, he added with engaging worldly aplomb: "think therefore, think, since all men are mortal, of some suitable expedient and provision for your

191

own safety, as well as of your privileges and property, and you will find me ready to comply with whatsoever may render us happy, by a nearer union of our interests. Review again your laws. Propose new ones, that you may better your circumstances; and what you do, do it quickly, remembering that the Parliament sits at the end of next month; and that the sooner I am there, the safer, I hope, we shall be here."

He then urged them always to remain well united, promptly expedite their affairs and pay their subsidies regularly. The representatives responded in affectionate and respectful tones but this response, which was brief, was accompanied by a request containing twenty-one articles, whereby they made it clear that they had certain reservations about his sincerity. Events well proved that the sentiments of his talk were not those of his heart. Things remained in their usual incertitude.

With regard to the new system of government, the proprietor finally presented it on October 28, almost at the moment of his departure, although as is evident by its date, it was ready on the 8th. The more essential changes consisted in the right to propose laws which would pass from the council to the representatives and, as for the election of the councilors, the proprietor took that right from the people and appropriated it for himself. A considerable change was made with regard to freedom of religion by this article: "All persons who make profession of believing in Jesus Christ can serve the government in all kinds of employment." Before this it had been sufficient merely to believe in God to enjoy all rights of a citizen. The representatives of the territory refused to adopt this new system. They walked out of the assembly, totally disgusted, and separated, never to meet again.

On leaving Penn left the unity of the colonies broken, and it was impossible for him to foresee what the consequences would be. This is one of the reasons why the author of the historical review considers it very strange that Montesquieu (10) gave Penn the title "A New Lycurgus." Penn's conduct toward the colonists was always the same. Agreements were never respected. To have money neither artifice nor deceit was to be spared, and sometimes even threats were employed.

The threats of the colony's Vice-Governor Evans, in 1704, were such that the representatives unanimously resolved to write to the proprietor in order to show Evans how much reason

they had to be discontented with his conduct and to encourage him to reform. The Assembly of 1707 wrote to the proprietor again on June 10 and reaffirmed what they had written previously, but all was useless.

In these complaints, they reproached Penn for the tricks he had used on them before and after emigration, for the extortions he resorted to in order to get money, for his shameful injustice in making himself judge of his own case, etc.

Those who desire more detailed information will find these reprimands at the end of this work, together with the 1701 plan of government, which lasted in Pennsylvania until the Revolution*.

Penn had some foolish and capricious ideas which placed him in constant need of money. To obtain this he had stooped to resort to extraordinary means, and his vice-governors were obliged, in order to maintain their positions, to make every effort to please him. He died in London in 1718, engulfed in debt, after he had already conveyed his property to a certain Gée and others and agreed to cede entirely all his rights to the Crown for 10,000 pounds sterling of which he had already received 2,000 on account. The contract was about to be signed when he died of a sudden attack of apoplexy, thus permitting Pennsylvania to remain in his family.

If William Penn had been the man several writers have described, the Colony of Pennsylvania would have prospered to greater advantage. They exaggerated its prosperity, for example, and when they said that it had never been at war with the Indians, and made other odd claims, they were being prompted by their imaginations. But despite the lack of scruples with which the proprietor violated agreements, and despite the disputes which existed continually between him and the Colonists, Pennsylvania prospered more rapidly than the other colonies. It is worthwhile therefore to examine the reasons.

We must consider, for one thing, the experience which the example the earlier settlements offered, and the help the Colony received in its infancy both from the foodstuffs with which it was supplied and the help it got when its frontiers were attacked.

*See *Notes*, Section A, p. 275.

The form of government which Penn had promised, and which he had the cleverness to publicize in London, as I have already said, made emigrants flock from everywhere.

Add the salutary effect of religious freedom, which made itself felt even after 1701, although the rights of citizens were reserved to Christians only. Since all the emigrants were Christians, no one suffered from the injustice done to other religions, and all enjoyed the advantage of not having any one religion dominate.

The Quakers, who in the beginning had been as fanatic as the Anabaptists, although they had become much more moderate, were not allowed either in Virginia or any of the colonies of New England, with the exception of Rhode Island; there were a few in the colonies of Maryland and New York, but in all a very small number.

The settled area of Rhode Island was much too small to attract European emigrants, and more than likely the difference that existed between this colony and the others of New England with regard to freedom of religion was not too well kown. Massachusetts, Connecticut and New Hampshire were governed arbitrarily by the Congregationalists; Virginia by the Anglicans. The territory of Maryland was not very great, and since the Catholics there had all the influence, as much because of their number as because of their proprietor, the Protestants did not go there very willingly.

The government of New York, dependent on James II, did not offer satisfactory assurance. The Protestants did not find themselves very happy there, and the few Catholics who went there under the indirect protection of James were not very well received; finally, after the abdication of James, they were banished by the law of 1691, as we have seen before.

Pennsylvania was therefore preferred by emigrants of all denominations and, above all, by the Quakers. There were among these last many rich people and, as their conduct was full of wisdom, especially in regard to business and thrift, and their example was always good in this regard, they were infinitely useful in the infancy of the Colony, which continues to reflect their efforts.

The first sowing sinks deep roots. The plants take strength, cover the land with their shadow and prevent the growth of those of a different kind that are in their vicinity.

THE FOUNDING OF
THE TWO CAROLINAS AND GEORGIA

Although the first settlement of the land which now forms the two Carolinas and Georgia preceded that of Pennsylvania by several years, we have had to speak about it at a later point because clarity requires that we discuss these three colonies together, without interruption, since the division of Carolina into two provinces followed [the settlement of Pennsylvania] by forty-six years and the foundation of Georgia by fifty.

On March 24, 1662, Charles II gave the charter for the lands situated between the thirty-first and the thirty-sixth degrees of latitude to eight persons, the Earl of Clarendon, the Duke of Albemarle, Lord Craven, Lord Berkeley, Lord Ashley, and Sirs George Carteret, William Berkeley and John Colleton. The land was called *Carolina* , some say, by order of and in honor of the King. Hewit ([11]), author of the history of southern Carolina and of Georgia, claims that it had been named Carolina a long time before by John Ribaud who, at the time of the civil wars in France, was sent to these parts by Admiral de Coligny with two ships bringing a very large group to found a colony, and he supposes that the intention of Coligny was to prepare an asylum for himself and his partisans in case he was forced to abandon his country.

Hewit says that Ribaud, having made the Indians understand that he was the enemy of the Spaniards, was well received by them, that after a kind of agreement made in France between the two parties, Coligny, who had not been able until then to aid his newborn colony, sent René Laudener with three ships and a considerable number of emigrants; that before his arrival, Ribaud had departed with all his people because of lack of supplies; that when Laudener was on the point of doing the same

thing and for the same reason, Ribaud returned from France with seven other ships; that when the Colony began to prosper, Pierre Mélandez, a Spaniard, killed Ribaud with seven hundred of his people and forced the others to return to France. He adds that Mr. de Gourgues of Gascogne avenged his compatriots some time later and gave rout to Mélandez, but that neither he, nor other Frenchmen ever attempted to found a colony there again*.

The charter of Charles II declared the eight associates, whose names we have mentioned, masters and absolute proprietors of the land with all rights of jurisdiction, royal privileges (etc.) The only restriction was that laws could not be made except with the consent of the freemen. In the same charter, after such ample concessions, the King reserved, both for himself and for his heirs and successors, sovereign authority over the whole territory. Whether these ambiguities are the result of chance, or whether they were intentional, it can be seen that they were then very much in style. Two years later, a new charter of June 30 extended the territory from the twenty-ninth up to the thirty-sixth and a half degrees latitude, declaring that it would be separated from Virginia by a straight line from east to west.

We have arrived now at the period of Locke's ([12]) system of legislation, a system more famous for the great name of the author, than for its intrinsic merits. It is claimed that the proprietors gave Locke the principal ideas on which the system was based. If this was so, Locke, it seems to me, should not have accepted such a commission for it endangered his own reputation. On the other hand, examining attentively all the parts of this system, which is extremely complicated, one comes to believe that the architect would not have employed so much time nor done so much work, if he had not deluded himself into believing that such foundations were stable and just.

Out of respect for the author, his system, if it were not so excessively long, would be inserted in its entirety at the end of this work. It contains one hundred twenty articles, for the most part very long, besides a supplement which sets down the rules

---

*The Spaniards hanged the French prisoners with this statement: *Not as Frenchmen, but as heretics.* De Gourgues had the Spaniards hanged with this other statement: *Not as Spaniards, but as assassins.*

of precedence. It is not possible, however, to make an extract to give an idea of the whole thing because the style is exceedingly concise. We must therefore limit ourselves to a summary of the most important points. Here are those which have seemed so to us.

The province shall be divided into counties of equal size.

Each county shall consist of eight signories, eight baronies and twenty-four colonies; each of these divisions shall consist of twelve thousand acres.

Six colonies shall form a district; consequently there will be four districts per county.

Each proprietor shall have a signory in each county.

He shall have there an hereditary nobility, consisting of a landgrave and two caciques per county, to which the eight baronies should belong, that is four to the landgrave and two to each of the caciques.

The oldest proprietor shall be Palatine, and shall preside at the proprietors' court, which will be the first of the eight supreme courts, and shall be called the Palatine court.

Each of the other seven shall be presided over by a proprietor, and they shall divide among themselves, at their choice, according to custom, the offices of grand constable, grand admiral, chancellor, chief justice, grand chamberlain, high-steward and treasurer.

Each of the seven courts shall be composed of a proprietor and six councilors and shall decide only the affairs of its own department.

Each proprietor can send a deputy to act in his place, as though he himself were present, except to confirm the decrees of Parliament and to create landgraves or caciques.

The decrees of the Palatine court cannot be valid without the vote of the Palatine or his deputy, and of three proprietors or their deputies.

If the Palatine goes to the army, the grand constable is obliged to relinquish the command; if he goes to any other supreme court, the proprietor or his deputy must also relinquish the place and be just one of the councilors.

The grand council, consisting of the Palatine and seven other proprietors, with the forty-two councilors of seven courts, has the exclusive power to declare war and peace, alliances and trea-

197

ties, to prepare all that shall be proposed in Parliament, and to resolve the disputes which could arise among the different supreme courts.

Thirteen members of the council suffice to act, provided that in this number there be a proprietor or his deputy.

The signories and baronies must always be indivisible, and after the year 1700, inalienable.

If a proprietor dies without heirs, the other seven must elevate to this position a landgrave who will succeed to the signory of the deceased, and his four baronies shall pass to his closest heirs.

Lacking heirs, either of landgraves or caciques, the proprietors shall appoint them; and if they fail to appoint those who are lacking, proprietors, landgraves or caciques, Parliament must appoint them in the time and manner prescribed by the system, so that their number always be complete.

Parliament shall be composed of the proprietors, landgraves, caciques and of a representative from each district, all of whom sit in the same chamber.

The election of representatives shall be every two years. It is necessary to possess five hundred acres of land for the right to be a representative, and fifty to enjoy that of voting.

Parliament shall discuss business proposed by the grand council and does not have the right to propose [business itself]. In order for its resolutions to become laws, they must be approved in the same session by the Palatine court in the chamber of Parliament.

If before being approved, a proprietor or his deputy opposes them, the proprietors, landgraves, caciques and representatives must retire into their respective chambers to deliberate separately on this point. If the majority of any of the four chambers support the opposition, it suffices to invalidate them.

After their approval, they last only until the next Parliament, if in the meantime they are not confirmed by the Palatine court, which confirmation the proprietors shall make in person, as we stated in the beginning.

Besides presiding over the supreme court of law, each proprietor has jurisdiction and presides over each of his signories, each landgrave and cacique in his baronies, and each district at its particular court. There is, in addition, the county court, to

which individual courts can appeal, just as the county court and all others can appeal to the supreme court, provided one pays, for the proprietors' benefit, certain sums designated within the government framework according to the various cases.

The Palatine's court can, in addition, erect manors and give the owners the same privileges which the landgraves and the caciques enjoy in their baronies.

The said manors shall consist of not less than one thousand acres, and not above twelve thousand, in one entire section within the limits of one colony. These shall be as inalienable as the baronies. But no portion of land, no matter how large it be, can constitute a manor, if the Palatine court has not given it this title.

I shall end by saying that article 96 of the system, declares that the Anglican religion is the only orthodox religion and that it should be maintained by the government. It is claimed, however, that Locke placed all religions on the same level, and that he said to one of his friends, to whom he gave a copy of his system, that article 96 had been inserted there by one of the proprietors.

Such are the most important points to be known in order to understand the true causes of the disputes between the people and the proprietors, whom one could more appropriately call sovereigns.

The area extends over more than five hundred miles along the coast and about six hundred inland. It is no less profitable or fertile than the other colonies. The proprietors should, according to Locke's system, possess the fifth part of all the territory in perpetuity, without being able to sell the smallest part. The territorial proprietorship would then be about eight million acres for each one. As soon as the land was well populated, the simple profit from real property would bring to each proprietor a revenue worthy of a sovereign. The four other fifths would belong equally to the proprietors, who could dispose of it as they judged most suitable to their financial interests or political purposes, sell or give the baronies, sell, give or rent the territory of the colonies. I pass over in silence other perpetual rents. This detail would lead me too far astray.

The proprietors, not being obliged to render an account, have control of the entire administration of public monies; they preside over all the highest offices, as well as in the General As-

sembly which proposes the laws; they have the absolute and exclusive power to approve them and to suspend them after having approved them. Finally, they do not lack the most efficacious means to corrupt individuals and dispose of their votes in case of need. And added to this is the interest of the nobility in supporting the proprietors, since each landgrave has the hope of becoming a proprietor, and each worker of becoming a landgrave. The more one examines Locke's system, the more one sees clearly that it tends to form an oligarchy, as extraordinary and as tyrannical as the human spirit can conceive. If anyone should doubt this, he just has to read one point after another to be convinced.

In 1667 the proprietors sent William Sayre to inspect the land. On his return, the King, acceding to their request, granted them possession of all the islands situated within the twenty-second and the twenty-seventh degrees latitude, and in 1669, they sent him back as governor, together with a very large number of emigrants. One of their first cares was that of approving a plan to construct a city which they decided to call Charles-Town [Charleston] in honor of the King.

The first emigrants were very discouraged. On landing, they found only vast, uncultivated plains, almost all covered with stagnant water. For this reason, the insects, characteristic of hot countries, were more numerous and more bothersome. Their knowledge of agriculture, in a climate so different from that which they had left, hindered the progress of nature instead of helping it; and the Indians often made unannounced visits attacking them with their arrows, which was fair enough, because the proprietors did not even consider buying their lands. The plans of the proprietors were very grand, and as extraordinary as they were lacking in justice.

The Duke of York became, as we have said, ruler of New Belgium, and his manner of governing prompted many people to emigrate. Some Hollanders decided to go to Carolina. The proprietors accepted their request and sent two ships to take them. The arrival of the newcomers gave courage to those who were already there. Their example urged others from Europe and from America to go there also, so that in 1674 the people were able to elect their first representatives.

The regulations established by Locke's system were not fol-

lowed completely. Their extreme complexity, which would have made carrying them out difficult at any time, made it impossible in the early days. One may add to this by saying that the government made no effort to win the sympathy of the people, and the proprietors administered everything through their substitutes, who were people who rarely knew how to win respect. Dissensions and disorders developed rapidly. Religion as usual played a great part in this. Although they formed the smallest number, since they knew of the proprietors' preference for their religion and their interest in making it the dominant one, the Anglicans attempted several times to eliminate the others. The partiality of the proprietors and their followers, who made it appear clearly that they were favoring this sect under all circumstances, augmented jealousy, envy and animosity.

It is known that at that time the sea was overrun with pirates, and that Charles II had made Henry Morgan of Wales a knight. Morgan was the famous pirate who had plundered Porto-Bello and Panama. The King's example contributed much to the fact that pirates were well received as much in their European domains as in some parts of America.

Carolina, because of its proximity to the Spanish possessions, was the most suitable place for the pirates. By distributing silver which they had acquired with so much facility, they succeeded without difficulty in befriending the people, who obtained very little from their badly cultivated lands. This gave rise to an infamous commerce. The proprietors had not yet made any treaty with the Indians. Consequently the wars, or rather the skirmishes, between them and the inhabitants of Carolina, were very frequent. The pirates would buy Indian prisoners and re-sell them on the islands. This abominable commerce lasted for some time, and there was much difficulty in abolishing it entirely.

Finally, the bad administration of James II and the revocation of the Edict of Nantes came to the assistance of this new-born colony. The persecution caused a large number of respectable families to rush there, both from France and from England, giving them a new life. Of course people who renounce the comforts of their native land to go in search of liberty must be very different from those recruited by companies of adventurers.

These last emigrants soon realized that the interests of the people could not be those of the proprietors. Their observations on the bad principles of government began to spread and justly impress others.

If the proprietors had been present, they would perhaps have changed their absurd system. But they resided in England and, from their privileged position, they sent their sovereign orders to America. Their agents, either out of prudence or necessity, in some cases went along with the inhabitants, disregarding the proprietors' instructions. However, this was no real remedy, because the proprietors never approved what deviated from their own preferred plans.

Governor Morton, a man in all respects worthy and very esteemed in the colony, lost the love of the people without retaining the favor of the proprietors because the duties of his position were in opposition to what his moderation dictated; he could not fully satisfy either of the two parties. In 1687, James Colleton, (brother of the proprietor) who was made landgrave by the Palatine court in order to give him more importance, became Morton's successor to the government. Colleton, although he desired to follow the instructions of his superiors in all things, understood the necessity of enacting some laws which deviated a little from their instructions.

The Palatine court sent these back to him without approving them and with precise orders to conform to their own instructions. But the people observed the new laws anyway and the governor was not obeyed.

During this kind of anarchy, Secretary Paul Grimball irritated the people with his over-ardent zeal in defending the interests of the proprietors. The people placed him in prison, took possession of the archives, refused to pay the quit-rent for the lands which they could not yet cultivate, and convoked an Assembly in order to oppose the government.

Colleton reacted shrewdly. He assembled the militia, as if the country were in danger and, placing himself in command, declared martial law. After the people were assured that there was no appearance of invasion and that the governor had invented this pretext to intimidate them, the Assembly gathered and decreed that Landgrave Colleton was incapable of exercising any civil or military office in the province and that he be obliged

to depart. Later the Assembly notified him of his exile ànd of the time that it had established for his departure. This event took place in 1690. The proprietors named a certain Philip Ludwell of Virginia as governor, who established as much order and tranquility as possible and contrived a new plan of government, by means of which the representatives achieved the right to propose laws.

The Anglicans, who always tried to make their religion the dominant one, looked upon this new plan with pleasure, and they exalted its merits, because it would have been impossible to attain their ends if the government of the proprietors had been destroyed. Among the nonconformists, there was a large number of French Protestants. To diminish the strength of the opposing party, the Anglicans began to open attack on them and try to deprive them of their rights as citizens. In this regard the English laws were favorable to them and they had recourse to them every time the local laws were silent. Animosities grew; [the Anglicans] began to say that [the French Protestants] did not have the right to possess lands, and that their marriages would no longer be valid. With regard to the last two points, the proprietors thought differently, but they did not have the courage to displease the Anglicans, who were the only support of their government.

Among the French refugees, there were many who had bought vast expanses of land from the proprietors, at twenty pounds sterling for each thousand acres, with an annual tax and in perpetuity a shilling of quit-rent for each hundred. They had already brought their agriculture to the point of their being able to live there comfortably and of being able to take pride in bequeathing to their children honest affluence. Ludwell's conduct in general, and his regard for them in particular, made many people decide to remain there in the hope that things would take a favorable turn. Some, however, who could neither bear the insolence of the Anglicans, nor tolerate the fear that their children would one day be declared bastards and excluded from their paternal inheritance, went to Pennsylvania and were also followed by some Dutch, and by some English nonconformists.

The weakness of the government gave rise to the return of the pirates, and they began again to sell the Indians. Ludwell, despairing of being able to establish good order, wrote to the

proprietors to send another governor, and he returned to Virginia. Hewit says that the proprietors removed him from office, because he did not defend their prerogatives as they had expected. He had as successor Landgrave Thomas Smith, and it was at the beginning of his government that the first grains of rice were brought by chance into Carolina by the Captain of a brigantine that stopped there on its way from the Island of Madagascar to England. Two years later, Smith resigned of his own accord from the government, because he could not maintain order and advised the proprietors to send one of themselves. In 1695, they sent as governor the proprietor John Archdale, a Quaker who, during the year that he remained, remedied the abuses a little but could neither prevent the landing of pirates, nor entirely abolish the custom of selling the Indians; he was also obliged to agree that the French refugees should enjoy neither the right to appoint their representatives nor the right to vote.

Archdale, on his return to London, made the proprietors understand the necessity of abolishing many of the articles of their system of government. They sent a new plan to Carolina, which, however, did not please at all. The Assembly rejected it with such indifference that they showed almost openly their firm conviction that they had no need of the proprietors. The religious disputes for the moment had abated somewhat and there no longer remained support in keeping the Anglicans in the proprietors' party.

After the Assembly of the people had acquired more stability, they advised the French refugees to present a request to the Assembly that they might be united with the other citizens, enjoy the same rights and form a united people. They had made many friends by their good conduct and their tranquility. The cessation of religious disputes had lessened the animosity a little and the majority of the inhabitants, in recovering their rights, manifested more generous sentiments. Thus their demands were accorded without difficulty.

While the events began to take a good turn, Lord Grenville, one of the greatest fanatics that the Anglican sect had ever had, became the ruler. The spirit of bigotry made him believe that everything was permissible in order to establish the preeminence of this religion. It would be too long to trace all the illicit means used for this purpose. Finally, in 1702, an election of the repre-

sentatives was held under the protection of the government, but without having first observed the legal formulas and in a disorderly manner. It is easy to guess the consequences. An Assembly which had not been elected with the free votes of the people made the law which established the preeminence of the Anglican religion and the whole area was in revolt. The peers of the English kingdom disapproved of the conduct of their colleague the Palatine and addressed to the nonconformists a memorandum from Queen Anne, who answered in these terms:

"I thank the Chamber for having explained this problem to me with such clarity. I am convinced that these plantations are of great importance for England, and I shall do all that is within my power to alleviate my subjects in Carolina and to protect them in their just rights."

Some progress was made and apparently the oppressed would have finally triumphed if the war which was on the brink of breaking out with France had not distracted attention. External wars are the most efficacious remedy for domestic dissension. In Carolina the discontent was extreme. The nonconformists made up almost three-fourths of the inhabitants. Some left the area and their departure heightened still more the resentment of the others. But an invasion on the part of the French and the Spanish which threatened this colony reunited the two parties for their mutual defense, and there was no longer the question of religion.

In 1708, many persons of the Palatine court resolved to emigrate to Carolina. They contacted the proprietors who sent ships to take them there and accorded them one hundred acres per person on condition that, at the end of ten years, they would pay annually a sterling coin per acre in perpetuity. These were established on the Roanoke River and the neighboring area, at a short distance from the Virginia boundary. A number of these founders of northern Carolina proved themselves most industrious. Unfortunately, a short time later, about one hundred thirty of these worthy men were suddenly attacked during the night and massacred with many others by Indians of various tribes, who had united to take revenge for past injustices, confusing, perhaps without knowing it, the innocent with the culprits.

The government of the proprietors continued to be insecure, their power lasting for only short, fleeting intervals. Their stub-

bornness in retaining their power increased the hatred of the people. Finally, in 1719, the people resolved to rid themselves of it entirely. The governor then was Mr. Robert Johnson, a man of much merit and respected by the inhabitants for his qualities. The Assembly notified him of the resolution which the people had taken to free themselves from the arbitrary and oppressive government of the proprietors, and assured him at the same time of their desire to have him as governor, provided he would recognize no superior other than the King. Not only did he refuse, but he made every possible effort to preserve the rights of his superiors.

The Assembly then elected Mr. James Moore as governor *pro tempore*, and sent an agent to the King to defend the rights of the people. When the agent arrived in London, George I was in Hanover. The Regency espoused the cause of the inhabitants of Carolina and at the beginning of 1721 sent there as governor, in the name of the King, a General Nicolson, who was received with enthusiastic acclamation.

Seven proprietors sold all their rights to the King; Lord Grenville reserved for himself the ownership of the land which had been assigned him in the most northern part. The charter was returned in 1728. Since a large settlement was being formed in the environs of Roanoke, consequently quite far from Charles-Town, the land was divided into two provinces called, as they are still called, South Carolina and North Carolina, each under a separate and distinct government.

Johnson had remained in Carolina after the election of Moore and had never ceased to oppose the aspirations of the inhabitants under all circumstances and to support the interests of his superiors, by whom however he was very badly received on his return to London. He was able to console himself for this ingratitude, however, when in 1731 he was appointed by the King to be the governor of South Carolina. The people of Charles-Town recalling his merit, taking into account what he had done for his superiors and indignant at their conduct toward him, received him as the people of Rome had received Cicero on his return from exile.

At the termination of the proprietary government, Carolina had only fourteen thousand inhabitants, although many people had arrived from Europe. Population cannot grow where people

are not happy. After the government was changed, the colony began to prosper.

In 1732, another vast expanse of land was taken from South Carolina to form a third colony, which was called Georgia, in honor of the King [George II]. The charter dated June 9 was granted to a company of twenty-one persons, who united, not for the purpose of personal gain, but only with the aim of founding an asylum for the unfortunate. They formed a foundation with their own funds which was greatly increased by the liberality of many others and which was destined solely to help the poor.

James Oglethorpe, one of the founders, was the first to come to this area; he brought with him one hundred six persons, who landed in Charles-Town [Charleston], where the inhabitants vied with one another to give these poor people proof of their sentiments of humanity. They gave them food and, in addition, pigs, cows and other animals to breed. To encourage them, some accompanied them to the Savannah River, on the shores of which Oglethorpe began to construct a town to which he gave the name of the river.

A second person to lead a large number of emigrants there was a certain Pierre Pury, a Swiss. He arrived with one hundred seventy of his compatriots, founded Purisbourg, and was later followed by two hundred more.

The founders were rich persons and respected for their intentions. Their enterprise confirms this and their zeal induced Parliament to grant a sum of money to encourage them. Hewit says that they received 36,000 pounds sterling, others say 10,000. It is perhaps to this contribution that one can attribute the widely propagated error in Europe that the colonies were founded at the expense of the mother country. The Americans were not aware of it and the English never troubled to correct this impression. The Abbé Raynal* expresses himself thus, in the face of all truth: "This settlement which in a very short time had received five thousand inhabitants, had cost the treasury 1,485,000 pounds." One must point out that the contribution of Parliament was a work of charity, and that it did not give any greater right of sovereignty over Georgia than the money sent to

*Ibid., Vol. 9, p. 114.

Portugal, on the occasion of the Lisbon earthquake, gave sovereignty over that kingdom.

The possessors of the charter could have been called protectors or benefactors, rather than masters or proprietors. Moreover, their regulations furnished a new proof of the difficulty to govern well these distant lands. Notwithstanding the best possible intentions, combined with repeated assistance, and notwithstanding the good will of the poor emigrants, among whom there were numerous industrious families from Scotland and from Germany, the colony did not prosper at all. The difficulties occasioned by regulations, made only with the idea of doing good, obliged a large number to depart. The majority did not go very far. They crossed the river, and established themselves in Carolina. They needed only to change government in order to prosper.

Finally these worthy benefactors of humanity, persuaded by experience that their help did nothing to render men happy, if one did not let them choose the means to become happy, abandoned their tutelage entirely. In 1752, they gave the charter back to the King, and the government of Georgia was placed more or less on the same footing as the others*.

---

*The Abbé Raynal says (*Ibid.*, Vol. 9, p. 115): "They had abandoned the jurisdiction as well as the ownership of Georgia to private individuals." And later on, alluding to the defects of the government: "The British ministry thus entrusted public interests to the avarice of private interests." Respectable men do not deserve such judgment.

CONCLUSION

There is no need to add anything else to give an idea of the foundation of the Thirteen Colonies, of the character of their people and of their relationship with Great Britain, in order to understand the true cause of the Revolution. The wars which they had with neighboring Europeans and Indians, and the political and economic matters are pertinent if one wants to trace the complete history. And were this history to be written in the most concise manner, it could not be instructive without being voluminous.

The character of the founders of the Colonies appears obvious from what I have said. The reasons which made the majority of them leave Europe and the behavior which they consistently displayed in America have been made sufficiently clear to the reader to render superfluous all the reflections which I might make on these points. It is easy to imagine what opinions they had to transmit to posterity.

It was said and written in Europe, and it was believed, that the Colonies were in large part peopled by criminals who were transported there from England. If this were true, their descendants should only be the more esteemed, unless one would like to attribute to the climate or to the soil the virtue of improving mankind. Whatever conclusion one wants to draw, it refutes that of those who spread such opinions in order to discredit that land. However, let us examine these points according to the facts, ignoring the lies resulting from politics or malice which are given credence only through ignorance.

In 1666 there appeared in England the first law which condemned to being transported to the colonies those who were convicted of having been bandits in the county of Northumber-

land. This county, as everyone knows, borders upon Scotland. Old animosities still existed between the two nations, and frequent damages which the inhabitants of Northumberland suffered at the hands of their turbulent neighbors gave rise to this law.

In 1670, the same law included those who were convicted either of stealing, during the night, linens which had been spread in the open fields to whiten or of having taken royal objects entrusted to them. Toward the end of this same year, the law was extended to include those who, during the night, had set fire to piles of grain or wheat or who had slaughtered animals.

Before 1717, transporting criminals to America except for the above-mentioned crimes was not permitted and, according to general opinion, none was brought there. This same year, to lessen the severity of criminal laws in certain cases, a law was enacted which permitted the judge to commute the death penalty to that of transportation to the colonies.

At this period, the population of the colonies was about eight hundred thousand. Probably there were never more than one hundred criminals transported each year. Some returned to England after their term was completed and the majority of these were vagabonds who could not make up their minds to work. Others, who because of poverty rather than the natural inclination had been forced into some small crime, finding themselves in a country where work was well paid, became good citizens. In general, because of prejudice against them, there were few who were able to marry.

Now the reader can judge if the Abbé Raynal was correct in saying*, "a second class of Colonists was at one time composed of criminals who were condemned by the state to be transported to America, and who had to do forced labor, from seven to fourteen years, for the plantation owners who had bought them from the tribunals of justice. Everywhere one is disgusted with these corrupt men who are always ready to commit crimes again."

Abbé Raynal's manner of expressing himself would lead the reader to conclude that he was misinformed in stating that criminals have contributed much to populate that country. It seems that the author deferred too easily to the common opinion, or

*Ibid., Vol. 8, p. 176.

rather that he let himself be induced into error by the assertions of some writers who, either through ignorance or Anglomania, have asserted that the intention of Parliament, in making this law, was to populate the colonies. It is as if one would send several buckets of water into the Potomac and Delaware Rivers in order to make them larger so that navigation would be facilitated.

Abbé Raynal is mistaken in saying that the tribunals were selling the services of the criminals. On the contrary, their transportation cost the government two pounds sterling per person. It is not true that the time of this service was seven or fourteen years. The law limited it in the beginning to seven and, later, it was increased to fourteen or twenty-one, or even to life according to the crime. It is also false that the Colonists were disgusted with the results. They complained as soon as the law was made. In some colonies they always refused to receive them. In others, they received them in order to avoid difficulty with England. As often happens one gives in to some disagreeable things in order to avoid others which would be still more so.

In New York, toward the year 1766, they arrested someone who had landed illegally. His case was brought to court; he was condemned *to be transported to the old England.* Consequently, he was placed aboard a ship and sent back. The very moment he landed, he was arrested and imprisoned. When brought before the tribunal, the judge asked him why he had returned: "I have been transported," he responded. —"But do you not know that the law condemns to be hanged whoever comes back before his term is up?" —"I know it, my Lord. —"Why then have you come back?" —"My Lord, because I have been transported." The judge, who did not imagine that one could be condemned to be transported from America to England, did not comprehend at all what the man was saying. The misunderstanding, one of my friends who had been present at this scene told me the same day, was the occasion for a very strange dialogue between the so-called culprit and the judge, which attracted the attention of all the spectators. Finally, when the judge made him understand that he would be hanged, he pulled out of his pocket the authentic copy of the sentence of the court of New York, the reading of which elicited general laughter, and it ended up with the man being set free.

211

The law for the transportation of criminals tended to discredit the Colonists, to give a frightening idea of a country where men were sent for punishment, and consequently to discourage emigration. When the House of Commons resolved to employ criminals in the arsenals, the House of Lords objected, that it *naturally tended to discredit the arsenals of the King.* The politics of Parliament was the same as in various parts of Europe and consisted in spreading everywhere, through newspapers, anything imaginable to the prejudice of the United States. Politics on the other hand was ineffectual, because the Europeans needed to emigrate to America to find happiness—in a word the only Europeans we needed were people who did not know how to read, or who had no time for it.

Abbé Raynal is no nearer the truth when he speaks of the increase of the population. After stating, that the rapid multiplication of the inhabitants of the Thirteen Colonies *must have two sources,* he adds: "The first is this crowd of the Irish, the Jews, the French, the Waldenses, the Palatines, the Moravians, the Salzburgers, who, tired of the political and religious persecutions they endured in Europe, have been looking for tranquility in these distant climates."* The inhabitants of Great Britain, of whom he does not speak, contributed to populate the Thirteen Colonies perhaps more than all the other nations together, including the Irish. As far as the French are concerned, we are not acquainted with any other emigration than that which was occasioned by the revocation of the Edict of Nantes. Only when France ceded Acadia to Great Britain, does one see some come from there. With regard to the Jews, we believe that they never reached one hundred in all the United States before the Revolution and that even now they do not reach one thousand. "The second source of this extraordinary multiplication (the author continues) is to be found in the very climate of the colonies." The internal growth, which greatly surpasses that which was the result of emigration, derives from the abundance of land and the cheapness of its price, with which the author himself agrees.** One cannot conceive how he can attribute this to the climate,

* *Ibid.,* p. 90.

**Ibid.,* pp. 191-192.

which he himself paints in various other places with the most unfavorable colors.

Let us now make several observations on the relations that the colonies had with the Kings of Great Britain and on the demands of Parliament.

We have seen how the foundation of the colonies was made at the expense of particular individuals; each Colony proves this clearly in its history. As far as the colonies of New England are concerned, we find the following testimony in a resolution of the House of Commons that the secretary addressed to the governor of Massachusetts. "Whereas the plantations in New England have had, by the blessing of the Almighty, good and prosperous success, without any public charge to this state, etc."* Finally England intervened in the affairs of the colonies only very late, and when she saw with certitude that there were advantages to be derived, after expenses were satisfied and difficulties surmounted.

Without examining how little founded was the pretension of the Kings of England to the right of sovereignty in America and without probing any further into the political reasons which persuaded the founders of the colonies to accept their charters,

---

*Abbé Raynal, speaking about the first two companies, '(Ibid.,'Vol. 8, p. 313) says: "Although they were granted help from the first lottery that was made in England, their progress was so slow that in 1614 they only counted four hundred persons in the two settlements." In this period there was only one settlement. The first attempts made in New England ended in 1608 and the second began in 1620, as we have seen. This grant from the lottery must have been yet another fable on the long list of those which the inaccuracy of Abbé Raynal made him adopt. In the Foedera [Vol. 19, p. 242], one finds that in 1630 Charles I gave a charter to a certain David Ramsey to bring to London and to Westminster the waters of some distant sources a mile and a half from the Hudson into Hertfordshire, with the power to establish a lottery in order to enable himself to meet the expenses. Mr. [Adam] Anderson ([13]), in his history of commerce, says that this lottery is the first which was mentioned both in the Foedora and in the statute books.

The Foedera is a collection of public acts and of historical records compiled by Thomas Rhymer. Under the title of Foedera, conventiones, litterae, etc., it contains pacts, agreements, letters, and all the other public acts which passed between the kings of England and all the emperors, kings, popes, princes, or republics, from the reign of King Henry I to that of Charles I inclusively. As to the history of commerce by Mr. Anderson, it is well known.

we must agree that they recognized the kings as sovereigns as soon as they received the charters and that the two parties were mutually obligated by virtue of the clauses which they contained. It was therefore with the King, and not with the nation, that the colonies contracted agreement. England never had the right to make laws for them. Each of the colonies adopted separately the parliamentary laws it liked, as it could have adopted those of the Koran, provided they were not contrary to the laws of England, which was one of the clauses contained in the charters. The error, diffused almost generally in Europe, that England founded the colonies and that she had the right of sovereignty, perhaps arose for different reasons. England satisfied her own self-love by letting it continue. With her monopoly of commerce, she prevented correspondence among the colonies and the other nations of Europe and, before the Revolution, the latter did not believe the colonies interesting enough to examine their history closely.

The kings, following the law of the strongest, often violated their pacts with all the colonies, with more or less audacity, depending on the circumstances. The colonies made protests. They never recognized the arbitrary right, but sometimes out of weakness, sometimes to avoid disputes, they let themselves be dominated. Compromises increased the desire to continue to exploit the colonies and the kings wanted to prove they had that right. It is like someone patiently letting himself be struck, thus giving the striker a legal right to hit him again for as long as he likes.

Acts of oppression were so numerous that one could not, without lingering too long, attempt to give a full account. The reader will see them in detail in the Declaration of Independence.* I would only observe that Charles II and James II, his brother and successor, had resolved to take back all the charters. They arbitrarily took away that of the Colony of Massachusetts, and the death of Charles, as well as the abdication of James, happened at the opportune moment for the peace of the colonies. The successors of James (William and Mary), believing they must give a charter back to the Colony of Massachusetts, made

*See *Notes*, Section B, p. 214.

214

sure that it was not so favorable to the people as the preceding one. At any rate the charters always demonstrated, even after they had been changed, that the colonies had relation only with the Kings and that the nation did not have the least right. Barnard, the next to the last governor of Massachusetts under the royal government, and one of the greatest enemies of the freedom of the colonies, wanting to show to the English government the necessity for reducing them to slavery, says, in his letters printed in England, "If the charters can be pleaded against the authority of Parliament, they amount to an alienation of the dominions of Great Britain, and are, in effect, acts of dismembering the British Empire and will operate as such, if care is not taken to prevent it."

OF THE TRUE CAUSE
OF THE REVOLUTION

After Charles I had been beheaded, the Parliament, having taken possession of the royal power as successor to the rights of the king, demanded sovereignty over the colonies. In 1650, a law was enacted prohibiting the colonies from having commerce with other nations. This was the beginning of the parliamentary demands. This would seem incredible when one makes the following reflections.

According to the English constitution, the deliberations of Parliament must be approved by the king in order to have the force of law. At the restoration of Charles II, it was assumed that his reign had begun at the death of his father. Thus the year in which he ascended the throne is called the twelfth of his reign instead of the first. The year 1650 was therefore the second, and in this period, since he was traveling in foreign lands, he could not have given his consent to the law of which I have just spoken. Finally, Parliament itself declared null, as we have already seen, all that which had been done under Cromwell; however, it was this law which opened the door to the parliamentary demands. Charles, in order to revive them, put no difficulties in the path of their enforcement, and that to which he gave his consent is precisely the same as the law of 1650.

We have seen that when Virginia surrendered to the arms of Cromwell in 1651, it was agreed that she would continue to enjoy the freedom of commerce with all nations. However Charles did not make any distinction between Virginia and the other colonies. If the capitulation made with Cromwell belongs in the number of laws declared null, how can one look upon the demand of Parliament founded on what was contrary to the rights of the King? The kings never had any more right to make the colonies submit to English Parliament than they had to make other countries submit to their laws.

By virtue of the law of the strongest, they exercised everywhere the right to regulate commerce and some colonies finally, convinced that there was, as the ministers of Great Britain affirmed, a pact of reciprocal agreement, consented to that. But even if all had accepted this pact, what would it prove? That Parliament had acquired through this the right of sovereignty? If through fear, or believing to make a better exchange, I allow you to take some of my clothes, would you thereby acquire a legal right to the rest as well as to all I possess in the world? Is it not, on the contrary, according to all justice, that I take back what you have taken from me by force or deceit, as soon as circumstances permit me? This truth needs no proof.

As long as the unjust demands referred only to particular things, one protested, one disputed, but preferred to suffer rather than cause a rupture. It is difficult to foresee what could have happened if the English ministers had continued to increase their demands. If luck had been with the colonies, stubbornness would have prevailed over politics. The ministers, however, openly declared that they had the right to subject us to all their laws. There remained for us then only this alternative: either separate ourselves from Great Britain or suffer under the most shameful and most terrible slavery. What purpose would our assemblies have served? It would have been a loss of time and money to convoke them, since a foreign legislative body could annul all that had been done and decree the opposite. It would have been better for us to be under the domination of an absolute prince, because the sovereign of two nations does not have an immediate interest in ruining one of them in order to save the other; but it is not thus in the case where one of the two exercises sovereignty over the other, since the whole burden she imposes on the one under her power is a relief for herself. It is impossible to disagree that the greatest misfortune which could happen to a nation is that of becoming the subject of a Republic.*

*This truth is perfectly understood in America. Political pretenders, who prophesy the future conquests of our states, either do not know in what consists the true well-being of nations, or suppose that we ourselves are ignorant of it. It may happen that one day the inhabitants of the United States will aid their neighbors to become free, but it is improbable that they will let themselves have the desire, no less imprudent than unjust, to have subjects.

218

The important help which the colonies furnished the mother country during the war of 1756 made the ministers hope, after the peace treaty of 1763, that they could increase the public revenues by subjecting the colonies to some new taxes. Besides they saw in this the increase of their own influence, since they would have the possibility to portion out new employment. While the subjects of Great Britain were overburdened with taxes and duties, the colonies, because of the obstacles which impeded freedom of commerce, contributed indirectly beyond their share. The ministers—either believing so or feigning not to believe so—enacted the well-known laws by which Parliament demanded the colonies submit to the taxation by means of revenue stamps on writing paper, glass, dye and tea. Everyone knows with what energy the Americans opposed them. This is not the place to report various facts which were the result of this opposition—for example, the case of the revenue stamps which were ignominiously thrown into the fire as soon as they landed at Hampton in Virginia.

Then the ministers changed the system. Parliament revoked the Stamp Act. But in another act, which it had previously issued, it had declared that it had the right to make the colonies obey all its laws and in all circumstances. It is this last act, the execution of which would have made even the shadow of freedom disappear, that alone provoked the revolution. Parliament then revoked the laws concerning writing paper, dye and glass, and only in order to continue to claim its right, contented itself with leaving a miserable duty of three deniers sterling per pound of tea.

If the British government had invited the colonies to impose on themselves a much more considerable tax to benefit the mother-country, no one would have refused it. As long as it was not demanded by law the colonists would have given all that England could possibly desire. During the war of 1756, they had contracted a debt of about ten million pounds sterling to help the metropolis in an efficacious manner, which earned them a gratification of three hundred thousand pounds sterling from Parliament. This gift was received with transports of joy, because the colonists regarded it as a recognition of their zeal toward the country of their ancestors, and not as a sum of money, which was infinitely less than the sacrifices they had made and

which, because of the misappropriation by those through whose hands the English government passed the money, was only partially paid. Among those who profited by it, one notices, particularly, the governor of Virginia, Dunwiddie; but the assembly, which was not ignorant of it, closed its eyes.

The smallness of the tax which they had placed on tea contributed to convincing the Americans that the ministers according to their custom had formed a project to establish their claimed right. In addition, it was learned in America that the ministers had plotted with the directors of the India Company. Some people claim to know what took place secretly on this occasion between the ministers and the directors. For my part, I shall keep to the known facts.

The company, whose charter did not permit any sale except in the public market and with certain formalities—with the assurance of the government which undertook to ask Parliament, in this regard, to pass a decree of indemnity—imported to America in 1773, for its own particular profit, a large quantity of tea, as any merchant would have done. The minister can act at his own pleasure against the laws, provided he has the majority of Parliament in his favor. It is wrong to believe that the Prime Minister of England is obliged to have regard for the people's opinion. He is less subject to their resentment than the minister of an absolute prince, because the sanction of Parliament serves him as a shield, much as the Roman Senate served as a shield to the ministers of the early Caesars.

The over-abundance of tea that existed at that time was very favorable to the interests of the ministers, who in order to captivate the Americans, wanted to sell it to them at a better price than they would have paid if smuggled in from anywhere else. In Boston, the tea was thrown into the sea; in New York and Philadelphia, the ships which carried it were not allowed to enter the ports.

When the news reached London, the shipment which was to go to all the other colonies was canceled, for it was thought that everywhere the tea would be received in like manner.

The difference of behavior between Boston and the other places was the result of circumstances. In Boston, the ships were in the port and the tea was addressed to the merchants, who had agreed with the governor to take it and pay the taxes, conforming

with the decree of Parliament. The inhabitants obstructed the unloading of it and wanted the ships to sail back home. But the governor forbade them to leave. After seven or eight days of useless debate, the governor insisted on keeping the ships in the port. The inhabitants, fearing that some English or Scotch merchant would eventually find the way to bring in the tea and pay the taxes, went aboard and threw all of the tea into the sea, using all possible precautions to make sure there be no other disorder. In Philadelphia and New York, the merchants bound themselves not to accept it. They offered the captains water and foodstuffs which they would need to return home and they ordered them to leave without unloading anything. The opposition of the colonies had therefore as its object the new system which Parliament had adopted to make them submit to its laws. It is clear that the help they furnished to the mother country made the English ministers perceive that, notwithstanding the obstacles in commerce, the colonies were growing rapidly in strength and vigor. We know that one of them* whose opinion was of great importance, revealed that the colonies were already too powerful and that it was time to control them. Some claim that the ministers' intention was to force the colonies to rebel in order to have a pretext to deprive them of their charters and to treat them as a conquered country. A well-informed historian will be able to demonstrate this probability without difficulty and perhaps even its certainty. He could also go back to the true motive of such conduct and make us see that the aim of the authors of this plan was to use the subjugation of America as a means to totally suppress freedom in England.

The English ministers wishing to justify their conduct, principally before the eyes of the nation, used every effort to prove that the Americans had premeditated the revolution for a long time, and that the reasons they advanced were purely pretexts. Nothing is more false. It is true that they knew that their forebears and they themselves had allowed many of their rights to be usurped, but it is not likewise true that they did not dream of restoring them. What one does not find difficult to believe is that what made them plan and for some time prepare the way to

*Lord Hillsborough in his counsel to the King, toward the end of 1771 or the beginning of 1774.

shake off the yoke was in the nature of a yoke itself. It was so revolting, that one could hardly conceive how an enlightened people, who had sucked with their milk the sentiments of liberty, could have endured being treated in this way, if one could not see that it shows an affection for the country of their ancestors that bordered on the most blind devotion.

The prohibition made to the colonists to manufacture certain objects for their own use, so as to oblige them to obtain all those articles from English manufacturers* and pay a great deal for them, is one of the laws which one cannot imagine without adopting the maxim that whatever is expedient is also just and honest. This example suffices to give an idea of the manner in which they tried to extend the right to regulate commerce. In the meantime, the Americans bore this burden patiently as they did numerous other similar ones, and they would not have ceased bearing them if the English ministers, mistaking the obedience of the colonists for pusillanimity, had not ended up breaking the bonds by trying to strengthen them.

We could report here several facts to prove that the Americans by no means ever dreamed of breaking them. But we are content to say only that the states, in their second petition, which England did not answer any more than it had the first, asked the King to place them back into the position they had been immediately after the peace treaty of 1763, which is a manifest proof that they were no longer complaining about former burdens, no matter how heavy and unjust, and that they also did not want any new ones.

*Listen to the Earl of Chatham, better known by the name of William Pitt, one of the most zealous defenders that America had in England. Speaking one day in the House of Lords against the ministers with regard to the subject of taxation about which we have spoken, he cried out: "But if America were to consider manufacturing a stocking or a nail for a horseshoe, I would want to make her feel all the weight of the power of the [mother] country." We leave the deduction to the reader.

PERIOD BETWEEN THE MONARCHIC AND THE REPUBLICAN GOVERNMENT

When the English governors began to neglect their duty and unscrupulously abuse their authority; when some because forced to and others by choice forsook their offices, as happened toward the end of 1773 in some colonies, and at the beginning of 1774 in others, the Americans still did not dream of seceding from Great Britain, and did not even imagine that she could one day push them to such extremity. The desire they had to remain united with her made them hope that the ministers would relinquish their claims and matters would be settled. To achieve this end, it was necessary to assert their rights which could only be done by maintaining a state of defense; but it was not possible to proceed legally under the constitution then in force, and they did not consider making a new one. It was therefore necessary to have recourse to measures that, without destroying the government whose power was suspended, could maintain good order. This would be accomplished by making all the inhabitants responsible for what would have to be done during this kind of interregnum. Since all the colonies adopted the same system, with only very slight differences, which could not after all have any influence on its general organization or results, the description of the particular conduct of only one of them will suffice to show how all the others conducted themselves.

The different governments were a mixture of monarchy, aristocracy and democracy, with the exception of the governments of Pennsylvania and Delaware which had no aristocracy. These Colonies had the same governor, always taken from the Penn family, the proprietor of both. This governor and Maryland's named by the heirs of Lord Baltimore, to whom the colony belonged, had to be approved by the King, which approval

had never been refused. The governors of Connecticut and Rhode Island were elected by the people. The King named all the others. The governors represented the monarchy. The aristocratic upper house was appointed by the King, except in New England; the people elected it in the governments of Rhode Island and in Connecticut (*); while in those of Massachusetts and New Hampshire, the representatives did. Everywhere the lower house was elected by the people.

Each colony was divided into districts, generally called counties. Virginia has about sixty counties which were not of equal size at all. Each of these counties sent two representatives to constitute the lower house, called, as it still is, general assembly (**).

The difference in the size of the counties was the result of the policy of the English government, which wanted to have a larger number of representatives in places accessible to its warships. A proof of this was given in these recent times. The frontier counties extended up to the boundaries of the colony. When the population grew and spread to the point that the inhabitants could not assemble any longer without much inconvenience, then one county would be split in two: but as the number of representatives from places away from the sea and navigable rivers, would have become predominant, the last English governor (the

(*) The Colonies of Rhode Island and of Connecticut were almost independent even before the Revolution, since the King could not even veto their laws. The charter of Massachusetts was originally similar to that of Connecticut; but Charles II nullified it in 1684. The colony continued to use it until 1686, at which time James II took it away from them, and governed arbitrarily during the short time his reign lasted. About the same time, Sir Edmond Andros, of whom we have already spoken, began making the same change in Connecticut; but one night as they were discussing the matter in Hartford, one of the spectators extinguished the lights, took the charter and hid it. It is thus that it was preserved and is still extant.

(**) The word *assembly* has always been considered less expressive than *parliament;* and for this reason when the new government was established, some people proposed to change the word; but after due consideration, they realized that names are only a passive thing and decided to leave it. After all, the word *emperor,* which, before Julius Caesar, had a less comprehensive meaning than king, signified much more when later on it served to designate the master of about two thirds of the known world.

Earl of Dunmore) was ordered to no longer permit the subdivision of any county, except on condition that the new counties would renounce the right of sending representatives. The governors of the other colonies received the same order. Congress speaks of it in its Declaration of Independence.

Besides the two representatives for each county, there were four others in Virginia, one each named by the city of Norfolck [sic], the city of Williamsburg, which was then the capital of the colony, the college of the latter city, finally by Jamestown, which had been the capital before Williamsburg, and where no more than two or three families were left (*).

Since like the King of England he had the power to dissolve the lower house (**), the governor did not hesitate to do so when the representatives, in May of 1774, at the news of the Boston blockade issued a declaration rebuking the conduct of the English ministers and making known the intention of the Virginians not to remain idle spectators of the persecution of their brothers.

The frequent outrages of the English government against the rights of the colonies, especially after the treaty of 1763, the various means used to foment discord among them, and the all too evident design to attack them separately, had induced the representatives of the people to form, on March 12, 1773, a committee of seven of them to keep in touch with those of other colonies. This had to be done if they were to follow Virginia's example and they lost no time in doing so. Thus whatever happened

(*) The present government did not leave to both Jamestown and Williamsburg College the right to send representatives. Privileges showing partiality and therefore unjust, whether originally given to a small number of men, or reserved when seats were vacant helped make corruption easy. It is therefore not surprising that in England the friends of freedom raised their voice against the right of sending representatives from the already depopulated villages.

(**) Because there could be no new election unless called by him, the governor's power did not end with keeping the colony without representatives, as it turned out on this occasion for about an entire year; it reached the point of keeping in office those with whom he was satisfied as long as he governed; for if he would not order a new election, it was necessary to wait, to be able to proceed legally, for either the arrival of a new governor, or the death of the King. They had no regard for time.

of interest in one, would be immediately communicated to all other colonies (*).

America owes its liberty to these committees, the consequences of whose activity the English ministers seem to have foreseen as soon as they were informed. The governor of Virginia received very strong reprimands for not having dissolved the lower house on this occasion.

In vain the English ministers had deluded themselves into thinking that the other ports, naturally jealous of the importance of Boston's, and especially the port of Salem which they had favored, did nothing but dream of a chance to profit by its disgrace, and that the other colonies would regard this circumstance as very favorable in order to obtain from the mother country some recompense for their filial submission. In all the counties of the [Massachusetts] colony, as also in all the neighboring colonies, the inhabitants took up arms, and flew to Boston's aid. So great was the display of activity, that a large number of horses could be seen arriving, each carrying two men, and some three. The more distant colonies hastened to make known to Massachusetts their resolutions pledging to support the common cause and to help with all their power. They were told that no men were needed, but foodstuffs, principally because of the interruption of farming. Since help consisted of private gifts, it is impossible to know the exact amount. What we definitely know is that soon abundance reigned there. The quantity of rice received from South Carolina was prodigious, and in Virginia I often witnessed what solicitude was used in order to obtain room on some ship for a cargo of wheat or Indian corn. Several persons got together to make up a cargo, and it was a privilege to be able to join the group, considering the large number of competitors. Some who had already loaded their commodities to be sold on the islands, ordered the captains to set sail for Boston. Others who had small ships of which they were sole owners wanted the cargo to be their own and refused to have any partners. If osten-

(*)The person who first suggested this committee was Dubney Carr, esquire, of Goochland county, a man respected for his very rare qualities. One of his relatives to whom he was tenderly attached has consecrated his memory with an inscription engraved on his tomb. He died at the age of thirty.

tation entered here in some way, circumstances rendered it at least worthy of excuse.

After the governor had dissolved the lower house, the representatives of the people returned and hastened to alert their constituents to the evils that threatened their country. Then all the inhabitants believed themselves equally obliged to watch over public safety and to maintain it. Everywhere they elected their representatives, as it was customary to do in ordinary times. It was only college professors, all English with the exception of one, who abstained from voting. Under these circumstances, the voice of the country called upon many citizens, who for some years had given up participation in public affairs in order to enjoy the pleasures of retirement.

When times are critical, the people fix their eyes on men of true merit, and the common good outweighs every other consideration.

[In Virginia] The name *Convention* was given to the assembly of representatives to show that it was a temporary body, created because of need, and not at all to disparage the name of *assembly,* the legislative body whose function was only suspended; for it was believed then that this body would soon resume its sessions (*).

The only general instruction that they received was to provide for public safety in the best possible manner, acting jointly with the other colonies. They assembled on August 4, 1774 at Williamsburg, and here are the results of the meeting.

It elected twelve persons to form a *committee of safety.* The functions of this committee were: 1. to execute the deliberations of the *convention*; 2. to keep in touch with the other committees of safety, or with all persons to whom the public administration was entrusted; 3. to provide with circumspection, in the intervals between sessions of the *convention*, for all that would be judged necessary.

(*) In Connecticut, Rhode Island, Pennsylvania and Delaware, there was no need to have recourse to the expedient of the convention, because the nature of their constitutions permitted the election and the convening of the assemblies without it being necessary to obtain the direct or indirect consent of the Crown.

It decided that the inhabitants of each county would choose among themselves twelve persons to form a committee, whose functions would be to watch over the good order, to correspond and plan with the committees of the other counties, and to carry out the instructions they would receive from the committee of safety.

Because it was very important to be ready to march, to rush to where need would require, and since the authority to command the military would belong to the English governor, it recommended that the citizens arm themselves and form companies of volunteers, which were called independent companies; each volunteer would sign the terms which he would promise to observe; namely:

That when the number of volunteers reached twenty-four, a company would be formed, a captain would be chosen from among them, as well as two lieutenants and an ensign, leaving the nomination of sergeants and corporals to the captain.

That they would march, and obey all the captain's orders, provided that the order to march came from the county committee (*).

That when there were several companies, the nomination of the colonels, lieutenant-colonels and majors, would be up to the county committee.

That when there were several regiments, the nomination of the general officers, would be up to the committee of safety.

After electing seven persons to represent Virginia, in the Congress of all the colonies, and stipulating that the committee of safety would inform each colony privately, the Convention adjourned; the second session was set for March 20, 1775, and it was resolved that it would be held in Richmond .

In the meantime the other colonies had made the same resolutions, so that many of the couriers crossed each other along the route. All had chosen Philadelphia for the Congress, as the most convenient and the nearest to the center. There were only delegates from eleven colonies present when Congress assembled

(*) In this period, every good citizen was a soldier, and one dreamed only, if I may say so, of the preparations for war. Despite this, the Americans never lost sight of the obedience everyone owed to the civil authority.

for the first time on September 5, 1774. Those from North Carolina did not arrive until the 14th of the same month and Georgia's position would not permit sending of hers until the following July. Consequently, they were there, for the first time, on the 5th of September 1775, the day on which the third session began.

Congress had to administer all the affairs of the war. Its power did not extend much beyond that. Often its decrees were only recommendations, which the colonies always respected and followed as much as possible.

Each colony appointed the officers of its regiments, and Congress nominated the general. George Washington, one of the delegates from Virginia, was elected unanimously on June 17, 1775, as commander-in-chief of the troops of the united colonies. Among the more southern delegates, there were at least seven who were perfectly acquainted with his military ability, of which he had given proof during the War of 1756, as well as with his prudence and competence. The delegates of the other colonies, either because they also knew him or because they were aware of the necessity to preserve perfect unity, concurred in his choice without the least difficulty. Perhaps the reader will not be displeased to see the commission which was given to him on this occasion, *addressed by the delegates of the united colonies to George Washington, esquire* [June 19, 1775]: ([14])

"We, reposing special trust and confidence in your patriotism, valour, conduct, and fidelity, do, by these presents constitute and appoint you to be General and Commander-in-Chief of the army of the United Colonies, and of all the forces now raised, or to be raised by them, and of all others who shall voluntarily offer their service, and join the said army for the defence of American liberty, and for repelling every hostile invasion thereof. And you are hereby invested with full power and authority to act as you shall think for the good and welfare of the service.

"And we do hereby strictly charge and require all officers and soldiers under your command to be obedient to your orders, and diligent in the exercise of their several duties.

"And we also enjoin and require you to be careful in executing the great trust reposed in you, by causing strict discipline and order to be observed in the army, and that the soldiers be duly exercised and provided with all convenient necessaries.

229

"And you are to regulate your conduct in every respect by the rules and discipline of war, (as herewith given you), and punctually to observe and follow such orders and directions from time to time as you shall receive from this or a future Congress of these United Colonies, or Committee of Congress.

"This commission to continue in force until revoked by this or a future Congress."

Eighteen months later, as circumstances required that the commander have more extensive power, Congress gave him, so to speak, those of a dictator, but his use of it was such that the majority of the inhabitants of the United States still do not realize that he ever had it.

The power of Congress, of the Assemblies, of the Conventions and of the Committees, was unlimited.

This kind of government, which exercised its power in the most moderate way (*), lasted until the creation of the republican government.

Internal affairs were conducted with rare tranquility. Debtors would not wait for their creditors to annoy them for payments. The sense of honor was prevalent.

The conviction is widespread that the payment of debts was much more punctual and more notable than it had been in any other period when the courts were functioning, and, in the places where they were not closed, the creditors' moderation rendered them useless.

It would be wrong to suppose that the debtors were influenced by local considerations. Those who had debts in Europe, used all possible means to discharge them, as long as exportation was permitted.

This is why the merchants of Great Britain have rendered public testimony.

In the petition (15) of the city of Bristol, that Mr. [Edmund]

(*) The power was without reservation; the exercise of it was truly paternal. Those to whom authority had been entrusted, never had need to make use of it. A simple recommendation was sufficient; everyone obeyed. Although no one commanded, only a very small number of men neglected their duty. The only punishment ordered was to publish their fault, a terrible punishment, because they were almost entirely ostracized from society.

Burke, a member of Parliament, presented to the King on September 11, 1775, we find the following:

"We owe a Testimony of Justice to your Colonies, which is, that in the midst of the present distractions, we have received many unequivocal proofs, that our Fellow Subjects in that part of the world are very far from having lost their ancient affection and regard to their Mother Country, or departed from the principles of commercial honour and private Justice. Notwithstanding the cessation of the Powers of Government throughout that vast continent, we have reason to think, judging by the Imports into this city, and by our extensive correspondencies, that the Commodities of American growth, enumerated by Acts of Parliament, have been as regularly brought to Great Britain, as in the most quiet times. We assure your Majesty that the Trade of this Port, and the Subsistence of a great part of your Kingdom, have depended very much on the Honourable, and, in this Instance, amicable Behaviour of your American subjects. We have in this single City received, within one year, from the first of September 1774 more than one million of bushells of wheat, to say nothing of the great quantity of other valuable commodities essential to our navigation and commerce."

The petition of the London merchants was lengthier. It mentioned among other things that after the Americans had closed their ports to the merchandise from Great Britain, their payments had been much more sizable than previously for the same period of time. Notwithstanding all my efforts, it has not been possible for me to obtain this document, or several others. It is very difficult to procure what would serve to demonstrate how much the language then used in this country on the question of America, was different from what it is now.

All the operations of this year were limited to the payment of debts which had been in arrears; as it was no longer permitted for merchandise from England to enter America. When to enable debtors to pay their debts it was proposed to allow exportation although importation was forbidden, there was more than one politician who, standing on the great principle, *salus publica suprema lex esto,* supported the contrary opinion maintaining that by such a policy we would be extremely weakened: we ourselves would be furnishing our enemies with the resources to make war on us, even more we would be augmenting to our detriment the

231

forces that they would have to employ; but the noblest sentiments prevailed. Some time later General Lee had a ship bound for England stopped on the James River because of the large amount of money it had on board. At the same time he tried in vain to persuade those in charge of matters to prevent its departure; the ship received orders to set sail.

This shows that the Americans had a very different spirit from that which is now attributed to them in Europe. This point will be discussed when we consider the present state of affairs in the United States. It is enough for me to say here that many facts, which would undoubtedly be of interest to a historian, are very often not even mentioned.

Although this book is meant to give only an idea of the conduct of the Americans in times so critical, and not to present a complete history, it will not be out of order to call attention to the fact that while we were preparing to defend ourselves, the last English governor [Lord Dunmore] had not yet departed. Moreover, he was using his right to command the militia without anyone opposing it, because it was still hoped that matters would improve, and found himself at the head of three thousand men in the country of the old inhabitants (commonly known by the name of *Indians*), unjustly fighting the Sciuaneese [Shawnees] tribe. Before his departure on this expedition, he knew that the *convention* had to assemble at Williamsburg. During his absence he was informed of all that went on, and he learned that they would meet for the second time at Richmond during the following month of March. In the interval he ordered the election of representatives for the Assembly; everywhere the people had the prudence to elect the same ones they had elected for the *convention;* and the first day of June 1775, after the Assembly had met by his order, he retired aboard a frigate, pretending that he was not safe on land; finally, a short time afterwards he openly began hostilities against the country. (*)

Since it is not our intention to write a complete history here,

(*) See Section C, p. 292. The conditions he set down to return to his government, and the positive resolution of the General Assembly, which had already sent a delegation to him on the frigate.

this, as I have just said, is enough to give you an honest idea of the conduct of the colonies during the interval between one government and the other.

VIRGINIA SECEDES
FROM GREAT BRITAIN

On May 15, 1776, the Virginia Convention, as a result of the general vote of its constituents and of the power which it had received from them, resolved to separate from Great Britain, and expressed it in the following manner ([16]):

"Forasmuch as all the endeavours of the United Colonies, by the most decent representations and petitions to the King and Parliament of Great Britain, to restore peace and security to America under the British Government, and a reunion with that people upon just and liberal terms, instead of a redress of grievances, have produced from an imperious and vindictive (*) Administration increased insult, oppression, and a vigorous attempt to effect our total destruction. By a late act, all these Colonies are declared to be in rebellion, and out of the protection of the British crown; our properties subject to confiscation; our people, when captivated, compelled to join in the murder and plunder of their relations and countrymen; and all former rapine and oppression of Americans declared legal and just. Fleets and Armies are raised, and the aid of foreign troops engaged to assist these destructive purposes. The King's representative in this Colony hath not only withheld all the powers of Government from operating for our safety, but having retired on board an armed ship, is carrying on a piratical and savage war against us, tempting our slaves, by every artifice, to resort to him, and training and employing them against their masters.

In this state of extreme danger we have no alternative left but an abject submission to the will of those overbearing tyrants,

(*) *Vindictive* refers here to some unfounded grievances, and not to just complaints. This is the meaning which this word has in the original English.

or a total separation from the Crown and Government of Great Britain, uniting and exerting all the strength of America for defence, and forming alliances with foreign powers for commerce and aid in war.

Wherefore, appealing to the Searcher of hearts for the sincerity of former declarations, expressing our desire to preserve the connection with that nation, and that we are driven from that inclination by their wicked counsels, and the eternal laws of self-preservation:

Resolved, unanimously, That the Delegates appointed to represent this Colony in General Congress be instructed to propose to that respectable body to declare the United Colonies free and independent States; absolved from all allegiance to, or dependance upon, the Crown or Parliament of Great Britain (*), and that they give the assent of this Colony to such declaration, and to whatever measures may be thought proper and necessary by the Congress for forming foreign alliances, and a confederation of the Colonies, at such time and in the manner as to them shall seem best. Provided, that the power of forming Government for and the regulations of the internal concerns of the Colony, be left to the respective Colonial Legislatures.

Resolved, unanimously, That a Committee be appointed to prepare a Declaration of Rights, and such a plan of Government as will be most likely to maintain peace and order in this Colony, and secure substantial and equal liberty to the people."

The declaration prepared by the committee by virtue of the above resolution, after having undergone some small changes, upon being examined during the Convention, was approved unanimously at Williamsburg on June 1, 1776, as a basis for the new government. It is thus conceived:

(*) Since Parliament had exercised the right to regulate commerce, notwithstanding the protests of the colonies, it is believed proper to make a declaration to remove all doubts.

A DECLARATION(17)

of rights made by the representatives of the good people of Virginia, assembled in full and free convention; which rights do pertain to them and their posterity, as the basis and foundation of government.

1. That all men are by nature equally free and independent, and have certain inherent rights, of which, when they enter into a state of society, they cannot by any compact deprive or divest their posterity; namely, the enjoyment of life and liberty, with the means of acquiring and possessing property, and pursuing and obtaining happiness and safety.

2. That all power is vested in, and consequently derived from, the people; that magistrates are their trustees and servants, and at all times amenable to them.

3. That government is, or ought to be instituted for the common benefit, protection, and security of the people, nation, or community; of all the various modes and forms of government, that is best which is capable of producing the greatest degree of happiness and safety, and is most effectually secured against the danger of maladministration; and that when any government shall be found inadequate or contrary to these purposes, a majority of the community hath an indubitable, unalienable and indefeasible right to reform, alter or abolish it, in such manner as shall be judged most conducive to the public weal.

4. That no man, or set of men, are entitled to exclusive or separate emoluments or privileges from the community, but in consideration of publick services; which, not being descendible, neither ought the offices of magistrate, legislator or judge to be hereditary.

5. That the legislative and executive powers of the state should be separate and distinct from the judiciary; and that the members of the two first may be restrained from oppression, by feeling and participating the burthens of the people, they should, at fixed periods, be reduced to a private station, return into that body from which they were originally taken, and the vacancies be supplied by frequent, certain, and regular elections, in which all, or any part of the former members to be again eligible or ineligible, as the laws shall direct.

6. That elections of members to serve as representatives of the people in assembly, ought to be free; and that all men having sufficient evidence of permanent common interest with, and attachment to the community, have the right of suffrage, and cannot be taxed or deprived of their property for publick uses, without their own consent, or that of their representatives so elected, nor bound by any law to which they have not, in like manner, assented for the public good (*).

7. That all power of suspending laws, or the execution of laws, by any authority without consent of the representatives of the people, is injurious to their rights, and ought not to be exercised.

8. That in all capital or criminal prosecutions a man hath a right to demand the cause and nature of his accusation, to be confronted with the accusers and witnesses, to call for evidence in his favour, and to a speedy trial by an impartial jury of his vicinage, without whose unanimous consent he cannot be found guilty; nor can he be compelled to give evidence against himself; that no man be deprived of his liberty, except by the law of the land or the judgment of his peers.

9. That excessive bail ought not to be required, nor excessive fines imposed, nor cruel and unusual punishments inflicted.

10. That general warrants, whereby an officer or messenger may be commanded to search suspected places without evidence of a

(*) In Virginia the right to vote has always included that of being a representative.

238

fact committed, or to seize any person or persons not named, or whose offence is not particularly described and supported by evidence, are grievous and oppressive, and ought not to be granted.

11. That in controversies respecting property, and in suits between man and man, the ancient trial by jury is preferable to any other, and ought to be held sacred.

12. That the freedom of the press is one of the great bulwarks of liberty, and can never be restrained but by despotick governments.

13. That a well-regulated militia, composed of the body of the people trained to arms, is the proper, natural and safe defence of a free state; that standing armies in time of peace should be avoided as dangerous to liberty; and that in all cases the military should be under strict subordination to, and governed by, the civil power.

14. That the people have a right to uniform government; and, therefore, that no government separate from, or independent of the government of Virginia, ought to be erected or established within the limits thereof.

15. That no free government, or the blessings of liberty, can be preserved to any people, but by a firm adherence to justice, moderation, temperance, frugality and virtue, and by frequent recurrence to fundamental principles.

16. That religion, or the duty which we owe to our Creator, and the manner of discharging it, can be directed only by reason and conviction, not by force or violence; and therefore all men are equally entitled to the free exercise of religion, according to the dictates of conscience; and that it is the mutual duty of all to practise Christian forbearance, love, and charity towards each other.

It is on the principles contained in this declaration, that the new government was established.

The preamble explains the reasons which made us secede

from Great Britain; these reasons are all found in the Declaration of Independence of the United States, which I have omitted to avoid repetition. It is moreover almost entirely the same in its phraseology since one of our citizens who wrote it was also entrusted to write the Declaration of Independence [sic] ([18]) in which there are some points added because of some grievances which were not common among all the colonies.

Five of the most able citizens were charged with reviewing and correcting the code of laws. They were, in a word, to make the changes, additions and curtailments which they judged necessary, and to give them all the degree of perfection of which they were susceptible, rendering them analogous to the principles of the new government; but since this required a work of several years (*), they resolved, in the meantime, to leave the old laws in force, with the exception of some whose defects seemed to need to be corrected without delay.

I have already said at the beginning that all the states, during the interval between the two governments, adopted the same regulations, and that exceptions consisted only in very slight differences not at all essential. The preceding Declaration served also as a basis for other new governments. Everywhere the spirit was the same; but the means employed to arrive at the goals envisioned differed more or less in each state, and it is probable that good will result; each one will have some matters to compare, and each one in this way can more easily discover one's own defects. Finally, adopting whatever is better in their neighbor, they can all, with time, aspire to the highest degree of perfection possible, and resemble one another perfectly.

In passing it may be recalled that the united colonies declared their independence unanimously on July 4, 1776, and took the name of the *United States of America.*

(*) This was truly a prodigious work, since these men, full of intelligence and of wisdom, convinced that every code has something good, examined all those they could obtain, ancient and modern, without even forgetting the Koran; and one of the things to which they bound themselves principally, was to render this great work as short and as clear as possible.

GOVERNMENTS OF
THE UNITED STATES

Whoever examines, with an attentive and impartial eye, the nature and spirit of our governments will understand without difficulty, that the most imperfect of them is closer to the principles of liberty than the government of any ancient or modern republic—although the best still does not approach the point which can satisfy the philosopher and the legislator. However, we have no reason to be proud for having done less badly than others since, despite the disasters of war, we have found ourselves in a situation more advantageous than did other nations (at least according to what history teaches us) when they were forming their governments.

The foundations on which the liberty of our republics rests are, more or less, as we shall now examine them. Sovereignty resides in the mass of inhabitants who entrust power to representatives whose number must neither be so large as to interfere with discussion in depth of matters for deliberation, nor so small as to give too much influence to any one individual. Members of the legislature are chosen according to a proportion that, although not the same in all states as it could and should be, is nowhere so unequal as to be likely to cause a dangerous majority. The term of office is short. Their salary does not exceed what is necessary to remunerate them for their expenses. They are empowered to make the laws, from which they are no more exempt than any other citizen, and nominations to fill a few important positions. None of them can accept one of these positions while he is a member of the legislative body. Their power can never be dangerous to liberty. Besides the brevity of its duration, the people have the right at all times to withdraw it by electing other persons and authorizing them especially to review, reform or reestablish the constitution as if it had suffered some attack.

This power, however, cannot be rendered ineffective. Each member of the assembly votes according to his own private opinion without needing the consent of his constituents, although all are obliged to follow their instructions when they have been given in advance on some particular matter: though this is very rare (*).

The right to vote and to be a representative is extended to almost all those who live in the state. There is no one who could not hope to obtain office by means of his industry and thrift, and to obtain as well any work there is in the republic. According to law, what qualifies is not one's birth, but property, especially landed.

There is only one class of citizens. Titles of nobility any newcomers might possess, do not give them preeminence among us, and even the constitution of Georgia has taken a wise precaution on this point. It requires that one solemnly renounce this odious distinction before being able to accept a public office in the state.

Not only can the representatives of sovereignty not hold any other office but all important offices are separate and distinct, so that the same person could not occupy more than one at the same time, and several states have already provided that no one be allowed to have two paid offices, regardless of their nature.

The military (**) and ministers of religion are not eligible to any of the three branches exercising the legislative, executive and judicial power.

All posts which can influence the government are of short duration. The appointments are not sufficiently lucrative to encourage avarice. As to power, there is only enough to maintain good order.

Freedom of the press has no limits except the exclusion of libel.

(*) A vote would be valid even though contrary to the instructions of the constituents. However, it is not likely that such a violation would occur, because the least evil that could result for its author would be to lose esteem and gain the ill-will of his constituents.

(**) By the word *military*, we mean only those who are with the regular troops. Here, all citizens, as soon as they are of age, belong to the militia, as we have already noted.

The exercise of any form of religion is perfectly free and is not subjected to any hateful or puerile distinction.

No one is obliged to contribute to the maintenance of ministers of a religion which he does not profess. No state has an official religion. No one is deprived of the right to vote because of religion. However, in several states it is necessary to be Christian, in others Protestant in order to be a member of the legislative body and to occupy certain other offices. In some, for example in Virginia, contributions are voluntary, even for the maintenance of the religion one professes, and all that is required to hold any public office is to swear to be faithful to the republic.

As for the confederation the power entrusted to Congress is not curtailed by any limitations. Congress needs the consent of the member states only to regulate cases unforeseen by the Articles of Confederation. Each state has its voice in Congress where it deliberates through its representatives. In matters of little consequence the majority of votes is enough, even if by only one vote. But it is not the same in the case of more important questions. For example, when it is a question of declaring war or making extraordinary expenditures, a majority vote of the states does not suffice. It is still necessary to have the majority of popular vote. Thus, since, as it might happen because of the difference in population between states, there might not be a majority of the popular vote, although there might be that of states, it has been calculated that nine votes would be necessary to be always sure of a majority vote.

There are, therefore, some cases in which seven votes suffice and others when it is necessary to have nine.

It is only in matters on which the Articles of Confederation are silent that the unanimous vote of the states in Congress, as well as the consent of each state separately, is required.

Fortunately for us, the Revolution did happen before the English ministers considered us worthy of their titles and blazons. Pride did not permit them to introduce among us this aristocratic poison, the only thing that might have influenced vain men. This hateful distinction would have prevented the union to which we are principally indebted for liberty.

Not having before us any of those things which so easily blind men and make them incapable of understanding the perfect equality that exists among them as to the rights of a citizen,

it is not surprising that at the moment of the abolition of the old government, when it came to establishing a new one, the right of voting on a matter of such importance was generally recognized. But since the absurdity and the impossibility of exercising this right personally was also known, a small number of citizens, who were judged the most suitable to lay the foundations of a just and stable government, was chosen and the right was delegated to them.

The right to vote was exercised only by those who enjoyed it under the former governments.

Some people might think that the moderation shown was attributable, at least in part, to circumstances. But it is certain that the American people have great veneration for law and order, and they are convinced that abuses are never remedied in the midst of tumult.

The committee of delegates declared, in precise terms, the natural and inalienable rights of man, as we have seen in the Declaration of Rights and to make them permanent they wrote certain phrases which future legislators can never ignore. One must distinguish between the purpose of this assembly, called *convention,* which framed what is called the Constitution, or form of government, and the duties of the future assemblies charged with ordinary legislative power, which can not, as we have stated, nullify any of the principles established in the Constitution (*).

When we consider that our century is one of Philosophy—at least in comparison with those we know—that the rights of man are infinitely better understood than they have ever been before, that we have had the advantage of valuable experience, through observation of the defects of ancient and modern republican

(°) In almost all the state constitutions, it is expressly declared that ordinary legislative power must not be taken away, and that every time it is believed necessary to change something, the people must elect a special commission. In Virginia, this clause does not exist; and it could not be inserted legally because the *convention,* which formed the government, did not receive from the people a special assignment to that effect, so that what was established would be considered as done *pro tempore.* In New Hampshire, the last time the constitution was rewritten the clause which we have discussed was inserted with all due solemnity.

governments, and that we have not had to fight class distinction, the worst obstacle to the establishment of a free and just government, it would seem that our governments might have come closer to the perfection of which they are capable. It is true that disturbances distracted our attention, but it is no less true that general danger unites men and disposes them to sacrifice their private passions for the common good. We must also consider that the American people are very docile and have the greatest confidence in those to whom they entrust the care of their affairs. Thus I do not presume to censure my compatriots, when I lament the fact that our governments have not the degree of perfection I would desire and I hope that they will achieve it one day. My hope rests, in this regard, on the free and sane manner of thinking that has characterized our beginnings. Whoever has known the prime movers and has had the opportunity to listen to their discussions cannot doubt their intention to do their best possible. Unfortunately, the majority of these men, for the most part in advanced age, could not be convinced that certain principles, which from their infancy they were accustomed to regard as excellent, could be bad, especially since they saw that their own passivity had hindered consideration of these principles at the time of the old government.

ON THE RIGHT TO VOTE AND
TO BE A REPRESENTATIVE

The delegates who were charged with framing the new constitution declared, unanimously, in all the states, that *all men are born equally free and independent.* It is a truth to which prejudice has not been able to oppose anything. When afterwards it came to the right to vote and of being elected to office, a matter which is the first step in the foundation of a free government and on which liberty principally rests, this indisputable principle was not scrupulously observed. Everywhere abuses were more or less corrected but in no area completely.

The States of Virginia, Connecticut and Rhode Island are the only ones where the right to vote is not separated from the right to being elected and where anyone having the right to vote cannot be declared ineligible to any post in the republic; but in Connecticut, and I believe also in Rhode Island, to have it, one must own lands worth two pounds sterling or forty pounds in personal property (*); and in Virginia it is necessary to possess real estate consisting of one hundred acres of uncultivated lands, or twenty-five acres with a house on it, or finally, either a lot (**) or a house in some city. In Georgia it is enough to have a trade to enjoy the voting right.

To be eligible as a representative the possession of two hun-

(*) The old regulation still exists. When it was passed, for two pounds sterling one could buy more land than was necessary for a family.

(**) Cities are divided into sections called *lots* in English, and generally of a half acre. The French word *lot* does not have the same meaning, so I have believed it my duty to avoid using it.

dred fifty acres of land is required or personal property valued at two hundred fifty pounds sterling. In Pennsylvania it is sufficient to be a resident for a period of one year and to have paid taxes in order to enjoy the right to vote. To be eligible as a representative, a two-year residence is required and similarly to have paid taxes. Finally, to enjoy both these rights, one must be the son of a landowner. In Pennsylvania and Georgia, the right to be eligible as a representative includes the right to hold any public office. In the other states, there are differences in varying degrees. In some a larger capital is required to be a member of one branch of the legislative body rather than of another and a still larger amount to hold certain offices in some departments of the executive branch: for example, the State of Massachusetts requires three pounds sterling of revenue on lands, or a capital of sixty pounds sterling of some other nature, to have the right to vote; land worth one hundred pounds or personal property valued at two hundred pounds is required to be a member of the house of representatives; land worth three hundred pounds sterling or personal property worth six hundred pounds, to be a member of the other branch of the legislative body, called the senate, or of the state council, and one thousand pounds to be governor or vice-governor. In the State of New York the difference extends to the right to vote in various elections. To have the right to vote at the election of representatives, one must have land worth twenty pounds sterling or pay two pounds in rent per year. To vote for election of members of the senate or for governor or vice-governor, one hundred pounds sterling is needed.

As for determining these rights, unanimity was required in each of the states and they have all expressed themselves in more or less the same terms. The reason for this is found in the freedom they had on this point and also in their dedication to the careful examination—without prejudice—of these most important truths. Later, however, when it was necessary to deal with individual cases, old customs, old doctrines reappeared on the scene and reason was obliged more than once to yield to these powerful enemies. This variation in the sacred right to vote and be elected to office, this odious, unjust and shameful distinction, was the deepest and the most dangerous wound inflicted to those rights. Bias in favor of riches has no other foundation than ancient injustice and is very similar to that which in various cir-

cumstances exists in favor of the stronger sex. Anyone willing to rid himself of prejudices and become himself again, will not find any satisfactory justification for such discriminations.

But, they say, is it not necessary to have money to govern a state? And since the property owner contributes more to the public fund, should he not participate in the government in proportion to his riches?

I deny that the property owner, as an individual really pays more than anyone else. All that he pays extra is the contribution he owes for the property he possesses, which is protected by the public, which defends it by arms from invasion from without, and by its laws from invasion from within. The property owner is, in this regard, like the tenant on his own property, who would pay the same sum to any person owning it, and little does it matter to the public if it belongs to one rather than another. Property does not render any personal service to the public and money must make up for this deficiency. Thus the Quaker, whose religion prohibits him to carry arms, is obliged to pay someone to perform the service in his stead.

I now speak about another opinion which is only too common: the interest, they further say, that individuals have in the prosperity of a state is in proportion to the riches that they possess. My response is very simple. If a millionnaire could spend only an instant in the place of a poor man whose ten coins are his entire fortune, he would realize that this small sum is as dear to the latter as his treasures are to him.

And those who own nothing, it is added, what interest can they have in the prosperity of the state? My answer is that if they must be regarded as indifferent to it, then the state must not order them either to enter its service or bear arms and fight for its defense.

"But they get great benefits (reply those who depriving them of the rights of citizens would want them to bear at the same time the burdens of the state): they benefit by filling their needs more easily than elsewhere. They are protected by the impartial laws of a good government. In a word they enjoy liberty as do the others."

These are the same benefits, as dear to their hearts as riches themselves and which keep them so attached to the country that was to render sacred all their rights as citizens. To deprive them

of these rights, without a crime to cause the deprivation, is an obvious injustice to horrify anyone convinced that *all men are born equally free and independent* (*).

Every citizen has an equal right to the benefits and honors of his country and cannot be deprived of them except for some crime and after being judged by his peers. Only those may be exempted from this rule who, living on public alms, are in the care of the state instead of contributing to its revenues.

Stripping the poor of their rights as citizens is justified on the grounds: 1) that they do not have the means to educate themselves and become capable of filling certain offices and 2) that the rich could easily bribe them. Some even cite the second as reason enough for depriving them of the right to vote.

But is it so rare to find good parents who, though owning no property, have acquired, through hard work and thriftiness, the means of educating their children and thus making them capable of holding the most important offices? Furthermore, is it not unjust as well as absurd to exclude such men from such offices? If instead of making such praiseworthy use of their money, these fathers had bought property, ignorance would have prevented their children from qualifying for those posts.

They say that an unworthy man, although rich, will have difficulty in obtaining the majority of votes. But experience has only too often demonstrated the contrary. Riches dazzle and hide defects in those who possess them, while poverty encumbers him whose extraordinary merit is not publicized.

(°) It is with this great truth that the declaration of our rights begins. This foundation of American liberty contains all the principles necessary to preserve it. These principles are on the lips and in the hearts of all Americans, who have a religious respect for it. It is on this declaration that my hopes rest. As the clouds of old prejudices are dispelled, the pen of one wise and zealous citizen will suffice, perhaps, to provide an efficacious remedy for the greatest disorder. In the Thirteen States people read and are avid for instruction. It will be enough to give them proof of the transgressions of their representatives for them to order them to do their duty. If these principles had not been expressed with a clarity that makes them easily understood by everyone, then the disputes, sustained on the one hand by all the cleverness of bad faith and on the other by the enthusiasm of patriotism, could have rendered the people unsure and consequently kept them inactive. But the declaration of rights will serve as a rule and point of departure for zealous citizens and dispel their doubts.

They also say that the poor will always be prone to give their votes to their equals although these may be incapable of filling the posts to which they aspire.

Whoever thinks so, does not know the human heart. A man of poor estate—provided oppression does not bind him to his equals by common interests—always sets his goal above himself.

During the entire period when the Roman patricians insisted on enjoying exclusive right to governing the republic, it seemed as if the plebeians would accord all offices to men of their own class the moment they were free to do so. But when they were allowed to vote, they ridiculed those among themselves who presented themselves as candidates for election as military tribunes and did not elect any. Many years passed before the people found in their own class a candidate worthy of their choice. Common people exercise strict censure in regard to their equals. They do not weigh the merits of the rich with the same scale. If a partial law were compatible with liberty, it would have to be stopped rather than favor the ascendancy of the rich. Poverty already obscures merit too much without its being afflicted by unjust and barbarous laws.

As for susceptibility to corruption, I admit that the man without a fortune does not have to sacrifice as much as one who has plenty. But when rights are equal for all citizens, as they should be, where will one find a citizen so rich that he can buy plurality? One might add to this impossibility that of the temptation to conduct secret maneuvers where the number is so great. Finally, one should not lose sight of the fact that there are other means of bribing the rich which are impractical for the poor. There is, besides, an easy way to avoid the sale of votes: use either ballots or some other secret form.

We must now consider whether our governments offer any temptations capable of exciting the ambitious to use their fortune in order to win in an election. Here it is not a question of becoming a pretor and then pillage conquered provinces, nor of selling one's talents to members of Parliament in the hope of gaining an office worth five or six thousand pounds sterling per year. It is a matter of being the agent of one's equals for the period of only one year with the right of giving one's viewpoint on public affairs in the midst of a large assembly, with the obliga-

tion to make that viewpoint known to one's constituents, and to agree or refuse to assent to the enactment of laws to which one must be subject as are all citizens. One receives, only for the time of his service and related trips, a fixed sum to cover expenses, provided that these are incurred economically. In the states where the people have reserved for themselves the right to other elections, besides those of the legislative body, questions of temptation cannot be very great, since even in other departments, none of the Thirteen States offers any office which could satisfy ambition or greed.

As for the difference that has been made between real and personal property, as also for the idea commonly shared that land owners are more attached to their country—that is, that real property renders them more interested than others in the country's prosperity—these seem to me false opinions which, uttered at first by men perhaps very learned in other respects, are regarded as axioms. Errors, by being repeated, develop deep roots, and too much respect for their authors prevents reflecting upon them.

The attraction of property flourishes because it provides us with subsistence and satisfies our tastes. Thus personal property produces the same effect as lands; but it is claimed that lands have a more seductive attraction. In the first place, it is not certain that that is inborn; on the contrary, it is probably only a prejudice from education, for we are seriously taught this principle, and an infinite number of others equally false, at a most tender age. Even if there were a natural predilection, would this be justifiable?

They say that whoever has no property, has no homeland. Also an individual and his property are easily transported from one country to another, but this is not true of real estate.

However, there are not too many possessions that can be easily transported without loss. When one wants to change environment, in general, one takes the chance of selling.

In case of war, the enemy has no other purpose than to place the country under its domination, personal property will be as safe as real property. If the enemy wants to act as a brigand and strip individuals, he will confiscate everything, without making distinction between properties. If he takes pleasure in devastation, movable property will be more exposed than the real, not-

withstanding the possibility of rescuing some part from destruction. If the new rule is not liked and one wishes to change allegiance, the real as well as personal property can be sold.

Some object to my saying that the real cannot be sold as readily as the personal and that, being subject to perish as easily as the personal either because of devastation or for other reasons, as stated above, there results a preference for the latter.

First of all we must note that the difficulty of selling real estate is generally the result of defects in the government rendering commerce difficult, burdensome and subject to risks. But it is not true that this is universal because defects are not the same everywhere and in several areas they are redeemed by various particular benefits greatly facilitating sale. It is further to be noted that this difficulty is certainly no reason for preference: on the contrary, it is likely to produce the opposite effect.

If there exists preference in favor of real estate, it is encouraged by the solidity of this kind of property even though it may yield a lesser revenue. Moreover, this fact does not invalidate my thesis, which is not concerned with the preference for the nature of property but only with the influence that it may have on the spirit of its owner in relation to arousing him to the defense of his country. If private interest is what directs the actions of man, then the zeal of an individual for the public cause will be in proportion to the damage he fears his property will suffer if it [i.e., the public cause] loses. In this case, personal property will be preferable to real estate.

Also to be opposed is the idea that, at present, in America it is so easy to acquire extensive lands that the number of those who have no real estate must be very small and therefore worthy of little attention. Although their exclusion from the rights of citizens might thus be justified, one should at least have regard for their descendants. With time, we shall see in our country what has happened elsewhere, namely that many people worthy for talents and virtues, are not in a position to acquire property. We shall see others obliged to sell what they have in order to learn a profession which seems more useful to themselves and to the country.

Love of country in each individual is in proportion to the benefits he receives. Anyone who would like to give free rein to his reflections, renouncing his deep-rooted prejudices, could not

be persuaded that the benefits of good government and other favorable circumstances have more to do with love of country with the owner of real estate, than with the man who has only personal property or who exercises a profession, noble or base, profitable or of mediocre revenue.

Is it probable that a doctor, a lawyer, a manufacturer, etc., who has to leave his country, does not suffer as much as the owner of a tract, a house, a farm? Why should not a craftsman, a journeyman, a teamster, also feel interested in defending their homeland where they enjoy the rights of citizens and earn their living with more freedom than they could hope to have elsewhere? Why would they not love such a good mother, just as much as a rich property owner? The latter knows that, if he wants to leave the country, the price for the sale of his lands will procure for him an honest subsistence wherever he decides to retire. Do those who live on possessions now know that by emigrating they expose themselves to the risk of dying of hunger, before finding their occupation?

The one thing which could lessen their zeal for their country is the disgrace of being deprived of a citizen's rights. In this case, it is not with them that one must find fault. Only those who are deprived of these rights do not actually have a country. If it were possible to justify such a deprivation, nothing would be more unjust—I repeat this once again—than to make them waste time in the army and risk their lives in the defense of a country in which they would be considered as foreigners, and consequently should be exempt from the duties of a citizen since they could not share in the benefits. In addition it would be illogical to depend upon men believed to be indifferent to the welfare of their country.

The history of all ages offers an infinite number of examples of the indifference and cowardice of the rich, occasioned often by the fear of losing their property. But there are even more examples of the heroic courage of native, less fortunate citizens. In America, we have had sufficient proof of this.

The revolution in Genoa, during the war of 1745, gave us an astonishing spectacle in this regard. Since the government was aristocratic, the enthusiasm of the people was of pure, disinterested patriotism. In this instance, the nobles, although having sovereign power, suffered the loss of their authority with amaz-

ing resignation. But the people could not bear the idea of losing the name *Republic* and of not seeing the cherished motto *Liberty,* on the gates of the city in many other places. Needed only was the illusion produced by these two words, *Republic* and *Liberty,* to encourage the people to save Genoa. Not only did the nobles not mingle with them, but they also stooped to feign to disapprove of the people's conduct. All that they did, not to force the people to abandon the walls for lack of food, was to supply a large quantity for them. They themselves brought it to them by night in the squares and on the streets and they were helped only by those domestics with whom they felt safe. There is no doubt that, if the enemy had re-taken the city as the nobles feared and had discovered that the nobles had had some part in the resistance, it would have cost them a great part of their riches. This fact in itself proves that riches were dearer to them than the life of the people.

If the illusion of freedom alone often renders people enthusiastic, what will it be when they feel that they really can enjoy their rights? More than once specious arguments have been used to give value to the injurious accusations against them. But the very disorders that occurred in these republics as the result of popular riots, instead of giving proof against the rights of the populace, in the end confirm what I have affirmed because there would not have been disorders if their rights had been respected.

We have seen the populace resenting wrongs endured and taking revenge. We have never seen it to be the aggressor. The fear of evil is only too often an excuse not to do good; so clever are the interested politicians in disguising injustice. The most acclaimed systems have been unable, up to the present, to find a remedy for many of the terrible situations. Till now, there has not been tried the only system that is totally just—that is a system exempt from all kinds of partiality. To prevent its being tried, the alleged partisans of liberty may very well not run out of sophisms; but they will not have one single solid reason.

Finally—and here I apologize to several famous writers who would have had more respect for humanity if their opinions had been less favorable to the great—I maintain that the sanest statesman is the one who does not deviate from strict law, and, if he has some case where he might deviate a little for the sake of

equity, then it must be said that it is above all for the poor man, who must be helped by diminishing the weight of his duties, instead of depriving him of his citizen's rights.

Despite the partialities existing in the right to vote and of being elected to office—discriminations which one must hope to see one day abolished—there is not one of the thirteen states where these rights are no longer equal and more extensive than they have ever been in any other republic (*). Furthermore (which is more consoling), no individual can be, properly speaking, excluded in his country from any office, since everybody can by means of industry and thriftiness reach all offices, as we have already said.

(*) To render equal the right to become a representative, it is not only necessary that all citizens, without exception, benefit, but it is also necessary that, where possible, the number elected be in proportion to that of the electors. Some of the states, like Massachusetts, New Hampshire and South Carolina, have already done this, and have provided for maintaining the equilibrium with the precaution taken to require that a census of voters be taken from time to time; and in proportion to the result of the census, the number of representatives be decided. In other southern states, there still exists great inequality, even if much diminished by means of the subdivision of very large counties.

THE LEGISLATIVE POWER(*)

The more a machine is complicated, the more it is subject to getting out of order; this is probably the strongest reason why many persons have believed the government by one ruler, as the better one. In fact, if it were exercised by a prince, just and wise, and consequently attentive to his duty, with the assurance that the successors of this prince would resemble him, it would be impossible to have a more excellent government.

According to this principle Pennsylvania has entrusted its legislative power to only one body of men. It seems that Georgia thought the same, although she has taken the precaution to establish that the resolutions of the legislative assembly could not become laws before being reviewed and amended by those who, with the exception of the governor, make up the executive power.

The other states thought that the entire assembly, like an individual, could be prompted by caprice and passions, and for this reason it must be checked.

A citizen of Virginia proposed the division of representatives of the counties equally into two houses, that is, admitting into each of these two houses a representative from each county, since to validate the resolutions of one, the approval of the other would be necessary. In this way the inconveniences would have been remedied without losing the advantages of a united sys-

(*) The legislative power is not designated in all the states by the same name. In several it is called *General Assembly,* in others *General Court.* In New Hampshire, it had the name of *Congress;* but with the constitution approved on October 31, 1783, it was decided that from then on it would be called *General Court.*

tem; for the resolution that one house would pass in the enthusiasm of a dispute, would have to pass in the other under the revision of men not prejudiced and cool headed. It was really advantageous to avoid a complicated system both in regard to our stability, and also because the smallest distinction could sow the seeds of aristocracy.

It is said that people, at least those of America, are naturally prone to prefer the qualities of the soul to those of the mind; and that, to have wise representatives it would be necessary to adopt a method capable of assuring us that there be some men of superior intelligence in the two houses. This could be achieved without making the system more complicated. It would suffice that the voters in each county instead of electing two representatives, would elect fifteen or twenty persons, or even more, who would choose from among themselves. But it is feared that through such an election the talents of the mind would have more influence on the choice of the representatives than the qualities of the soul. It has been thought that the superior talents of an assembly of men entrusted with all the legislative power could easily become dangerous, if virtue were not equal to it.

After evaluating all the advantages and disadvantages of each method, the eleven states decided that it is better to divide the legislative power between two different bodies.

The more numerous body is called in Virginia and in Maryland the *House of Burgesses,* and in the other states the *House of Representatives.* The other body is called Senate almost everywhere; in New Jersey, it has the name of Legislative Council; in Connecticut the House of Representatives is called *Lower House,* and the *Upper House* is the other body which consists of the governor, the vice-governor, and twelve assistants. In Virginia, it was agreed that the Senate should be composed of twenty-four persons. A citizen of great judgment, the same one [Jefferson] to whom we owe the first and best model of the Declaration of Rights, proposed for the election of the Senate a method similar to the one envisioned by the one who had desired to preserve simplicity in the system [Mazzei]. The counties, which are now about eighty, were divided into twenty-four districts: he proposed that in each county, after the ordinary election of two representatives, the people should elect twelve persons who, meeting with the twelve of each of the other coun-

ties of the same district, would choose only one among them, to form, with the twenty-three colleagues elected in the same manner, the other branch of the legislative power. This project was not adopted; the election takes place in the same manner as the other and, consequently, as the advantage of a second choice was lost, so too was lost the possibility of assembling a body of men endowed with the greatest possible wisdom. On the other hand, since it is not probable that the majority know the people of the greatest merit in the other counties as well as the twelve mentioned could have: and since they are more subject to local prejudices, it is to be feared that the election will always be won by the county where the number of voters is greatest. We shall see that this objection is not the only one which should be obviated, when the constitution is framed on stable and permanent foundations.

I say stable and permanent, because the present form of government has been put together hurriedly without the special delegation required for this purpose. The idea that the least delay would have been dangerous in this very critical period, convinced the representatives of the people to count on the docility and trust of their constituents, instead of returning to their respective counties and waiting for a new election: our government [Virginia] was established first and the other states were able to profit by our mistakes, just as they profited from our Declaration of Rights. The present Constitution should therefore be considered the fruit of necessity, which sometimes gives birth to rules. However, the obligation to return to constituencies the moment circumstances permit it is preserved. The best minds of Virginia have always considered it temporary. At the same time there appeared an article by a citizen [Mazzei] which pointed out the objections. His work was approved by the inhabitants of his county: finally today everywhere there is thought of changing it with due solemnity, and in some way we will benefit by the other constitutions.

There is no doubt that the same power concentrated in a small number will work with more force than if divided among a larger number; concentrated force does not work only in the physical sense. It is perhaps because of this fear, or because of other less plausible motives, that the right to initiate legislation has not been accorded to the Virginia Senate, but only the right

259

to approve or reject the resolutions passed by the other House (*). From this comes an infinite number of elements, which could be useful to this body—the result of conceit or zeal for country. It is natural to desire to use one's talents in an assembly when one can contribute to the public good in whatever manner possible, rather than want to be reduced to only a negative good. One should, as much as possible, prevent the aristocratic seed to take root, without at the same time losing the fruit of the superior talents which distinguish such men. From this body should be removed all the exterior pomp which, without having any validity, serves only to foment vanity and blind the multitude. Since this might little by little have very fatal consequences, it would be necessary to give this body a simple and modest name, call it the second branch of the legislative power, and give precedence on all occasions to the other. The contrary has been done, perhaps because men persuade themselves with difficulty that such formalities could have a real influence or continue old prejudices.

One must attribute to this last cause the policy of not according to this body the right to change any of the resolutions of the other House which relate to financial affairs. Their right is limited to disapproving them entirely, if they do not want to approve them just as they have been sent by the House of Representatives. In England, where the members of one of the two Houses transmit their rights by succession, one could have some good reasons for admitting such a distinction in financial affairs. But, among us, one cannot find one reason, since the two bodies of the legislative power have equally the representatives of the people, and have no separate or distinct interest. The distinction in financial matters, however, has been adopted in all the states where the legislative power is divided into two branches. No state permits the Senate to propose laws on these matters, although it has in all, with the exception of Virginia, the liberty to make changes.

The other states have had the wise precaution not to imitate

(*) If something is to be amended, the proposal must be returned to the other House and start another discussion, since no resolution has the force of law, except when it is approved by the Senate without the least change.

the prohibition which Virginia made to this body to propose laws on any matter that existed.

As for the manner of election, the State of Maryland is the only one that has more or less adopted what was proposed in Virginia: and has already experienced its advantages several times.

The interval between the elections of this body is not the same in all the states. In Maryland, the election is held every five years; in South Carolina, every two years; in the other states, every year. In several, only a number of those who make up the body is chosen each year, for example, in Virginia, six are chosen, so that the complete election is held in four years.

The election of the other body is, I believe, annual everywhere, except in South Carolina, where it is held every two years, and in Connecticut where it is held every six months.

In Pennsylvania, one cannot be a member of the legislative body for more than four out of seven years. Elsewhere the people can always elect the same ones. Many of the reasons which invite us to change frequently those placed in other offices of the Republic are not at all applicable to the members of the legislative power. However, after weighing the pros and cons and glancing into the future, I would prefer Pennsylvania's system.

The sessions of the legislative houses can take place whenever the members consider it opportune. According to the constitutional law, they must be convoked at least once a year everywhere, and in Connecticut every six months. If the need is urgent, members of the executive body have the right and the obligation to meet.

In order to enact laws, some states require a majority vote in the two Houses; others, to avoid delay, have established a number which is below the half. In some states, as in Massachusetts and in New Hampshire, to be elected one must have the majority vote of all those who have the right to vote; in others, a plurality suffices, as in England, even if only of one vote.

The caution shown on these matters of such great importance is worthy of praise. Steps must be taken to avoid whatever could lead to negligence. It seems to me that the people could refuse to obey laws passed without the participation of the majority of its representatives. The same reflection is applicable to elections.

261

THE EXECUTIVE POWER(*)

Each of the thirteen states has entrusted its executive power to a magistrate assisted by a fixed number of councilors. In no place are the councilors less than five, or more than twelve. Ten states have given to this chief magistrate the name of *governor*: Pennsylvania, Delaware and New Hampshire are the only ones which have abolished this meaningless name, a ridiculous reminder of the monarchy.

The title of Excellency, perhaps the most unbecoming that the vanity of men has ever invented, is given to the chief magistrate in almost all the states, sometimes because of law (**), sometimes because usage holds sway. Men believe in honoring the person, and have not reflected that the name of the office is the only truly honorable one, since it brings with it testimony of the good opinion that the country has had and still retains for the one who is invested with it. Besides the ridiculousness which cannot be separated from all kinds of titles, it is well to observe also that the title *Excellency*, being so common in Europe, whence it came to us, tends rather to degrade than honor the chief magistrate of a free people.

(*) The executive power is also called government. This classification is improper, and it is the result of an ancient usage. Its functions are about the same as those of European governments, except that it does not meddle in anything that concerns the legislative and the judicial branches. The functions include the direction or control of foreign affairs, of finances, of war and of sea affairs.

(**) The constitution of Georgia wants that the title of Honorable be given; according to Massachusetts and New Hampshire, he must be addressed as *Excellency*.

The chief magistrate enjoys in several states, such as Massachusetts and New Jersey, some prerogatives which he should not have. In Virginia, fearing to give him too much power, we have made him an almost insignificant personage: he is completely under the tutelage of his councilors. Several other states, and particularly New York, seem to have managed better to give him nearly all the influence that is appropriate. The objection I see in the State of New York and in many others is the possibility of being reconfirmed in office without time limit. The triennial election which this state and Delaware have adopted may be at present preferable to the annual election; but this kind of reelection, opening the way to perpetuate men in these offices, is dangerous, although at the beginning it may have its usefulness (*).

The greatest danger that Virginia and some other states have a just reason to fear, as regards the chief magistrate, comes from having placed him in the condition of being, for at least the first two years, under the influence of the legislative power which, besides determining his salary, elects him annually, and can continue him in office for three consecutive years. In Massachusetts and in many other states, he is elected every year, but by the people. In New York, he is elected for three years, as we have said, and also by the people. However, it is not probable, unless the state is closely knit, that the mass of people know as well as its representatives how to evaluate the merits of the person most worthy of this office.

The influence of the legislative power in Virginia is extended to all the members of the executive branch since of the eight councilors, two have to leave office every three years, not according to seniority of service, but because voted out by a majority of votes of the General Assembly. This system was envisioned so as to have the means of excluding the least worthy; but it is defective for several reasons. One of the principal ones is the possibility that those desirous of being continued in office would slavishly support the views of the General Assembly, or rather of single members of this Assembly who would seem to them to have an influence capable of keeping them there.

(*) Several constitutions established that the chief magistrate, after a certain lapse of time, cannot be elected for the same period. Others require a greater interval.

To correct this shortcoming in an efficacious manner, it would be necessary first that the chief magistrate, as well as the councilors, be elected for all the time that they must serve. Their salaries moreover should not have to depend at all on the caprice of the ordinary legislative power. These salaries should be established by constitutional law, and regulated from time to time in line with the price of some products of prime necessity. The value of money will never be safe from vicissitudes, so long as gold and silver mines furnish for circulation a quantity disproportionate to the consumption.

The constitution of New York requires that the governor, the chancellor, the judges of the supreme court, or at least two among them, meet to examine the resolutions of the legislative power, which must be submitted to this committee before they become laws.

The objections of the committee to a proposed law, or to some part of a law, must be written and sent to the legislative power; and, if it persists in its first opinion, then the concurrence of two-thirds of the vote in each of the two Houses would be necessary, to remove the effect of the objections. Massachusetts has entrusted the same power to the governor: this magistrate alone can do therefore what fifty votes in one of the two Houses can do, prevailing over ninety-nine of the same House, and the unanimity of the other.

It is easy to see which of the two regulations merits preference, although perhaps that of New York can be improved by substituting other persons for the governor. It is always a serious mistake to give to anyone too much authority. After all, a man can possess, to the highest degree, all the qualities necessary for the chief magistrate of the Republic, and still not qualify him to revise the laws.

One of the advantages of this regulation is to make the formulation and the repeal of laws more difficult; some small faults are not as dangerous as the instability of the law, and when the faults are considerable, one must not fear to apply the remedy.

Various superfluous formalities, which are largely the remains of a monarchic government and which tend to support and nurture pride and vanity, are found more in the constitution of Massachusetts than in the others. One can cite, for example, the manner with which the General Court is dismissed, the day

265

preceding the new election, which is done by means of a procla-
mation by the governor, though the law could easily provide for
it without useless pomp, as in Virginia and in some other states.
Considering that perhaps nowhere is there a republican spirit
more generally diffused and more profoundly felt than in Massachusetts, I am inclined to believe that this comes from feeling
too much security. The great equality which has always existed
in that state has generated the feeling that probably such formalities were necessary to insure a respect for the chief magistrate of the Republic, without suspecting the evil effects that
they could produce. It is however to be hoped that the most zealous and most intelligent citizens of that state, particularly those
who have had occasion to visit Europe, will make, out of consideration for their descendants, all possible efforts to bring about a
prompt remedy.

In Virginia the chief magistrate is, as we have said earlier,
absolutely under the tutelage of his councilors. This is the other
extreme, which must be avoided no less than its opposite. The
obligation he is under to follow their instructions in all cases
limits his authority too much, and in critical moments, his
obligation to consult them can also be very dangerous. The
slowness of the resolutions and the uncertainty of secrecy are
two inevitable objections to the legislative department. With regard to the executive, they are not as insurmountable. A magistrate who has no part in the legislation and who is subject to give
an account of his operations, must have the freedom to act
promptly and secretly. On the other hand, how can he be held
accountable for his actions when he is ordered to follow the
advice of others? He needs no lawyer to defend him. All he has
to do is to present in writing the resolutions of his councilors
and the law which commands him to execute them. Such a regulation can on the contrary serve as protection for a cheating and
scheming man, who knows how to sway the minds of his councilors. In truth, all the members of the executive power can be
equally called to give an account of their conduct; but the very
large number of accused would make the punishment more difficult for several important reasons.

In the State of New Jersey, the executive power can pardon
all the condemned. Elsewhere it has the right to suspend execution in certain cases and in others to grant pardon. The differ-

ence one finds on this point among the various states is important enough to dwell upon. Everywhere the legislative power has the right to pardon criminals. So long as the least vestige of the old laws remains with us, which reflect only barbarism and bloodthirstiness, the power to mitigate them or to suspend entirely their effects, will be very useful.

But I hope that we shall be soon free of them; that the legislature, following the advice of Beccaria ([19]), will become in everything indulgent and humane, and that in its turn the executive power will become inflexible (*).

(*) All punishments must be proportionate to the nature of the offense. No branch of the legislative body will demand for crimes of theft, fraud, and similar offenses the same punishment as for murder and treason. Wherever the same norm is used for all offenses without any distinction, men are prone to forget the real distinction of the crimes and commit the greatest with as little scruple as the smallest. It is for this reason that laws which are too cruel are, at the same time, contrary to polity and justice, the true purpose of all punishments being to correct and not to destroy men (article 18 of the declaration of rights of New Hampshire, October 31, 1783). These very just and very humane reforms are the result of the Revolution.

THE JUDICIAL POWER

The judicial power is, in each state, exercised by two classes of judges. Some are called *justices of the peace,* and the others *justices of the supreme courts.*

The number of the first group is not limited. It is more or less large, according to the size and the population of the county, of the city or of the district under their jurisdiction, which extends to both criminal as well as civil cases. The judges are chosen from among the most esteemed persons of their district, for the purity of their morals and the extent of their knowledge. An effort is made to place them in a way that all the inhabitants can have access to some of them without too much inconvenience. In Virginia, and in some other states, they serve gratuitously. I believe that in all the states they were at one time chosen by the people; that it was also the people who chose them originally under the new government; that they received and must receive from the executive power, or only from the chief magistrate, their confirmation and their commission. There are several states, for example Virginia, where vacant seats have been and are being filled with people nominated by those already in office. It seems to me that such a method could, with time, become dangerous; since it tends to create small oligarchies. The method used in Pennsylvania and in some other states is according to my judgment infinitely better.

Every justice of the peace can judge matters of little importance alone and where it is not subject to appeal. In Virginia, if the amount reaches the value of four and one sixth piastres, the case must be discussed and judged publicly in the county seat, and there must be at least four justices. One can, in civil matters, appeal to the supreme courts, every time the dispute is over ten

pounds sterling. If it is over, or if it is a question of land titles or boundaries, one can appeal from the start.

The jurisdiction of the justices of the peace in criminal matters, does not extend to the death penalty. If the crime is a capital crime, and if the accused is believed guilty, they send him to the prison of the supreme court before which he must be judged.

When a matter pending before the justices of the peace has reference solely to the [meaning of the] law, they judge it themselves; if crime is involved, the jurors decide it; if it is complicated, the jurors give their opinion and ordinarily send it to the judges for a decision as to the law. However, this referral depends on their prudence. But if the matter concerns civil liberty, or centers on a point in regard to which bias is suspected among the justices, the jurors pass sentence on everything.

Literally speaking, there are four supreme courts in each state. The one called *admiralty court,* takes care of only maritime cases. The tribunal called in Virginia *General Court,* and known in the other states by the name that corresponds to that, tries all the civil common law matters (*) and all criminal matters. But the question of crimes must be judged by twelve jurors, and in criminal matters there is no appeal.

The *court of chancery* embraces all that which concerns minors and equity.

The fourth tribunal is called *court of appeals.* In Virginia, it is composed of all the judges of the three supreme courts. They assemble to judge in a final effort the cases which are brought there by those who are not pleased with the sentence of one of the three courts, and sometimes in doubtful cases, the judges themselves present them.

(*) Common law code had its origin in England, where it was born during the heptarchy, and was so called because the laws contained in it were common to all the seven kingdoms. Before the thirteenth century, it was lost; but its substance remained in the minds of men, and the same laws were found later from time to time in the decisions of judges and in the treatises of jurists. After the barons had obtained from King John, at the beginning of the thirteenth century, the great charter (*Magna Charta)* the parliamentary laws began to form a second code. They called the old one, common law, and the new one, statute law; but since both contain laws which are binding, they are both classified as *common law,* when it is a question, as here, of distinguishing this court from the chancery court.

In Virginia in the common law court there are five justices. In the other two courts, there are three. Whatever was the motive for the difference in number and the preference for an uneven number, I hope that in revising the constitution with due formality, the number of justices will be established at four in all of the three courts. In cases that are not very doubtful, it is hardly possible that out of four, three are not on the side of reason; and when there is doubt, it is better to try the case again because of an equal division of opinion rather than deprive someone of what he possesses by a majority of only one vote.

I would still want that in the court of appeals the justices of the court appealed from would have no vote, except when the justices themselves bring the case there.

The constitution of some states requires that the salaries of justices be sufficient to assure that people of merit will accept the office; but since the ordinary legislative power is renewed each year, and could change its opinion, to avoid its having the slightest influence in a branch of such importance for the security of goods and all individuals, the salaries of justices should be established by the constitution just as we said should be done for the members of the executive branch.

Much is needed for the nature of our governments to resemble the description given by the Abbé Raynal (*) "Each province had an assembly, formed by the representatives of various districts, in which resided the legislative power. Its president had the executive power. His rights and his duties were to listen to the citizens; to convoke them when circumstances required it; to provide for arms, to maintain the troops, and to plan operations with their chiefs. He was placed at the head of a secret committee which would be in constant liaison with the general congress. The period of his administration was limited to two years; but the laws would permit a longer period."

If the author had paid attention to our constitutions, or at least to the Declaration of Rights, he would not have confused the legislative with the executive power. The other rights, and the other duties which he attributes to those whom he calls the president of the legislative power, are so many errors brought

(*) *Op. cit.*, Vol. 9, p. 304.

271

forth by fantasy. In a word, this description presents the very opposite of the truth; however, when the author wrote, it was very easy for him to obtain correct information through the Americans who resided in Paris, and whom he visited often.

CONCLUSION

In Virginia, the people reserved for themselves only the election of the members of the legislative body, for it was thought, and I believe with reason, that the majority of the inhabitants of a large state cannot know the particular merits of the persons most suitable to fulfill the functions of the different offices. The legislative body elects the members of the executive and judicial branches, the representatives of the state in Congress, the treasurer, the attorney general, the auditors, in a word all those who must fill the most important state offices.

In other states the methods for the different elections resemble each other so little, that a detailed description would be too long and tiresome; however there is no place where the justices are not chosen, either by the legislative, or by the executive, or by both of them together. The same happens for the other offices considered which are dependent on the legislative, or the executive power, with the exception of those of secretary and of treasurer in Connecticut, where the people have reserved the choice for themselves. The present secretary of this state and the late Governor Trumbull, are so much proof that the people, when they are well served, are not so inconstant as some writers who study men in office have assumed. Trumbull who died last year, and who two years before his death had returned, on his own initiative, to private life, was elected governor eighteen consecutive years; as for the present secretary, he has been in office forty years without interruption, and the secretariat has been in his family for the past three generations.

It is not necessary to add anything to give you an adequate idea of the foundations on which the governments of the United

273

States are built. This is not the place to talk about useful reforms contained in the various constitutional laws, such as, for example, the one abolishing the barbarous law regarding suicide brought against the heirs, a law which no longer exists in any state. Anyone who would like to see a particular aspect of these governments, can do so by reading the *various constitutions*, translated into French, and printed in Paris with scholarly notes by a translator. I advise you however that to acquire a minute and complete knowledge, it would be indispensable to consult a well-informed citizen of each of the thirteen states. Each state has written its constitution only for its own inhabitants. Thus many of the things known perfectly by all have been passed over in silence, as superfluous to mention.

The two following passages, the first taken from the constitution of Virginia, and the second from that of New Jersey, prove this clearly.

"The right to vote will continue in the same way that it is presently exercised."

"All the laws proclaimed recently by Mr. Alinson, will be in effect, except, etc., etc."

Of all that one reads in the constitutions of Connecticut and of Rhode Island, one understands only a very small part.

That of New Hampshire was revised toward the end of 1783, as we have already said, and consequently it has not been translated and published with the others.

As for the particular observations on the governments and the laws of the United States, we shall consider later what might stimulate the curiosity of a foreigner. The confutation of the nunumerous errors of the Abbé de Mably would require lengthy discussion so that if one would speak of each separately, there would be many repetitions.

NOTES

Section A, page 193, line 12.

CHARTER of Privileges accorded by William Penn, Esquire, to the Inhabitants of Pennsylvania and Territories, the 28th of October 1701 [20].

Here are in substance the principal articles which it contains, namely: That, because no people could be truly happy, though under the greatest enjoyment of civil liberties, if abridged of the freedom of their consciences, as to their religious profession and worship, no inhabitant, confessing and acknowledging one almighty God, and professing himself obliged to live quiet under the civil government, should be in any case molested or prejudiced in person or estate.

That all persons professing to believe in Jesus Christ the Saviour of the world, promising, when required, allegiance to the King, and taking certain attests by a certain provincial law provided, should be capable to serve the government either legislatively or executively.

That an assembly should be yearly chosen by the freemen, to consist of four persons out of each county, of most note for virtue, wisdom, and ability; or of a greater number, if the governor and assembly should so agree, upon the first of October, and should sit on the 15th following, with power to choose a speaker and the necessary officers, to be judges of the qualifications and elections of their own members, sit upon their own adjournments, appoint committees, prepare bills, impeach criminals, and redress grievances, with all other rights and privileges of an assembly, according to those of the freeborn subjects of England, and the customs observed in any of the King's plantations in America.

That two-thirds of the freemen so chosen should have the full authority over the whole.

That the said freemen in each respective county, at the time and place of meeting for electing representatives, might choose a double number of persons to present to the governor for sheriffs and coroners, to serve for three years, for as long as they should behave themselves well, out of whom the governor was to nominate one for each office, provided his nomination was made the third day after presentment, otherwise the person first named to serve and, in case of death or default, the governor is to supply the vacancy.

That three persons should be nominated by the justices of the respective counties, out of whom the governor was to select one to serve for clerk of the peace within ten days, or otherwise the place to be filled by the first so nominated.

That the laws of the government should be in this style to wit, *'By the governor, with the consent and approbation of the freemen in general assembly met.'*

That all criminals should have the same privileges of witnesses and council as their prosecutors.

That no person should be obliged to answer any complaint, matter, or thing whatsoever, relating to *property*, before the governor and council, or in any other place but in ordinary course of justice, unless in appeals according to law.

That the estates of suicides should not be forfeited; that no act, law, or ordinance whatsoever should at any time hereafter be made or done to alter, change or diminish the form or effect of this charter, or of any part or clause therein, according to the true intent and meaning thereof, without the consent of the governor for the time being, and six parts in seven of the assembly met.

That the first article relating to liberty of conscience should be kept and remain without any alteration inviolably forever.

That the said William Penn, for himself, and his heirs or assigns, does he hereby solemnly declare, grant and confirm, that neither he, his heirs, nor assigns, should procure or do any thing or things whereby the liberties in this charter, contained and expressed, nor any part thereof, should be infringed or broken and, that if any thing should be procured and done by any person or persons contrary thereto, it should be held of no force or effect.

Excerpts from the Remonstrance that the Pennsylvania Assembly addressed to William Penn in 1704*:

The minutes of the Assembly and other papers, as well as living witnesses attest that, soon after thy arrival here, thou, having obtained the Duke's (Duke of York) grant for the three lower counties (that is to say the *territory*) prevailed on the people of the province to unite in legislation and government with those of the lower counties; and then, by subtle contrivance and artifice—too deep for the perception of some while the circumstances gave others no time for consideration—thou found a way to lay aside that first charter, and to introduce another, which thou completed in the year 1683. . . .

And as to the union of the province and lower counties, we cannot gainsay it, if the King had granted thee the government as the Duke had done the soil; but, to our grief, we cannot find that thou had any such grant; and if thou had, thou would not produce it, though often requested so to do; therefore we take it the harder that thou, who knew how precarious thy power was to govern the lower counties, should bring thy province into such a state and condition that, whenever the crown had assumed that government, or the people there revolted, or refused to act with us in legislation, as they often did, that then the said second charter should become impracticable, and the privileges thereby granted of no effect to the province, because the representatives of the lower counties were equal in number with those of the province, and the charter required a greater number than the province had, or by charter could elect for members of council and assembly; and our numbers, by the charter, could not be increased without the revolters' consent. . . .

The motives which we find upon record, inducing the people to accept that second charter, were chiefly two, viz. that the number of representatives would prove burdensome to the

*Documents of this nature cannot be translated literally. However, we have tried to be faithful to the original text. The reader will not be surprised to find very long and, sometimes, ambiguous sentences.

277

country; and the other was, that, in regard thou had but a *treble vote*, the people, through their unskillfulness in the laws of trade and navigation, might pass some laws over thy head repugnant thereunto, which might occasion the forfeiture of the King's letters patent, by which this country was granted to thee; and wherein is a clause for that purpose, which we find much relied upon, and frequently read or urged in the assembly of that time; and security demanded by thee from the people on that account.

As to the first motive, we know that the number of representatives might have been very well reduced without a new charter; and, as to the laws of trade, we cannot conceive that a people so fond of thyself for (their) governor, and who saw much with thy eyes in those affairs, should, against thy advice and cautions, make laws repugnant to those of trade, and so bring trouble and disappointment upon themselves, by being a means of suspending thy administration; the influence whereof, and hopes of thy continuance therein, induced them, to embark with thee in that great and weighty affair, more than the honor due to persons in those stations, or any sinister ends destructive to the constitution they acted by. Therefore we see no just cause thou had to insist on such security, or to have a negative upon bills to be passed into laws in general assemblies, since thou had by the said charter (pursuant to the authority and direction of the King's letters patent aforesaid) formed those assemblies and, thereupon reserved but a treble vote in the provincial council, which could not be more injurious to thee than to the people, for the reasons aforesaid.

Thus was the first charter laid aside, contrary to the tenor thereof, and true intent of the first adventurers; and the second charter introduced and accepted by the General Assembly held at Philadelphia, in the first and second months, 1683, where thou solemnly testified, that what was inserted in that charter was solely intended by thee for the good and benefit of the freemen of the province, and prosecuted with much earnestness in thy spirit towards God at the time of its composition.

[Mazzei adds:] *We do not comment on their complaints when Penn left for London, and on the laws and the new constitution of which he had neglected to get approval by King James; we also omit that which refers to the period when Penn was without a charter. . . .*

Upon thy being restored to the government, thou required thy lieutenant to govern us according to charter, which, by reason of Fletcher's interruption, became impossible before thy orders reached us, and so the government fell into great confusion again. Nor was the administration of thy propriety much better managed, because thou put some in that commission with whom the rest would not act; and at last the office of property and surveyor-general came to be shut up, and thou kept them so whilst thou sold lands to the value of about two thousand pounds sterling, and gave thy warrants in England for surveying the said land, and also got great tracts of land laid out or secured for thyself and relations, besides several valuable parcels which should have been laid out for the purchase, but were reserved by thy surveyors, whether for thee or themselves we know not; however thou appropriated those lands to thyself, by the name of *concealed lands*, whereas in truth they were concealed from the purchasers, who were to have their lands laid out contiguous one to another, and no vacancies left between them; and thou wast to have only thy tenth, as it fell, according to the concessions thou made with thy first adventurers; and if thou took it not up so, it was thy own (not their) fault, but the other was a manifest injury to many of them.

After all the hardships and disappointments we had labored under, we hoped to enjoy the fruits of thy former promises and engagements; instead of that, we found thee very full of resentment, and many of our applications and addresses, about our just rights and properties, were answered by recriminations or bitter invectives; and we found that the false insinuations and reproaches, that our adversaries had cast upon the province, with respect to false trade and harbouring pirates, had made so great an impression upon thee, that thou rather believed them than thy honest friends.

And when thou entered upon legislation, thou wast pleased to repeal all the laws that were made in Colonel Fletcher's time, which were approved by the King or Queen, as we were informed, and as some of us gathered by the account thou gave of them, viz., that Chancellor Somers had sent for thee to know what thou had to object against any of those laws; and if it had not been for thee, none of them had passed, or words to that effect. And not only so, but the people being minded to surren-

der the said second charter upon thy promise to give them a better in lieu of it, and under pretence of passing an act for confirming and securing their lands, etc., thou obtained liberty to re-survey all the lands in the province, and to bring the people to terms for the overplus; so that by this stratagem, the warrants, surveys, and new patents cost the people as much, and to some more, than the first purchase of their lands, besides their long attendance upon thy secretary and surveyors to have their business done; but before thou would pass that act, it must be accompanied with an impost or excise, and a two thousand pound bill besides. And all this thou esteemed but inconsiderable, when thou compared it with the vast charge thou had been at, in the administration and defence of this government, since the year 1682, though we know thy stay here at first coming was not above two years, but went home about the difference between thee and Baltimore, concerning the bounds of the lower counties, and did not return till the year 1699, excusing thy stay by thy service to the nation of England in general, and to thy friends there in particular, (as appears by thy letters from time to time) whilst the interest of this province was sinking, which might have been upheld by the many wealthy persons that were inclined to transport themselves here, after the rout of Monmouth, if thee had then come over according to thy repeated promises. And how far thy stay has either effected what thou went about, or contributed to the establishment of the inhabitants here in their just rights and liberties and properties, we leave thee to demonstrate and the world to judge. In the meantime, we desire thee to consider better what to place to the account of this province; and do not forget that no part of thy pretended charges was expended in paying some of those who acted under thee, in the administration here, one of whom, viz. Thomas Lloyd, served thee in that station about nine years of thy absence, which thou leaves, it seems for the country to discharge.

After thou had managed these points, and was sent for to England, thou granted the third charter of privileges*, by which

*This remonstrance does not mention the second charter, given to Chester in December, 1682. Perhaps the changes contained did not seem so important as to warrant a new charter. This is why the third charter is called the second and the fourth is called the third.

we are now convened; as also a charter to incorporate the city of Philadelphia, and signed a charter of property, but refused to order thy seal to be affixed thereunto, till thou had advised upon it in England; nevertheless, thou promised under thy hand, that thou would confirm the first part of it relating to titles of land, but thou sent thy order, under hand and seal, dated within six months after, to countermand the sealing thereof.

After the laws were completed for raising all the said taxes and imposts, thou proposed, that, if thy friends would give thee a sum of money, thou promised to negotiate their affairs at home to the best advantage, and endeavour to procure the approbation of our laws and a general exemption from oaths. We find that considerable sums have been raised by way of subscription and benevolence for that service; part thou received before thou went, and more have been received since by thy secretary; but we had no account that our laws are approved, nor had we as much as a letter from thee, nor any other intimation, but by thy secretary's letters, which he thought fit to communicate by piecemeal, whereby we understand, that thou hast been making terms for thyself and family. And, by what we gather, thou hast been upon surrendering the government; nor are thy friends here eased of oaths, but, on the contrary, an order from the Queen, requiring oaths to be administered to all persons who are willing to take them in all judicatures, whereby the people called *Quakers* are disabled to sit in courts.

By the last Charter of Privileges, thou established an annual election of representatives for assembly, and that they should continue and sit upon their own adjournments; yet, by thy commission to thy present deputy, John Evans, thou did, in a direct opposition to the said charter, give him power, not only to call assemblies by his writs, but to prorogue and dissolve them as he should see cause; and also reserved to thyself, though in England, thy final assent to all bills passed here by thy deputy. We suppose thou hast not forgot, that what rendered the former charter inconvenient if not impracticable, was chiefly, that Colonel Fletcher's interruption had halted the rotation of the council, and, next to that, the proposals of laws by the council, in presence of the governor; as also the instability of the Lower Counties, which we had before experience of, and whose result was then doubted, as hath since happened. But that annual standing

assemblies, liable only to the dismission and call of the governor as occasion required, was never found an inconveniency, nor assigned as a reason for changing the said form for the present charter; and, should that of dissolution be introduced, it would frustrate the constitution, because, if a dissolution should happen, the province might be a great part of the year without an assembly, and the governor without power to call one, whatsoever commands from the crown, or other occasions, may happen; for that the election being fixed by charter, which is in nature of a perpetual writ, and has the authority of a law, if it could be superseded by the governor's writ, which is but an act of state, and merely temporary, it would be of pernicious consequence to the province as well as thyself; and of this thou seemed very sensible, when, being desired by the assembly, upon the close of the session in the year 1701, to dissolve them (being then called by writs), thou told them, thou wouldst not do it, for that thou couldst not answer to the crown to leave the province without a standing assembly.

As the exemption from any dissolution or prorogation seems to be an inseparable consequent of thy grant, as well as our constant practice upon the former charter, which this was by thy promise to exceed, so, upon an attempt made by the council to prorogue us in October last, we have thought it our duty to prepare a bill for ascertaining, explaining, and settling our present constitution; which we having presented to thy deputy for his assent, he finding that the power of dissolution and prorogation is not in express words granted away by charter, as also the inconveniency thereof with his said commission, after several conferences thereupon, had with him and his council, he thought fit to advise us to forbear the further pressing it, till we should hear from thee; therefore, he being unwilling to pass the said bill by us judged so necessary, and the very foundation of our present constitution, we could not think it proper to proceed to perfect any other business, whilst that remained unsettled. Nor do we suppose any thing will be done in legislation either by the present or succeeding assemblies, till the difficulties we labor under herein be removed, either by thy speedy order, or by thy deputy without it, seeing to proceed upon other matters would be to raise a superstructure before the foundation were well laid; nor do we look upon it very advisable for us to proceed far in legisla-

tion, until thou repeals those parts of thy lieutenant's commission, relating to prorogation and dissolution of assemblies, for the reasons before given, as also concerning thy final assent to laws, which we conceive to be very unreasonable in itself, and a great abuse and violation of our constitution, that thou should offer to put three negatives upon our acts, whereas by our first charter we had none but that of the crown; and how thou gained another to thyself, we have before showed thee, but now to bring us under three seems a contrivance to provoke us to complain to the Queen, that thou art not effectually represented here, and make that a motive for her to take us under her immediate care and protection, which would make thy surrender in some measure our act, which, if thou should do without the consent of the landholders and inhabitants of this province first obtained, would look too much like treachery.

It appears, by several petitions now before us, that very great abuses have been and are put upon the inhabitants, and extortions used by thy secretary, surveyors, and other officers, concerned in property as well as courts, which might have been prevented or sooner remedied, had thou been pleased to pass the bill proposed by the assembly in the year 1701 to regulate fees; as also the want of a surveyor-general, which is a great injury and dissatisfaction to the people, as is likewise the want of an established judicature for trials between thee and the people. For if we exhibit our complaints against thee, or those who represent thee in state or property, they must be determined by or before justices of thy own appointment; by which means, thou becomes, in a legal sense, judge, in thy own cause, which is against natural equity. Therefore we propose, that a man, learned in the laws of England, may be commissioned by the Queen, to determine all matters, wherein thy tenants have just cause to complain against thee, thy deputies, or commissioners; or else restore the people to the privilege of electing judges, justices, and other officers, according to the direction of the first charter, and intent of the first adventurers, and as the people of New England have, by King William's charter. That thy commissioners of property, are very unwilling to make good the deficiencies of those lands thou hast been many years ago paid for (though thou gave them power so to do), and so great is the difficulty and trouble to get satisfaction in this particular, that it is better for one to

forego his right, than wait on and attend the commissioners about it, unless the quantity wanting be very great.

We have many other things to represent to thee as grievances; as thy unheard-of abuses to thy purchasers, etc., in pretending to give them a town, and then, by imposing unconscionable quit-rents, makes it worse by ten-fold than a purchase would have been; also the abuse about the bank, and want of common to the town, and not only so, but the very land the town stands on is not cleared of the Swedes' claims.

These are the chief complaints which we thought fit at this time to lay before thee, earnestly intreating thy serious consideration of them, and that thou will now at last, after we have thus long endured and groaned under these hardships (which of late seem to be multiplied upon us), endeavour, as far as in thee lies, to retrieve thy credit with us thy poor tenants and fellow-subjects, by redressing these aggrievances, especially in getting our laws confirmed, and also to be eased of oaths, and giving positive orders to thy deputy to unite heartily with us upon our constitution; and that the charters thou granted us for city and country may be explained, settled, and confirmed by law. And we further intreat, that effectual care be taken for the suppressing of vice, which, to our great trouble we have to acquaint thee, is more rife and common amongst us since the arrival of thy deputy and son*, especially of late, than was ever known before. Nor are we capable to suppress it, whilst it is connived at, if not encouraged by authority, the mouths of the more sober magistrates being stopped by the said late order about oaths, and the governor's licensing ordinaries not approven by the magistrates of the city of Philadelphia, and the roost chiefly ruled by such as are none of the most exemplary for virtuous conversation. Thy positive orders in the premises, will be absolutely necessary to thy deputy, who thinks it unreasonable, and a great hardship on him, to give sanction to laws explanatory of thy grants, or to do any thing by way of enlargement or confirmation of aught, save what is particularly and expressly granted by thee, it being by some of his council urged as an absurdity in us to expect; and we desire that thou would order the licensing of ordinaries and tav-

*Penn had sent his son as a deputy.

284

erns to be by the justices, according to thy letter dated in September, 1697; and we hope we need not be more express in charging thee, as thou tenders thy own honor and honesty, or the obligations thou art under to thy friends, and particularly thy first purchasers and adventurers into this province, that thou do not surrender the government, whatsoever terms thou may by so doing make for thyself and family, which we shall deem no less than a betraying us, and at least will look like first fleecing, then selling; but rather use thy utmost interest with the Queen to ease us in the premises; and if, after thy endeavours used to keep the government, it be per force taken from thee, thou will be the clearer in the sight of God, and us the representatives of the people of this thy province, who are thy real friends and well-wishers, as we hope is evident in that we have dealt thus plainly with thee.

Excerpts from another
Remonstrance of June 10, 1707

We, and the people we represent, being still grieved and oppressed with the maladministration and practices of thy deputy, and the ill carriage, unwarrantable proceedings, and great exactions of thy secretary, are like to be destroyed by the great injustice and arbitrary oppressions of thy evil ministers, who abuse the powers given thee by the crown, and we suppose have too much prevailed upon thee to leave us hitherto without relief.

The assembly which sat here on the 26th of the sixth month, 1704, agreed upon certain charges or particulars, which, according to the order of that day, were drawn up in a representation, and was signed by the speaker, and sent thee by a passenger in John Guy's brigantine, who was taken into France, from whence the same representation was conveyed to thy hands; whereby thou art put in mind, upon what score the purchasers and first adventurers embarked with thee to plant this colony, and what grants and promises thou made, and the assurance and expectations thou gave them and the rest of the settlers and inhabitants of this province to enjoy the privileges derived from thy own grants and concessions, besides the rights and freedoms of England; but how they were disappointed in several respects, appears, in part, by the said representation, to which we refer, and become supplicants for relief, not only in matters there complained of, which are not yet redressed, but also in things then omitted, as well as what have been lately transacted, to the grievous oppression of the Queen's subjects, and public scandal of this government.

We are much concerned, that thou conceived such displeasure as thou did against that assembly and not in all this time vouchsafe to show thy readiness to rectify those things which they made appear were amiss; nor hast thou showed thy particular objections to the bills, which, with great care and charge, were then prepared, for confirming thy charters to this city and

country, respecting both privileges and property, and for settling the affirmation instead of oaths. But, on the other hand, we found, to our great disappointment, that thou gave credit to wrong insinuations against them, as appears by thy letter from Hyde Park, dated the twenty-sixth of the twelfth month, 1704-5, wherein thou treated some particulars very unfriendly, and without any just grounds blamed the people's representatives, who, we perceive by their proceedings, were ready to support the government under thy administration, and desired nothing but to have their just rights, privileges, and properties confirmed, the judicatories regularly established, the magistracy supplied with men of virtue and probity, and the whole constitution so framed, that the people called *Quakers* might have a share with other Christian people in the government, which thou always gave them an expectation of, and which they justly claim as a point of right, not for the sake of honor, but for the suppressing of vice, etc.

The compiler of these authentic decrees adds the following:

To wade through the whole of this provincial controversy, repeatedly renewed and lasting until Gookin was superseded in the year 1717, and replaced by William Keith, would be a task of great prolixity, and what consequently might prove as tedious to the reader as laborious to the writer.

Enough has been said, to show upon what terms Mr. Penn was first followed by his flock, as a kind of patriarch to Pennsylvania; as, also, what failures in his conduct towards them were complained of by them; and as to the conduct of the several assemblies, which, in the several periods of this interval, maintained this controversy, a bare perusal of their proceedings is in general sufficient for their justification.

Section B, page 214, line 31.

DECLARATION [21]

Delivered by the representatives of the United States of America, assembled in General Congress the 4th of July 1776.

When in the Course of human events, it becomes necessary for one people to dissolve the political bands which have connected them with another, and to assume among the Powers of the earth, the separate and equal station to which the Laws of Nature and of Nature's God entitle them, a decent respect to the opinions of mankind requires that they should declare the causes which impel them to the separation.

We hold these truths to be self-evident, that all men are created equal, that they are endowed by their Creator with certain unalienable Rights, that among these are Life, Liberty and the pursuit of Happiness. That to secure these rights, Governments are instituted among Men, deriving their just powers from the consent of the governed. That whenever any Form of Government becomes destructive of these ends, it is the Right of the People to alter or to abolish it, and to institute new Government, laying its foundation on such principles and organizing its powers in such form, as to them shall seem most likely to effect their Safety and Happiness. Prudence, indeed, will dictate that Governments long established should not be changed for light and transient causes; and accordingly all experience hath shown, that mankind are more disposed to suffer, while evils are sufferable, than to right themselves by abolishing the forms to which they are accustomed. But when a long train of abuses and usurpations, pursuing invariably the same Object evinces a design to reduce them under absolute Despotism, it is their right, it is their duty, to throw off such Government, and to provide new Guards for their future security. —Such has been the patient sufferance of these Colonies; and such is now the necessity which constrains them to alter their former Systems of Government. The

history of the present King of Great Britain is a history of repeated injuries and usurpations, all having in direct object the establishment of an absolute Tyranny over these States. To prove this, let Facts be submitted to a candid world.

He has refused his Assent to Laws, the most wholesome and necessary for the public good.

He has forbidden his Governors to pass Laws of immediate and pressing importance, unless suspended in their operation till his Assent should be obtained; and when so suspended, he has utterly neglected to attend to them.

He has refused to pass other Laws for the accommodation of large districts of people, unless those people would relinquish the right of Representation in the Legislature, a right inestimable to them and formidable to tyrants only.

He has called together legislative bodies at places unusual, uncomfortable, and distant from the depository of their Public Records, for the sole purpose of fatiguing them into compliance with his measures.

He has dissolved Representative Houses repeatedly, for opposing with manly firmness his invasions on the rights of the people.

He has refused for a long time, after such dissolutions, to cause others to be elected; whereby the Legislative Powers, incapable of Annihilation, have returned to the People at large for their exercise; the State remaining in the meantime exposed to all the dangers of invasion from without, and convulsions within.

He has endeavoured to prevent the population of these States; for that purpose obstructing the Laws for Naturalization of Foreigners; refusing to pass others to encourage their migration hither, and raising the conditions of new Appropriations of Lands.

He has obstructed the Administration of Justice, by refusing his Assent to Laws for establishing Judiciary Powers.

He has made Judges dependent on his Will alone, for the tenure of their offices, and the amount and payment of their salaries.

He has erected a multitude of New Offices, and sent hither swarms of Officers to harrass our People, and eat out their substance.

He has kept among us, in times of peace, Standing Armies without the Consent of our legislature.

He has affected to render the Military independent of and superior to the Civil Power.

He has combined with others to subject us to a jurisdiction foreign to our constitution, and unacknowledged by our laws; giving his Assent to their Acts of pretended Legislation:

For quartering large bodies of armed troops among us:

For protecting them, by a mock Trial, from Punishment for any Murders which they should commit on the Inhabitants of these States:

For cutting off our Trade with all parts of the world:

For imposing Taxes on us without our Consent:

For depriving us in many cases, of the benefits of Trial by Jury:

For transporting us beyond Seas to be tried for pretended offences:

For abolishing the free System of English Laws in a neighbouring Province, establishing therein an Arbitrary government, and enlarging its Boundaries so as to render it at once an example and fit instrument for introducing the same absolute rule into these Colonies:

For taking away our Charters, abolishing our most valuable Laws, and altering fundamentally the Forms of our Governments:

For suspending our own Legislatures, and declaring themselves invested with Power to legislate for us in all cases whatsoever.

He has abdicated Government here, by declaring us out of his Protection and waging War against us.

He has plundered our seas, ravaged our Coasts, burnt our towns, and destroyed the Lives of our people.

He is at this time transporting large Armies of foreign Mercenaries to compleat the works of death, desolation and tyranny, already begun with circumstances of Cruelty and perfidy scarcely paralleled in the most barbarous ages, and totally unworthy the Head of a civilized nation.

He has constrained our fellow Citizens taken Captive on the high Seas to bear Arms against their Country, to become the executioners of their friends and Brethren, or to fall themselves by their Hands.

He has excited domestic insurrections amongst us, and has endeavoured to bring on the inhabitants of our frontiers, the merciless Indian Savages, whose known rule of warfare, is an undistinguished destruction of all ages, sexes and conditions.

In every stage of these Oppressions We have Petitioned for Redress in the most humble terms: Our repeated Petitions have been answered only by repeated injury. A Prince, whose character is thus marked by every act which may define a Tyrant, is unfit to be the ruler of a free People.

Nor have We been wanting in attention to our British brethren. We have warned them from time to time of attempts by their legislature to extend an unwarrantable jurisdiction over us. We have reminded them of the circumstances of our emigration and settlement here. We have appealed to their native justice and magnanimity, and we have conjured them by the ties of our common kindred to disavow these usurpations, which, would inevitably interrupt our connections and correspondence. They too have been deaf to the voice of justice and of consanguinity. We must, therefore, acquiesce in the necessity, which denounces our Separation, and hold them, as we hold the rest of mankind, Enemies in War, in Peace Friends.

We, therefore, the Representatives of the united States of America, in General Congress, Assembled, appealing to the Supreme Judge of the world for the rectitude of our intentions, do, in the Name, and by Authority of the good People of these Colonies, solemnly publish and declare, That these United Colonies are, and of Right ought to be Free and Independent States; that they are Absolved from all Allegiance to the British Crown, and that all political connection between them and the State of Great Britain, is and ought to be totally dissolved; and that as Free and Independent States, they have full Power to levy War, conclude Peace, contract Alliances, establish Commerce, and to do all other Acts and Things which Independent States may of right do. And for the support of this Declaration, with a firm reliance on the Protection of Divine Providence, we mutually pledge to each other our Lives, our Fortunes and our sacred Honor. Signed by order of and in the name of Congress,

John Hancock, president, [22]
Attested by, Charles Tompson, secretary.

Section C, page 232, line 33.

Response ([23]) *of the governor of Virginia, to the address which the Council and the House of Burgesses sent to him on the occasion of the message which His Excellency left as he boarded the ship of war, the Fowey.*

"Gentlemen of the Council, Mr. Speaker, and
Gentlemen of the House of Burgesses.

In answer to your joint Address, presented by your deputies yesterday, I acquaint you, that it appears to me the commotions among the People, and their menaces and threats (an enumeration of which I forbear, out of tenderness) have been of such public notoriety, that you must suppose many of his Majesty's subjects in this Colony, whether they meditated or not, have at least manifested, such an inveteracy as justifies my suspicion that they would not hesitate to commit a Crime, which, horrid and atrocious as it is, I had just ground to apprehend. And when the disposition which the House of Burgesses have shown towards me, the returns they have made to the respect and civility which I have been forward to offer to them, the countenance they have given to the violent and disorderly proceedings of the People, his Majesty's magazine having been forced and rifled in the presence of some of the members of the House of Burgesses, and, by the information of the Committee of the House appointed to inspect the Magazine, no other endeavours have been used than to prevail on the People to return the Arms taken out, but not to commit the Persons in whose possession they were found, in order that they might be brought to the punishment due to so heinous an offence, no less against the peace and good order of the Country than the dignity and authority of the King; when a body of Men assembled in the City of *Williamsburg*, not only to the knowledge, but with the approbation of every body, for the avowed purpose of attacking a party of the King's forces, which, without the least foundation, it was reported were marching to my protection, and which, if true, ought to have been approved

292

and aided, not opposed and insulted, by all good and loyal Subjects; when especially the House of Burgesses, or a committee of the House (which is the same) has ventured upon a step fraught with the most alarming consequences, in ordering and appointing guards, without even consulting me, to mount in the city of *Williamsburg*, as is pretended, to protect the Magazine, but which may well be doubted, as there then remained nothing therein which required being guarded; but if otherwise, this step nevertheless shews a design to usurp the executive power, which, if it be persisted in, subverts the constitution: I say, when these circumstances are duly considered, I may submit it to your own judgment whether I could reasonably expect any good effect from communicating the ground of my uneasiness to you.

But as you are pleased, Gentlemen, now to assure me, that you will cheerfully concur in any measure that may be proposed proper for the security of myself and family, I leave to your own consideration whether that can be effected any other wise than by reinstating me in the full powers of my office, as his Majesty's representative, by opening the Courts of Justice, and restoring the energy of the Laws, which is all the security requisite for all parties; by disarming all independent companies, or other bodies of Men raised and acting in defiance of lawful authority, and by obliging those who have taken any of his Majesty's public store of Arms to deliver them up immediately; and, what is not less essential than any thing by your own example, and every means in your power, abolishing that Spirit of persecution, which, to the disgrace of humanity, now reigns, and pursues with menaces and acts of oppression, all persons who differ from the multitude in political opinion, or are attached from principles and duty to the service of their King and government; by which means, the deluded People never hearing but the disfigured side of a Story, their minds are continually kept in that ferment which subjects them forever to be imposed upon, and leads to the commission of any desperate Act, and endangers the general safety. For the more speedy accomplishment of these ends, and the great object and necessary business of the Sessions, I shall have no objection to your adjourning to the Town of *York*, where I shall meet you, and remain with you till your business be finished.

With respect to your entreaty that I should return to the Palace, as the most likely means of quieting the minds of the People, I must represent to you, that, unless there be among you a sincere and active desire to seize this opportunity, now offered to you by Parliament, of establishing the freedom of your Country upon a fixed and known foundation, and of uniting yourselves with your fellow subjects of *Great Britain* in one common bond of interest, and mutual assistance, my return to *Williamsburg* would be as fruitless to the People, as, possibly, it might be dangerous to myself. But if your proceedings manifest that happy disposition, which is to be desired ardently by every good friend to this as well as the Mother Country, I assure you, in the warmth of my heart, that I will return, with the greatest joy, and shall consider it as the most fortunate event of my Life if you give me an opportunity to be an instrument of promoting your happiness, and a mediator between you and the supreme authority, to obtain for you every explanation of your doubts, and the fullest conviction of the sincerity of their desire to confirm to you the undisturbed enjoyment of your rights and liberty; and I shall be well pleased, by bringing my family back again, that you should have such a pledge of my attachment to this Country, and of my wishes to cultivate a close and lasting intimacy with the inhabitants."

DUNMORE
June 10, 1775

To His Excellency the very honorable John, Earl of Dunmore, lieutenant of His Majesty, governor general of the colony and the domain of Virginia, and vice-admiral of the same place.

Address of the House of Burgesses. ([24])

"My Lord,

We his Majesty's dutiful and loyal Subjects, the Burgesses of *Virginia*, now met in General Assembly, have taken into our Consideration the joint Address of the two Houses of Parliament, his Majesty's answer, and the Resolution of the Commons which your Lordship has been pleased to lay before us, wishing nothing so sincerely as the perpetual continuance of that brotherly love which we bear to our fellow subjects of *Great Britain*, and still continuing to hope and believe that they do not approve the measures which have so long oppressed their brethren in *America*, we were pleased to receive your Lordship's notification that a benevolent tender had at length been made by the British House of Commons towards bringing to a good end our unhappy disputes with the Mother Country. Next to the possession of liberty my Lord we should consider such a reconciliation as the greatest of all human blessings. With these dispositions we entered into consideration of that Resolution: we examined it minutely; we viewed it in every point of light in which we were able to place it; and with pain and disappointment we must ultimately declare it only changes the form of oppression, without lightening its burthen we cannot, my Lord, close with the terms of that Resolution for these Reasons.

Because the British Parliament has no right to intermeddle with the support of civil Government in the Colonies. For us, not for them, has government been instituted here, agreeable to our Ideas provision has been made for such Officers as we think necessary for the Administration of public affairs; and we cannot conceive that any other legislature has right to prescribe either the number of pecuniary appointments of our Offices. As a proof that the Claim of Parliament to interfere in the necessary provisions for support of civil Government is novel and of a late

295

date we take leave to refer to an Act of our Assembly passed so long since as the thirty-second Year of the Reign of King *Charles* the second intituled *"An Act for raising a public revenue and for the better support of the Government of this his Majesty's Colony of Virginia."* This Act was brought over by *Lord Culpeper*, then Governor, under the great Seal of *England* and was enacted in the name of "the King's most excellent Majesty by and with the consent of the General Assembly."

Because, to render perpetual our exemption from an unjust taxation we must saddle ourselves with a perpetual tax adequate to the expectations and subject to the disposal of Parliament alone. Whereas we have right to give our Money, as the Parliament to theirs, without coersion, from time to time, as public exigencies may require. We conceive that we alone are the judges of the condition, circumstances and situation of our people, as the Parliament are of theirs. It is not merely the mode of raising, but the freedom of granting our money for which we have contended. Without this we possess no check on the royal prerogative; and, what must be lamented by dutiful and loyal Subjects, we should be stript of the only means as well of recommending this country to the favours of our most gracious sovereign, as of strengthening those bonds of Amity with our fellow-subjects which we would wish to remain indissoluble.

Because, on our undertaking to grant Money as is proposed, the Commons only resolve to forbear leaving pecuniary taxes on us; still leaving unrepealed their several Acts passed for the purposes of restraining the trade and altering the form of Government of the Eastern Colonies; extending the boundaries and changing the Government and Religion of *Quebec*; enlarging the jurisdiction of the Courts of Admiralty, taking from us the right of trial by jury; and transporting us into other Countries to be tried for Criminal Offenses. Standing Armies too are still to be kept among us, and the other numerous grievances of which ourselves and Sister-Colonies, separately and by our representatives in General Congress have so often complained are still to continue without redress.

Because at the very time of requiring from us Grants of money they are making disposition to invade us with large Armaments by sea and land, which is a stile of asking Gifts not reconcileable to our freedom. They are also proceeding to a repeti-

tion of injury by passing Acts for restraining the Commerce and Fisheries of the Provinces of *New England,* and for prohibiting the trade of the other Colonies with all parts of the world, except the Islands of *Great Britain, Ireland,* and the *West Indies,* this seems to bespeak no intention to discontinue the exercise of this usurped power over us in future.

Because, on our agreeing to contribute our proportion towards the common defence, they do not propose to lay open to us a free trade with all the World: whereas to us it appears just that those who bear equally the burthens of Government, should equally participate of its benefits. Either be contented with the monopoly of our Trade, which brings greater loss to us and benefit to them, than the amount of our proportional contributions to the common defence; or, if the latter be preferred, relinquish the former, and do not propose, by holding both, to exact from us double contributions. Yet we would remind Government that on former emergencies when called upon as a free people, however Cramped by this monopoly in our resources of wealth, we have liberally contributed to the common defence. Be assured then that we shall be generous in future as in past times, disdaining the Shackles of proportion when called to our free Station in the general system of the Empire.

Because the proposition now made to us involves the interest of all the other Colonies. We are now represented in General Congress by members approved by this House, where our former union it is hoped will be so strongly cemented that no partial applications can produce the slightest departure from the common cause, we consider ourselves as bound in honor as well as interest to share one general fate with our Sister Colonies, and should hold ourselves base deserters of that union to which we have acceded, were we to agree on any measures distinct and apart from them.

There was indeed a plan of accomodation offered in parliament, which though not entirely equal to the terms we had a right to ask, yet differed but in few points from what the General Congress had held out. Had Parliament been disposed sincerely as we are to bring about a reconciliation, reasonable Men had hoped that by meeting us on this ground, something might have been done. Lord *Chatham's* bill on the one part, and the terms of the Congress on the other, would have formed a basis for nego-

tiation, which a spirit of accomodation on both sides might perhaps have reconciled. It came recommended too from one whose successful experience in the art of Government should have ensured to it some attention from those to whom it was tendered. He had shewn to the World that *Great Britain* with her Colonies, united firmly under a just and honest government formed a power which might bid defiance to the most potent Enemies. With a Change of Ministers however, a total Change of Measures took place; the component parts of the empire have from that Moment been falling asunder, and a total annihilation of its weight in the political scale of the World seems justly to be apprehended.

These, my *Lord,* are our sentiments on this very important subject which we offer only as an individual part of the whole Empire. Final determination we leave to the General Congress now sitting, before whom we shall lay the papers your Lordship has communicated to us. To their wisdom we commit the improvement of this important advance; if it can be wrought into any good we are assured they will do it. To them also we refer the discovery of that proper method of representing our well founded grievances which your Lordship assures us will meet with the attention and regard so justly due to them. For ourselves, we have exhausted every mode of application which our invention could suggest as proper and promising. We have decently remonstrated with parliament, they have added new injuries to the old; we have wearied our King with supplications, he has not deigned to answer us; we have appealed to the native honour and justice of the British nation, their efforts in our favor have been hitherto ineffectual. What then remains to be done? That we commit our injuries to the evenhanded justice of that being who doth no wrong, earnestly beseeching him to illuminate the Counsels and prosper the endeavors of those to whom America hath confided her hopes; that thro' their wise direction we may again see reunited the blessings of Liberty and Property, and the most permanent Harmony with *Great Britain.*"

June 15, 1775

REMARKS

Addressed to the People of the United States, by the Author of these Enquiries, etc.

Probably the exercise of the legislative power will be nearly the same in all the States. In all will be found, at least in part, the objections I have always observed in Virginia. At the beginning of the sessions the least important matters are treated. Many do not care about going to the assembly before they begin to discuss those things which are most interesting. Others fear arriving before there is a sufficient number of their colleagues to begin the session. Indeed the number is scanty, and thus time passes uselessly.

When the session begins to become interesting, it requires painful diligence for which the health of some members is not equipped. Often night comes before the discussions are finished. Certain things have to be examined in committees before they are discussed in the General Assembly. Those who form these committees are obliged to take care of matters in the evening to continue the same work of the morning, and often to go to the Chamber of the Assembly without a break. After drawing up their deliberations in legal form for discussion by the entire legislative body, the state of lassitude to which their minds are reduced prevents them from examining with sufficient attention the changes proposed, which thus, although dictated by the desire for improvement or the achievement of certain objectives, have no other effect than to alter or to obscure the meaning. It is not rare that the General Assembly is obliged to wait for some committee to begin the discussions. Finally, because of this delay it often happens that the sessions last longer than they should, the members of the legislative body are all fatigued, some finding it impossible to continue their work until the end of the sessions and very important decisions being rushed through without sufficient discussion.

To obviate these inconveniences, we think that a standing committee of six persons should be established, whose only function would be to prepare the material for each coming session of the General Assembly. In this manner a great part of the work would be done in advance, the laws would be drawn up much better and, although the Assembly could change or reject the proposed articles and deliberate on others which had not been presented, presumably the handling and expediting of business would be greatly aided.

The president [Dr. James Blair] ([25]) of the University of Williamsburg is the author of this idea which he communicated to me two years ago. It appeared to me a good one, but instead of limiting the six persons to only these functions, it seems to me that several other advantages would be obtained from them.

In order to maintain a free government, a very essential point is that the offices which the nation entrusts to its agents have precisely only the necessary degree of power and authority. When too much power is given to them, one is exposed to tyranny; when too little is given to them, anarchy is to be feared.

I believe that vigilance in not gathering in the same individual all the advantages of authority and power would contribute infinitely to public security. In my opinion, power should reside in the legislative body, and esteem in the six of whom we have spoken and whom we might call elders or rather guardians or preservers of liberty.

To prevent them from having too much facility in enacting or revoking laws, the six might have the right to give the legislative body their objections in writing, and these objections could not be nullified except through a two-thirds or three-fourths vote. Everytime the legislative body refuses to examine the laws proposed by the six, or rejects them after having examined them (for this a simple majority would suffice), or better, every time the required majority of two-thirds or of three-fourths would enact others or revoke them, their only right and duty should be to inform the people on the matter.

The legislative body should do the same thing, so that the people have time, before the following session, to examine the subject and to weigh the reasons of the two parties, and thus they would be able to give the proper instructions to their representatives for the next session.

I should also like that, in the case of difference of opinion

between one body and the other, the number of *ayes* and *nays* be published, with the names of those who so voted, so that the people could know the capabilities and the intentions of each voter. I believe that this would serve to calm passions and render differences rare.

Such an institution, by adopting the system of dividing the representatives of the people into two Chambers, would obviate the objections to the simplicity of the system in the legislative branch, as we have discussed at the beginning of our remarks on governments.

Our constitutions declare, with reason, that the three powers, the legislative, the executive and the judiciary, must be separate and distinct, and absolutely independent of one another, but they do not indicate the manner of resolving the differences which could rise among them. Therefore it would be necessary in such a case to have recourse to a national body and, as the citizens have had the wisdom to renounce their right to vote personally on particular matters, it would be necessary to elect members of a *Convention,* which could occasion decisive delays. By approving the establishment of the six, these differences could be judged by them and by an equal number of members of a neutral department delegated by their colleagues.

The six could intervene also in particular lawsuits, civil and criminal, when one of the parties would be judged in one of the supreme courts. Partiality among colleagues is always to be feared, and this can give rise to suspicions injurious to a conscientious judge, who must make an announcement in someone's favor. I would like therefore that in such a case each party would be able to require that the affair be judged by the six and by an equal number of judges drawn from the various supreme courts.

The six could also still be useful in the executive branch. I would not want them to have the right to meddle in it but only to be obliged to help the first magistrate of the Republic with their advice whenever requested. I have already mentioned, speaking of the executive power, the reasons for which I think that the first magistrate should have the liberty to act without the intervention of councilors*. To have recourse to the council of the

*Colleagues of the first magistrate in the executive branch are called *councilors.*

301

six, who would be obliged, because of the nature of their functions, to reside in the capital, would render very rare the occasions when the first magistrate would have to have recourse to the counsel of his colleagues, who could then occupy themselves with their own private affairs, and in place of fixed salaries would content themselves with a remuneration proportionate to their work—at all times that they would be dedicating their time to the service of the public.

Various motives could render necessary the revision of the constitution. Experience can make it known as insufficient or defective, and some dangerous innovations can be introduced in it. Everyone has the right to inform his fellow-citizens, and to encourage them to convoke a *Convention.* But perhaps much time will pass before the majority of the counties and the districts of a state decide to make this decision. The extreme confidence that the people have in their representatives can easily lead them to suppose that their delegates would not neglect business of such great importance or neglect to pay attention to the advice of some individuals. The lack of trust in one's self could impede a citizen from venturing his own opinion.

Pennsylvania has wisely thought that such an objective as the simple right must not be abandoned, but that it is necessary to make of it an obligation. She has therefore established that a Council of Censors should be elected every seven years, their principal duty being to examine whether the Constitution needs reform, whether the legislative power should be rejected, or for any other reason, and if it does [need reform], the Council must order that a *Convention* be elected for this purpose.

The principle is as good as this manner of executing it is bad. Experience proves that it is dangerous to set a time for such an operation. Discontent and the desire for novelties are increased when a revision is certain; often this creates needs and intrigues, and cabals begin to use every effort two or three years in advance. Vigilance must be steady and not sporadic. Therefore it is necessary to entrust the care and to impose the obligation on persons whose employment is always constant. One could, for example, charge the six jointly with the legislative, executive and judicial branches, in the following manner: Two of the four bodies would have the right to order the first magistrate to convoke a *Convention,* for the purpose of reviewing the Con-

stitution; but in the legislative body, the relative majority should, to my mind, be sufficient; and in each of the others, the two-thirds would be necessary. Such an action should neither be too easy nor too difficult. Every individual can invite his fellow-citizens to convoke a Convention, but the right to make this convocation must not be given to too small a number of persons.

The six should be elected by the legislative body, and none of them should be dismissed without a trial on which the judges of all the supreme courts preside. Since they dedicate themselves entirely to the service of the country, their salary should be of a nature to enable them to earn enough so that with their families they have the means for an honest livelihood. These six offices should be regarded as an honorable refuge for those who would distinguish themselves by their talents and their virtues, and there is much room to believe that the representatives of the people, obligated to elect these guardians who should be considered as the fathers of the nation, would select men for whom they have sentiments of esteem.

The spirit of economy that reigns in America, as regards public expenses, must not fear the extra expense that would be caused by the proposed system, since the savings alone that would result from the prompt execution of the affairs of the legislative department would be sufficient to compensate for these expenses.

Such an institution would also be suitable to a people that would adopt the system of legislation, contained in the four letters of the citizen from New Haven.

The formation of grand juries, without whose approval one could not conduct a trial—such as those which may occasion capital punishment—must be recognized among the salutary laws that our ancestors have brought from England. There exists in the small Republic of Lucca [Italy] a similar precaution for civil affairs that I would desire to see adopted in our constitutions. Six of the most distinguished persons, because of their merit, are entrusted to examine the nature of a trial, before it can be presented in court. Their opinion has great weight and many trials are avoided in this way.([26])

TRANSLATOR'S NOTES

1. (p. 132) Marie-Jean-Antoine-Nicolas Caritat, Marquis de Condorcet (1743-1794), philosopher, mathematician and politician. In a letter to Madison from Paris, Mazzei wrote (August 14, 1786) that the four letters by M. de Condorcet would appear at the end of his book. Actually these letters are at the end of the first volume of Mazzei's book as it was finally printed. They are called "Lettres d'un Bourgeois de New-Heaven à un Citoyen de Virginie, sur l'inutilité de partager le pouvoir legislatif entre plusiers corps." Condorcet's name does not appear as the author of them. See Mazzei, *Recherches historiques*, vol. 1, pp. 267-371.

2. (p. 135) Michel René Hilliard d'Auberteuil (1751-1789): *Essais historiques et politiques sur les Anglo-Américains* . . . Bruxelles: 1781–1782, 2 vols.; *Essais historiques et politiques sur la Révolution de l'Amérique Septentrionale* . . . Paris: 1783, 3 vols.; *Histoire de l'Administration de Lord North (1778–1782) et de la guerre de l'Amérique,* London and Paris: 1784; and *Miss MacRae,* roman historique, Philadelphia: 1784.

3. (p. 135) Guillaume-Thomas François Raynal, historian and philosopher (1713-1796): *Histoire Philosophique et Politique des Établissements et du Commerce des Européens dans les deux Indes,* Amsterdam: 1770, 6 vols.; *Révolution de l'Amérique,* London: 1781; *Tableau et révolution des Colonies anglaises de l'Amérique Septentrionale,* Amsterdam: 1781, 2 vols.; *Considerations sur la paix de 1783,* Berlin: 1783.

4. (p. 135) Gabriel Bonnot de Mably, French philosopher and historian (1709-1785). The book to which Mazzei refers is: *Observations sur le Gouvernement et les Lois des États-Unis d'Amérique,* Amsterdam: 1784.

5. (p. 144) David Hume (1711-1776): *The History of England,* London: 1754-62, 6 vols.

6. (p. 156) Ferdinando Gorges (1565-1647): *A Brief Narration of the Original Undertakings for the Advancement of Plantations in America,* London: 1658.

7. (p. 159) William Hubbard (1621-1704): *The Present State of New-England,* London: 1677.

8. (p. 170) Jeremy Belknap (1744-1798): *History of New Hampshire,* Philadelphia: 1784-92.

9. (p. 178) William Smith (1728-1793): *The History of the Province of New York, from the First Discovery,* London: 1757 and 1776.

10. (p. 192) Charles Louis de Secondat, Baron de Montesquieu (1689-1755): *De l'Esprit des lois,* Geneva: (Barrillot et Fils), 1748.

11. (p. 195) Hewit [Alexander Hewatt] (1745-1829): *An Historical Account of the Rise and Progress of the Colonies of South Carolina and Georgia,* London: 1779. (Hewat himself spelled his name with one "T". See: *Dictionary of American Biography,* Vol. 8.)

12. (p. 196) John Locke (1632-1704): *The Works of John Locke,* London: 1727.

13. (p. 213) Adam Anderson (1692-1765): *An Historical and Chronological Deduction of the Origin of Commerce, from the Earliest Accounts,* London: 1787-89.

14. (p. 229) George Washington's Commission reprinted in: Schroeder, John Frederick, *Life and Times of Washington,* Albany, N.Y., M.M. Belcher, 1903, Vol. 2, 732-733.

15. (p. 230) Edmund Burke (1729-1797): *The Remembrancer: or Impartial Repository of Public Events.* Seventeen volumes were issued from 1775 to 1784.

16. (p. 235) Resolution of May 15, 1776, of the Virginia Convention is from Peter Force's *American Archives,* 4th ser., v. 6, in the 1972 reprint issued by the Johnson Reprint Corp. in New York.

17. (p. 237) See: Henry Steele Commager, *Documents of American History,* 8th ed. New York, Appleton-Century-Crofts, 1968, 103–104.

18. (p. 240) Declaration of Rights. (See pp. 237–239.)

19. (p. 267) Cesare Bonesana, Marchese di Beccaria (1738-1794), Italian economist and criminologist: *Dei delitti e delle pene,* Milan: 1764.

20. (p. 275) F.N. Thorpe, ed. *Federal and State Constitutions,* Vol. V, p. 3076 ff. The Frame of Government of 1682, proving cumbersome and unsatisfactory in detail, was replaced by the Great Charter and Frame of April 2, 1683. The following year Penn returned to England. He soon fell into disfavor with King William and in 1692 his colony was taken away from him and placed under the authority of Governor Fletcher of New York. Two years later it was restored to Penn, but Penn was not able to return to America until 1699, and meanwhile affairs became thoroughly unsatisfactory and disorganized. Under these circumstances, Penn agreed to the appointment of committees from the council and assembly to draft a new frame of government. This charter, finally agreed upon October 28, 1701, remained in force until the Revolution.

21. (p. 288) Text of Declaration of Independence in Revised Statutes (ed. 1878). Facsimile of the engrossed copy in Force's *American Archives,* Series V., I., 1597.

22. (p. 291) After the Declaration of Independence was signed by John Hancock as President, the following names were appended to it:

New Hampshire: Josiah Bartlett, Wm. Whipple, Matthew Thornton.

Massachusetts Bay: Saml. Adams, John Adams, Robt. Treat Paine, Elbridge Gerry.

Rhode Island: Step. Hopkins, William Ellery.

Connecticut: Roger Sherman, Sam'el Huntington, Wm. Williams, Oliver Wolcott.

New York: Wm. Floyd, Phil. Livingston, Frans. Lewis, Lewis Morris.
New Jersey: Richd. Stockton, Jno. Witherspoon, Fras. Hopkinson, John Hart, Abra. Clark.
Pennsylvania: Robt. Morris, Benjamin Rush, Benja. Franklin, John Morton, Geo. Clymer, Jas. Smith, Geo. Taylor, James Wilson, Geo. Ross.
Delaware: Caesar Rodney, Geo. Read, Tho. M'Kean.
Maryland: Samuel Chase, Wm. Paca, Thos. Stone, Charles Carroll of Carrollton.
Virginia: George Wythe, Richard Henry Lee, Th. Jefferson, Benja. Harrison, Thos. Nelson, jr., Francis Lightfoot Lee, Carter Braxton.
North Carolina: Wm. Hooper, Joseph Hewes, John Penn.
South Carolina: Edward Rutledge, Thos. Heyward, Junr., Thomas Lynch, Junr., Arthur Middleton.
Georgia: Button Gwinnett, Lyman Hall, Geo. Walton.
Mr. Ferdinand Jefferson, Keeper of the Rolls in the Department of State, at Washington, says: "The names of the signers are spelt above as in the facsimile of the original, but the punctuation of them is not always the same: neither do the names of the States appear in the facsimile of the original. The names of the signers of each State are grouped together in the facsimile of the original, except the name of Matthew Thornton, which follows that of Oliver Wolcott."

23. (p. 292) Lord Dunmore's response to the joint address of the Council and the House of Burgesses, read in the House of Burgesses on June 10, 1775. (See *Journals of the House of Burgesses of Virginia 1773-1776,* Richmond: 1905, xxiii, 301 p., edited by John Pendleton Kennedy.)

24. (p. 295) *Ibid.* Address of the House of Burgesses presented to Lord Dunmore, read on June 15, 1775.

25. (p. 300) According to *The History of the College of William and Mary . . .* prepared by the faculty of the College, 1874, p. 45, Dr. James Blair, a native of Scotland, and an Episcopal clergyman, was the first president of the College.

26. Notes on Colonies.

   A. *British Sovereigns during the Colonial Period:* Elizabeth I, 1558–1603; James I, 1603–1625; Charles I, 1625–1649; Commonwealth, 1649–1660 (Council of State, 1649–1653; Oliver Cromwell, Lord Protector, 1653–1658; Richard Cromwell, Lord Protector, 1658–1659); Charles II, 1660–1685; James II, 1685–1688; William and Mary (Joint rule), 1689–1694; William III, 1694–1702; Anne, 1702–1714; George I, 1714–1727; George II, 1727–1760; George III, 1760–1820.

   B. *Royal Charters cited by Mazzei*—Elizabeth I: March 25, 1584; Henry IV (France): 1603, 1606; James I: April 10, 1606, May 23, 1609, November 3, 1620, 1624; Charles I: 1629, June 10, 1632; Warwick: 1641, 1648; Charles II: April 23, 1662, June 8, 1662, March 12, 1664, June 24, 1668, June 29, 1674, March 4, 1681, March 24, 1662, 1667, June 9, 1728, 1732, 1752. Sub Charters—Cartier: 1683; William Penn: February 28, 1701.

   C. *Boundaries of Territorial Patents of the English and French Monarchs*

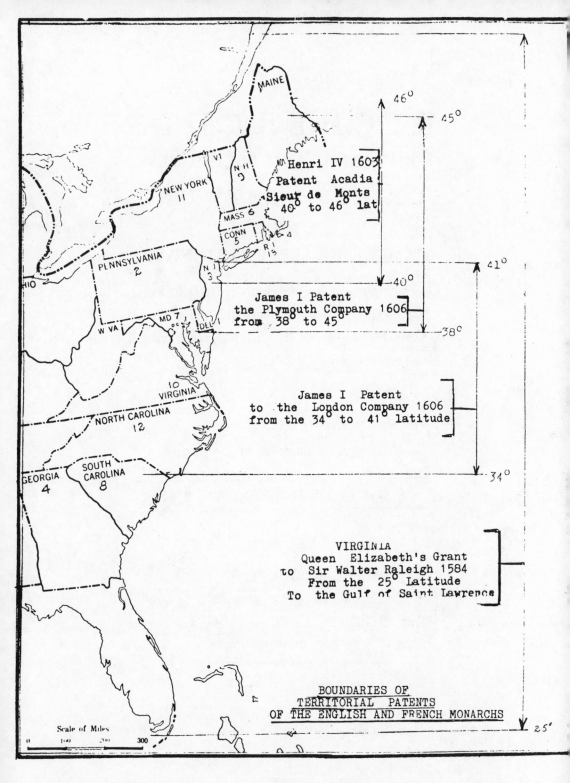

BOUNDARIES OF
TERRITORIAL PATENTS
OF THE ENGLISH AND FRENCH MONARCHS

307

RECHERCHES

HISTORIQUES ET POLITIQUES

SUR LES ÉTATS-UNIS

DE

L'AMÉRIQUE SEPTENTRIONALE;

Où l'on traite des établiſſemens des treize Colonies ; de leurs rapports & de leurs diſſentions avec la Grande-Bretagne, de leurs gouvernemens avant & après la révolution, &c.

PAR UN CITOYEN DE VIRGINIE,

Avec quatre Lettres d'un Bourgèois de New-Heaven ſur l'unité de la légiſlation.

PREMIÈRE PARTIE.

A COLLE,

Et ſe trouve A PARIS,

Chez FROULLÉ, libraire, quai des Auguſtins ; au coin de la rue Pavée.

1788.

DES COLONIES

QUI ONT DONNÉ NAISSANCE

AUX

TREIZE ÉTATS-UNIS

DE L'AMÉRIQUE.

Une Histoire complette de l'établissement des colonies, auxquelles les républiques américaines doivent leur origine, intéresseroit peu ceux qui n'ont aucune raison pour desirer d'en connoître toutes les particularités. Il y a beaucoup de chofes qui ne font faites que pour être conservées dans les dépôts publics. Nous croyons donc qu'une idée nette, sûre & précise des commencemens & des progrès de ces établissemens, sera suffisante. Ce qu'il importe le plus de connoître, c'est le caractère de ceux qui en jetèrent les fondemens, & leurs

Part. I.   A

DES

---

xvj   *INTRODUCTION.*

ciffemens & d'entrer dans des détails; deftinés tout-à-la fois à rendre les fujets plus intéreffans, & les réfutations moins arides. D'ailleurs, ces difcuffions peuvent fervir à réfuter les écarts des autres Ecrivains.

Some pages of Mazzei's *Recherches* . . . *(Courtesy, University of Pennsylvania Library)*

TABLE

ERRATA.

Page 104, note, au lieu de L.E, lisez L.F.

TABLE

DE LA QUATRIÈME PARTIE.

Title page and foreword of the German translation of Mazzei's *Recherches* . . . *(Courtesy, University of Pennsylvania Library)*

314

VERMISCHTE SCHRIFTEN.

PARIS, bey Froulé: *Recherches historiques & politiques sur les etats unis de l'amerique septentrionale.* 4 Bände. 1788. 8. (3 Rthl. 12 gr.)

Der Verf., ein geborner Virginier, der Europa und einen Theil der Levante durchreist ist, will in diesen Untersuchungen die falschen Nachrichten und Urtheile widerlegen, die durch Raynal, Mably und andere französische und englische Schriftsteller über die Geschichte der dreyzehn amerikanischen Freystaaten, ihre Beschaffenheit und ihren letzten Kampf mit Grosbrittannien, ins europäische Publicum gekommen. Er fühlte sich um desto mehr zu dieser undankbaren Arbeit verpflichtet, da er, wie seine Schrift aller Orten zeigt, sein Vaterland genau kennt, und häufig Zeuge war, wie man, vorzüglich in Frankreich, durch jene Schriftsteller verleitet, die sonderbarsten Meynungen von Nordamerika hegte. Im Ganzen betrachtet, wird keiner, der sich über den neuen Freystaat unterrichten will, dieses Werk ohne Nutzen durchlesen, wenn gleich der Patriotismus unsern Verf. zu oft hinreist, bey kleinen Unrichtigkeiten, einseitigen Urtheilen und Declamationen die Ehre seiner Landesleute angetastet zu glauben, und manche oft nicht genug gewählte Ausdrücke und Uebereilungsfehler mit zu grossem Geräusche, und zu vielem Wortaufwand als Beleidigungen, oder höchst gefährliche Irrthümer, widerlegt. Er würde auch seinem Werke einen höhern Werth in Europa verschafft haben, wenn er zuweilen bey seinen Widerlegungen tiefer in die Materien gedrungen, und Schriftsteller, die in Jedermanns Händen sind, wie *Jeffersons* Notes on Virginia, *Adams* Schrift gegen Raynal etc., weniger oft für sich hätte reden lassen. Wir zweifeln auch, daß es dem Verf. gelingen dürfte, durch die Geschichte der amerikanischen Revolution, der dabey vorgefallenen grossen Handlungen und edlen Züge ungeachtet, die der Streit für Freyheit und Vaterland so oft erzeugte, ähnliche Scenen der alten Geschichte, und die so lange bewunderten Thaten griechischer und römischer Helden, (so sehr dies auch

seine Absicht zu seyn scheint,) zu verdunkeln, oder sie so allgemein zu verbreiten, als jene Vorfälle durch öftere Wiederholungen in so vielen Jahrhunderten unter cultivirten Menschen bekannt geworden sind.

Der Verf. fängt mit einer kurzen Geschichte eines jeden Freystaats, und der ersten Nordamerikanischen Colonisation durch die Engländer an. Da er hier nicht vollständiger Geschichtschreiber seines Vaterlandes seyn, sondern nur eine anschauliche Uebersicht ihrer allmähligen Entstehung geben will, so rügen wir den Mangel an Detail nicht, das andere Schriftsteller über America vor unserm Verfasser voraus haben. Bey Pensilvanien haben wir indessen viel eigenes gefunden, und nach unserm Verf. verdient der Stifter dieser Colonie die Lobsprüche nicht, die man seit hundert Jahren ihm so freygebig ertheilt hat. Penn suchte keinesweges die Freyheit in Pensilvanien, sondern nur seine Gewalt, auszubreiten. Er belegte daher gleich nach seiner Ankunft die den Colonien zugetheilten Ländereyen mit einer beständigen Abgabe, worüber bald heftige Streitigkeiten zwischen beiden entstanden, selber aber trug er nichts zu den Landesabgaben bey, auch erlaubte er deswegen nicht, Privatcontracte mit den Wilden wegen Ländereyen zu schliessen, damit er nur das von ihnen unter öffentlicher Autorität erkaufte Land desto theurer wieder ausbringen möchte. Pensilvanien kam, dieser und andern vermeynten Bedruckungen ungeachtet, schneller empor, als andere Colonien, (die Ursachen werden auch davon angegeben,) auch thut der Vf. Herrn Penn bisweilen offenbar unrecht. So glaubt er, daß Penn seine Colonie von der königlichen Taxation absichtlich nicht habe befreyen wollen, und daher in seinem Freybrief setzen lassen, der König soll von Pensilvanien keine Taxen von Grundstücken oder andern Artikeln haben, *ohne Einwilligung des Eigenthümers oder der Assembly von Pensilvanien.* Allein dies sagt Penns Charter nicht, sondern hier steht mit dürren Worten, *that we* (Carl II) *shal at no time cause to set any imposition, custom or other taxation, unless with the Consent of the proprietary and assembly.* — Auch den ersten Anbau von Carolina,

und

First page of a four-page review of Mazzei's *Recherches* in a German literary magazine. *(Courtesy, New York Public Library)*

NOUVELLES LITTÉRAIRES.

RECHERCHES Historiques & Politiques sur les Etats-Unis de l'Amérique Septentrionale, où l'on traite des Etablissemens des Treize Colonies, de leurs rapports & de leurs dissentions avec la Grande-Bretagne, de leurs Gouvernemens avant & après la révolution, &c.; par un Citoyen de Virginie; avec 4 Lettres d'un Bourgeois de New-Heaven, sur l'unité de la Législation. 4 Vol. in-8°. A Colle; & se trouve à Paris, chez Froullé, Lib., quai des Augustins, au coin de la rue Pavée.

PREMIER EXTRAIT.

Depuis l'instant où les premiers regards de l'Europe se font tournés sur l'Amérique Septentrionale; une foule d'Ecrivains s'est efforcée de développer les causes, & les circonstances de la révolution qui a rendu à la liberté cette partie du Nouveau-Monde.

G 3

Mais, plus jaloux de satisfaire à la hâte la curiosité publique, que d'être utiles aux hommes par la justice & la vérité, la plupart n'ont fait que répandre en Europe des préjugés plus ou moins dangereux sur la conduite des Américains, & sur l'état de leurs Gouvernemens. Les uns, entraînés par une imagination déréglée qu'ils prenoient pour la force de l'ame, ou dominés par une humeur inquiète qu'ils croyoient être la sagesse, n'ont vu dans les objets que ce qu'ils avoient dans l'esprit, ont exagéré les motifs de leurs craintes & de leurs espérances, & ont mêlé a des évènemens chimériques ou faux, des éloges peu raisonnables & des critiques injustes. D'autres, guidés par des principes de politique absurdes, ou par des vues d'intérêt mieux déterminées, ont dénaturé volontairement tous les faits pour en calculer l'influence, d'après leurs idées ou d'après leurs passions. Presque tous, placés à une distance immense du théâtre de la révolution, étrangers aux Loix, aux mœurs, aux usages, aux opinions, à l'Histoire de ces Peuples qu'ils avoient la prétention de faire connoître à l'Europe, ont puisé, sans défiance & sans choix, dans des Papiers publics livrés à la corruption & à l'esprit de parti, tous les détails, toutes les réflexions dont ils ont formé leurs Ouvrages.

Ainsi se font répandues & se répandent encore chaque jour, sur les principes des

Beginning of lengthy book review by Condorcet, *Mercure de France*, February 23 and March 1, 1788. *(Courtesy, New York Public Library)*

First page of a four-page letter written by Mazzei in 1788, in which he derides the late Abbé de Mably. *(Courtesy, Dartmouth College)*

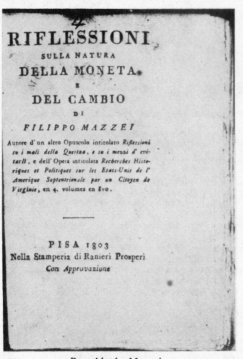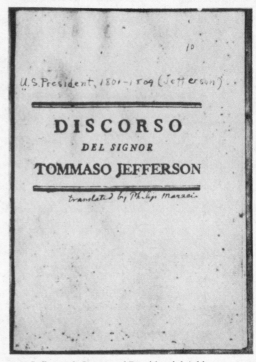

Pamphlet by Mazzei. Jefferson's Inaugural Presidential Address.

Title page and Index of pamphlet by Mazzei. *(Courtesy, Library of Congress)*

Veduta del Poggio a Cajano

Dear Sir.   New York. April 5. 1790.

On my arrival in Virginia after a short & pleasant passage I found my name announced in the newspapers as Secretary of state. I was surprised because I had answered negatively, to the question whether I would accept any post in the domestic adminis- -tration. I did not yet know that that answer had been so long on it's way that the nomination had taken place. still I thought I should easily decline it. but in the correspondence which took place between the President & myself, I found that while he left me constantly at perfect liberty to return to France, he wished me to undertake the new office, and indeed that the public, or so many of them as think of these things, wished I should do it. so I agreed after 3. months suspence to take the place which had been assigned me, and am now here in it's exercise. the short stay I made at home has doubled my propensity to return.

The diary I inclose of your affairs will let you see as much as I have been able to learn of them. on my arrival here I was at once immersed in such a mass of accumulated business, that I have not been able to enquire after Dohrman the answer as to his matter shall come with those of Blair & Randolph whenever I can get them.

I see no prospect of your professions in Virginia ris- -ing in value; on the contrary, they will continue to lose in value as they go more to ruin. I would advise you therefore to sell

Mr. Mazzei   them

Jefferson's letter of April 5, 1790, from New York, to Mazzei about his position as Secretary of State. *(Courtesy, Dartmouth College)*

them immediately, for whatever they will bring. were you to come to Colle yourself, all your arrangements would be to begin anew, & the money that will sell for will buy a smaller peice of better land. be so good as to do something definitive as to Anthony's claim for his passage. I was presented on the part of mr Bowdoin with a note of mine given for a debt of my brother's, which when settled by the table of depreciation came I think to about £ 18. I do not find this entered in your account & mine, tho' that account comprehends the period of it's date. I thought it possible therefore that it might have been settled in some other way. what increased my suspicion was that you have not assigned the bond to Bowdoin. I therefore refused to account to him for it, saying I would write to you, and consider myself as accountable to you alone. the shortness of time allowed me to write my letters and the multiplicity of them, public & private, prevents my entering into the subject of news. I must therefore only add assurances of the sincere esteem of Dear Sir

your friend & servt

Apr. 6. P.S. I sent your letter to Dohrman last night with information that if he chose to send an answer it must be here by noon to-day. it is now 9. aclock P.M. and no answer.

Th: Jefferson

321

1757–1834

From a French print made in 1781.

Letter from Lafayette to Mazzei. (Courtesy, Library of Congress)

Notes jotted down by Mazzei on a letter he received from Jefferson, dated April 3, 1790.
(*Courtesy, Dartmouth College*)

STANISLAUS AUGUSTUS PONIATOWSKI,
Last King of Poland.
From an engraving by Leney.

1732–1798

Excerpts from letters and reports of Philip Mazzei to King Stanislaus of Poland: a. Report no. 186 which speaks of American affairs and of Mazzei's imprisonment by the British; b. Report no. 221 in which Mazzei transcribes an *Anecdote concerning Mechanics*, sent by Franklin to De la Rochefoucauld; c. Letters of July 23, 1792, August 18, 1792, August 22, 1792. *(Courtesy, Biblioteca Nazionale di Firenze)*

parlò molto del Rè e della Pollonia con vero amichevole interesse. Mi accolse con istraordinaria gentilezza, mi fece comprendere ch'io non gli ero straniero, et dimostrò un gran piacere di sentire che ò l'onore di servire Sua Maestà.

Isaura, che ancora è qui, e che ripartirà per Nizza tra otto o dieci Giorni, à ricevuto una lettera dalla Principessa Marasciallo, nella quale gli dice che va a Torino, ma che pensa di ritornare a passar l'inverno a Nizza. Prima ch'ei ne partisse, essa aveva dichiarato che a — volova certamente andare in Pollonia, ed egli lo credeva, su di che mi burlai alquanto di lui. Ell'è cosa veramente inescusabile in uno che la conosce da tanto tempo il contare sulle di lei determinazioni. Egli pensa ch'Ella abbia avuto paura della guerra.

Il Conte Giuseppe Torelli mi fornì, a norma degli ordini di Sua Maestà, la formula dei ringraziamenti da farsi à Mr. de la Tour du Pin, e i materiali per servirmi di base onde giovare al Conte Ioacco. Iersera ebbi su di ciò una lunga conferenza col Conte di Gouvernet. Ò pronto il memoriale; ma esso mi consiglia a non darlo a suo Padre prima che l'Ass. Nazionale abbia dato l'ultima mano allo Stabilimento militare, e che si sappia in conseguenza qual che potrà farsi. Andrò per altro mercoledì prossimo a ringraziar Mr. de la Tour du Pin, da parte del Rè, per quel che à fatto a favor del Conte Giuseppe, conforme ò convenuto col figlio, a cui ò detto che dev'esser mio mentore, oltre il sollecitar l'affare presso il Padre. Son persuaso che, tanto il Padre che il figlio faranno il possibile, con buona grazia e con vera soddisfazione, per compiacere Sua Maestà.

I fogli stampati che pullularono, relativi alla gran giornata del 14, son generalmente male scritti, molti ripetono l'istesse cose, e niuno dice forse la centesima parte di quel che vi sarebbe da dire. La gente anche più scioperata à trascurato di leggere una gran parte di quelli che à comprati. Per uniformarmi al comando di Sua Maestà ne manderò qualcheduno, quando vi troverò, come nell'incluso, qualche cosa ch'io non abbia mandato stampata o manoscritta. La relazione contenuta nell'incluso è veridica senza esagerazione. Fortunatamente, il solo sbaglio che vi conosco, esiste nel disastro supposto al fine riguardo al ponte, poichè il vecchio Maresciallo di Mailli è vivo e sano, e un sol'uomo fù casualmente e molto leggermente ferito. Son persuaso che un'uomo attivo e intelligente potrebbe far due volumi bene interessanti, raccogliendo e mettendo in buon'ordine tutto ciò che è relazione direttamente o indirettamente alla festa della Confederazione. Nell'ultimo Mercurio si leggono i due seguenti versi; che un certo Mr. Lasquet, Aide Major dans l'armée patriotique Bordeloise, et député à la fédération générale, fece al ballo nel recinto della Bastiglia, la sera del 18.

» Autrefois dans ces murs, la honte de la France,
» On y trouvait la mort; aujourd'hui on y danse.

Se due lettere del 5 e del 9 Luglio, senza numero, sono di Mr. Faure, non di Mr. Gallois, il quale, conforme avevo detto nel mio Nº 209 del 16, era nel punto d'andare anch'esso in campagna.

Nel do. Nº 209 dissi: " Gradirei che il Piattoli

39

» sapesse chi è l'Autor del bullettino, e che me ne » dicesse il suo parere, tanto più che lo svanimento » della mia testa m'à impedito di avvertir Mr. Faure » di serbarmene la copia." Se non fosse troppo incomodo, sia per il Piattoli, o per qualcheduno dei Segretarj, bramerei d'aver una copia d'ambidue i Bullettini di Mr. Faure. Quanto agli originali, come pure ai 16 che scrisse Mr. Gallois nel mese d'Aprile, parmi che vi si potrebbe aggiugner nel margine d'ognuno Annesso (al Nº al quale appartengono, poichè dalla Campagna ò scritto sempre il giorno avanti) e aggiugnerli ai detti numeri, potendo forse un giorno esser utili per la ricerca di qualche notizia istorica.

Il Duca di Liancour, sapendo con quanta benignità il Rè accoglie le sue produzioni all'Assemblea Nazionale, mi pregò ieri di mettere ai suoi piedi l'incluso Troisième rapport du Comité de Mendicité. Eramo in casa della Duchessa d'Enville in numerosa compagnia, ove parlando della domanda fattami da Sua Maestà (riguardo ai nomi da darsi loro in futuro) e della mia risposta (quei di prima) il Duca della Rochefoucauld andò nel suo studio, e ritornato con un'aneddoto scritto di mano del Dr. Franklin, me lo diede dicendo: " potete mandarne una copia al Rè di Pollonia; probabilmente non gli dispiacerà."

Anecdote concerning Mechanics

In Philadelphia where there are no Noblesse, but the Inhabitants are all either Merchants or Mechanics, the Merchants about 40 years since set up an Assembly for dancing; and desiring to make a distinction and to assume a Rank above the Mechanics, they at first proposed this among the rules for regulating the Assembly; that, no mechanic or mechanic's Wife or daughter should be admitted on any terms. These rules being shown by a Manager to a friend for his opinion, he remarked that one of them excluded God almighty. How so? says the manager. Because, replied the friend, he is notoriously the greatest mechanic in the Universe. The intended new Gentlemen became asham'd of their rule, struck it out, and no ~~such~~ such distinction has ever since been made there.

Quantunque il Rè non mi abbia mai detto nulla, riguardo ai 2 piccoli scritti di Franklin, dei quali (per mancanza dell'originale) mandai la traduzion

* Copia dell' indicato articolo: " Quand Monsieur Mazzei sera à Vienne, ditez lui que je lui ai envoyé une lettre qui m'est venue
  " de Paris pour lui à Leipzig, car je croyais qu'il devoit y aller. Ditez lui, que j'ai reçu sa lettre n.o 1. de Cracovie du 23 Juillet
  " que je ne crois pas qu'il soit à propos de faire aller à sa destination l'autre lettre dont il m'a inclus le projet, et que si je ne lui
  " écris pas aujourd'hui moi même, c'est que cela m'est réellement impossible aujourd'hui, tant je suis accablé des affaires."

Dear Sir,   Monticello   Sep. 8. 95.

The first copy of my letter of May 30. went soon after that
date. a second copy accompanies this. soon after that date I
received letters from Mr Blair & Mr Madison, extracts from
which I now inclose you. by that from mr Madison you
will perceive that Dohrman alledges some deductions from
the sum claimed, if he accedes to mr Madison's proposition
of paying up what he acknoleges due, the money shall be
immediately remitted to Messrs. Van Staphorsts. if he does
not, it will afford a presumption that delay is his object.
and the whole sum must be demanded by legal process,
leaving to him to prove his discounts.

Considering your situation as stated by yourself & that
such feeble remittances (could only) be made from your
other resources, Mr Blair & myself concluded it better that
your stock in the funds should be sold. you will perceive
by the inclosed extract from him that the 2359.12 of all
descriptions mentioned in my letter of May 30. have sold
for 1972.56 including interest. Mr Blair has now delivered me
Wm Hodgson's bill of exchange on Messrs. Robinson, Saunderson &
Rumney of Whitehaven for £300. pounds sterling payable in London
to Ichabod Hunter or order who has endorsed it to Messrs. Van
Staphorsts & I this day inclose to them the 1st. of exchange, the
2d. & 3d. being to follow by other conveyances. this bill expresses
to be for £420. Virginia currency (1400 D.) received. but Mr Blair
tells me there is to be in fact a deduction of a few dollars in
                                                          your

Philip Mazzei

Jefferson's letter of September 8, 1795, from Monticello, to Mazzei in Pisa. *(Courtesy, Dartmouth College)*

your favour. he will invest the balance of the 1972:56 as soon as he can find a good bill & it shall be immediately transmitted to the Van Staphorsts.

Giannini's law suit is not yet come to trial.

We have no small news interesting to you since the date of my last. a treaty which has been concluded with England ^by the federal executive. through the agency of Mr Jay has excited a more general disgust than any public transaction since the days of our independance. it is thought to have stipulated some things beyond the power of the President & Senate, and that this will place us in an embarrassing situation. preferring now tranquility to every other object. I determine to take no part in the passions of the day, but to pursue my farm and my nailery, pay my taxes and leave public measures to those who have longer to live under them. I wish your Italy only lay on the other side of Chesapeak bay, that I might go and see it. if I were to take another voyage on this side the Styx, it would certainly be to see that. be this as it may, I am and always shall be with great & sincere esteem Dear Sir

Your affectionate friend
& sevt
Th Jefferson

330

All' Cittad.o Americano
à Pippo l'Ortolano } Mio caro Amico
Genova 15: Marzo 1804

L'Egregio Sen.r Paolo Celesia, mi comunica una vostra lettera, che sembra scritta all' Età di 30: Anni, eppure io so che avete i capelli bianchi come me = Mi congratulo della vostra Salute di Corpo, e della gioventù di Anima che mostrate = Iddio vi conservi = Il Guardo che avete fatto il Paese è tutto al natu= rale, e ciò è stato un colpo doloroso al mio Cuore = Voi Sapete, che la Toscana fu la mia Innamorata, ed io non ho potuto sgombrare il mio cuore da questo affetto quantunque la mia Bella amata mi abbia fatto un bosco di corna = Io non l'ho amata p me, ma totalm.e p lei, ed ero contento di vederla felice, anche ingrata = Io l'Amo benche la vedo corrotta, e guasta, e mi affligge spesso il sentire che non hà più i suoi costumi, che la facevano ammi= rare dagl' Esteri = Compagnie di ladri orga= =nizzati, Società di divoratori che si arricchiscono delle sue spoglie, e perfidi spioni che si fanno ingiuriare, non erano oggetti conosciuti in quel Paese = Sì che la Guerra corrompe tutto, ma la guerra si vidde cessare, è la Corruttela progre= =disce = L'Ignoranza si estende, e le Scienze che formano lo Spirito vanno decadendo, non si insegnano, ò si insegnano mascherate ò sboscia te e non si Studiano = L'Insegnam.to e lo Studio si Distinguono alle materie che promettono i profitti d' mestiere, e non Sarebbe poco, ma i lumi che coltivano e formano gli Spiriti, Res= =tano sepolti, e non Rinascono Senza prepare un periodo di funesta Barbarie che è Sempre troppo lungo = Questa è l' Idea che mi ha data

il mio

331

Caro e Amato Scipione,   Pisa, 5 Luglio, 1805.

Mazzei's letter to Scipione Piattoli, Pisa, July 3, 1803, signed "Pippo," (his nickname).
(Courtesy, Columbia University)

" an ironical eye to the modern detractions against Philosophy."

Le ragioni, o per dir meglio, i motivi che anno dato luogo a una gran parte di quel che dice Jefferson nel suo discorso, si vedono in un altro pezzo di gazzetta americana, che più è egualmente mandato; ma per ben comprendergli si richiedono notizie locali, che non potrei descrivervele in molti giorni quando ancora io fossi bene al fatto di tutte. Troverete la discussione sulla libertà della stampa di vostro vostro genio, ammirerete l'accennata sua opinione, che non dovrebbesi punirne legalmente nessuna la più sfrenata licenza, dopo d'esserne stato egli stesso il bersaglio. Dopo che codesto grande e degno soggetto ebbe letto 3 anni sono ai suoi amici il suo primo discorso inarguale, e quello dell'anno seguente nel quale propose al Congresso tante riforme salutari, e un articolo di lettera da Filadelfia scritta ad giorni dopo letta in Congresso le sue proposizioni, ove si vedeva il molto che era stato già fatto, e che tutto vi faceva unanimamente in ambedue le camere dissi con trasporto di gioia accennando il d° articolo di lettera) già si vede quanto bene può fare un sol uomo che unisce merito e cuore. Ora lo dirà, o piuttosto lo ripeterà con trasporto maggiore, e parteciperà della consolazione, che deve aver provata il suo e nostro Amico, per la stupenda notevole testimonianza ricevuta dagli abitanti di 17 Stati. La sua rielezione a avuto 162 voti contro 14. Macchiavelli ebbe ragione dicendo, che il Popolo nei particolari non s'inganna, e Jefferson l'à parimente, sostenendo che l'errore non può mai tenersi dove la discussione è libera. — Non mi maraviglio, Amico, di quel che mi dite di codesto Paese. Vi dissi io pure a Laubigow, che ci sarei rimasto, se fossi stato in età da potermici acclimatare. Non vedo altro Paese dopo gli Stati Uniti e la Russia, ove chiunque pensa e sente, come noi possa vivere con qualche soddisfazione. Scrissi tempo fa per sapere come potrei avere in America la pensione accordatami dall'Imperatore, mentre mi risolva d'andarvi a terminare i miei giorni. Fatene ricerca voi, vi prego, e ragguagliatemene. Datemi ancora qualche ragguaglio su quel che vi scrissi riguardo alla mia lettera al Conte Severino, relativamente al residuo del mio credito col suo fratello. Mandatemi sempre le lettere dirette a Diomede con i 2 // sul canto inferiore sinistro della soprascritta, e non le includete ad altri. Seguì un piccolo inconveniente per avvisi inclusa la vostra dei 13 Maggio a Marchisio. Amatemi, come vi amo, caro Amico, e adopratevi per sollevarmi, ne o realmente bisogno. Il vostro Pippo.

N.B. Unitamente al discorso di Jefferson, un breve Bullettino riferirà la pace conchiusa tra gli Stati Uniti e il Bey di Tripoli, e parlerà dell'imminente gita dello scrivente a Roma per commissione venetagli d'America.

À Monsieur

Monsieur Scipione Piattoli,

St Petersbourg.

Mazzei's letter to Thomas Jefferson, from Pisa, February 13, 1811, followed by first draft of the same letter. *(Courtesy, Columbia University)*

In quella dei 29 Marzo 1808

" Termino col raccomandarle al suo tenero cuore le 2 povere disgraziate sorelle
" del fù nostro Amico Bellini. Per ridurle a memoria l'occorrenza le includo
" le 2 lettere di Mr. Bracken, nella p.ma delle qli vi è l'abbozzo d'una mia ri
" sposta. Non comprendo un sì lungo silenzio, mentre non sia morto, come
" seguì di Mr. Andrews. Se ciò fosse, potrebbesi commetterne la cura a qualche
" altro Amico in Williamsburgo. Dopo una tanto lusinghevole aspettativa, un sì
" lungo ritardo, senza veruna notizia, rende quelle infelici giustamente impa
" zienti, e forse dubbiose della mia onestà. In una delle mie lettere mandate
" a suo mezzo a Mr. Bracken, lo pregai di mandare qualunque somma
" se riscossa, senz' aspettare d'aver il totale, poichè ogni piccolo soccorso è d'
" importanza per loro."

          e ✻ in quella dei 28 8bre, anno d.o

" Più volte Le ò parlato dell'infelice stato delle povere sorelle del Bellini ed
" ò richiesto la sua intercessione per dispor Mr. Bracken a mandar qualche pic
" cola somma, che abbia potuto ricavare dagli effetti lasciati dal nostro defunto
" Amico, il quale mi scrisse poter produrre circa mille talleri. Subito ch'Ella sarà di ritor
" no alla vita privata, spero che si degnerà di prendere a cuore questo caritatevo
" le affare."

          A tutto questo che dissi nelle mie citate lettere, aggiungerò solamente la
preghiera, la conclusione delle ✻ che l'interesse di quelle povere disgraziate sia preferita al mio proprio.

          Il 13 7bre 1807 Le scrissi per mezzo del mio buon' Amico Sig.r Federigo
Wollaston, il quale partiva per Filadelfia sul bastimento americano the Dispatch,
Cap.n Jacob Bewer, Le mandavo il seme di fragola d'ogni mese in una boccetti
na ben chiusa, e 12 bottiglie di moscadello di Montalcino, in una cassetta, dell'
istesso dei 30 fiaschi che Le avevo mandato in una cassa l'anno precedente, seg
giungendo che il d.o Amico era erudito, ingegnosissimo, di ottimo cuore, somma
mente prudente, e di una dolcezza di carattere veramente singolare. Se Ella
ne sa, o può saperne qualche cosa, La prego di liberarmi dal tetro timore,
che ne sia seguito quel che seguì del povere Timpanari.

          Questo desiderio (alla mia età) parrà chimerico e stravagante; ma un Marche
se Rinuccini fiorentino, stato Ministro di Toscana in Londra in tempo di Giorgio Primo
avanti che principiasse la corruzion parlamentaria, dopo d'esserne partito, soleva ogni
anno (finchè visse morì vecchissimo) andare a Londra per mare, e dopo 2 mesi
circa tornarsene per l'istessa strada, quantunque la navigazione sia molto più pe
ricolosa che nel traversar l'Atlantico, e non di rado più lunga, mediante la varietà
dei venti che vi bisognano. In somma, Car.mo e Stim.mo Sig.re ed Amico, l'unica mia e
gran consolazione sarebbe il lasciar, morendo, la vedova e l'orfanella in Patria
libera! Accetti intanto i miei sinceri ardenti voti per la prosperità sua e di tutta la
sua famiglia, e mi creda con sincera e costante amicizia, e venerazione per la
sua virtù,
                    Tutto suo,
                    Ct. M.

P.S. Quando ricevei il modello dell'Aratro, il Fabbr. era stato chiamato a Parigi
come Membro del Consiglio Legislativo; poi fu fatto Maitre de Requete coll'incom
benza di sovrintendere tutto quel che riguarda strade, ponti, &c di quà dall'Alpi, ed io

Car.^{mo} e Amat.^{mo} Signore, Pisa, 15 Febbraio, 1811

11

3.

L'anno passato in questo istesso mese, mi pervenne col modello del suo Aratro la graditissima sua data Washington 10 Febbraio 1809, ed io non ò mai potuto trovare alcun mezzo per farle pervenire la mia risposta, colla Procura che Ella mi richiede à la bontà di richiedermi. Ella dice: "In one of my former letters I advised you to sell your house and lot &c." Me ne ricordo bene, e Le ne mandai la Procura Duplicata, che (da quanto ella mi dice) congetturo che non le pervenne. Ora è tornato finalmente da Napoli Mr. Appleton il quale mi fa sperare di farlene pervenire per mezzo del nostro Ministro in Parigi. Per maggior cautela ne mando 3 copie. Io Le son molto grato della premura che mi dimostra per la mia figlia, che avrà 13 anni il 22 del prossimo Luglio; è grande per la sua età; la sua figura piace; à molto talento, e criterio; parla passabilmente bene la lingua francese; a impara con gran facilità a ricamare, a suonare il piano-forte, e a disegnare. Riaprendosi la comunicazione marittima, Le manderò qualcheduno dei suoi disegni. Ma quanto più volentieri La condurrei costà! Son 2 anni e 5 giorni, che VS. mi scrisse: I am panting for the tranquillity of Monticello. Io terminai gli 80 anni il 25 del passato dicembre; ma, (riaprendosi la comunicazione fra questo e codesto Paese, se Ella VS. volesse allontanarsene per venire a veder l'Italia, come in altro tempo desiderava) io ben volentieri L'accompagnerei per farne il giro, venderei quel che non potessi portar meco anche la metà del valore, e verrei con Lei portando meco tutto quel che à mobile) per aver la consolazione di lasciare alla mia morte la vedova e l'orfanina in Albemarle County nelle vicinanze di Monticello. Sei mesi potrebbero bastare per venire, vedere, e tornare.

Due volte Le ò parlato nelle mie lettere delle povere sorelle del Bellini, dopo d'averla notificato d'averne spedita la procura a Mr. Braker, il quale ne l'aveva chiesto, e d. che vi sarebbe stato da ricavare circa mille talleri. Nella mia dei 22 Giugno 1807 (che Ella mi dice d'aver ricevuto) La pregai di far notificare a Mr. Braker, che ne aveo ricevuta una dalle povere vecchie sorelle del Bellini, che dimostra la loro estrema miseria; e di pregarlo che avesse avuta la bontà di rimettermi qualunque piccola somma egli avesse realizzata senza aspettare d'aver realizzato il tutto. E del 10 Marzo 1808, io risposi come segue nella quale Ella mi dice: "In one of my former letters I advised you to sell your house & lot in Richmond &c." Io risposi all'indicata lettera, "Io includo la Procura che à la bontà di richie

quel tempo, io veduto, una sola volta in casa mia, dove venne la sera, e partì la mattina seguente. Quantunque le sue incombenze pubbliche sieno qua, se gli fa passare la massima parte del tempo in Parigi. Gli mi raccomando caldamente la traduzione dei fogli che lo riguardano, e di dargli tutta la pubblicità possibile. La traduzione è fatta, ma non perfettamente, perché ne ignoro i termini tecnici. Per me vi è anche l'ostacolo delle figure, nel l'Aratro che egli è intelligentissimo. Bisogna dunque ch'io aspetti Lui a poterlo rendere utile in questo paese. Intanto gradirei di sapere, se Ella à trovata la maniera di fare i 3 solchi nel tempo stesso.

Philip Mazzei's Death Certificate, March 19, 1816, Pisa. (*Courtesy, Comune di Pisa*)

PHILIPPO MAZZEIO
DE PODIO A CAIANO
VIRO FRUGI ATQUE INTEGERRIMO
CIVI OPTIMO VEL TEMPORIBUS MALIS
QUI
MORES HOMINUM MULTORUM
VIDIT ET URBES
IN FOEDERATIS SEPTEMTR. AMERICAE
PROVINCIIS CIVITATE DONATUS
LEGATIONE PRO IPSIS IN GALLIA
ET UNIVERSA EUROPA FUNCTUS EST
DEQUE REBUS IPSARUM PUBLICIS
COMMENTARIA SCRIPSIT EGREGIA
HUMANISSIMO POLONIAE REGI
STANISLAO PONIATOWSKI
A CUBICULO FUIT SECRETIORI
...... GALLOS ACCEPIT
...... REGNO ET REPUBLICA
NONNULLA DESUNT

...... DOMINI ......
OBIIT PISIS DIE 20 MARTII 181...

DIED—At Piza, in Tuscany, March 19th, in the 86th year of his age, Philip Mazzie, formerly a citizen of the United States, and author of a political and historical work on North America.

Mazzie was descended of respectable parentage in Tuscany, and received the best education its universities afforded. He early applied himself to medicine, a science, however, to which he was not attached, and it does not appear that he ever made any great acquisition in it. Endowed with a mind free and independent, and disdaining to reside in a country where superstition, bigotry, and tyranny opposed a barrier to all generous efforts in the cause of liberty and freedom, his affections were soon directed from the place which gave him birth.

After travelling over the eastern part of Europe, and acquiring a little fortune by trade, he established himself in business at London. But the ordinary routine of commercial transactions was little calculated to engross a mind like that of Mazzei, which sought a wide display for its talents. The rising colonies of Great Britain attracted his notice, and he was induced to embark his fortune for Virginia, where he attempted to introduce the culture of the vine, olive, and other fruits of his native country. In a short time after his arrival, hostilities commenced in which he manifested an enthusiastic zeal in favor of the cause of liberty. In 1779, he was sent by the state of Virginia on a secret mission to Europe. In 1785, he returned to America, but shortly afterwards re-embarked for France. We next find him at Paris, a member of the "corps diplomatique," at the French court, in the service of the king of Poland. The revolution in France drove him to Warsaw, in 1792, where he was made privy counsellor to Stanislaus Augustus. The subsequent dismemberment of Poland, and the misfortunes of its virtuous monarch, were productive of many changes in the affairs of Mazzei, who finally retired to Pisa, where, from a life of temperence, and a happy climate, he attained an advanced age.

Mazzei was a distinguished politician. In principles he was a republican, and a confessed enemy to tyrants, both of church and state. His work on America furnishes ample proof of his adherence to the best principles in politics.

He was possessed of a great ingeniousness of character, and simplicity of manners. His knowledge of mankind was extensive; and he was a profound adept in the science of human nature. Towards the United States his affections were entirely devoted; and his principal consolation in the decline of life, was derived from seeing that country flourish, of which he was proud to consider himself an adopted citizen.

Mazzei's obituary in the Richmond, Virginia, *Argus*, June 26, 1816.

340

1740–1799

Engraved by P. Maverick from a drawing by J.B. Longacre from Copley.

Annapolis 26th June 1774

Gentlemen

The inclosed Resolutions, which we are directed to communicate, contain the Sense of this Province of a Union and general Plan of Conduct, in Defence of the Liberties of America, in the present dangerous and truly alarming Crisis— We feel ourselves happy in the firm and steady Spirit which animates the People of this Province to pursue those Means, which they judge the most speedy and effectual to prevent the Fall of Boston and the Massachusetts Government; and by such Prevention to save America from Destruction.— It is our most fervent Wish and sanguine Hope, that your Colony has the same Disposition and Spirit, and that by a general Congress such a Plan may be struck out, as may effectually accomplish the grand Object in View.

We are also directed to propose, that the general Congress be held at the City of Philadelphia, the twentieth of September next. The Limits of our Province and the Number of its Inhabitants, compared with yours, afforded an Opportunity of collecting our general Sense, before the Sentiments of your Colony could be regularly ascertained; and therefore, as this Province had the first Opportunity

Resolution of the Committee of Correspondence for Virginia, dated June 26, 1774. One of the Signers was William Paca—also a Signer of the Declaration of Independence—whose ancestors were originally from Italy. *(Courtesy, The Pierpont Morgan Library)*

it has taken the Liberty of making the first Proposition.

We request that you will forward our Resolutions and Proposition to the Colonies Southward of you.— If any Circumstance unknown to us should render the Time or Place inconvenient to your Colony, you will oblige us by advising us of it, as soon as possible, and mentioning a Time and Place more agreeable.— We shall be thankful for a speedy Communication of every thing you may think of Consequence.

We are, Gentlemen,
with the utmost Respect,
Your most Obedient Servants

W. Johnson Jun.

Robt. Goldsborough

Wm Paca

Samuel Chase

To the Committee of Correspondence
for Virginia

343

A Declaration by the Representatives of the UNITED STATES OF AMERICA in General Congress assembled.

When in the course of human events it becomes necessary for one people to dissolve the political bands which have connected them with another, and to assume among the powers of the earth the separate and equal station to which the laws of nature & of nature's god entitle them, a decent respect to the opinions of mankind requires that they should declare the causes which impel them to the separation.

We hold these truths to be self evident; that all men are created equal; that they are endowed by their Creator with inherent & inalienable rights; that among these are life, liberty, & the pursuit of happiness; that to secure these rights, governments are instituted among men, deriving their just powers from the consent of the governed; that whenever any form of government becomes destructive of these ends, it is the right of the people to alter or to abolish it, and to institute new government, laying it's foundation on such principles & organising it's powers in such form as to them shall seem most likely to effect their safety & happiness. prudence indeed will dictate that governments long established should not be changed for light & transient causes. and accordingly all experience hath shewn that mankind are more disposed to suffer while evils are sufferable, ~~than to right~~ themselves by abolishing the forms they are accustomed. but when a long train of abuses & usurpations, begun at a distinguished period, & pursuing invariably the same object, evinces a design to reduce them under absolute despotism, it is their right, it is their duty, to throw off such government & to provide new guards for their future security. such has been the patient sufferance of these colonies; & such is now the necessity which constrains them to expunge their former systems of government. the history of the present king of Great Britain, is a history of unremitting injuries & usurpations, among which appears no solitary fact to contradict the uniform ~~tenor~~ of the rest; but all have in direct object the establishment of an absolute tyranny over these states. to prove this let facts be submitted to a candid world, for the truth of which we pledge a faith yet unsullied by falsehood. He has refused his assent to laws the most wholesome & necessary for the public good: he has forbidden his governors ~~to pass~~ laws of immediate & pressing importance, unless suspended in their operation till his assent should be obtained; & when so suspended, he has neglected utterly to attend to them: he has refused to pass other laws for the accomodation of large districts of people, unless those people would relinquish the right of representation in the legislature, a right inestimable to them & formidable to tyrants only:

Mazzei received what Jefferson called "the original" draft of the Declaration of Independence. (Courtesy, New York Public Library)

NOTIZIE DEL MONDO
Num.   SABATO 14. Settembre 1776.   74.

Italian translation of the Declaration of Independence in "Notizie del Mondo," Florence, Italy, September 14, 1776. *(Courtesy, New York Public Library)*

IN CONGRESS, JULY 4, 1776.

The unanimous Declaration of the thirteen united States of America.

When in the Course of human events, it becomes necessary for one people to dissolve the political bands which have connected them with another, and to assume among the powers of the earth, the separate and equal station to which the Laws of Nature and of Nature's God entitle them, a decent respect to the opinions of mankind requires that they should declare the causes which impel them to the separation.

We hold these truths to be self-evident, that all men are created equal, that they are endowed by their Creator with certain unalienable Rights, that among these are Life, Liberty and the pursuit of Happiness.—That to secure these rights, Governments are instituted among Men, deriving their just powers from the consent of the governed,—That whenever any Form of Government becomes destructive of these ends, it is the Right of the People to alter or to abolish it, and to institute new Government, laying its foundation on such principles and organizing its powers in such form, as to them shall seem most likely to effect their Safety and Happiness. Prudence, indeed, will dictate that Governments long established should not be changed for light and transient causes; and accordingly all experience hath shewn, that mankind are more disposed to suffer, while evils are sufferable, than to right themselves by abolishing the forms to which they are accustomed. But when a long train of abuses and usurpations, pursuing invariably the same Object evinces a design to reduce them under absolute Despotism, it is their right, it is their duty, to throw off such Government, and to provide new Guards for their future security.—Such has been the patient sufferance of these Colonies; and such is now the necessity which constrains them to alter their former Systems of Government. The history of the present King of Great Britain is a history of repeated injuries and usurpations, all having in direct object the establishment of an absolute Tyranny over these States. To prove this, let Facts be submitted to a candid world.

He has refused his Assent to Laws, the most wholesome and necessary for the public good.

He has forbidden his Governors to pass Laws of immediate and pressing importance, unless suspended in their operation till his Assent should be obtained; and when so suspended, he has utterly neglected to attend to them.

He has refused to pass other Laws for the accommodation of large districts of people, unless those people would relinquish the right of Representation in the Legislature, a right inestimable to them and formidable to tyrants only.

He has called together legislative bodies at places unusual, uncomfortable, and distant from the depository of their public Records, for the sole purpose of fatiguing them into compliance with his measures.

He has dissolved Representative Houses repeatedly, for opposing with manly firmness his invasions on the rights of the people.

He has refused for a long time, after such dissolutions, to cause others to be elected; whereby the Legislative powers, incapable of Annihilation, have returned to the People at large for their exercise; the State remaining in the mean time exposed to all the dangers of invasion from without, and convulsions within.

He has endeavoured to prevent the population of these States; for that purpose obstructing the Laws for Naturalization of Foreigners; refusing to pass others to encourage their migrations hither, and raising the conditions of new Appropriations of Lands.

He has obstructed the Administration of Justice, by refusing his Assent to Laws for establishing Judiciary powers.

He has made Judges dependent on his Will alone, for the tenure of their offices, and the amount and payment of their salaries.

He has erected a multitude of New Offices, and sent hither swarms of Officers to harrass our people, and eat out their substance.

He has kept among us, in times of peace, Standing Armies without the Consent of our legislatures.

He has affected to render the Military independent of and superior to the Civil power.

He has combined with others to subject us to a jurisdiction foreign to our constitution, and unacknowledged by our laws; giving his Assent to their Acts of pretended Legislation:

For quartering large bodies of armed troops among us:—For protecting them, by a mock Trial, from punishment for any Murders which they should commit on the Inhabitants of these States:—For cutting off our Trade with all parts of the world:—For imposing Taxes on us without our Consent:—For depriving us in many cases, of the benefits of Trial by Jury:—For transporting us beyond Seas to be tried for pretended offences:—For abolishing the free System of English Laws in a neighbouring Province, establishing therein an Arbitrary government, and enlarging its Boundaries so as to render it at once an example and fit instrument for introducing the same absolute rule into these Colonies:—For taking away our Charters, abolishing our most valuable Laws, and altering fundamentally the Forms of our Governments:—For suspending our own Legislatures, and declaring themselves invested with power to legislate for us in all cases whatsoever.

He has abdicated Government here, by declaring us out of his Protection and waging War against us.

He has plundered our seas, ravaged our Coasts, burnt our towns, and destroyed the lives of our people.

He is at this time transporting large Armies of foreign Mercenaries to compleat the works of death, desolation and tyranny, already begun with circumstances of Cruelty & perfidy

their country, to become the executioners of their friends and Brethren, or to fall themselves by their Hands. — He has excited domestic insurrections amongst us, and has endeavoured to bring on the inhabitants of our frontiers, the merciless Indian Savages, whose known rule of warfare, is an undistinguished destruction of all ages, sexes and conditions. In every stage of these Oppressions We have Petitioned for Redress in the most humble terms: Our repeated Petitions have been answered only by repeated injury. A Prince, whose character is thus marked by every act which may define a Tyrant, is unfit to be the ruler of a free people. Nor have We been wanting in attentions to our British brethren. We have warned them from time to time of attempts by their legislature to extend an unwarrantable jurisdiction over us. We have reminded them of the circumstances of our emigration and settlement here. We have appealed to their native justice and magnanimity, and we have conjured them by the ties of our common kindred to disavow these usurpations, which, would inevitably interrupt our connections and correspondence. They too have been deaf to the voice of justice and of consanguinity. We must, therefore, acquiesce in the necessity, which denounces our Separation, and hold them, as we hold the rest of mankind, Enemies in War, in Peace Friends.

We, therefore, the Representatives of the united States of America, in General Congress, Assembled, appealing to the Supreme Judge of the world for the rectitude of our intentions, do, in the Name, and by Authority of the good People of these Colonies, solemnly publish and declare, That these United Colonies are, and of Right ought to be Free and Independent States; that they are Absolved from all Allegiance to the British Crown, and that all political connection between them and the State of Great Britain, is and ought to be totally dissolved; and that as Free and Independent States, they have full Power to levy War, conclude Peace, contract Alliances, establish Commerce, and to do all other Acts and Things which Independent States may of right do. — And for the support of this Declaration, with a firm reliance on the Protection of divine Providence, we mutually pledge to each other our Lives, our Fortunes and our sacred Honor. —

John Hancock

Button Gwinnett
Lyman Hall
Geo Walton.

Wm Hooper
Joseph Hewes,
John Penn.

Edward Rutledge.
Tho° Heyward Jun°
Thomas Lynch Jun°
Arthur Middleton

Josiah Bartlett
Wm Whipple

Saml Adams
John Adams
Rob° Treat Paine
Elbridge Gerry

Step Hopkins
William Ellery

Roger Sherman
Sam° Huntington
Wm Williams
Oliver Wolcott

Matthew Thornton

Robt Morris
Benjamin Rush
Benj° Franklin
John Morton
Geo Clymer
Jas Smith
Geo. Taylor
James Wilson
Geo. Ross

Caesar Rodney
Geo Read
Tho M:Kean

Wm Floyd
Phil. Livingston
Frans Lewis
Lewis Morris

Richd Stockton
Jn° Witherspoon
Fra° Hopkinson
John Hart
Abra Clark

Samuel Chase
Wm Paca
Thos Stone
Charles Carroll of Carrollton

George Wythe
Richard Henry Lee
Th Jefferson
Benj° Harrison
Thos Nelson jr
Francis Lightfoot Lee
Carter Braxton

The Declaration of Independence from the engraving, by Durand, of the picture painted by John Trumbull for the rotunda of the Capitol at Washington.

Mazzei's name is in the 6th column of this list of Virginians who renounced allegiance to George III on April 21, 1779. (*Courtesy, Virginia Historical Society*)

Other books by Margherita Marchione:

L'Imagine Tesa (The Life and Works of Clemente Rebora). Preface by Giuseppe Prezzolini. Rome: Edizioni di Storia e Letteratura, 1960; enlarged edition, 1974.

Carteggio di Giovanni Boine, Volumes I-VI. Edited by Margherita Marchione and S. Eugene Scalia. Rome: Edizioni di Storia e Letteratura.
Vol. I, *Boine-Prezzolini (1908–1915).* Preface by Giuseppe Prezzolini, 1971.
Vol. II, *Boine-Emilio Cecchi* (1911–1917). Preface by Carlo Martini, 1972.
Vols. III-IV, Boine-*Amici del "Rinnovamento" (1905–1917).* Preface by Giancarlo Vigorelli, 1975.

Twentieth Century Italian Poetry (A Bilingual Anthology). Preface by Charles Angoff. Rutherford: Fairleigh Dickinson University Press, 1974.

Carteggio di Clemente Rebora, Volumes I-II. Preface by Carlo Bo. Rome: Edizioni di Storia e Letteratura, 1975.

Distribution U.S.A.: Religious Teachers Filippini
Villa Walsh
Morristown, N.J. 07960

Distribution abroad: Edizioni di Storia e Letteratura
Via Lancellotti 18
00186 Rome, Italy

The author gratefully acknowledges
the sincere dedication that marked the guidance
and assistance so ably rendered by
Mr. Mario De Vita, President,
Commercial Multicolor Corporation,
653 Eleventh Avenue
New York, N.Y. 10036

This book was typeset by
Unitron Graphics, Inc., New York, N.Y.,
in Times Roman and Caledonia
on a Linotron 505.

Where it is a duty to worship the sun it is
pretty sure to be a crime to examine the laws of heat.
John, Viscount Morley

SYNDICATE

IN THE SUN

by Hank Messick

THE MACMILLAN COMPANY, NEW YORK

To Richard E. Jaffe
A Very Special Agent

CONTENTS

PROLOGUE

I DEFY THE BUZZARDS

AND BREAK MY WORD

*

There was one slot left in the parking lot off Flagler. I put the VW into it, remembering wryly the warning that all cars in that lot were checked by sheriff's deputies. The white Mustang that had tailed me from Fort Lauderdale halted outside the lot as if the driver were undecided. I watched until he pulled onto the next side street and double-parked there, his motor idling.

Had proof been needed that a crisis was at hand, the expert tail job was evidence enough. In recent weeks the boys had become careless, or contemptuous, apparently considering it great sport to see how close they could stick to me. But the Mustang had hung far behind and it wasn't until I again took to I-95, after my fruitless detour by the Pink House, that I could be sure he was following.

I locked the car on getting out of it. One nice thing about a VW—when you lock the door you lock the gadget that unlocks the hood. And the gas tank is beneath the hood. Back in Newport a few years ago some unfriendly person put sugar into my tank, ruining the motor and leaving me stranded. The newspaper sent a plane to pick me up and I made my deadline, but it was a lesson I remembered. With this car they'd have to wreck the body to reach the tank.

Moving to the street, I looked east along Flagler. On the right, the narrow windows of the new Federal Building resembled gun slits in a massive concrete slab. I smiled at the thought, which was an old one. The building was a fortress in a sense, a citadel, standing strong against the organized cor-

1

ruption that a syndicate in the sun had created along the Gold Coast of Florida.

On the other side of the street was the Dade County Courthouse, tallest structure in Miami. I turned to face it. While waiting for the light to change, I looked upward at the weird pyramid topping the building. The vultures were out in force —black buzzards above the halls of justice.

Dodging a Cuban in a Cadillac, I crossed the street and ascended the long flight of stairs to the first floor lobby. The stink was the same as in county courthouses in Kentucky—a blend of urine, stale cigars, sweat, and fear. The crowd was larger than usual, much of it apparently an overflow from the sixth floor, where in a packed courtroom the highest-paid reporters of the nation were covering the farce they breathlessly called the Candy Mossler trial.

But my business was on the fifth floor, where the Dade County Grand Jury was sitting in emergency session.

No one was around as I got off the elevator. Apparently no editor knew the jury was meeting. Possibly not more than a hundred gangsters knew of it either. Par for the course, and as far as I was concerned all for the best. At least no one would scoop me if I got indicted.

The possibility I would be indicted was very real. We had been playing a dangerous game. A multimillion-dollar crime empire was at stake, and the time to put up or shut up had arrived. When Sam failed to make the meet that morning, I knew I had no choice. Someone had to give the jury the truth —today. It seemed that I was elected.

At the door of the grand jury chambers, I pressed the button. A buzzer sounded within, and an elderly bailiff opened the door. He knew me, but his face was expressionless.

"The jury wants to hear me," I said.

"Wait here," he replied, closing the door in my face.

I waited, puzzled. It was customary for witnesses to be admitted. Inside was a large room where they usually waited, safe from the prying eyes of reporters or gangsters, until

called into an inner chamber where the jury met. Why was I being kept in the hall? Was another witness ahead of me—someone they didn't want me to see?

I learned the answer later. While I waited in the hall, a bailiff entered Room 633 on the floor above. He approached the table where State Attorney Richard Gerstein sat with his assistants and gave Gerstein a note. The crowd of reporters who watched every move speculated the message might concern a new development in the Mossler case. Their interest grew as Gerstein whispered something to his aides, then left the courtroom. But no reporter followed to see where he was going. After all, Candy was the principal attraction, and she remained in the courtroom.

Gerstein descended to the fifth floor by way of a back stairs. From the stairwell a side door opened into the grand jury area. The door was used occasionally by witnesses hoping to escape press photographers. Today, Gerstein used it to escape me.

Perhaps ten minutes after I was told to wait, the door to the hall opened, and the bailiff motioned. There was no more delay. We passed through the empty waiting room, and the bailiff pulled open the first of the two doors that led to the jury. I pushed the second door open and stepped into the presence of the twenty-three individuals who composed the jury.

The foreman, sitting at what ordinarily would have been the judge's bench, stood up to greet me. I felt the eyes of everyone, but I was looking too. In the split second as I turned to face the foreman, I spotted my man.

State Attorney Gerstein sat at the very rear of the room, almost hidden behind a mass of jurors. The light gleamed on his bald head, and I glimpsed the grim expression he had made into a trademark.

I kept my face impassive. If Gerstein wanted to play games, let him—but my stomach signaled my brain to be careful. At the witness stand there were the usual formalities: the oath to

tell the truth, the oath to keep secret all testimony, and finally, the signing of a waiver that surrendered my constitutional rights against self-incrimination. Anything I said could be used against me.

At an earlier appearance before a Dade Grand Jury, I had refused to sign such a waiver on the grounds it had become a tool to prevent juries from hearing the truth. Surely, I agreed, it would be nice if only persons with clean hands could be permitted to accuse others—but such honest citizens seldom have the inside knowledge needed for such accusations. To learn much about corruption it is necessary to hear from the corrupters.

I still felt the same way, but with Bad Eye—as Gerstein was known to gangsters—staring from the rear of the room, it was no time to be arguing principles. I wanted to be heard, and I signed the waiver without a word.

Sy Gelber, a studious young assistant state attorney, much admired by some of my newspaper colleagues, rose to question me. From the witness chair I could see his boss, still half hidden behind the jury. To hell with it. I cut short Gelber's preliminary questions and turned to the foreman. My words spilled out, angry, biting. I don't recall exactly what I said, and I couldn't legally report it if I did, but the gist of my remarks concerned conspiracy.

Yes, I said, there was a conspiracy—a conspiracy to penetrate the insulation with which the grand jury was surrounded and supply the jurors with the truth. The fact that honest men had to conspire like criminals to achieve such goals was, I said, quite a commentary on conditions in general and the state attorney's office in particular.

Gelber, somewhat desperate with his boss watching, interrupted me, tried to stem the flow of words with a counterattack. But I wasn't having any. I continued to talk, always aware of that silent, half-crouching figure at the rear of the room. And when at last I had made my point, I opened my

briefcase. Even Gelber shut up as I produced two sheets of paper and tossed them on the table in front of me.

"You want evidence, not hearsay," I told the jury. "There it is."

All eyes fastened on those pieces of brown copy paper—so innocent in appearance, so deadly in potential. Consisting of only three short paragraphs each, they could blow apart the invisible government that ruled Dade County, if properly used. There they were on the table. I had not planned to present them in this fashion. Indeed, I had promised not to make them public. But promises to me had been broken by frightened men, and I had no choice. It was in their interest as well as mine.

The foreman delivered a brief lecture. It was at once an apology, a defense, and a complaint. I scarcely heard it. What the jury thought of me was unimportant. What they thought about my evidence was all that mattered. When he was through, I walked stiffly to the double doors. The first one opened inward. I took a step forward and reached for the second door. Behind me I sensed movement. Deliberately I paused to look back. State Attorney Gerstein was on his feet, towering above the seated jurors. The "fighting DA" expression was firmly in place. His voice sounded crisp and cold.

"I have a statement to make."

Moving forward he became aware I was still at the door. He halted. Our eyes met. I laughed. Even to my own ears it sounded strange. He turned back toward the front of the room. I went out the door.

Moments later I felt the heat rising from the sidewalk as I left the building. And suddenly I felt empty. The strain of five months of investigation, of intrigue, drained my body. I found myself wondering why I had made the effort. No one was going to clean up this cesspool. It was like trying to empty Biscayne Bay with a leaky spoon. For too many years corruption had been a way of life here. The boys had become too

deeply entrenched. For three decades they had ruled the Gold Coast.

The feeling stayed with me as I crossed to the parking lot, where once more I looked at the top of the courthouse. Against the bright blue of the sky the buzzards were still circling. Somehow, there seemed to be more of them.

ONE

The job began in August. On the advice of various well-informed persons who understood the potential problems, I selected Fort Lauderdale as home and headquarters. The city is in Broward County, some twenty miles north of Miami. It has palm-shaded canals, beautiful ocean beaches, and, more uniquely, an honest and efficient police department.

Shortly after settling in an old house in the Rio Vista section, I called on Chief Lester Holt and presented certain credentials. The chief, a little man with a big reputation, accepted them without comment and promised to call. Two days later his aide Captain Floyd Hall telephoned, and I knew my home base was secure.

There were other problems. August is a bad month to begin life in south Florida. Away from the beaches the heat is intense and there is little breeze. Air conditioning is a necessity. There are insects, sudden rain squalls, and the threat of hurricanes to worry about as well.

Added to the natural discomforts were the tensions of beginning a new assignment. The editors of the Miami *Herald* were cooperative if skeptical. Managing Editor George Beebe was blunt:

"I'm told," he said, "that if I give you a free hand you'll surprise me. I doubt it. I think we have the crime situation pretty much under control, but I'm willing to be shown. Good luck."

He had given me that free hand as an "independent con-

tractor" assigned to investigate crime in south Florida. The newspaper couldn't tell me what to investigate or what to write, and I, in turn, couldn't require them to print anything I wrote. It was a good deal, but the contract allowed me only thirteen weeks in which to "surprise" Beebe.

The deadline didn't worry me after I inspected the newspaper's files. They contained no current information about organized crime. Apparently little of importance had been found to report since the Kefauver Committee hearings of 1950. Yet my assignment just completed—a two-year study for the Ford Foundations—had convinced me the Miami area was the crime capital of the country. The material was here. My problem was to dig it up in the time allotted. Once a start was made there would be new opportunities and the digging could continue.

I called at several offices where my reputation had preceded me and received unofficial, off-the-record briefings. They were rather general, but they confirmed my belief that organized crime ruled south Florida. Almost every racket known to man was operating: gambling, prostitution, abortions, organized jewel snatches, narcotics, protection, extortion, etc. Syndicate gangsters owned major hotels, restaurants, nightclubs and were heavy investors in service industries. Corruption was nearly complete. Anything and almost anyone was for sale, if the price was right.

The jewel snatches, alone of all the rackets, had recently created a degree of public indignation. After all, a retired executive resented the invasion of his plush home by gangsters, who tied up him and his family and ransacked the house at leisure. Occasionally, torture was employed, when hidden jewels were not easily located.

While the public muttered about the jewel thefts, the experts, not too surprisingly, considered the biggest problem to be illegal gambling. It provided the funds with which to corrupt officials. The annual "handle" of the numbers racket alone was estimated at one billion dollars. But the angry citi-

zens who waxed wroth about house burglaries never seemed to understand the basic fact—a cop bought by gamblers can also be bought by burglars. Gambling in south Florida still possessed more than a tinge of the respectability it enjoyed in the pre-Kefauver days of the S & G Syndicate. And now, as then, it financed a veritable civil service of crime. Officials came and went, but there was little change in the invisible bureaucracy operating just beneath the official surface. Old bagmen such as Houston (Red) Rainwater were still around, more powerful than ever.

My advisers were openly pessimistic. While wishing me luck, they doubted any dent could be made in the vast apathy of Gold Coast citizens. I didn't argue the point, but I had seen in Newport, Kentucky, what determined men could do in a similar situation. After a century of open vice, Newport revolted and largely cleansed itself. Many of the uprooted gangsters moved to south Florida. If they could be beaten once, they could be beaten again. The immediate problem was where to begin.

According to the men who should know, the numbers racket was the key. How then to penetrate it? Officially, no one could help me. Unofficially, however, it was another matter. I might not know why or how, but help would come. Go back to Fort Lauderdale and wait.

I accepted the situation. In the past on occasion I had received confidential data in plain envelopes and bearing no identification or signature. It was a rather awkward way to handle the problem of releasing information, but apparently it was considered safe. All I wanted, after all, was to be pointed in the right direction. I would get my own facts, draw my own conclusions.

Two days passed. The mail brought me nothing except elaborate invitations to avail myself of the services of one broker or another. I was flattered until I learned all newcomers to Fort Lauderdale receive similar letters. Apparently

the notion persists that only the wealthy can afford a home on
the Gold Coast.

Just as I was becoming impatient, a call came. The caller
was brusque and guarded. He asked questions to establish
my identity and my interests. We touched briefly on the
ground rules for confidential informants. Satisfied at last, the
caller proposed a meet. He named the time, the place, the
make of car he would be driving, and the color of the shirt he
would be wearing. He also gave me a warning:

"Make sure you're not tailed. They know all about you."

It bothered me. How could "they"—whoever they were—
know anything about me? As yet, I had made few contacts
outside of federal agencies and the Fort Lauderdale police.
Only three men at the *Herald* knew of my existence. Was the
leak there? It seemed unlikely. But so had the lack of current
information on crime seemed unlikely. What about Chief
Holt? He was highly recommended by federal agents. If he
was "wrong," then so were they. Was that impossible? Just a
few weeks earlier the head of the federal narcotics bureau in
Miami had been arrested on bribery charges and was awaiting
trial. In south Florida nothing was impossible if money was
involved.

It was a question only time could answer. Perhaps the unknown caller could tell me more about the leak—if any.
There was only one way to find out. Someone *had* told him
about me.

Down I–95 I drove, past the exits to Dania, Hollywood,
and Hallandale. In north Dade, I turned west as directed and
soon parked at a drugstore off State Road 7. Five minutes
passed before a white Buick pulled alongside. A round-faced
man with curly black hair leaned out and spoke through my
open window.

"Mr. Messick?" And then, "Were you tailed?"

Assured no one had followed me, the man still seemed to
be debating something. Possibly he was wondering if I would
know a tail when I saw one. Or, perhaps, he was just gather-

ing his courage. I have seen other men hesitate before saying the words that take them beyond the point of no return. Deciding to turn informer is a bit like getting married. Once certain things are said, you're committed.

When at last my new friend spoke, it was as if he was in a hurry. "Get in my car. We'll go somewhere and talk."

It was my turn to hesitate. The sun glistened on a puddle of water, survivor of a recent downpour. Two girls wearing skintight white shorts passed in front of my car. I caught a fragment of conversation. "He's a real swinger."

My companion was backing out even as I closed the door. He watched the rear-view mirror, and I watched his face. The car turned smoothly this way, then that. Soon I was lost. Within a minute we were away from the urbanized highway strip and into the wilds. Florida visitors who stay near the coast may be surprised to learn that only a few miles inland are vast stretches of semiswamp where homes are few. Stagnant canals crisscross the land, giving it form and character. The scattered small lakes only contribute to a sense of desolation.

So it was when the driver at last stopped the car under a huge live oak at the side of an unpaved road, my first comment seemed appropriate. "Looks like a good place to dump a body."

The driver chuckled. "They don't do much of that down here. It ain't necessary."

We faced each other. I saw a man of about my own age, short and stocky. His dark complexion hinted at what I later confirmed—he was of Greek descent. His clothes—knit shirt, slacks—were good but not flashy. I looked at his pinkie. The diamond that is the mark of a syndicate hood or a crooked cop was not present.

"Call me 'Charley,'" he said. "It ain't my real name, but it'll do for now."

"Call me 'Hank,'" I replied. "It isn't my real name either, but I'm used to it."

Formally we shook hands. He had a firm, warm clasp. It was the beginning of a relationship that would ultimately shake the Gold Coast. But I felt no premonitions. The stink of swamp was in my nostrils, and I was hot—sticky hot.

"I hear you want to know about the numbers racket," said Charley. "I can tell you all about it."

I said, "Before you do, tell me something else. What's your angle? What are you after?"

"Revenge," said Charley promptly. "Just plain revenge. I'm no do-gooder. I just figure they owe it to me."

"Why?"

The smile was gone now. "For eleven years I paid those bastards. Every week I'd get a call from Red Rainwater. 'When do we eat?' he'd say. Or, 'When's the party?' And I'd scrape up my ice payment and take it to him on his boat or wherever the damned drop happened to be. For eleven years I paid and then the pressure started and the numbers all went bad. I missed just three payments and the cops raided me. Fourteen cops, by God. You'd thought I was Trigger Mike Coppola or somebody."

"This pressure—where did it come from?"

Again Charley seemed to be debating something. Again caution was defeated. The words came as before in a rush. "It came from Fat Hymie Martin," he blurted. "From Fat Hymie and the syndicate."

One of the few rewards of crime reporting is the satisfaction that comes when assorted facts suddenly fit neatly into a pattern. The name, "Fat Hymie Martin," dropped snugly into a pattern I had recently spent a year developing.

My study for the Ford Foundation of the so-called Cleveland Syndicate touched the early career of Martin. In 1931, when the Cleveland boys were just beginning the transition from rum-running to gambling, Hymie played a key role. In those days he had been known as Pittsburgh Hymie, a sharp dresser and a lean and hungry hood.

When an ex-official of Cleveland was found murdered in a rented room, a wave of indignation swept the city and forced the usually tolerant police force into unwonted activity. It was established that the official, William E. Potter, had fallen on hard times prior to his death. The theory developed that Potter had been attempting to recoup by shaking down high members of the syndicate. His weapon was knowledge of their gambling operations.

Ultimately all signs pointed to Martin as the actual gunman. When finally captured some months later, he denied his guilt but was convicted in a sensational trial. Convictions meant as little then as later in the days of Dr. Sam Sheppard, and eventually Martin won a new trial. By the time he again appeared in court, some witness had vanished and others had changed their stories. Martin was acquitted the second time around and the question newspapers continued to ask— Who killed Bill Potter—was never officially answered.

Martin went back to Pittsburgh where he remained identified with the gaming activities of the expanding syndicate. Shortly before Prohibition officially ended, the syndicate joined with Meyer Lansky and others of the New York mob to form Molaska Corporation and produce a huge volume of illicit alcohol. The operation continued until 1937. Meantime, gambling casinos in Ohio prospered and in 1940 the syndicate moved into Newport, Kentucky. It also crossed the Ohio River at Huntington, West Virginia, and moved into the Wheeling area as well. Soon syndicate big shots were running casinos in the Miami area during the winter season. When new opportunities arose in Las Vegas, the old rum-runners were on the scene with the plush Desert Inn as a starter. Later they added the Stardust Club and moved on to establish a vast complex of related businesses. With Lansky's aid, they moved into Havana in the 1950's and operated the Nacional Casino. Unlike Lansky, however, they unloaded their property just before Castro took control.

If Martin was running the numbers racket in south Florida,

the chances were good that behind him were ex-rummies who once paid him to guard their boats on Lake Erie. Charley's figures confirmed the guess. Martin had muscled into the numbers racket to the point he now controlled 80 per cent of the action along the Gold Coast. On a given Saturday he might make $350,000, but if the number was "hot" he could lose a million. That kind of action required a bigger bankroll than a Fat Hymie could acquire on his own.

My suspicions became convictions when I checked some of my more official sources. Information was limited, but two of Martin's backers were known—George Gordon and a representative of the Eastern Syndicate.

Gordon I knew. Like Martin he had accompanied the syndicate in its growth since those days of generation on Lake Erie. In the 1940's he had been associated with the syndicate's plush Pettibone Club near Cleveland. In the 1950's he had been listed as a junior partner in the equally fabulous Beverly Hills Club near Newport. I had heard of him there in 1958 while covering that sin city for the Louisville *Courier-Journal*. In those days Gordon was considered little more than a high-ranking courier, carrying cash to syndicate members about the country from the gold mine that was Newport.

The other man I had heard of as a lieutenant of such men as Vincent (Jimmy Blue Eyes) Alo and Meyer Lansky. The fact that Gordon and the lieutenant were cooperating in supplying Martin with cash could only mean that the south Florida numbers racket was but another of those joint ventures within the framework of the National Syndicate. Such a development was logical enough. Miami had long been considered an "open" city. No one group or faction was permitted to dominate the area. Alo and Lansky maintained homes in nearby Hollywood—just up the road in Broward County. Gordon and his pal lived near each other in the little town of Surfside. Near at hand were two of Gordon's top bosses, Sam Tucker and Morris Kleinman. It was a comfortable arrangement all around.

To evaluate my new facts I made a special visit to the library of the Miami *Herald*. It was not a great shock to learn that Martin had apparently managed to keep his name out of the newspaper. As far as I could determine it had never appeared in public print in Florida. A little original research seemed overdue. I decided to return to Charley. His motives might be questionable but his information was current.

The next few weeks were busy ones as I was introduced to the man-made jungles of Miami and Dade County. Day and night blurred, as I sought to obtain as much information and insight as possible before my first story alerted the underworld and restricted my snooping.

In less than a day Charley and I achieved an empathy of purpose. He was eager and uncomplaining, asking nothing in return for the time and information he was providing. Occasionally he discussed a proposed venture into the tomato business with his brother-in-law, and spoke of the need to support his two children in college, but it was apparent revenge had the highest priority.

The question of how he learned of my activity continued to puzzle me long after I dismissed the possibility of a trap. A little probing was necessary to get the story. Charley was worried lest he compromise a friend, but as he gained confidence in me his fears began to evaporate. The story, when finally I heard it, raised as many new questions as it answered.

A gambler known as "Shoes" called Charley to a meet one day and told him of an experience in Fort Lauderdale. It seems Shoes had stopped for gasoline. While his tank was being filled he headed for the men's room but found it occupied. Two men were inside and they were talking. Shoes heard enough to understand that a secret agent was in town. The agent was posing as a writer and was calling himself "Hank Messick." He was going to expose the numbers racket. Something would have to be done about him before he learned too much.

Charley said Shoes identified one of the men as an agent of Fat Hymie Martin and the other as a Broward deputy sheriff.

Somehow, the story didn't ring true although it was obvious that Charley accepted it. Such things were routine enough in the strange world of the numbers racketeer. He explained further that Shoes passed the word on because Shoes knew that he, Charley, was bitter about the treatment he had received. After thinking about it for two days, Charley called person-to-person in Fort Lauderdale and, somewhat to his surprise, got through to me.

It still sounded strange. If Fat Hymie knew so much, what was he doing about it? And how about this "secret agent" jazz? That sounded like a certain friend of mine with a peculiar sense of humor?

Two months later my hunch was confirmed. Charley arranged for me to meet Shoes at the inevitable Howard Johnson's Restaurant. In south Florida the favorite spot for "meets" is a Howard Johnson's. As we left the restaurant, Shoes spoke for my ear alone. "We've got mutual friends," he whispered. "They asked me to help you so I gave Charley the word."

As it turned out I was glad to be so late in learning that Shoes was an informer. Spurred by Charley's very real fears that "they" knew all about me, we took special precautions. At the time they were designed to prevent Charley from being linked with me, but they proved valuable later when the invisible government made a serious effort to backtrack and learn how I got my information.

One phase of our security program required us to meet each day in a new place. Thus it was weeks before Charley took me to his home where I met his plump, red-headed wife and their three children. The two boys were getting ready to return to college, and the daughter was looking forward to her last year of high school. That their father had been a gambler engaged in illegal activity all his adult life didn't

seem to bother them nearly as much as the fact he was currently an unemployed gambler. Money was very short in that household and the pressure was on Charley to provide, somehow, the scratch that would enable his family to keep up with the Prokos boys. John and Chris Prokos were the two most successful gamblers of the Greek colony, and pillars in the local church.

Insight into the status system came one day as I waited for Charley to change his shirt. His wife excused herself to make a telephone call. She explained she had to ask the "preacher" about a church social. The "preacher" was out, but the maid wanted to talk.

"She asked what number is going to fall Saturday," said Charley's wife, hanging up with a satisfied smile. "Sometimes even the preacher asks. They think I have inside information."

Later, as we were driving toward the central Negro district of Miami, Charley commented bitterly, "It shows what the syndicate has done. Used to be everybody had a little confidence in 'Cuba.' Maybe they didn't trust bolita much, but they figured 'Cuba' was honest. Now they just don't know. They see outsiders running the show, and they think maybe there's a fix in somewhere."

I said, "But they keep on betting."

We swerved to avoid a stretch of broken pavement. "Yeah," said Charley. "They ain't got much else to do."

I looked around at the slums: at children with shirts on their backs and naked bottoms, at identical little houses with tiny porches, at the concrete and the two-foot strips of grass. Even the occasional palm trees seemed sickly, dispirited.

Charley was right—the people didn't have much else to do. But, I noted, in his voice no feeling of regret that such things should be. As I had learned, Charley had as healthy a contempt for Negroes as a New York Jew had for a Mississippi white man.

Well, no point in seeking to arouse compassion here.

Charley had problems of his own. Instead, I backed up a little to the business of our partnership.

"You say the Negroes think 'Cuba' may be fixed? Could they be right? Is it fixed?"

Charley laughed. "It ain't fixed unless Castro is fixing it. The boys tried to make a deal with Batista several years back. Offered him a cool million for just four numbers, and the bastard wouldn't take it. Said the Cuban National Lottery was sacred or something."

"Sacred?" I chuckled. "I didn't know Batista considered anything sacred. What was he talking about?"

Charley grinned as if I was betraying a secret knowledge worthy of a secret agent. In the tones of a man playing along with a joke, he continued, "That lottery has been running since 1909. Cubans live and breathe it. For years it was their one chance to make big money. Take that chance away— cheat just once—and you'd have a revolution. Even Batista didn't risk it. Castro tried to stop it when he took over, and couldn't. It was bigger than he was."

"Maybe he found a use for it," I muttered, but Charley's attention had been diverted. The time had come to see rather than hear. It was Saturday morning and we were about to visit some number writers at their "stations." In an hour or so the winning number would fall in Havana, and bettors had to move fast to get their dimes and quarters down.

We stopped in front of a three-story apartment house. The building was shaped like a "U." Balconies provided exterior hallways on the second and third floors. Grouped around the stairs at every landing were knots of men and a few women. Ragged children played in the courtyard where the original flowering shrubs, set out when the building was constructed, had abandoned all hope of a healthy life.

Charley had done much business in the district. He knew Negroes, and was usually accepted by them with a strange combination of respect and hostility. Respect, I assumed, because as a gambler and a white man he represented money.

Hostility, perhaps, because of the lingering conviction of the Negro that he was being cheated by white men.

It was a potentially explosive situation, and in the next few minutes I was to have dramatic proof.

The crowd on the stair moved their legs aside just enough for us to get by them. We climbed to the first landing and found the greatest concentration of people waiting outside the first door on the balcony. They were facing the door, their backs to us, and for a moment we were unnoticed. The entrance to the room was blocked. We were pushing forward into the crowd when I heard a low whistle from the stairs. Instantly faces turned backward, and we were spotted. The knot of men began to dissolve, and the way ahead was suddenly clear. I could see into the room—see an enormously fat woman seated on a couch.

The customers were retreating now to the balcony. We moved into the room. A white telephone sat on the couch beside the woman. It was an oddly jarring note in the dark room. There was also an open notebook on the couch. As we approached the woman reached out calmly to cover the notebook with a red towel.

Charley called the woman by name and introduced me as a friend interested in learning the business. The fat woman wasn't impressed. Her several chins jiggled as she shook her head.

"You'd better go. You're scaring my friends."

Again Charley tried as I made quick mental notes. The room was small but cluttered with furniture. The most conspicuous item was a large color television set. On the wall hung the famous picture by Karsh of John and Jacqueline Kennedy.

"Your friend looks like a cop," said the woman loudly. "My friends don't like cops."

There was a growl behind us. I glanced hastily over my shoulder. Three men had re-entered the room and others were crowding to the door. Two of the men were smiling. The

other held a knife. I couldn't be sure but it looked like a switchblade. Anyway, the blade was open. Briefly I wondered what Martin Luther King would say in such a situation. The man with the knife had no such problems.

"Beat it, white men," he snarled. "You've done been paid."

So they really thought I was a cop on a shakedown mission. Or was that just an excuse? Charley cursed in Greek, then very slowly pulled a hammerless .38 pistol from his pocket. The men watched as he raised the gun and gently scratched his head with the muzzle.

"We'll be going," he said in conversational tones.

Again there was motion as men stepped backward and to one side. A narrow lane formed and down it we walked. Charley led the way, still scratching his head as if bothered by an acute attack of dandruff.

The balcony and the stairs were still crowded but the path was open. No one spoke or sought to stop us. Only after we reached the courtyard did Charley put away his gun. I looked back. Most of the men had returned to the station. Only one man watched as we walked to the street.

"What was wrong?" I asked as we neared the car. "I thought for a minute we might cause a riot. Wasn't she one of your old writers?"

Charley said nothing until we were in the car and moving. When he spoke his voice was tired.

"She's a good writer. Makes $150 a week easy. She ain't about to take any chances with the syndicate. She knew damned well we weren't cops. That was just for the customers' benefit."

I did some mental arithmetic. Writers were allowed to keep fifteen per cent of total bets sold. That meant the fat old girl collected at least $1,000 a week from her "friends." And the bulk of the action came on Saturday mornings. No wonder she resented the interruption.

The next stop was on a narrow side street in front of a grocer. The owner, a balding Negro, was friendly enough.

Albert, the regular writer, was in the hospital. An ambulance came right up to the door and carried him away.

Two men who sat on empty soft-drink cases nodded their heads in mute agreement. Albert was gone, all right. But unasked questions hung in the air.

"I'm thirsty," said Charley. "Let's get a Coke."

We followed the owner into the hot dimness of the store where Charley fished around in a cooler and extracted two bottles. They were only slightly cooler than the air, but they were wet. Taking his time, Charley made small talk as we drank the Cokes. Finally, unhurriedly, he asked the key question. Who was handling Albert's business?

"He's out front," was the reply.

A young Negro stood up as we returned to the sunlight. Apparently a signal passed, but I couldn't detect it. Without a word the Negro led the way across the street. We followed him to a house. Planks had been nailed across the front door, and windows and a sign proclaimed the dwelling had been condemned as unfit for human occupancy.

The writer walked to the left, where a path had been worn in the brown grass. It led to the rear. The house was of the design known locally as a "Choo Choo"—consisting as it did of only three rooms, each behind the other in the fashion of railroad cars. A bullet fired through an open front door would pass out an open back door.

The back door was boarded up too, but the nails were loose in their holes and the planks could be lifted out easily. The writer lifted them out, and led the way through the rear to the central room. The only furniture there was a card table and a chair. On the table were pencils and a cigar box containing bills, change, and bet slips. A dog-eared "dream book" was on the floor.

Sitting down primly, the writer picked up a pencil and a "book" of bet tickets, then looked up expectantly.

"What's your pleasure?" he asked, speaking for the first time.

I put down one dollar on the number "43"—why, I don't know. The Negro wrote the ticket quickly, handing me the original and putting the carbon in his cigar box. Charley invested another dollar of my money in a parlay—picking numbers "14" and "41." If, when the number fell in Havana, my bet won, I would collect seventy dollars. If Charley's parlay was lucky, he would collect $2,000.

As we drove away Charley explained that the odds against his winning—even assuming an honest, unrigged drawing—were astronomical. The first prize number in Havana would have to end in "14," and either the second or third prize numbers would have to end in "41." Considering that 46,000 numbered balls were used in the lottery, the chances of hitting two out of the first three winners seemed rather remote indeed.

When I wondered if anyone ever won a parlay, Charley was quick to quash my doubts. Enough people won often enough, he said, that an ordinary independent operator would not accept more than a three dollar bet on a parlay. Men banked by the syndicate, however, would accept up to twenty dollars on a parlay and it was possible to place identical twenty-dollar bets with at least five of Hymie Martin's lieutenants.

"You can see why a man could clean up if he could fix 'Cuba,'" Charley said. "Five twenty-dollar parlays would mean a $200,000 payoff and that ain't bad for a day's work."

"But would Hymie pay off if he got hit like that?"

"Yeah," grunted Charley. "At least he ain't failed yet. Course nobody's hit him that hard, but there's been a few times when a hot number like 07 or 100 fell, and it cost the syndicate a mint. They had to delay the pay day a couple of times so they could send in the cash from Las Vegas."

Unlike the numbers game as played in New York, suckers in south Florida bet on two-digit numbers instead of three. The only exception is the hot "100." In addition to the Satur-

day drawing in Havana, there is also action based on a Monday drawing in San Juan, Puerto Rico. However, "PR," as it is known, was a new development, dating back to 1961.

Play on "PR" began, I learned, after the syndicate attempted to make a deal with Castro to control the Cuban lottery. Unwilling to bargain with the persons he had ousted from Havana's casinos, Castro flatly refused. Syndicate leaders were undiscouraged. To be consistently profitable, it was necessary to control the action. If Castro wouldn't cooperate, the only thing to do was find a substitute. The Mexican lottery was considered. It had one big advantage—semiweekly drawings—but the reliable controls required could not be guaranteed. Puerto Rico was selected.

All syndicate writers were instructed to sell "PR" as well as "Cuba," and to promote it. To aid the campaign it was decided that a series of "hot" numbers should fall in San Juan. The news spread quickly—to make money bet "PR." The plan was ultimately, when enough bettors shifted allegiance, to halt action based on "Cuba" and concentrate entirely on "PR." The Golden Age would then arrive for the operators.

As yet, according to Charley, the time to switch had not come. Many people had been attracted to "PR," but "Cuba" remained king. Tradition was a hard thing to overcome, but the syndicate was being patient about it. Sooner or later it would get its way.

Shortly after noon, and several more bets with friendly writers, Charley called it quits and we drove to his home to listen to the number fall in Havana. The station came in so clearly one could hear the balls rolling down a chute to the judges. One judge would read aloud the number on the ball that reached him. His companion would pick up a second ball released at the same time and announce the prize it represented. Since there were hundreds of prizes, no one could be sure when the first of five $10,000 prizes would "fall." A degree of suspense was created.

I found it hard to understand the Spanish numbers and I wondered why the thousands of bettors in south Florida were not equally confused. Charley assured me a solution had been arranged. When the first prize fell, a judge would rap three times with a gavel. Sure enough, after some fifteen minutes I heard the three measured thuds. Charley said the number announced was 17409. As far as most bettors in south Florida were concerned, only the last two digits, the "09," were important. It was a hot number, one upon which many people often bet.

"It's days like this that make me glad I'm out of the business," said Charley with a smile. "The boys will be hurting over this one."

He flipped off the radio. "No use to wait for the other numbers. My parlay is already lost. Would you like to go to a bolita drawing? I think I can arrange it."

Darkness hid the slums and let the yellow light from window and open door seem homey and attractive. We were in the vicinity of Twenty-ninth Avenue and Fifty-seventh Street in the northwest section. A young Negro with a thin black mustache and long sideburns was talking to Charley through the car window.

"The drawing is at nine," he said. "You can drive through once and get the lay of the land, but be careful. They got peepers out."

Slowly we drove down the narrow street. I noticed nothing abnormal. Only a few persons seemed to be moving about. Ahead of us children played kickball in the light of the one street lamp in the block. The kids scattered reluctantly as we approached.

"Over there," said Charley. "The house on the corner."

I got only a glimpse. A huge tractor-trailer was parked directly in front of the house, blocking the view. I saw little more than a lighted television screen glowing from a back porch.

"Pretty quiet," I muttered.

Charley laughed shortly. "In fifteen minutes you'll see a change."

He drove on for another block before turning to the right and back around the square. The man with the moustache appeared out of the darkness as we stopped at our former spot.

"Get out," he said. "Pass these around. You've got the peepers excited. They might call it off."

He thrust a bundle of handbills into the car. I took half of them and laughed out loud when I read the print. I was now to advertise the "Original Chicken Scratchers" who were appearing at a Negro nightclub.

"C'mon," said Charley. "White men own the joint so it'll look okay for us to be passing these things out."

He went down one side of the street while I took the other. Dark figures materialized at every house. The handbills were taken—sometimes with a muttered thanks, usually in silence. Several persons called from parked cars which had appeared to be empty. Apparently the peepers were too curious to remain concealed.

Returning to the car, I found Charley and his friend waiting. "Maybe it'll be okay now," the stranger said. "I just don't know."

"You're a worrier," said Charley. "That KY House ain't afraid of anything. They figure they got connections."

"That's for sure," said the Negro. He looked at his watch. "Well, give it a try. It's time."

Again we drove down the dark street. But now the night was full of movement. People were hurrying along the sidewalks. Other figures were crossing vacant lots. Cars became more and more numerous. When we reached the house on the corner, I counted fifteen cars where before only the tractor-trailer had been parked. The television screen was blank now and the porch crowded with people. Through an open window I glimpsed still more.

Charley drove by the house without hesitation and continued into the next block. Only when the row of parked cars ended did he stop. I got out, feeling suddenly alone in an alien world.

"Don't forget these," said Charley. "They're your passport." He gave me a new supply of handbills. "Play up the Original Chicken Scratchers if anybody stops you," he ordered. "I'll keep the motor running."

I began the walk back up the street. Some one hundred feet from the car I spotted a dark figure in a yard. I moved over and gave a man a handbill. Another man appeared, then two more. Soon I was one of several moving in small groups toward the house on the corner. The few who noticed me accepted handbills and seemed satisfied.

Leaving the street as we neared the house, I ducked in between parked cars. There, unobserved, I watched as the lamps of an approaching car lighted the area. The car double-parked in front of the house. A white man got out and moved in front of his still burning headlamps. I saw the crew cut, the regular features. This was Charles Blount, pickup man for the KY House—a syndicate-banked operation.

A Negro came out of the house. As he approached, Blount stepped back into the shadows. Apparently his moment in the lamplight had been for recognition purposes. The Negro and Blount chatted, as around them other people moved toward the house.

Agreement reached, Blount stepped to the rear and opened the car trunk. The lighted interior was plainly visible from my position. On the carpet was a large brown paper bag. It was full of something. I didn't have to wonder what.

Blount reached for the bag, closed the trunk, and, with the Negro trailing went into the house. There was excited chatter, as if Santa Claus were being greeted. A few stragglers hastened their step. I waited until they should be gone.

Through the window I could see movement. People were forming a circle. And suddenly through the darkness I heard

a noise—shuffle, shuffle—like a bag of dried beans blown by the wind.

Temptation overcame caution. I slipped from between the cars and started across the yard. Halfway to the window I was confronted by a man who seemed to materialize out of the ground. Automatically I held out the handbills.

"I'll take them in for you," he said. "Now beat it."

The noise from the house was louder. The bolita balls were being shaken prior to being tossed. I glanced around the yard. No one was visible. All attention was concentrated in that living room where drab lives were being touched by hope. I swung my fist. The blow landed on the man's chin, sending pain up my arm to my shoulder. The "peeper" staggered. I hit him again and he went down. A light breeze was just strong enough to spread the handbills that fell from his hand.

I hurried to the window. There, crouched on one knee, ready to run if spotted, I watched a bolita drawing.

Blount stood at the top of a rounded line of men and women. A green cloth bag was being shaken by a woman on his left. Apparently it had made the entire round, being shaken by everyone in turn. As I watched, Blount pointed to a white-haired Negro to his right. The woman cackled, "Here it comes," and the bag of balls flew through the air to the "catcher."

Whether the old man was prepared or not, I couldn't tell. He caught the bag with one hand, clutching a single ball and holding on tightly as the weight of the other balls dipped the bag toward the floor.

Blount stepped forward and "tied off" the ball grasped by the man. He used a rubber band to segregate it. The players were buzzing with excitement. All eyes were on the bag as Blount carried it back to his position. The man, who, I assumed, had chatted with him outside, stepped up with an empty green bag. Blount poured the balls ninety-nine of them—into the new sack, then tossed the original bag with its one ball to the center of the floor.

The chatter redoubled. Blount's helper was busy taking last-minute bets. This was the "house book," the exclusive right of the writer whose station was used for the drawing. No one else could write a bet at this point.

Behind me I heard a groan. The "peeper" was reviving. It was time to go. As I reached the street, Charley pulled up beside me and opened the door. I jumped into the still moving car, and we left the area.

After a Jack Daniels and water in the better lighted section, I felt sufficiently recovered to wonder about the winning number. Charley smiled. "Sorta gets you, don't it?"

To learn the winning number we drove south to the Coconut Grove section and the home of Gooch the Root Man. Gooch, an ancient and very dirty Negro, appeared to be in a trance when we pushed into his ground floor apartment. Above a cluttered table was a small bulletin board, and on it was posted a sheet of paper listing the numbers drawn at five syndicate bolita houses that night.

The KY House had drawn a cold 68. The Club House had a warmish 01. The Dixie House advertised a 47 and the Cadillac House an 82. Winning number at the Reno House was 60.

"Leave a dollar for Gooch," suggested Charley. "It's the standard price. When he comes out of that trance there'll be a dozen customers here wanting to know what number to play tomorrow. He charges them a buck for the information and then writes the tickets for them. Not bad, eh?"

For the first time I smelled the incense. So Gooch really was in a trance. Well, so were a lot of people in south Florida.

T W O

I MEET A BROAD

AND ALMOST BUY A BROTHEL

*

Children wearing bathing trunks sailed miniature boats in a large puddle left by the latest shower. Charley swerved to avoid them. We were in the northwest section on a typical summer day of dark thunderheads and bright sunlight.

The interview just ended had been with another frightened gambler. An older man, Honey was full of threats against the syndicate and promises of cooperation. But, as usual, the cooperation would come later—"when it will do some good."

I was getting a bit tired of hearing the same story from men who had lived so long in the shadow of the fix, they had forgotten, if they ever knew, how to deal with honest people. Apparently Charley sensed my feelings. Perhaps he shared them.

In any case his voice suddenly brightened. "Got an idea," he said. "Up the street there's something you have to see."

"What now?" I grumbled. "You got maybe the guy who stole the Star of India?"

Charley grinned. "Nothing like that but you could use a massage, couldn't you? Or maybe you ain't interested in sex."

"I got a guy who wants to sell me a whorehouse," I replied. "It sounds like a good deal, but you've kept me too busy with bolita to check it out."

"Good," said Charley. "This'll be an introduction."

He swung the car to the right and splashed into a parking lot fronting a neighborhood-type shopping center shaped like an "L." Unlike most such centers, however, the stores faced outward. We parked on the long side, near the corner.

"There's a massage parlor around there," Charley said. "Why don't you go in and ask for a massage? I'll get some cigarettes."

By now I knew there was a reason when Charley sent me in alone. I got out of the car and stepped into a puddle. Even behind dark glasses, I had to squint. Rounding the corner, I walked along the short side of the "L" to a window bearing faded lettering. Surprisingly, the door to the shop was ajar. Cold air gushed out through the opening.

Bells jingled as I pushed the door wide and entered a tiny reception room. Two chairs and a small table filled the space. To the left was a short, waist-high counter, which blocked entrance to what appeared to be a hall running off at right angles to the front of the building. There was a gate in the counter, but as I moved toward it a girl came out of the hall. She had dark hair, which hung page-boy style about her shoulders, and she was buttoning a silk blouse of flowery design.

I asked, "Is this the massage parlor?"

She smiled. Her teeth were white, and her eyes were dark. "Yes, it is. The sign that said so washed off some time back."

There was nothing under the blouse, I decided. Nothing but girl. "I'd like a massage, please."

The smile widened. "Who sent you?"

This, I guessed, was the place for a code word. Well, I could only bluff. The girl seemed friendly.

"Nobody sent me, honey. I heard you were here and thought I'd have a look.'

Her voice was teasing now. "Is that all you want—a look?"

"Not now it isn't."

She sighed, and managed to make it seem sincere. "I'm sorry. You'll have to talk to Kitty. She makes all the appointments."

"And where is Kitty?"

"She went to the delicatessen to get something for lunch. She'll be back any minute."

"I'll wait—if you don't mind."

"It's okay with me." She was almost whispering. "But push that door open a little more, please. Kitty keeps this place like an ice box and I'm not dressed for it."

Her eyes met mine. She was still teasing me. Deliberately I leaned across the counter. The girl stepped backward to improve the view. My hunch was right. Except for the blouse she was naked.

Well, I had seen naked women before. I glanced down the hall and counted five doors, each only a few feet apart. Massage rooms, no doubt.

The girl's voice was suddenly hard. "If you've had your look, how about that door?"

"At your service, mam."

I pushed the door open. The heat hit like a blow. For a moment it felt good.

"Thanks," said the girl. "Now why don't you sit down and wait? If things aren't done by the rules, Kitty tells Red Vaught."

The name came out too pat, too casually. It was supposed to mean something. Another test? I checked the impulse to leave, and turned to a chair. On the table was a magazine. I picked it up. One of the articles listed on the cover was titled "Sex Techniques in Marriage."

"Who the hell is Red Vaught?" I asked.

The girl laughed. "Maybe you are on the level."

"If ignorance of Red Vaught is the way you figure it," I told her, "I'm not only on the level, I'm downright square. Who is the guy?"

"He's a son of a bitch," said the girl in the same conversational tones. "He's a big shot. He lives on a yacht and is a friend of the cops."

"Sounds like the bolita business," I muttered, but the girl ignored it. She had unbuttoned the blouse and it gaped open as she put her elbows on the counter and rested her chin on

her hands. Small, pear-shaped breasts moved freely in the opening.

"I like you, mister," she said suddenly. "Red Vaught is a son of a bitch, but I like you. Whatta you think of that?"

I opened my mouth to say something—I don't know what —but the sound of a car's motor stopped me. The car had parked just outside. I dropped the magazine on the table and glanced out the door. An elderly black Cadillac sat there and a woman was backing out of the front seat. She was clutching a large brown bag. The groceries had arrived.

Kitty proved to be middle-aged, bulky, and businesslike. She interviewed me while unpacking tomatoes, bread, cheese, onions, and salami. When I couldn't produce a reference, she said I'd have to come back later. When I asked for an appointment, she said she was too busy right now to add new customers.

The girl took a bite of the king-sized sandwich the woman handed her and shook her head to indicate my cause was hopeless.

"Close the door as you leave," said Kitty. "It's a sin to waste this cool air."

Charley waited at the wheel of the car as I rounded the corner. He flipped his cigarette into the puddle, which by now had shrunk considerably, and mopped his face.

"Have fun?"

I got into the car. "This Red Vaught—just who is he?"

Charley started the motor. "He's a son of a bitch."

That made it unanimous. "I'd like to meet him. Got any ideas?"

"Well," said Charley, "if you was a cop it wouldn't be no problem. I hear he provided the girls last month to keep the witnesses in the Mossler case happy. Most of them were out-of-town cops here for the pretrial conference."

"Who arranged things?"

Charley tossed me a quick glance. "Are you kidding? Word was the whole deal was set up by the top brass. In fact so

many showed up to share the fun, Red had to send for more girls. The boys appreciated his cooperation so much they set him home in a police car after he got too drunk to drive."

I had been in south Florida a month, but the statement didn't shock me. It was but part of the pattern, part of the amoral society.

"How can I meet him?" I asked.

Charley backed out into the parking lot. "Just buy that whorehouse you were talking about, and you'll meet him fast enough. He'll come by to collect your dues."

"Maybe you've got something there," I said thoughtfully.

As we drove past the massage parlor on the way to the street, I noticed the drapes move. Someone was watching us leave. Well, perhaps it was a farewell of sorts. Or maybe Kitty was just getting our license number.

The man I wanted to talk to was calling himself Vic this summer. Two years before, when a federal agent introduced me to him, he was using another name. I was pretty sure that in a few weeks or months he would seek a new identity.

Short, slim, with a red face and buck teeth, Vic was not physically attractive, but he had a glib tongue, a long memory and—as one man put it rather ruefully—"balls."

Vic also had a basic conflict. He was torn between a desire to be a secret agent and what at times seemed to be an overpowering impulse to be a con man. When he was able to reconcile the two and direct his contempt of people against crooks, he sometimes achieved spectacular results. I knew from independent sources he had played a key role in several important narcotics cases by posing as a buyer. I also knew he had been arrested on charges of impersonating an FBI agent.

His greatest weakness was also his salvation. After listening to him boast, most people concluded he was an irresponsible liar. This, I had long ago decided, was the one thing that kept him from being murdered. Frankie Dio once broke Vic's nose, but under the circumstances it amounted to little more

than brushing away a gnat. Had Frankie believed Vic was telling the truth, he might have taken more drastic action.

I was one of the few people who took Vic seriously. That didn't mean I accepted everything he said, but I had learned never to disregard anything he said. So, a few weeks before, when he told me of a brothel for sale, I listened. His scheme, as usual, exceeded the bounds of the practical. He wanted me to buy the brothel, install microphones and cameras, and collect the evidence as corrupt officials trooped in with their hands out. Where I was to get the money was a problem Vic left for me to solve.

Shortly after getting home from the massage parlor, I was called by Vic. This was no coincidence. He had been calling every night for a week always eager, urgent, and completely undiscouragable. And tonight I didn't try.

"Ever hear of Red Vaught?" I asked.

"Sure," said Vic, "but I know him as Red Beau."

I had to laugh. Never yet had I named anyone Vic didn't know. As a good con man should, he read the newspapers carefully and retained most of what he read. Each morning he spent hours on the telephone checking his "sources." Yet always there was at least a grain of truth in his version of events.

Tonight he ignored my laugh and elaborated. "Red's in the rackets, see? He's a friend of Bessie. All right? He's also tied in with Bla Bla. You know him, don't you? Lives in Hollywood and bosses prostitution for the southeastern part of the country. All right? I can introduce you. The Feebees want him bad."

"Feebee" was Vic's name for the FBI—an organization he resented, since they objected to his attempt to impersonate a special agent. "Bla Bla" was an old-time syndicate hood, but not quite a regional coordinator. Bessie was the gal who had the brothel for sale, so I backtracked to her.

"When are you going to introduce me to Bessie?" I demanded. "She sounds more interesting."

There was a long pause. Sometimes, I decided, even Vic was a little surprised to be taken seriously.

"You mean it?" he said. "You're ready to talk business?"

"Set it up," I ordered grandly. "I've got a little free time now. Call me back when it's arranged."

"Right," said Vic, and hung up fast.

Ten minutes later he called back. Bessie was, of course, too busy to see me tonight. But she could make it tomorrow afternoon. How about 4 P.M. at the South Pacific on the Boulevard? He could pick me up about three o'clock and brief me on the deal.

I made the date—sighing a little at the prospect of having to listen to Vic for an hour. But I had plenty of desk work to do. A visit with a madam should add an episode of interest to an otherwise dull day.

Promptly at 3 P.M. next day Vic arrived. He was resplendent in a new jacket of some bright but unrecognizable color. Beneath the jacket he wore a vest that buttoned on one side. I looked at his shoes expecting to see spats.

We got into the Cadillac he had borrowed for the purpose and headed south along U.S. 1, which on the Gold Coast is known generally as Federal Highway. Inside Dade County it becomes Biscayne Boulevard. During the drive Vic "briefed" me once again.

Bessie Winkle was a long-time madam, who operated various brothels in south Florida. Of late she had concentrated on two houses, one north and the other south of the Dade-Broward County line. But her husband, who was a safe-cracker of some note back home in Indiana, had recently been sent to prison, and Bessie wanted to get rid of the Broward brothel.

Vic, posing as the secret owner of a Hollywood cab company, became friendly with Bessie and had been promised a commission if he could find a suitable buyer for the property. "Suitable" was the key word, for, as I was to learn, money

was not enough. A man had to have character references as well.

As we pulled into the parking lot beside a straw hut, Vic had one last suggestion. "Let me buy the drinks. After all, you're my guest."

He held out his hand and I put a twenty-dollar bill in it.

The bar was dimly lighted and almost deserted. Over in a corner a fat woman stared at an empty beer bottle. Vic noted it too.

He ordered drinks for us and pointed to the woman. "Give the lady over there whatever she wants," he said, tossing my money onto the bar.

The woman raised a red face, smiled happily, and ordered a double bourbon instead of another beer. When it arrived, she lifted her glass in salute. Vic acknowledged the gesture with a bow.

The bartender discussed the Cuban situation with Vic, while I let my eyes adjust to the gloom. There was just enough light, I decided, to make a fake diamond ring I had purchased at Hot Springs look real. I stuck it on my pinkie in the best gangster tradition. The fat woman finished her drink and was looking hopefully at Vic, when two women entered and her chance was lost. Instantly, Vic was off the bar stool and rushing to greet them. After seating them at a table in a far corner, he returned to the bar and ordered two screwdrivers. I picked up my Jack Daniels and followed him to the table.

Bessie was short and rather dumpy, about forty-five, I guessed, and 150 pounds. She wore a smart black cocktail dress and displayed white teeth as she smiled. The woman beside her was a younger, slimmer version of Bessie. I was not surprised when Bessie introduced her as a sister just down from Indianapolis.

Vic made small talk, while I tried to appear preoccupied and indifferent to Bessie's probing glance. I noted she kept looking at my ring, so I waved it at every opportunity. The drinks came—a fresh round for everyone thanks to Vic—and

we drank a toast to "Business." The sister tried to offer one to
"Pleasure," but Bessie ignored her and we played like gentlemen and pretended not to notice.

It seemed like an eternity before Vic cleared his throat and
suggested we put all cards on the table. After all, he told
Bessie, I was a very busy man and it had taken considerable
persuasion on his part to get me to the conference table. I
smiled depreciatingly and asked Bessie how much she wanted
for her "establishment." There was no hesitation in her reply.
She had to have $48,500 in cash. It would cost $55,000 if I
bought it through a broker.

I shrugged. What was $48,500 to me? My big concern was
the protection. If I invested that much money I wanted to be
sure I could operate unmolested. Bessie shrugged. Nothing to
worry about there, she said. I pressed for details. Bessie was
largely noncommittal. We seemed headed for a stalemate.

Vic sensed the problem. He motioned to Bessie and took
her to another table where he talked fast with many gestures.
Meanwhile, the sister mentioned Louisville. I remembered a
bustout joint and she knew the operator. From Louisville we
skipped north to Newport. I knew all the crooks there and so
did the sister. By the time Bessie and Vic returned, we were
chatting like old friends.

Either the sister signaled Bessie that I was all right, or Vic
had been convincing. In any case Bessie was a changed per-
sonality. Gone was the distrust, the caution.

Protection was no problem, she assured me. She would
help arrange it. I would have to pay roughly $2,000 to open
for business. "Key money" it was called. Monthly "ice payments" would total $1,000, but there would be only one
bagman. He would collect for everyone.

As for girls, Bessie would supply two in the beginning and
others as business increased. I should keep an open mind on
prices, adjusting them to whatever the "John" could pay. A
supermarket-type of operation was more profitable than a
specialty house, she advised, but of course that was my busi-

ness. Girls living on the premises would split the take fifty-fifty. Girls living off the premises got 60 per cent because they had to pay their own rent. I should develop a call-girl service as well. Girls were plentiful and I would have no trouble getting fresh young faces. In fact, if the truth be told, there were more whores wanting to hustle than there were beds available.

I made appropriate noises while Bessie's sister added a touch of realism by pressing my foot. Fortunately she was on the other side of the table and her reach was limited.

There was no need to worry about competition, Bessie said in reply to a question. If one place got too busy the waiting "Johns" were sent to another house. Cooperation was the rule. And I would be real busy. As soon as the season started all the old customers who knew the house would be back, and the word would spread. If I desired, however, I could do a little missionary work in certain bars. She would give me some names. But I shouldn't make any deals with cab drivers. That was old stuff—attracted too much attention.

When at last Bessie paused and beamed upon me, I waved my fake ring and in a harsh voice said all that was fine, but, by God, I wanted concrete proof I wouldn't be raided the night I opened. I might not know much about the prostitution racket, but I'd been around. I knew how things were handled sometimes.

Bessie nodded approval. She didn't blame me a bit. If it would quiet my fears, she would arrange for me to meet a ranking member of the Broward sheriff's department. He could guarantee protection and at the same time settle the details of how large my protection package would be. Did I want her to arrange a meet?

Did I indeed? I liked the idea so much I ordered another round of drinks. Vic held out his hand beneath the table, but I tossed my last C-note on the waiter's tray and ignored his frown.

Bessie was smiling. She wanted me to know she had been a

little skeptical of me at first. That's why she had been reluctant to talk.

I picked up my change from the waiter, leaving the silver and a five-dollar bill as a tip, and assured Bessie I understood. After all, I knew nothing about the prostitution racket.

Again she smiled. "I know," she said. "Vic told me."

When at last we were out in the street again, leaving Bessie and her sister to eat steaks, I asked Vic just what it was he told Bessie during their private conference.

"Nothing much," he replied airily. "I had to say something to make her trust you, so I said you were a dope peddler who lost his connection when that 'Fed' was caught. That was enough."

It was more than enough in my opinion.

Days of confusion followed. I waited for a call to the meeting with Bessie and the Fuzz. Twice appointments were made, then broken. I concluded Bessie had smelled a rat—meaning Vic—and the deal was off. When at last the call came I was in Miami, where Charley had just shown me a shady lane leading to the bolita counting house of the gambler I was later to know as Sam. It was an intriguing view, a narrow path just wide enough for an automobile and disappearing into what appeared to be a mangrove swamp. I wanted to go in but Charley warned me the gambler was a dead shot with rifle or handgun, so instead we went to a drugstore, and I called the office to learn Vic wanted me urgently.

When I called the number I could visualize Vic dancing up and down in impatience. Bessie had telephoned an hour before, he said, and set a meeting for 4 P.M. If I didn't make it the chance might be lost.

Saying goodbye to Charley, who declined my invitation to come along, I drove north up I–95 to Hollywood, where Vic waited in a cab he had borrowed for the occasion. On getting in, I discovered we were to go south again on Biscayne Boulevard.

The rendezvous was at an Italian restaurant, which proved
to be closed for the season. But up front was a liquor store,
and a nice old lady took me back into the deserted bar and
sold me a miniature Jack Daniels. The glass and ice were on
the house.

Fifteen minutes late was Bessie. She entered through the
liquor store. In the sunlight of the doorway she looked much
younger than in the shadows of the South Pacific. The sleeve-
less dress was low cut, displaying her plump figure to advantage but also exposing the scars of bullet wounds on the neck.
A customer had shot her a few months before, but she carried
on from the hospital bed without losing a night's business.

After all, she merely supervised the operation, and with
well-trained girls it was possible to do that by telephone.

I realized I was almost glad to see her, but it occurred to
me that the hard-boiled ex-dope peddler Vic represented me
to be might resent being kept waiting. So I wasted no time
after ordering her a miniature Jack Daniels in telling her what
I thought of the melodrama and the delay. She quickly apologized, explaining that while she had been satisfied, some of
"the boys" wanted to make sure I wasn't a Fed in disguise.

We finished the drinks and went out into the brightness.
Vic and his battered cab sat at the rear of the parking lot, but
we climbed into a brand new white Cadillac parked at the
front. Bessie explained as we moved into Biscayne Boulevard
that on a recent trip to Indiana her old Caddy—two years
old, that is—developed engine trouble. She got "disgusted,"
she said, and bought a new model.

Even the air conditioner made little noise as we headed
south—away from Broward County, where my brothel-to-be
was located. I debated the matter and decided my dignity
could stand a question.

Bessie smiled. She had planned to take me to see a Broward
deputy, she said, but on sober second thought had decided it
was wiser to go through channels. We were going to see Red.
Only he could give me an "okay" to operate. Without his

"okay," no agreement with a deputy was valid. I would be raided. Only independents who tried to operate without Red's permission got raided. I should remember that.

I agreed to remember but pretended to be puzzled. Why were we going to see a man in Dade County for permission to operate in Broward?

Bessie sighed. Apparently I was stupid. The racket was well organized. Dade or Broward it made no difference. The same rules applied.

We were on the Seventy-ninth Street Causeway, a beautiful street leading across to Miami Beach and containing—so once I had been told—more gangsters per block than any street on the Gold Coast.

Then we passed a plush spa. I barely had time to remember that the spa had once been the property of the Cleveland Syndicate. I asked Bessie if the syndicate still owned it. She didn't know. Nor had she heard of Pussy, Meyer Lansky's representative, who had worked there. It was my turn to feel superior.

Beyond the spa we stopped at the crossed racquets of the Racquet Club—an appropriate name for the place. Red was inside, Bessie said. She would get him. I played dumb. Was it Red Rainwater? No answer. Was it Red Vaught? The smile left her eyes. Red Vaught, sometimes known as "Little Red"?

"I never heard him called that," said Bessie loyally.

I could have told her something else he was called, but she gave me no opportunity. Within two minutes she was in and out of the club. With her came a well-proportioned man of about fifty. He wore a sports shirt, slacks, and white sneakers. Beneath his tan were huge freckles.

Bessie got into the front seat. Red slipped into the rear. I was introduced as Johnny Williams by Bessie, who then offered to leave us alone.

"That's not necessary," said Red. His voice was well modulated. "But start the air."

Bessie apologized profusely and the air conditioner began

humming faintly. I noticed she was perspiring heavily. It wasn't that hot.

Red wasted little time. "I understand you want an okay to operate," he said. "Why do you want to go into the business?"

I blamed Vic and he nodded. Apparently Bessie had briefed him well. Had I ever been in the rackets? I assured him I had been around and mentioned Newport. Immediately Red was interested. Years ago, he said, he had worked at the old Lookout House at nearby Covington, Kentucky. I mentally thanked the Ford Foundation, and mentioned Jimmy Brink —the man who had operated the casino for the Cleveland Syndicate. Sure enough, Red knew Jimmy well. In fact, he had flown Jimmy's plane shortly before Jimmy crashed near Atlanta. Did I remember that? Certainly. That was the time all those hundred-dollar bills spilled out of the burning plane.

Bessie was beaming. I sensed Red's reserve was melting. I would like the prostitution racket, he said. Not only was it profitable, it was fascinating. Always something new.

Bessie chimed in to agree the racket was worth a degree in abnormal psychology. I had the feeling she had said the same thing before, but I admitted I was looking forward to the experience.

With the amenities out of the way, Red got down to business. It would cost $200 a week to the county, he said, and $500 a month to the state. As soon as I was well established, the weekly rate would increase to $300.

When I protested, Red cut me short. "The Broward scale is a helluva lot less than the one in Dade," he said.

I submitted without argument even when Red said I might have to shell out another $50 weekly to local cops. The motel was in unincorporated country, he said, but many of my customers would come from the strip joints of a nearby town.

The town is between Hollywood and Fort Lauderdale. Several bust-out joints, run out of Miami years ago, relocated there.

Payments to the cops aside, all other graft would be collected in one package on a monthly basis if I desired. And if

any cop or deputy showed up wanting free service, I could tell him to go jack himself off.

I nodded agreement and Red cleared his throat. There was one more detail to settle. Unless a man had enough money to operate a high-class joint, it was better not to let him start. Therefore, to prove my financial health as well as show good faith, I would have to pay a flat sum of between $2,500 and $3,000, before I could open.

This was not a deposit, he emphasized. It wouldn't be returned. Furthermore, if I received orders to close, I must instantly obey. My ice payments would continue regardless of how long I was closed.

This seemed unfair, and I protested. Bessie reassured me. She had been closed only two days in the past two years. It was no real problem. The organization had good control.

Slowly I nodded. I didn't know what I was getting into, but it sounded okay to me. I'd give it a try.

Red smiled. In that case, could I come to the Harbor Inn next day at 10 A.M.? He'd have the man from Broward there, and we'd arrange the final details and fix the amount of the key money. I agreed to come, and he wrote the address on a slip of paper. The inn, he said, was a seafood restaurant he maintained as a meeting place.

I put the address in my pocket and prepared to relax. With studied casualness, Red asked, "May I see your driver's license?"

It was a question I had expected from the first and I had my answer ready. After all the delay, all the fun and games, I had not known what I was getting into. Not only had I left my wallet behind, I had brought only enough cash to buy Bessie a drink.

The answer seemed to suffice. In fact, it proved I was a careful soul. Red pressed my hand in farewell.

"I've been operating in Miami for thirty years," he said. "I just finished the seventh grade, but I've done well by cooperating and playing by the rules."

With that hint, or warning, he slid out of the car and re-

entered the Racquet Club. Bessie heaved a loud sigh of relief.

"That's that. When can you get the cash?"

The epilogue was brief. Next morning I went to the Harbor Inn. The smell of fish was in the air. Across the canal was the Playboy Club. Up the street was the joint known as the Pink Pussycat.

Red was alone except for waiter when I arrived, and he wasted no time. Producing a small pad and a gold pencil, he ordered me to write my real name and address.

"Doesn't matter what city you're from," Red said. "We can check you out in a matter of a few hours."

I tried to make a joke. "Who do you use?" I asked. "The city cops or the sheriff's boys?"

Red didn't laugh. "Either or both," he said shortly. "Now write out your name and let's get down to business. I've got some people waiting to meet you."

We were seated at a table on the patio. I turned. Behind me a full dozen men had collected. They sat at other tables, but they weren't even drinking coffee. They were just staring at me.

All were strangers, but Vic, who was watching from a parking lot across the street, later said one of them was a Broward deputy sheriff and the other worked for the state attorney.

I turned back to Red and picked up the pencil. "Why all the precautions? I thought you people had things under control here. Is the heat on?"

The last question brought a derisive snort. "Hell no," said my host. "The heat ain't on, and it ain't going to be if I can help it. That's why we're careful—so there won't be any heat. Now if you're the right kind of guy, you can open your whorehouse tomorrow. If you ain't, then you'll never open."

Briefly I regretted I'd not had time to prepare a cover identity. For that matter, I should have arranged somehow to follow Vic's suggestion and actually buy the brothel. But the

Herald executives had not responded warmly to my tentative approach. In fact, to be truthful, they seemed shocked at the idea.

"Look," I said. "You got your reasons and I got mine. How about doing it this way? Let me give you some local references and you check them out. If the boys say I'm okay, will you let it go at that?"

"Certainly." Red was smiling now. "All we want to be sure of is that you're a high class guy. Who do you know?"

I threw out the names of a handful of bolita operators. Just for class I added the name of a top deputy. Red didn't blink.

"Fine," he said. "I know them all. We'll do it your way but it'll mean a delay. Soon as I check you out I'll be in touch."

"Good enough." I stood up and turned to face the "observers." They stared at me. I stared back, then walked by them to the street, where Vic in his borrowed cab appeared with perfect timing. The eyes watched as we drove away.

I told Vic the situation and was surprised to see him cross himself.

"You shouldn't have done it," he said. "He'll call those guys, and they'll know you made a fool of him. He won't like that a bit."

I shrugged. "So who cares? As soon as I write this story everybody in south Florida will know I made a fool of him, but the very publicity will protect me. He won't dare do anything then."

"All right," said Vic. "But what makes you think you'll be alive to write that story?"

We were on the causeway again. The stink of Biscayne Bay rose on either side. It was going to be another hot day, but momentarily I felt cold. Vic had a point, I decided.

THREE

I FIND A CHEESEBOX

AND FLEE A HURRICANE

*

The sky was as blue as usual, and the palm trees scarcely moved, but people were putting up storm shutters at houses along Biscayne Boulevard. Somewhere, not too far out in the Caribbean, Hurricane Betsy was on the prowl. The experts said she would skirt Florida's coast as she moved north and east, but some people obviously didn't trust the experts. Or perhaps they didn't believe in gambling.

I was on my way to visit someone who didn't believe in gambling—although he made a good living taking bets from people who did.

Downtown Miami seemed unusually deserted, but for this I didn't blame the hurricane. The area, built largely during the boom days of the twenties, had been dying for years as people moved to the suburbs where the action was. Ultimately, those businessmen who were so prompt to decry federal interference would accept urban renewal funds and rebuild the city's core area.

I parked east of Flagler and walked a block to a hamburger joint on a corner. It offered no place to sit down, but facing the street was an open counter where a customer might rest his coffee cup as he stood to eat his burger. My contact was waiting there, a tall, wiry man with a quiet, competent air about him. I bought a coffee and moved in beside him. He spoke out of the side of his mouth.

"He hasn't shown yet. Should be soon."

I yawned. Two days earlier I had turned in my first stories.

They were long, and they were good. I needed no one to tell me that. A three-part series covered the syndicate take-over of the numbers racket. A two-parter took care of the prostitution business as seen through the eyes of Red Vaught and Bessie Winkle.

The editors were cautious, afraid or at least unwilling to say much. But I could sense their excitement. Not since the days of the S & G Syndicate, had the *Herald* been given such stories. Publication would come just as soon as they checked out enough of my facts to know I deserved my reputation as a careful reporter. That was why I was out so early after a long night. It was important to get as much undercover work done as possible before the heat started. And I had another big story about wrapped up.

My companion moved beside me. "Here he comes. The short guy with the briefcase. Get going."

I put down the coffee cup and moved around the counter to the street. The short, dark-haired man was walking rapidly. I started down the street toward him. The timing was perfect. He reached the entrance to the Langford Building about three steps ahead of me. I followed him in.

The lobby was small. A door led to the stairwell, but around and to the rear was an elevator. John (the Greek) Prokos pushed the button as I studied the wall directory. With nine floors to choose from, which would he be using today?

A clatter and the elevator descended. The door opened. It wasn't automatic, I remembered. The elderly man who operated it also served as a lookout for Prokos. So did the guy in the shop across the street.

"Going up," said the operator loudly.

A woman walked by me and entered the elevator. Prokos was already aboard. I followed. The woman was plump and in her fifties. I saw nothing attractive about her, but the operator had better instincts. He began talking to her about the hurricane. I tried to be inconspicuous but Prokos looked at me steadily, incuriously.

Still talking, the operator closed the doors and started the machinery. No one called a floor, but almost as quickly as we started we stopped. The light above the door said we were at the second floor. Prokos got off here.

I got off too—and instantly knew it was a mistake. For Prokos stopped in the middle of the corridor and turned to face me. I was conscious the elevator had not moved. The operator had stopped talking too.

"Can I help you," said the little man. His voice was deep. There was no trace of an accent.

I glanced around as if looking for something. No light showed through any of the office doors. There was no sound. Either these offices were vacant, or no one had come to work. I couldn't bluff here. Prokos didn't intend to move until he saw where I was going. There was nothing to do but retreat.

"Got the wrong floor, I guess." I turned back to the elevator. Prokos didn't move. He was still standing there as the door closed.

"Who you looking for?" asked the operator. For the first time I noticed his yellow shoes. They were well polished.

"Alliance Air Conditioning," I said. "I thought it was on the second floor."

"It ain't in the building," said the operator. "You got the wrong building."

"Oh, hell," I said. "Well, take me down."

Surprisingly, he obeyed. The woman had not said a word and continued mute as she got a free ride to the ground floor. The operator made no move to take her up again as I stopped to study the directory. He watched as I wagged my head in disgust and left the building.

It was still a quiet morning. Very little traffic. I wondered if the lookout across the street would spot me. From my position, just to the right of the entrance, I could hear the rumble of the elevator, as at last the operator started upward. I waited until the sound died before re-entering the lobby.

The door to the stairwell was unlocked. I climbed rapidly.

Just outside the door to the second floor I paused to listen. In my mind's eye I could see Prokos still standing there. The illusion faded when I opened the door. The lobby was deserted.

I could feel the wetness of my shirt against my body as I moved around the lobby. At each door I crouched in turn, listening. The doors had old-fashioned keyholes. You could see as well as hear. Had Prokos fooled me by getting off on the wrong floor? Unlikely. If he had wanted to try that old trick, he surely would have gone higher and walked down.

At the fourth door, my ear was rewarded. I could hear the muted ring of a telephone. Peeping through, I could see light. This must be it. I waited. The phone rang again. Just once. Prokos was at work. The old-style handbook went out in 1961, when Bobby Kennedy got some new federal laws passed. Business these days is done by telephone.

I was across the lobby from the elevator. Another room adjoined the one where the phone was ringing. I tried the door. Locked, of course. Okay, so here went nothing. I pulled out the key I had been given. An old-fashioned key for an old-fashioned lock. Probably opened every room in the building. At least I hoped it would open this one.

It did, turning easily. I pushed the door open slowly. No sound. I released my breath. A reporter's life gets complicated. Briefly, I wondered what the *Herald*'s editors would say.

The room was empty. I closed the door quickly and glanced around. Almost no furniture—a table and chair. On the unswept floor were some cigarette butts and a copy of *Playboy* magazine. But even more attractive was the object on the table.

Built into an open briefcase was an electronic gadget. It looked like a radio, but it had no knobs. Some tubes were visible and lights glowed in them. The thing was functioning, whatever it was. Wires ran from the mechanism to the telephone on the table.

Even as I looked, there was a click. And somewhere a

telephone rang. Somewhere? It was in the next room. I moved
to the connecting wall. Now I could hear a man's voice. He
was quoting odds on baseball games.

And suddenly I understood. It had been explained to me
earlier, but it hadn't made much sense. The device in the
briefcase was a cheesebox—so called because the first one
found by federal agents was hidden in a cheesebox. An electronic device, it was designed to bypass a called telephone and
divert the call to another phone.

"We suspect it works like this," the man had said. "Prokos
gives a number to his customers. They call that number when
they want to put down a bet. The cheesebox is attached to the
telephone they call and it automatically switches the call to
another telephone. The phone Prokos answers may be in another room next door or ten miles away."

I had made some notes. The beauty of the arrangement was
in the safety it gave the bookie. Cops could learn the telephone number used by the bettors. But if they located it and
got a search warrant, a raid wouldn't catch anyone. The
bookie could move his phone from room to room, from floor
to floor. And in the huge Langford Building, only half occupied, he had plenty of rooms from which to choose.

Today, Prokos was in the next room. Presumably, if raid-
ing parties got warrants for both rooms and hit them at the
same time, they would get both the cheesebox and Prokos and
thus have a case. But until now the very existence of the
cheesebox had been but an educated guess. The chances were
good there were more of them. No bookie as big as Prokos
would operate with only one phone. Elsewhere in the building
other cheeseboxes might be diverting calls to other telephones
in the room next door.

The device clicked again. The little specks of light glowed
in the tubes. I watched and wondered. The device was complicated yet compact. Should Prokos want to move his operation, he would need only to disconnect the wires, close the
briefcase, and walk out with it in his hand.

"The Greek" was the biggest bookie in Miami. With his brother Chris he operated a cafe around the corner. It was there his customers came to collect their winnings and settle their accounts. They could do both while paying for a meal. A beautiful system, but not one depending entirely on secrecy. Many cops in Miami knew of the operation. It was the "feds" who worried Prokos. He was a big operator, handling millions in sports bets. In daily contact with top layoff bettors around the country, Prokos was bankrolled by the same syndicate bosses who financed Gil (the Brain) Beckley. Gil ran the largest layoff-betting business in the country from a plush apartment in the Blair House across the bay.

Years ago, Beckley operated in Newport where his head-quarters were located above the Tropicana Club on Monmouth Street. Beckley had been in Newport that fateful night in May, 1961, when a reform candidate for sheriff had been given a chloral hydrate cocktail and put to bed with a strip-tease dancer. Beckley supervised the early stages of the frame and then flew out of the Greater Cincinnati Airport about 3 A.M., leaving the details in the hands of young Tito Carinci —and Tito bungled the job.

George Ratterman survived the frame and when I persuaded the stripper to talk, his election was assured. The hoods left Newport before Ratterman took office, and among those departing for Las Vegas and Miami was Beckley. He set up shop in the Blair House and had operated undisturbed for almost four years.

I smiled. Here, in the beginning of a new campaign, I was dreaming of past victories. Already I had visited Beckley. He would be featured with Prokos in my next articles. Meanwhile, it was time to get out of here before—like Ratterman —I was caught with my pants down.

The lobby was empty, but as I closed the door to the room the sound of the elevator was suddenly loud. There wasn't time to get to the stairs if he stopped. And stop he did. When the door opened, the old man was holding a coffee pot. His

face changed as he recognized me. His mouth opened but nothing came out.

"Down, please," I said, and stepped aboard.

Still he stood there. I could see a fresh wound in his gums. Apparently he had just lost a tooth. I took the coffee pot. It was hot.

"Let's go," I said. "Down."

He didn't like it, but he obeyed. We clanked down the one flight. When he opened the door I returned the coffee pot. He didn't speak, and I had nothing to say either.

My contact was waiting in the arcade across the street. "You've got a tail," he said as I walked by. "I'll see you later."

When later we talked there was pleasure and disappointment. The use of the cheesebox had been confirmed, but now it would probably be moved.

"Go ahead with your story," I was told. "The Greek will probably be relieved to find it was just a nosy reporter. Don't say anything about the cheesebox. He'll figure you didn't know what it was."

I gave the man back his key. "Sorry I got spotted."

My contact smiled. "Don't worry about it. With the World Series and pro football coming up, the Greek isn't about to quit. We'll let you know when we're ready."

I turned to leave. He stopped me. "Got a message for you. Someone you've been wanting to meet is looking for a private eye. Give you any ideas?"

A gust of wind shook the window. Betsy was flicking her skirts, as the weather writers like to put it, but as I took the piece of paper with an address scrawled on it, I was suddenly thinking of a girl named Judy.

Two days had passed. I sat, or reclined, in what was allegedly a contour chair. Obviously, it was not designed for anyone with my contours. In front of me a vast picture window looked out on the Atlantic—or did on ordinary occa-

sions. Today the view was blocked by sheets of rain, which splashed like a river against the window.

It was just as well, for between me and the window a nude girl posed.

As far as I knew, her name wasn't Judy. My host, a little runt of a man, who fitted perfectly into the matched contour chair at any side, called her Honey when she arrived. He had called two girls who preceded her by the same name, so I was a little confused.

The third Honey stopped playing like a still life and began to move. It wasn't a dance, exactly, but it set everything to vibrating. The carpet was at least ankle-deep and yet her oversized breasts jiggled as if she were pounding a beat in brogans. Another fact of interest was now apparent—she was an unnatural blonde. I sipped the scotch the runty guy I will call Virgil (this is not his name) had given me and wondered what in hell I was doing here.

The curtain of rain fell away for a moment and I could see the ocean. It looked dirty, as if the sandy bottom for a thousand miles had boiled to the surface. Near the shore it was gray, topped with a white froth in which you could almost see the sand. Moving outward, the color changed to a bluish-black with only specks of white. Still there was a gritty feeling about it. Huge clouds were piled high and dirty, and the space between sea and sky was filled with a hazy mist. Soon the driving rain would resume.

Betsy was at hand.

The unpredictable storm skirted the coast as expected and moved north and east. But when about even with Jacksonville, she suddenly halted, hesitated for a few hours, and turned back. Now she was bearing down on Miami with winds in excess of one hundred miles an hour.

And here I sat in a penthouse overlooking the ocean, while Virgil selected his next playmate.

It looked as if the third Honey of the day was to win the

beauty contest. Virgil nudged me. "Be with you in a minute," he said.

I watched as he gestured to the girl. She stopped vibrating and walked over. He snapped his fingers and pointed to the floor. The girl sat on the red carpet, crossed her legs Indian-style, put her hands beside her bottom and leaned back with a smile I could only call expectant.

Virgil sipped his drink, placed the glass carefully on a table beside his chair, and leaned forward. His voice was soft, yet containing contradictions one might expect in a self-made southern businessman.

"Let's get it straight," he said. "You'll live here. I'll pay all expenses and give you a hundred a week. You can use the Cadillac. If you want to have a friend in, that's all right too. I'll always let you know when I'm coming down."

The girl nodded. "I dig, daddy," she said. Her voice was husky. No southern accent here. Well, perhaps he got enough of that back home in Alabama.

Virgil nodded. "There's just one thing. When I do come down, I'm king. You drop everything and everybody while I'm here. Understand? I'm king."

Her smile was wider than ever. "Yes, daddy."

For a second they stared at each other. I couldn't see his face but there was new color in his neck. The tip of her tongue appeared, flicked in and out. The wind blew a mighty blast and the rain returned with a crash. I coughed loudly, and Virgil relaxed.

"Okay," he said. "Take the car and go get your things. Be back here by dinner time."

She scrambled to her feet in one graceful motion. "Thanks, daddy. 'Bye now." And she was gone into the bedroom.

Virgil got smoothly to his feet. The Chinese dressing gown —or was it a smoking jacket—was a shortie. It came down only to mid-thigh. I looked at his legs. They were thin and hairy. He moved to the window.

"Excuse the delay," he said, "but I didn't think you'd mind.

Besides, it helped get the idea across. As you can see, I have
my own ideas of fun. Hell, I can afford it. Naturally, my wife
doesn't approve . . ."

He kept on talking. On his last trip down there had been
complications. At that time he kept a house. Well, he was
hardly inside when the wife called long distance. She wasn't
supposed to know the number. She had been tipped off by
someone. She caught the next plane down and spoiled his
vacation. In fact, she had made him sell the house at a loss.

"I found out who tipped her," said Virgil softly. "Honey
had this punk, and he was jealous. When she told him to get
lost because I was coming down, he called my wife."

Scorn was heavy in his voice. I felt I should comment.
"Narrow-minded fellow, wasn't he?"

"Intolerant," said Virgil. "That's the word. Intolerant.
There's nothing worse than intolerance." He turned to face
me. "But that's not the point. If the punk wants to poison his
soul that way, it's none of my business. What is my business is
the trouble he caused me."

I didn't say anything.

"Understand," he continued. "It wasn't even the girl. I can
find a honey any time and I rather enjoy looking." He paused
and smiled. "Matter of fact I used to insist on a test ride, but I
finally decided that was rather juvenile. After all, a man
should be able to judge by a careful inspection."

Again, I kept quiet. It seemed to bother him a little. When
he resumed, his voice was all business.

"Anyway," he said, "I bought this apartment and furnished
it my style. Everything is all set. But this time I don't want it
ruined. It upsets my wife for one thing. And it's rather expensive having to buy and sell houses and apartments."

I grunted and he seemed satisfied.

"This is the assignment. Find me a couple of Cubans and
have them break that punk's legs. Both legs, mind you. It'll be
an object lesson people will remember. I'll spread the word
why it was done."

I tossed my glass onto the carpet. It didn't even bounce. "What's wrong?" asked Virgil as I began an effort to rise. "I hear you can get the job done for fifty bucks. There'll be another fifty for you to make sure it's handled properly. Okay?"

The view from the chair was unreal: the plush apartment and, outside, the angry ocean, gray and white. On the horizon a freighter with a white superstructure and a black smokestack stood out against the bleakness, as it headed north into the storm.

Getting out of the chair was a problem I solved by rolling over to the floor. Virgil retreated a few feet as I climbed erect. I grinned.

"Sorry, Virgil," I said softly. "I'm afraid you've been had. I'm no private eye and I don't go around arranging to have legs broken."

I'm not certain what reaction I expected but it wasn't a smile. Yet Virgil smiled.

"This is interesting," he said. "If you're not an eye, then what are you? And why are you here?"

The man had guts. I began to like him a little. "Did you read the *Herald* this morning?" I asked. "Well, I wrote the big story."

His smile widened. "Oh, yes. The expose about Fat Hymie Martin. How very interesting indeed. Fascinating."

"I've got another series coming up soon," I told him. "All about Red Vaught and the prostitution racket."

"Good," said Virgil. He was literally beaming. "It's about time. That man treats his girls shamefully. He's not a gentleman."

It was my turn to stare. This guy was as full of surprises as a sportswriter is full of clichés. Now he was picking up my glass and pouring me a drink. I took it and sat down on the arm of a straight-backed chair.

"What can I do for you?" he was asking. "Darn clever of you to get in like this. I try to stay private, you know. I

suppose you heard I was asking about for an eye. In the past I went to the sheriff's department for little chores like that, but lately they've been rather unreliable."

When he stopped for breath I interjected, "I'm looking for a hooker named Judy. She used to live at [I named a place I'll call Purple Manor] in the Springs. I hear she has quite a story to tell about some of your friends in the sheriff's office."

He sipped his drink and eyed me carefully. There was no trace of the playboy now. This was a hard-nosed businessman closing a deal.

"I think I know what you mean," he said. "It's dangerous business. You could get killed."

"So I've heard," I admitted.

"I'm serious," he said. "Try checking the McFarland murder up in Fort Lauderdale. You'll see what I mean."

I made a mental note to do just that. But now he was smiling again. "If I help, you'll leave me out of it?"

"Naturally."

"And you won't say anything about all this?" He waved his hand.

"Not a word."

"Good enough." He put down his glass and went toward the master bedroom. It actually had a mirror in the ceiling. Upon arrival, I had taken a quick glance while Virgil busied himself with Honey number one who had just come in. Two minutes later he was back, a small, leather-bound notebook in his hand.

"I was once offered $10,000 for this," he commented.

I looked out the window. A new volley of raindrops was headed toward the window. They came in horizontally, like bullets, and they splattered against the glass like bullets, too. Then the first drops were submerged in a wave of water that obscured everything. The storm was getting worse and I was twenty miles from home. Virgil leafed through the book as I moved impatiently.

"Ah, here it is. Still calls herself Judy, I see, but the last

name has changed." He gave me an address in the northwest section.

I pulled out my own notebook. It wasn't leatherbound but it was valuable. "What can you tell me about her?"

"Nothing much. She's tall, skinny, got a big nose. Some people down here won't lay a girl unless she has a big nose. When I met her she was just starting out. Inexperienced, but a lot of ambition."

"Where did you meet her?"

He shrugged. "That's all I'm going to tell you. It's her story if she wants to tell it. Just be careful—you're getting close to something big."

I thanked him—and meant it. We moved to the door. As he turned the knob, a bell chimed. A girl was outside, her finger still pushing the button. She was short. Water dripped from a blue plastic raincoat and hat.

"Hi," she said. "God, it's wet. I almost got blown into the ocean."

She winked at me and slipped between us to go into the bathroom on the right. Virgil's face was a study in amused dismay.

"She's the muff I had last night," he explained. "I forgot to call her this afternoon after I picked Honey. Now what'll I do?"

"You'll think of something," I assured him. "Meanwhile, I've got to get out of here before Betsy shows up too."

"Hold on." He grabbed my arm and I thought I could guess what was coming. I tasted the idea in advance and found it not unattractive. The little one had been nice.

But I was wrong.

"If you run into anybody who'd break that punk's legs for me, give me a call," he said.

I felt cheated all the way down the elevator. After that, Betsy required my attention. It took two hours to get home.

Betsy continued to occupy my attention. She even inter-

rupted my series. The editors decided no one had time to read anything but hurricane news, and they held up the series after two articles. The storm finally came ashore a bit south of Miami, but the big eye reached to Fort Lauderdale. Yet despite the fear which gripped the Gold Coast for days, the storm did relatively little damage. People were buttoned down well in advance and with few exceptions suffered little inconvenience.

One exception involved Key Biscayne, an island off Miami. A string of barges was blown apart and into Rickenbacker Causeway. The island was cut off from the mainland for a while. Wealthy residents were annoyed, but the general public knew Key Biscayne only as the spot where millionaire Jacques Mossler was murdered in 1964.

When the storm passed and the streets were clear, the *Herald* resumed my series. And suddenly I was working harder than ever. From caution bordering on disbelief, the editors changed to an eagerness that was equally naive. They wanted more stories in a hurry—a new bomb every week.

I tried to oblige, but I refused to take chances. I knew, if the editors didn't, that one slip on my part would negate everything I had written. My stories were having an impact, I felt, because they were factual down to the smallest detail.

So I worked sixteen hours a day, seven days a week, and in the next few weeks the *Herald* printed more facts about organized crime than any newspaper in history in a comparable period. About the time I was beginning to suspect the editors wanted to squeeze me dry before my contract expired, I was informed they wanted me to sign a new one. They had decided, by God, that the job of cleaning up south Florida was a little larger than they had originally supposed. They were willing to give me another thirteen weeks to finish it.

I signed—all too aware the new contract would keep me on the payroll until just after the first of the year. After that, any stories wouldn't be considered for the 1965 journalistic awards such as the Pulitzer or Sigma Delta Chi. Well, good

luck to them. I'd had my shot at a Pulitzer years before in my less cynical days. Come to think of it, the episode had contributed a lot to making me cynical.

My unofficial assistant, the would-be bolita baron I called Charley, worked right along with me. I paid all expenses and managed to give him a little extra now and then, but my conscience was spared any acute pain by his obvious interest. Charley thought my stories the greatest thing since the adding machine. He was always confident the next one would cause all officials to quit en masse. I didn't share his optimism, but his faith in the power of the press was inspiring.

Under the circumstances there wasn't time to pursue the elusive Judy. But we talked about her at intervals, and Charley provided some insight.

Women, I was told, played an important role in the lives of officials. Old standards of morality, of values, had been dropped. An official, while perhaps salting away some cash reserves, believed in enjoying the present. This meant for him expensive clothes, the best of food, and a variety of women. The interest in sex was so overpowering as to be abnormal. I couldn't but wonder if these supposedly tough, sophisticated individuals, weren't trying to compensate for something—perhaps self-respect.

Charley took me to one official and convinced him I wouldn't use his name. The man, a lower-level law-enforcement officer, told me how he met Jackie. Shortly after his election, he said, a judge brought Jackie to his office and ordered her to hoist her skirts and show her wares. She was introduced as an "entertainer," the official said, "and I got the message."

Telephone numbers were exchanged. Thereafter, when Jackie needed the help of the law, she called the official. When he wanted a favor of another kind, he called her. Often they met at one of Frankie Dio's joints near the Dade-Broward County line. Jackie worked as a hostess and one of her duties was to keep certain officials happy. She knew many officials, she boasted.

The official talked freely to me because Charley had convinced him my friendship might be useful if, later, the sheriff was removed. The guy was eager to get the job and he assumed I would be glad to assist him in return for some information.

Charley thought the official's attitude reasonable. I didn't argue. In view of the political morality in vogue along the Gold Coast, perhaps it was reasonable. At any rate it was typical.

But always the conversation returned to Judy. She was, according to the rumor, the key to many things. At the Purple Manor she had lived across the patio from an apartment maintained by certain politicians. In that apartment in 1962 had been plotted a scheme to remove from office the incumbent sheriff and to replace him with Tal Buchanan, the chief of detectives. The plan succeeded—but then something happened. Buchanan double-crossed his friends and the syndicate, led by Fat Hymie, waxed stronger than ever.

Some people thought Judy had the answers.

I was all set one day to start in search of Judy, when the editors of the *Herald* called me in on an urgent matter. They had changed their minds, it seemed, and now thought I should accept a subpoena from the Dade Grand Jury.

For a week the jury had been attempting to subpoena me. I was entirely willing but the editors feared a trap. When deputies had appeared in the newsroom with the subpoena, they were told—correctly enough—that I was an independent contractor not subject to orders. When I might show up no one knew.

But State Attorney Richard E. Gerstein was persistent, and reports had it, he was also annoyed. This apparently alarmed the editors. I had my own opinion of Gerstein, but since the *Herald* had supported him for years and quoted him at every opportunity, I kept my opinions to myself. So I followed the editors' suggestion and remained in the city room, while someone phoned the state attorney's office to tip them I had just arrived.

The subpoena arrived within the hour. I was to appear next day before the grand jury. This discovery brought another full-dress editorial conference. I listened as the editors talked. Despite their faith in Gerstein—and their desire not to annoy him—they still felt I should keep my mouth shut and say as little as possible. Presumably, if Gerstein wanted to become annoyed with me, that was okay. They pointed out that by talking I might play into Gerstein's hands. He hadn't been consulted, as in the past, about my crime series, and he might feel it was directed at him. So the less said the better.

I listened, wondered a bit, and reserved judgment. Next day, arriving outside the grand jury chambers on the fifth floor of the old courthouse, I was not surprised to find one of the *Herald*'s attorneys. He was there, he assured me, to help if I fell into any legal trap.

As I entered the grand jury room I wondered once more—if Gerstein was a friend of the newspaper, how the editors must fear their enemies.

The jury was meeting in one of the many small courtrooms. At the bench sat the foreman and vice-foreman while the jurors were scattered about at small tables. This was the spring grand jury which had been convened in May. It had indicted, among others, Candace Mossler and Melvin Powers in connection with that famous murder on Key Biscayne. Actually, the jury was winding up its work. With its six-month term soon to expire, it seemed rather late to be starting a probe of organized crime and corruption.

But that is what it intended to do. State Attorney Gerstein said so as he rose to his feet—all six feet, five inches of him. His scarred face and artificial eye—result of war wounds—made him even more impressive. His words were measured, solemn.

I can't repeat what he said, but he conveyed the idea that both he and the jury were deeply concerned about conditions I had exposed. There wasn't much time, he acknowledged, but he felt this jury could act in a limited way, and he would ask the next grand jury to continue the probe.

As Gerstein spoke, I studied the jurors. They seemed interested, clean-cut, intelligent. One smiled and winked as our eyes met. The *Herald*'s warning was fresh in my mind but the voice of my own experience spoke louder. If anything was to be done in Dade County, it would have to start here. If not this jury, then another one. And this one had an advantage future ones would not have—it had been chosen back in the merry month of May before anyone had suggested something might be stinking besides Biscayne Bay.

I didn't doubt that Gerstein, like any successful district attorney anywhere, had gained the jurors' confidence and brainwashed them to a degree. But that was part of the gamble. I took a deep breath and began to talk.

It went very well. Soon I aroused enough interest to bring questions from individual jurors. I saw a woman making notes. It had taken me four years in Newport to get jurors to take notes. By those standards this was amazing progress.

Gerstein played it cool. His questions concentrated on the Red Vaught-Bessie Winkle episode. Perhaps he thought there was sufficient evidence there to take immediate action. I answered his questions fully but returned at every opportunity to the broader subject of crime and corruption. He didn't interfere and finally someone asked the questions I wanted.

"How did the situation get so bad? Why has nothing been done about it?"

There was no change of expression on Gerstein's face as I hit hard. At the heart of the problem, I said, was fear. Potential witnesses feared to talk because they didn't trust officials. They believed many officials were corrupt, and they didn't want to gamble on finding an honest one. Rightly or wrongly they didn't trust the state attorney's office.

There was more of this, and it opened some eyes. I became sure when Gerstein admitted I might be right. But he felt the distrust was illogical insofar as his office was concerned, and he was sure the problem would be overcome by the next grand jury.

I left the room with the thanks of both Gerstein and the

foreman following me. Reporters clustered around as I reached the hall. My shirt was wet. In south Florida it was always wet.

"Do you realize how long you were in there?" one reporter asked. "Almost two hours."

All I realized was a sudden awareness of fatigue. I was exhausted. The *Herald's* attorney wore a worried frown, but I ignored it. This was one day I was going to go home early.

A few days later the jury issued an interim report. The *Herald* featured it in a double banner across page one:

JURY SPOTLIGHTS S. FLORIDA CRIME,
BLAMES SHERIFF AND POLICE OFFICIALS

The report was a blast. The role of the syndicate was acknowledged. Prostitution and gambling were said to be operating openly without interference from police or sheriff.

The jury commented at one point, "It is evident police can not or care not to enforce the law . . ."

Herald editors were on cloud nine—or perhaps ten. Some sort of supreme compliment was paid me when one of them remarked, "I don't think we'll worry about you and grand juries in the future."

More than ever all signals were go, go, go. The editors wanted instant stories. Keep up the momentum, I was told. Take advantage of public interest. Strike while the iron is hot. Hit 'em again, harder, harder.

Two other reporters were assigned to the crime beat—but not to me. They worked under the city editor who was given the title "Crime Coordinator." Exactly what he coordinated, I never found out. But tips were flooding the city room as the public decided it had a champion at last. There was more information coming in than a dozen men could check.

Despite the pressure, the endless hours, it was a happy experience. A certain unity of purpose existed. Morale was high and fears restrained. We worked hard and enjoyed a sense of achievement.

Not everyone in the community was happy, of course. The afternoon newspaper started a series entitled "What's Good About Miami." Certain radio and television stations deplored the "hysteria" and speculated what it would do to the tourist business. Others called for legalized gambling. And one day I was called to the television screen to see Sheriff Buchanan. It was the first time I had ever seen the man, on or off the screen. He was big, I decided, and didn't look too bright; he didn't sound very bright either.

Buchanan was responding to a friendly question by saying he feared a conspiracy existed to undermine local law enforcement. He went on to slap Supreme Court decisions, which he said were part of the plot, and to deplore the acts of certain newspaper reporters who also served.

At this point he paused, as if to give added weight to his next remark. It concerned me. The sheriff said he was devoting all his spare time to finding out who was *really* paying me.

The statement came as no surprise. Since the day after the grand jury's report was issued, his deputies had been tailing me. My information indicated it was a joint venture with the Broward sheriff's office. In any case, they seemed to have plenty of spare time available for the purpose.

In fact, according to Charley, the smart boys were betting the sheriff would get me before the syndicate got around to it.

FOUR

I TALK TO A BAGMAN

AND PROBE A MURDER

*

It began simply enough. Judy was reported to be "in the islands" when I checked her apartment. I remembered Virgil's other suggestion that I look into the McFarland murder in Broward. And abruptly life became complicated.

In other cities, when I've needed to examine police files, I've gone to the office in question, identified myself as a reporter, and made my request. But in south Florida the name of the game is intrigue.

Dick Basinger was my first contact. A short, curly-haired Dutchman, Dick won the Democratic nomination for Broward sheriff in 1964. Considering that the Democratic politicians failed to support him, he ran a surprisingly strong race but was defeated by the incumbent, Allen B. Michell.

My old pal, Vic, introduced me to Dick, and instantly regretted it. Since my story about Bessie came out, Vic had been riding high. I tried to protect him in the story only to discover he was making the rounds identifying himself. He was also telling everyone who would listen—and a lot of people listened—that he was my personal assistant, and anyone wanting to contact me should apply to him.

There wasn't much I could do to shut Vic up, and I consoled myself with the thought that by the time he got through embellishing the facts I would be even more of a mystery. Nevertheless, I enjoyed the situation, as Vic—sensing a rival—glowered, while Dick offered to pull all kinds of strings to help me.

66

As a result of that talk and a telephone call I drove one
night to a gravel pit near the Everglades. Basinger was waiting for me there. I left my car and rode with him to a junction
in the middle of nowhere. Ed Clode, former Dade County
deputy and now chief deputy for Broward Sheriff Michell,
was waiting for us. We got into his car, drove some more,
switched cars somewhere else, and ended on the side of an
unknown road about midnight.

Clode was tall, thin, and nervous. He smoked cigarettes
constantly, kept the air conditioner going, and watched the
lights of an occasional car as if he expected Michell to turn up
at any moment.

I was also a bit nervous. Why was Michell's chief deputy
willing to talk? It didn't make sense.

Clode explained he had nothing much against the sheriff. It
was the sheriff's secretary, the Blonde Bombshell, that worried him. She had a lot to say about the running of the department, and of late she had been looking askance. She was
impulsive enough to demand Michell fire Clode, and Michell
was weak enough to do it. The Old Man just didn't have any
guts.

Other men had told tales of the Blonde Sheriff, as they
called her, so I could accept Clode's story up to a point. In
this case, the point was to ask questions, listen, and reserve
judgment.

I asked about the McFarland murder and learned it had
occurred in August, 1963. Floyd Earl McFarland, an elderly
service station attendant, had been reported missing from his
station on State Road 84, southwest of Fort Lauderdale. His
wife, who called occasionally during the early morning hours,
reported to police when he didn't answer the phone. At about
3 A.M. the station was inspected. Soap had been spread over
the concrete apron with a water hose. Inside the station
the cash register was untouched. A money-changer still
stocked with change was on a table along with a few small
bills. But there was no sign of McFarland. His car was parked
at the station, the keys still in the ignition.

A few days later McFarland's body was found on the side of a canal ten miles away. Two bullets had been fired at close range into the base of his skull. His wallet was gone, but if robbery had been the motive why had money been left behind at the station?

Clode personally investigated the case, he said, and ran down every lead. It was still as much a mystery as ever—one of many unsolved murders in Broward.

When I tried to probe deeper, Clode suddenly became evasive. He saw no point in wasting time on McFarland, but he could help me with another murder that would blow the lid off organized crime in Dade County. Again, as before, I let him talk.

It was back in 1960 when Louis (Babe) Silvers disappeared. Clode was working on the intelligence squad of the Dade sheriff's office then, and he was assigned the case. Well, it was sorta like the McFarland case in a way, only it was fifteen months later before any trace of Babe was found. And by then he was just a bag of bones somebody fished out of a lake. Identification was made by Silvers' dentist.

Everyone knew Babe was a bookie and associated with some real tough Mafia boys. Theory was, he had a disagreement over some money he had borrowed, and the shylocks had him bumped. But proving it was another matter.

Some of Babe's associates included Dave Yaras, Tommy Altamura, Benny Husick, John (Peanuts) Tronolone, Anthony (Chickee) De Meo, and John Parisi.

I whistled softly as Clode rattled off the names. Some of these guys were big-time all right.

Clode seemed gratified at my reaction. He kept working the case, he said, until 1963, when Tal Buchanan became sheriff of Dade County and fired him. As several other ex-Dade deputies were doing, Clode came north to Broward and found a job with Sheriff Michell. But he kept in touch with the investigation in Dade, such as it was, and quite by accident found the solution.

A car came slowly down the darkness, and Clode caught his breath. Lights touched us briefly and were gone. "It was the highway patrol," said Clode. "They know this car. Belongs to my bodyguard, Joe Mazur."

Briefly I wondered why a chief deputy needed a bodyguard and how much the job paid. The car was a new model Cadillac with all the extras. But Clode was talking again.

Exactly how he got the solution, Clode didn't make clear. But it came in a roundabout way from a federal prisoner in New York. The prisoner was almost a witness to the murder. Clode didn't have all the details, but it seems Charles Hedges —the prisoner—had been hanging out at a Hallandale motel when he met a friend, who asked him to help out with a little chore.

The chore consisted of cleaning up a motel room where Silvers had been murdered. Five shylocks were in that room, according to Hedges' friend. One of them hit Silvers with a tire iron and the others took turns stabbing him with an ice-pick. This joint venture was considered necessary to equally incriminate everyone. The body was cut up then.

According to Hedges, as related to me by Clode, he and his friend removed all bloodstains from the motel room, took the sheets and other evidence, along with the tire iron, and dumped them in the Intracoastal Waterway.

Clode became more excited as he talked, but his eyes kept cutting back to me, as if he could read my expression in the darkness. All he needed, he said, to solve the case was expense money to go to New York and get a signed statement from the prisoner. Would the *Herald* be willing to help?

I said that under the circumstances there was a good possibility. But why, I asked, won't the county send you?

The chief deputy gave a wry chuckle. These five shylocks had too much influence. In fact, if he solved the murder he would have to look for another job. Would the *Herald* be willing to guarantee one?

By now I could feel the short hairs standing on my neck. I

was ready to accept the general condition of corruption, but this seemed too much. A chief deputy afraid to solve a murder case for fear of losing his job? Possible, perhaps, but not likely. And if not likely, what was Clode trying to pull?

I promised to discuss the matter with the *Herald*. Clode could understand why I couldn't promise money and a job without consulting with them. Meanwhile, they were very anxious to learn more about the McFarland case. Sure, it sounded dull compared to Silvers, but they had asked for it. Could Clode help me there a little? Some evidence of his cooperation might swing the New York trip.

He wasn't eager, but with Dick Basinger chiming in from the back seat, he agreed. If I would present myself at his office next day—using a code name, of course—he would get the McFarland file. To protect his job, he'd have to tell the sheriff I was there, but he'd delay it until I had time to see everything there was to see. It wouldn't take long.

All the way back to the first car, we discussed the Silvers' case. When Dick and I were at last alone in his car, we discussed Clode. While puzzled, Dick was confident Ed Clode was on our side. I wasn't too sure—for a politician Dick seemed a little too honest to be a very good judge of character.

I resolved, however, to play it straight and give Clode every chance. Next morning I began by driving to the massive structure that is the new Broward County Courthouse. It smelled very much like the Dade Courthouse, but looked a lot cleaner. Up to the sixth floor I went, ducking in a side door, down a hall, and into the cubicle Clode had described.

He was there—along with his "bodyguard," Deputy Joe Mazur. A handsome, muscular young man, Joe was another refugee from Dade County. Apparently, someone had reassigned a lot of men to the northern provinces. I made a note to find out why.

Clode made a short speech, presumably for Mazur's benefit. Then he produced a rather thin manila folder. I sat down

at a table and began the routine task of making notes. Clode and Mazur huddled at the desk, pretending to talk but keeping an eye on me.

The case background was very much as I expected. A missing persons report described the scene at the station the night McFarland vanished. There were several reports describing the finding of the body. An autopsy report revealed a number of skull fractures, and there was confusion as to whether the bullets caused them or the victim had been struck over the head as well.

Suddenly, a gleam of blue caught my eye. I pulled a letter from the pile of papers—and held my breath. The letter was on the official stationery of State Attorney Richard E. Gerstein in Miami. It was addressed to Sheriff Michell and it was dated January 3, 1964. The body of the letter I hurriedly copied. It asked Michell if he had conducted an investigation to determine whether Sheriff T.A. Buchanan of Dade County was involved in a traffic fatality or some other crime in Broward County.

Clode and Mazur were openly curious now as I put away my pen. I ignored them and pulled from my pocket a tiny Minox camera. Using the attached knotted cord as a measuring device, I set the camera for a close-up and took three quick shots of the letter. Only then did I glance at my audience.

Mazur was grinning. "Ain't you the sneaky one?" he said.

"Very interesting letter," I commented. "Where's the reply?"

"Damned if I know," replied Joe. "I had forgotten that thing was in there."

Clode stood up. "I'd better tell the Old Man you're here," he said. As he walked by me, I noticed his face. He wasn't happy.

I was still checking the file and finding little of value when Clode returned. With him was a short, fat man in an expen-

sive suit puffing on a thick cigar. I stood up as Clode performed the introductions, but Sheriff Michell didn't offer his hand.

"Finding anything?" he demanded.

I tried to keep it light. "Nothing much. Just this letter from Gerstein. What did you say in your reply?"

"That's confidential," said the sheriff brusquely. He blew a cloud of smoke and flipped away some ash. It fell on the paper in front of me. "So you're the big-shot reporter. I've been reading your stories."

I didn't say anything this time. Clode moved nervously. Mazur still wore an idiot's grin.

"Ever hear of Jake Lingle?" asked the sheriff. "He was a big-shot reporter too—in Chicago. Know what happened to him?"

"He got murdered by the Capone mob," I said softly. "Are you threatening me sheriff?"

Again came the contemptuous wave of the cigar. "Just reminding you," he replied. Turning to Clode, he ordered, "See me in my office as soon as you're free."

With that he was gone, leaving a trail of smoke. Clode wiped his forehead, and Joe cursed softly. His smile had vanished.

"If you're through," said the chief deputy, "you'd better get going. The Old Man is pretty sore."

"Don't worry," I began. "The *Herald* will back you up . . ."

"Shh." He put his finger to his lips. "We'll talk later. Just get going."

There was much to think about as I went down the elevator and out to the parking lot. But, for some reason, I kept wondering about Jake Lingle. Interesting that Sheriff Michell should know of Lingle. By all accounts, Jake had been a crooked reporter. Maybe Michell was trying to insult as well as threaten.

Anyway, what next?

The *Herald* decided what next. I turned in a detailed memo based on my notes from the McFarland file, and the photography department developed my Minox film. The Gerstein-to-Michell letter came out sharp and clear, and was probably decisive.

At any rate, I was called to a full-flight editorial conference. Executives I had never heard of, let alone met, were present. The *Herald* had decided, I discovered, to shoot the works. It would offer a large reward for information leading to the conviction of McFarland's murder. The hope was that money would loosen tongues, quiet fears, and give us a quick and simple solution—in time for the Pulitzer awards.

Other editors had heard the whispered rumors linking Sheriff Buchanan to the case. The existence of an official letter naming him as a suspect, apparently clinched the matter. My advice was sought more or less as an afterthought.

As best I could, I tried to point out that no real evidence existed. The McFarland killing could be nothing more than an unrelated incident. Some bum might have attempted a holdup, got cold feet, and pulled the trigger too hastily. Frightened, he could have thought only of disposing of the body before someone pulled in for gas.

This theory was brushed aside by the excited executives. As one of them explained it, "We're just doing a public service. If Buchanan isn't involved, then any solution will prove his innocence. If he's not guilty, he should be grateful."

There was something to that, I decided, but I couldn't believe the sheriff would be very grateful. Nevertheless, I decided to shut up and learn a little more about the inner workings of a metropolitan newspaper. Interesting to see how bold the junior executives had suddenly become.

The only problem to be decided was the size of the reward. It was agreed to begin with $15,000 and go up, if necessary, to $25,000: caution of another kind.

I couldn't but wonder if we were being amoral. Silence, presumably, had been bought by fear. We were now going to

outbid the opposition by offering cash. And if justice couldn't be bought with one figure we'd go higher.

On the other hand, why should I discourage the executives? For years they had ignored crime and corruption. Now they were interested. Perhaps they knew the area and its people better than I.

I was ordered to write the first story, a factual account of the murder. No mention was to be made of the fact that the Dade sheriff was an official suspect. That could come later if the reward failed to bring the truth—and the evidence to prove it.

I wrote the story—solid, unimpeachable. Had not the *Herald* carried a front-page box announcing a $15,000 reward, it would not have attracted undue attention. But the edition was hardly on the street when the telephones started ringing. And everyone, it seemed, had the same answer. But they still lacked the proof.

Meanwhile, I went back to Broward County for a meeting with Basinger, and a gambler he wanted me to meet. Vic demanded he be permitted to "overlook the session," but we went ahead without him. The meet was set up for a lonely stretch of road in the grasslands west of Dania.

It was not until I was seated in the gambler's new Pontiac that I recognized him. My pal Charley had given me full information, and indeed, we had taken pictures of his home and of the shady lane leading to his bolita counting house. (His real name was Charles Robertson, but—to avoid confusion as much as anything—we decided to call him Sam.)

A Georgia redneck, Sam was a few years older than I. He had come to Florida in the 1940's and by 1950 was a big enough gambler to be mentioned in Kefauver Committee testimony. Of medium height, dark, with a gruff twang of a voice, he was notable by the scar on his face. I was to hear more of that scar later.

Sam owned, among other things, a "Catfish House" in north Broward near Pompano, and it was there Dick met him while campaigning. This didn't surprise me. If there were a

single voter in Broward whom Dick didn't know, I would have
been shocked.

After two roadside meetings Sam apparently decided he
could trust me. We left Dick behind and drove south to Dade.
The route took us by the counting house, whose entrance I
had photographed, but Sam didn't stop. Too many people
knew that location, he said. We went instead to the Pink
House—a two-bedroom frame house by a swamp. It got its
name from its color—Flamingo Pink.

As Sam explained it, he kept the Pink House in reserve for
the unlikely event law enforcement might stake out his regular counting house. And he used it for very special conferences and for social drinking.

I began to understand when I got inside and was introduced to a girl I will call Nan. Sam said she was a good hand
with an adding machine, but I guessed she had other talents.
In her late twenties, perhaps, she was slim, dark, and eager to
please. She was also well trained, sitting for an hour without
speaking, moving only to fix Sam a new drink or to light his
cigarette. He drank gin and orange juice in milk-shake-size
paper containers.

On this first afternoon at the Pink House, Sam consumed
five of his huge drinks, while he told me a tale which I came to
call "The Making of a Sheriff—Dade County."

The years following the Kefauver blight were quiet and
healthy, Sam said. The reformers and do-gooders were happy.
They thought they had cleaned up the county. Of course,
except for the closing of Meyer Lansky's plush casinos and
the collapse of the S & G Syndicate on the Beach, very little
actually changed. The bookies and the bolita operators
worked in comparative freedom and paid very little ice.

The system was controlled outside Miami and Miami
Beach by a bagman known as the "Smoker." Red Rainwater
collected inside Miami, as he had done for a decade. And on
the Beach a New Yorker known as the "Fruit Man"—he
operated several fruit stores—was nominally boss.

Sam ran the CB House. He, as many other bolita barons

had before him, took over the operation when the original
boss retired. He was unwilling to quote figures, but Charley
had already told me the CB House did $30,000 a week gross.
Even Charley admitted Sam had a reputation for honesty that
stood him in good stead when the syndicate began moving
into the area.

Again I heard the story of Hymie Martin and the syndicate.
By 1960 Martin had three of the largest operations—Fred
Chapman, Jack Rainwater, and Jimmy Christian. With the
election of Sheriff Michell in 1960, he expanded into Broward
County. Actually the Broward operations were but extensions
of the Dade houses.

The pinch began on Sam, and he turned to his friend, the
Smoker, for help. But the Smoker was having trouble control-
ling the sheriff. There had been a narrow escape in 1960–61,
Sam said, and Sheriff Tom Kelly was playing it safe. The
Smoker advised that it might be well to replace Kelly with
someone more cooperative.

Sam agreed. To aid in the project, he drafted a couple of
Metro commissioners, an ex-newspaper reporter turned political aide, and several ward heelers. Finding a candidate was
no problem—both Sam and the Smoker had known Tal
Buchanan for years. They used their influence to get him
promoted to chief of detectives. From every indication
Buchanan was not a serious thinker. He enjoyed good liquor
and other pleasures of an amoral society. The Smoker was
sure he would cooperate.

The project was made possible by the fact that Dade
County voters had adopted a metropolitan form of government. It was supposed to coordinate the work of some twenty-
six cities in the county and give the area an efficient government. Naturally, the experiment was not a complete success,
but it had resulted in making the office of sheriff appointive.
To speed acceptance, Tom Kelly was appointed to the post he
had originally won at the polls. He could be fired by the
county manager if the manager could be sure such abrupt

action wouldn't cause him to be fired in turn by the Metro commission.

According to Sam, the campaign began early in 1962. Various means were used to put Sheriff Kelly in a bad light with the county manager. The help of certain officials who were cooperative was indispensable, Sam said.

Campaign headquarters were set up in a villa at the Purple Manor in Miami Springs, Sam continued. And here I pricked up my ears. Five men had keys to that villa, but Buchanan spent more time in it than anyone else. He lived there for weeks at a time, Sam said.

When success was at last achieved on December 26, 1962, and Kelly was fired, Buchanan got the word at the Purple Manor. He was a little unhappy at the thought that he, as sheriff, would have to go home to his wife, Sam said with a hoarse chuckle.

All went well. Buchanan was in power and promising to do something about Hymie Martin as well as the KY House, which had suddenly reappeared. The KY House had been dead for years, and there had been a general agreement no new bolita houses would be permitted. But out of the blue came the revival—if that's what it was. Word was that the same syndicate bankrolled it, but the operators bypassed Martin and dealt directly with syndicate bosses. A veteran player, Hoke (Bookie Mac) MacClellan, fronted for the operation but—and Sam lowered his voice—word was the real operators were the top brass in the sheriff's department.

Charley had said the same thing so I wasn't so shocked as Sam thought I should be. He moved his legs aside as Nan, apparently bored, got up to "pick up the room." I watched as she emptied ash trays and dusted around the pistol on the table within reach of Sam. It didn't seem to bother her.

Life became complicated when ousted Sheriff Kelly managed to circulate a petition that caused a special election to be held to amend the Metro charter and make the sheriff's job

elective. Much to the surprise of everyone, including the *Herald*, Kelly carried the day. And suddenly, after only eight months in office, Buchanan found himself running for the office he had originally been given by appointment.

"They came to me," Sam said, "for campaign money. It was an emergency. If I didn't give it, they'd have to go to Hymie and make a deal. So I put up $25,000."

It was a close race, but Buchanan defeated Kelly and retained his title. But something happened. Now he was in office for four years. Without warning he dumped the Smoker. After being chief bagman for thirteen years, the Smoker was finished. And the pressure continued on Sam. The KY House grew by leaps and bounds, and Fat Hymie gobbled up everything else.

"I met with Tal," said Sam, "but it didn't do no good. He made promises, but he didn't keep them. Chief of Detectives Manson Hill was running things, and Buchanan couldn't seem to control him."

"Whatta you think caused it?" I asked.

"I'm not sure," said Sam slowly, "but they gotta have some strong hold on him—something real strong."

"Like what?"

"Like maybe the McFarland case," he speculated.

The Smoker knew more about the McFarland case than anyone else, Sam said. In fact, most of Sam's information came from him. The rumor was that the sheriff, while visiting a friend in Broward, had accidentally hit McFarland. He allegedly became frightened and carted the body off in his car. Later, or so went the story, some deputies hauled it back to Broward and fired the bullets into the head to disguise the accident. Many months were to pass before Buchanan publicly denied this rumor.

Roy O'Nan was the Smoker's name and he was part owner of a liquor store on the edge of the central Negro district. But

getting him to tell me anything might be a problem. Sam had some suggestions and I followed them.

It went exactly as Sam predicted. I drove out to the liquor store after making an appointment. O'Nan met me in the door. Tall, broad-shouldered, he had silvering hair and looked for all the world like a Chamber of Commerce executive. I learned later he had been president of a North Dade Chamber of Commerce before becoming a bagman.

We sat in a booth, and I inquired about his being a bagman and, especially, about a rumor the sheriff's car was found in O'Nan's driveway on the morning after the McFarland murder. The man turned white beneath his tan. It was all a lie, an unfounded, absurd lie, sir. He knew the sheriff, yes. In fact, he had campaigned for him. But his interest was only that of a good citizen eager to see the most qualified man elected to office.

I let him talk, then returned with the sharp questions. Did he have a key to Apartment 212 at the Purple Manor? Did he know a prostitute named Judy who lived across the patio? Why had he been replaced as bagman?

Roy lowered his voice. We were talking confidentially now. Sure, he knew a few things, but he couldn't talk. He had this big deal cooking. As soon as it was out of the way he would be happy to talk to me. After all, he had read my stories. I couldn't fool him. No ordinary reporter could come up with that stuff. I was a federal man. Right?

I denied it, but Roy's smile grew broader. He wanted to believe it. I searched my mind for a few scraps of information that, when posed in question form, might strengthen his conviction. Apparently, I achieved my goal. Roy promised to get in touch with me in the very near future. He wanted to tap a few sources first, but he'd be back.

Rather wearily, I gave up and went home. Next day I called the unlisted number—one of three Sam had given me—and got a report. Sure enough, Roy had called to tell Sam about the federal man. Sam had advised him to cooper-

ate. Could I come to a meet that afternoon at the Howard Johnson at the Golden Glades Interchange?

I made the meet—and several others in the weeks ahead. I saw Roy weep as I pushed for information. I saw him curse with an honest hatred that encouraged me. But most of the time he squirmed. Soon I learned the direct approach was the wrong one. Better to sit at the counting house—Sam never permitted Roy to know the location of the Pink House or to meet Nan—and listen to O'Nan and Sam talk about old times, the good old days. Some of their tales were fantastic, and the sight of a notebook choked off conversation. Roy developed a phobia about my streamlined briefcase. He was convinced it had a built-in "bug"—and remained convinced when I opened it.

I learned much of Dade County politics in the next few weeks, but I came no closer to solving the central issue. Soon I decided that neither O'Nan nor Sam really knew what caused Buchanan to double-cross them—they could but guess. Most of their guesses centered around the girl named Judy, and so when at last my spies informed me she had returned, I headed for her apartment.

The rain began in the night and by mid-morning it surpassed even the torrents of Hurricane Betsy. Twenty inches of rain were to fall in less than twenty-four hours that day, and I was in the middle of it.

There I stood, on a balcony outside the second story apartment. The overhang of the roof was just enough to protect me if I pressed against the door. Judy was inside that door, but she wouldn't open it. And I was afraid to leave, lest she again disappear.

It was a stalemate—and still the rain came slanting in upon me, and I cursed the Miami *Herald* and the distorted sense of duty that kept me waiting outside a prostitute's door.

Help came unexpectedly, when I recognized a special agent of the Internal Revenue Service. He had once questioned me about my dealings with Red Vaught, and I learned he was

investigating Vaught's income. Well, as far as I knew, Judy worked for Red. At any rate, she should know something about him.

I called the agent over and explained the situation. I knew the girl was there, but I couldn't get her to open up the door. She might even be sick—or dead.

The IRS man, small and intelligent, knocked on the door. When no one answered he went in search of the building manager. The sight of a badge did more than a press card, and when Judy refused to respond to the manager's knock, a passkey was inserted.

The door opened on a chain. A face topped by dark hair and featuring a big nose appeared in the small space. My friend showed his badge again, and asked for an interview. I identified myself and asked for an interview. She told me to get lost but she promised the agent to come to his office next day. I started to argue and delay things a moment as the manager and the agent moved away.

When they were out of hearing, the girl hissed, "I'll call you later. I don't want the sheriff's people to see us talking."

The door closed. I stepped out into the rain and looked down into the parking lot. The deputies weren't hard to spot. They were parked in two cars at angles that gave them a view of the balcony, while permitting them to observe all cars coming and going.

I was too wet to care. One car followed as I crawled east to I–95. I assumed the other followed the agent back to town— but I assumed wrong.

The interview took place in a motel—a Howard Johnson, naturally. It was Judy's idea. The deputies would think she was attending to business. We met in the lobby and I signed for a room—using my name as well as the *Herald*'s on the card. Dick Basinger volunteered to stand guard outside the door, and City Editor Pete Laine dropped in on his way to work. He assured me he wanted only to be sure no one

crashed in with cameras, but I figured he really wanted a look at the girl.

The conversation inside the bedroom was a little strained. After all, when you're talking about prostitution to a prostitute, a nearby bed can't help but bulk large in your subconscious. And Judy didn't help matters much. Oh, she was decorous enough, up to a point. But she kept crossing her legs and remarking wistfully how she really liked "mature men."

Determinedly, I returned the conversation to business. She explained that I had hardly left her room when the deputies appeared at her door, after calling to say they were coming up. They took her, she said, to headquarters, where Chief of Detectives Manson Hill personally questioned her about my visit. Then he took a statement in which she denied ever having seen Sheriff Buchanan at the Purple Manor or anywhere else. Finally, she was escorted into the sheriff's personal office and asked in front of witnesses if she knew him. Needless to say, she swore again she had never seen Tal before.

The deputies brought her home then, after warning her strongly that she was to report any effort by me to contact her.

Why then did she contact me? Why was she talking? The woman shrugged her skinny shoulders. Steve was responsible. Who was Steve? Well, that was a long story. Besides, I wouldn't believe it.

So I leaned back and listened. She was only nineteen, she said, when she moved into the Manor. She was working in a bank. She was a square, a real square. All she wanted was to find another nice square, settle down, and have kids—seven kids.

The trouble was—this roommate was a professional. Her name was Judy too, Judy B. People called them Judy B and Judy C to tell them apart. Actually, they looked alike—same age, same size. Hair was different, but with today's wigs, that didn't mean anything. A lot of people got them confused.

Judy B didn't have a full-time job. She worked at odds and

ends at the Manor—dated the son of the owner. He was wild but she loved him. In between, she slept with other men. The boy understood it was business.

The Manor was a swinging place. Two nightclubs ran all hours. One office was fixed for gambling. You could buy almost anything, including narcotics. A lot of airline people stayed there—it was near Miami International Airport—and you met a lot of swingers.

Life with Judy B could get exciting. On one occasion Judy B brought in a pregnant girl. A doctor performed the abortion right there in the motel room. He had dirty fingernails and he botched the job. The poor girl almost died. It was two weeks before she could leave.

When I interrupted to ask if Judy C—by then I was doing it—got acquainted with the people who lived across the patio in Apartment 212, the girl smiled. Naturally. He was one of Judy B's frequent visitors. In fact, he was largely responsible for saving Judy B's life.

I shut up and listened. Judy C had been dating Steve. He was a college boy spending the summer in Miami. Real nice. She got home about 4 A.M. The room was dark and Judy B was apparently asleep on the twin bed. Judy C was undressing in the darkness when a loud knocking sounded. A man's voice demanded Judy open the door. It made other suggestions as well, said Judy with a wry smile.

When Judy B didn't answer, Judy C turned on the lights and discovered her roommate was unconscious. A suicide note explained Judy B was pregnant, unloved, and unwilling to live. She had taken sleeping pills.

Police arrived. Someone next door reported the disturbance by the nocturnal visitor, and a car had been in the vicinity. A car was usually in the vicinity, I discovered later. Even as the officers walked Judy B back and forth and forced a raw egg down her throat, the neighbor in Apartment 212 called with an invitation. The officers took the call, then checked

with the switchboard to make sure the caller was in the apartment across the patio.

When Judy B revived a little, one officer took her to Jackson Memorial Hospital. The other man, Bob Tenan, went to Apartment 212 and identified the occupant.

"Naturally," said Judy C, "when they found who he was they didn't arrest him. I heard later they called Manson Hill to come and get him."

Judy B recovered, had an abortion, and shortly thereafter moved. One report had it she lived awhile in Broward County before going to Houston and a job in a club there. Judy C really didn't know, for Steve—"my college boy"—moved in and spent the rest of the summer with her at the Manor.

"He'll always be my college boy," said the girl wistfully. Her regret for what might have been was believable, but it passed. "Of course, I like mature men now," she said coyly and looked at the bed.

I thanked the girl and assured her Steve would be proud of her sentimental gesture. City Editor Laine had given up the vigil, but faithful Dick was still guarding the door. I introduced Dick to Judy and made my excuses. All the way to Miami Springs I wondered if Dick would meet Judy's specifications. There was a lot of silver in his curly hair.

A confused but rewarding period followed, as I checked every lead. To my surprise I got cooperation from the Miami Springs police department. The Manor was still a headache, they said, despite its reorganization after bankruptcy. They would be happy to see it closed.

Ultimately, I wound up in the home of off-duty policeman Bob Tenan. His new bride, a poised and striking brunette, served coffee as I explained my mission. Bob required little convincing. He had read my stories but, even more important, was the memory he carried. I left his home with an affidavit that identified Sheriff T. A. Buchanan as the man in Apartment 212 on the night Judy B almost died.

I also took along official police reports that listed Buchan-

an's car as having been found near the Manor twice on the night in question. There was another report detailing the attempted suicide.

As I headed toward the *Herald* with my goodies, I felt a quiet satisfaction that is the real reward of investigative reporting. We had already obtained the Broward end of it. Now I had the Purple Manor story in documented detail. All that remained was to connect up the two sequences. And on this sunny afternoon the task seemed possible.

My mood changed at the *Herald*. Deep gloom cloaked the city room. An editor handed me a long story that had just come in on the teletype from the Broward bureau.

State Attorney Quentin Long was quoted as saying a second autopsy on the recently interred body of Floyd Earl McFarland produced no evidence to sustain a theory McFarland was a hit-and-run victim.

The autopsy had been ordered, Long added, to quiet vicious rumors circulating about the case. The Broward sheriff's office probe was continuing.

There was much more, but I tossed it aside. As far as I could see, nothing had changed. I had no more confidence in Quentin Long than I had in Chief Deputy Ed Clode.

But I was wrong. The *Herald*'s attitude had changed. Barring a miracle, the story was dead. The entire plan of action originally designed would be abandoned. We couldn't take a chance on giving anyone grounds for a suit.

I presented my new evidence and argued, the McFarland case aside, that here was a good story in its own right. The editors rejected my argument but they were delighted. This was fine work, indeed. If a suit did come, the fact we had such a story and had not used it would prove a lack of malice on our part. What better evidence of good faith than facts withheld?

The conference ended with everyone in a much better humor—everyone but me. I kept thinking of Judy C and Bob Tenan. Because of me their necks were stretched way out.

FIVE

I PLAY SECRET AGENT

AND NEARLY LOSE MY SECRETS

*

It was almost dark when I left home, but across the tiny park on Rio Vista Drive I could see the parked car. The idiots were using Joe Mazur's white Cadillac again. Stupid, but perhaps Sheriff Michell's austerity program didn't permit maintaining a fleet for surveillance purposes.

I got into the Mustang I was renting this week and headed down Tenth Street toward Federal Highway. The Cadillac turned on its lights and followed. Apparently my "tails" didn't yet realize I was aware of their presence. Later, when they learned otherwise, they became quite open, but at this stage they still tried to be subtle. That presented me with a problem —how to get rid of them without being obvious.

Turning north on Federal, I went through the New River tunnel and on toward Pompano. At Oakland Park Boulevard I turned east. It was impossible to tell in the growing darkness if any of the hundreds of lights behind me belonged to a white Caddy, but I had a feeling it was there. I lost that feeling in the parking lot of a restaurant so snobbish it specialized in steaks although located on the ocean. Dick was waiting there. We went south in his car on A1A, hoping the feint to the north would divert the Broward sheriff's office.

Ultimately, we got back on Federal Highway and ended up in West Hollywood—a racially mixed community where people carry guns when answering the doorbell at night.

"There's no law in West Hollywood," Basinger said. "I know—I live here."

Our subject for the night was a former Broward deputy
sheriff who, upon being fired, attempted to work as a private
detective and was now sacking groceries in a supermarket. In
helping me, through Dick, he hoped to win back his badge
when, and if, Dick ran again for sheriff and was elected.

Jim was impressively large, with a balding head, white
teeth, and a hearty smile. We drank coffee. The air conditioner hummed. I suppressed a yawn. These days I was always
sleepy—until I got to bed. Then ideas would churn around
until, in desperation, I would raid the refrigerator. With belly
full, the mind at last would relax, and sleep would come.
Already, despite the frantic pace, I had gained fifteen pounds.
It worried me.

It began to look like a wasted evening. Dick got excited
about several things, but I saw little I could use. Just as I was
about to suggest we leave, Jim produced the report.

I settled down to read it, as Jim and Dick continued to talk
about the current situation. And abruptly their conversation
and the four walls of the comfortable living-room seemed to
fade. I was back in a jungle.

It was 1961. Sheriff Allen B. Michell had just taken office.
A former police captain in Philadelphia, Michell had been in
Broward County only eighteen months when he was elected.

Leo Hart, a real-estate promoter among other things, "discovered" Michell and sold him to the local newspaper. Years
before, the same newspaper had supported Sheriff Walter
Clark during his long rule. The Kefauver Committee ruined
Clark when it revealed he operated slot machines and bolita
from the sheriff's office and worked closely with Jake Lansky,
who bossed syndicate casinos in south Broward. Since Clark
was forced out, the newspaper had been looking for a new
sheriff and Michell seemed to be the man.

Shortly after election the inevitable happened. Even as two
years later in Dade, Sheriff Buchanan booted out bagman
Roy O'Nan, Michell in 1961 turned on his campaign man-

ager. Jim, the deputy who four years later wanted his badge
back, was assigned to investigate Hart.

According to Jim's report, he was told Hart "had entered
into some private contracts with individuals for the operation
of bolita and other types of lotteries and gambling in Broward
County."

What's more—and probably more to the issue—Hart had
allegedly made separate arrangements with rival groups for
the same "franchise" and had been collecting from both. This
was considered unethical.

In quest of information, Jim went first to some of Gulfstream Park's on-track bookies—men who are permitted to
accept bets from individuals who don't want to use the pari-
mutuel system for one reason or another. The bookies were
cooperative and directed the deputy to other bookies in
Miami.

Again cooperation was achieved. The gamblers pointed
out, however, that since Hart came from East St. Louis, it
might be wise to arrange things through Buster Wortman,
"head of the syndicate there." They put a call through to
Wortman but were unable to reach him. Jim was told to go
home, and that Hart would be taken care of later.

In fact, the report added, the gamblers said they felt it
would be better to take care of Hart in Mexico City—cause
less heat.

Not wanting to leave any stone unturned, Jim arranged to
meet, as he put it, "another individual of great renown—
Mandy Capone, the brother of Al Capone."

Despite Capone's promise to lend a hand in a good cause,
the deputy arranged for a Dade officer to introduce him to
"Jules Levitt, former syndicate man from East St. Louis."
Levitt listened sympathetically to the tale of woe and also
promised to help. Four days later he became ill, however, "and
we have received no further information from him."

Undismayed, Jim tried again. This time he contacted
"Tony Gobbels alias Tony Ricci, a syndicate man," and got

his promise to call Wortman "and see if he could come up with something which could stop Hart's attitude and loud and boisterous actions in this county."

The deputy added that he later learned that Ricci talked to Wortman on two occasions. "Mr. Ricci advised me," he wrote, "that we need not worry about the man, that things would be taken care of in the proper manner."

I glanced across the room at this point. Jim was in heavy conversation with Basinger. He was asking for a future appointment to the sheriff's vice squad.

The report continued with details of Hart's activities since the sheriff took office. The report noted:

"One of the most interesting of these was his connection with Joe Sonken and Hymie Martin. Mr. Martin being a known syndicate man and former big time hood, and Mr. Sonken being the same and also having a business in this area called the Gold Coast Lounge in Hollywood on A1A . . ."

I raised mental eyebrows here. Sheriff Michell disclaimed any knowledge of Martin when questioned prior to the publication of my first story. Yet Martin was identified in a 1961 official report. Sonken and his joint were familiar too. Back in 1957, syndicated columnist Jack Anderson described the Gold Coast Lounge as "the underworld message center in the Miami area." He noted it was "run by blimp-bellied Joe Sonken who, police say, was formerly a partner in the Chicago call-girl racket with Peter Arnstein, alias Petey Arnold. The pair came to Miami a few years ago and opened Mother Kelly's night club . . ."

Anderson didn't say so, but another partner in Mother Kelly's was Irving (Nig) Devine, a former Newport hood now in Las Vegas.

I checked myself. That organized crime was organized, I had long ago decided. I would drop in soon on Joe Sonken and see if he was still blimp-bellied. Meanwhile, back to the report:

"From the information I received from very reliable

sources," it continued, "Mr. Hart, Mr. Martin and Mr. Sonken had numerous amounts of visits in the city of Hollywood on many occasions, due to the fact that he guaranteed them protection for a bolita operation to be conducted by them in Broward County. The amount of money involved, according to the informant, was $5,000 per month to be paid to Hart by Mr. Sonken and Mr. Martin . . ."

So there it was—an official sheriff's report confirming what I had already written. Hymie Martin and the syndicate bought protection in Broward County. Michell might claim he wasn't party to the agreement, but the fact remained—Martin got the protection he paid for.

The report concluded with an optimistic note—the gamblers that Jim first contacted had reported back. They gave assurances, he wrote, that "Hart would be removed from South Florida in the very near future and would not be here to bother this department, or the sheriff, in any manner."

The deputy added his conviction that the gamblers "will live up to their particular part of this bargain, as I have always found them to be very honorable men in any type of dealings."

"Jesus Christ," I muttered, and the conversation in the room ceased.

Jim, a smile masking the anxiety on his broad face, asked, "Whatta you think?"

I grinned. This was hardly the place to tell Jim what I thought. Instead, I asked to borrow his report. He agreed readily enough when I promised to return it.

"Way I look at it," said Jim, "it's sorta like insurance."

"What happened to Leo Hart?" I asked. "Did he have any insurance?"

Jim grinned. "Not that you'd notice. Few days after I turned in this report, the sheriff posted a notice on the bulletin board saying nobody was to take orders from Hart no more. Next thing we heard, Hart went to Mexico City for some reason and while he was there he had an accident. Broke both his legs."

I thought of Virgil and his quest for people with leg-breaking talent. He had asked for Cubans. Was there a reason why folks south of the border excelled in such arts?

"What happened next?"

Jim shook his head. "I don't rightly know. I got indicted after the state boys hit this VFW Club I was in, and they said I was running the gambling. It wasn't so. I was there because the sheriff had told me to warn them. But that didn't stop Michell from firing me. He's got no more loyalty than an alley cat."

We moved to the door. Jim's final handshake was strong. "If the paper needs a private eye," he said, "call on me. I've still got some contacts and I sure as hell need the money."

I promised to do my best, and tightly clutching the thick report, I hurried to the car. Dick sensed my eagerness to be gone and wasted no time. The night was dark and on the side streets of West Hollywood, there was little traffic. I sat pensive for a few blocks, marveling not so much at the events described in the report but at the fact they should be officially recorded.

We were going north and already were in the outskirts of Dania. When I noticed our position, I got an idea. "Swing by the Paradise Club," I suggested, "and let's check the action."

Within two minutes we were on "Bolita Boulevard," a wide street separating the cities of Dania and Hollywood. The area was largely populated by Negroes and the numbers writers had long ago learned to move back and forth across the street, according to which city was applying heat.

Somewhere in the vicinity of the Paradise Club, a Negro night spot, the "Dania Night Number" was thrown each night. Unlike Dade, where each operation conducted its own bolita drawings, in Broward the Dania Night Number served everyone. Hymie Martin, shortly after his deal with Leo Hart, used his power in Broward to force its acceptance.

We drove down an alley between the Paradise Club and the Liberty Heights Housing Project, a row of dingy apartment buildings. People were everywhere, milling around. The sight

of a car containing two white men attracted absolutely no attention.

The crowd was thickest outside the fourth building. When I noticed a huge air conditioner on the window of a ground-floor apartment, I knew we had found the action.

Dick stopped the car. A tall man with shiny black hair and a red shirt was walking by. He was grinning broadly.

"Hey, man," I called, remembering Charley's techniques. "Has the number fell yet?"

It seemed impossible, but the grin got wider. "Yeah, man, it has, and I got it. Fifty-one. I sure dreamed right last night."

I turned to Dick. "Mr. Basinger," I began, "if you had been elected sheriff last year, do you think you might be able to deduce that something is going on around here?"

"Well, Mr. Messick," said Dick. "I'm aware that people with evil minds might decide something is going on, but you must remember this is inside the city of Dania. Chief Smith tells me the bolita situation is under control down here, and of course, I must accept his word."

I jotted down the license numbers of two big cars parked at the side of the alley. The first numeral was 1, indicating the cars were from Dade County.

"Your caution does you credit," I remarked. "I suppose you would never consider checking out those tags to see just who is visiting here at this particular time? Some people might even think it necessary to tail these cars and see where they go."

"My dear sir, the sheriff's department has neither the time nor the manpower to waste on idle speculation. All my available men are being employed in keeping tabs on a certain wild-eyed reporter the communists sent down here to destroy faith in local law enforcement."

That was worth a laugh or two. Then we pulled out and circled the area. As we again entered the alley, one of the Dade cars was moving out. Dick needed no suggestion from me.

The car, a blue Buick with two white men it it, went south

to Hollywood Boulevard and turned east. By the time it crossed the Intracoastal and reached A1A, I guessed where it was going.

Sure enough, the men pulled into the parking lot flanking the Gold Coast Lounge. We started to follow them in, then decided the deputy watching my car north of Fort Lauderdale might get a little suspicious if I didn't return soon.

But a visit to Joe Sonken's joint had achieved high priority.

A subpoena was brought to my home by two deputies. I recognized Joe Mazur but followed his lead and gave no sign. The other deputy seemed quite pleased with himself—so I asked, "How did you find me?"

"We're detectives," he replied, grinning broadly.

I didn't tell him I knew Mazur had been watching my house for days. I didn't even mention that to find it in the first place one needed only to dial information and ask. I said nothing about the fact that last July, when I bought the house, a picture of it was carried in the real estate section of the local newspaper.

The subpoena was an "Instanter," which meant I was supposed to present myself instantly. I changed shirts and drove over to the courthouse. There was only a short wait—the jury was in a hurry.

State Attorney Quentin Long, tall, smooth, and bland, welcomed me into the jury room. Mentally I contrasted him to Dick Gerstein, and found him wanting. Where Gerstein was stern, Long was genial. Both were tall men, but Gerstein was by far the more imposing.

Yet, I quickly discovered, Long was as adept as Gerstein at controlling a grand jury. At least he had this one completely in the palm of his hand. The individual jurors were little more than faces, as Long explained that some of my recent stories had interested the jury. Specifically, they wanted to know a bit more about Sheriff Michell and Leo Hart.

I pointed out that the current jury had very little time in which to conduct the type of investigation the situation war-

ranted and required. Long smilingly agreed. This was true, but nevertheless the jurors wanted to make a beginning. He would see that the next jury was fully briefed and it would carry on.

Heads nodded. A nondescript man with gray hair spoke up. "Mr. Long is right, Mr. Messick. But could you hurry? Some of us have to get home to supper."

I concealed a smile. This was a challenge. Could I in thirty minutes outline the history of syndicate activity in Broward County and perhaps create a measure of interest in additional investigation?

When I finished, I searched the faces. Perhaps one or two were interested. One old man was angry—he had voted for Walter Clark in the old days, he said, and he didn't want anyone running Walter down—especially since Walter was dead and couldn't defend himself.

Long stepped in smoothly. We should be concerned, he said, not with Clark but with Michell. Personally, he found my account of events rather shocking, and he intended to see that the next jury carried on.

Smiles were back as Long shook my hand. "We'll be reading your future stories with interest," he said. "And perhaps you'll read our report with interest too. Thank you, very much."

Against my better judgment, I was almost convinced. The man was smooth, but perhaps he was also sincere.

Outside the jury room, reporter Jim Savage of the *Herald's* Broward bureau was waiting. Jim was young, but I had been impressed with his work from reading the Broward edition in recent months. He had a capacity for getting the facts, of seeing beyond the appearance of things.

"Keep an eye on the jury," I told him. "Long indicated they might come out with a pretty hot report."

Jim looked doubtful. "I just got word they're going to quit tonight," he said. "The judge has been notified to stand by."

I shrugged. "He talks a good fight anyway."

The sun was setting across the parking lot as I went out to my rented Mustang—a green one this week. To the west the sky flamed in various shades of red as grotesque cloud formations came alive with fiery light. Florida sunsets were always an experience, and this was one of the best.

Over to one side a man seemed to be having trouble unlocking his car door. I gave him one glance. The sunset was more interesting. It wasn't until much later I learned he was the official photographer of the Broward sheriff's office. My midnight companion, Chief Ed Clode, made the assignment after I arrived at the courthouse in answer to the subpoena. For good measure he sent the photographer out to make pictures of my house.

The shots of me were rather flattering—which was just as well since almost every hood in south Florida wanted a copy.

I arrived a little early at Joe Sonken's Gold Coast Lounge. The dining room was almost empty so I sat down at the bar. The bartender, a handsome first-generation Italian, seemed out of place polishing glasses. He was big enough to serve as bouncer.

The telephone—the same one described by Jack Anderson in his 1957 column—rang loudly. The bartender picked it up, then circled the bar and went out into the dining area where a short, fat man sat alone at a table. He whispered in the man's ear, and I watched Sonken put aside his cigar and waddle back to the telephone. Blimp-bellied was right—he weighed three hundred pounds if an ounce.

The telephone conversation was one-sided. All Joe did was grunt. Then he went back to his table.

I finished my drink and was about to order another one when a waiter happened by. Apparently he wasn't looking where he was going for he jostled my elbow.

"A thousand pardons," he said in a voice so accented I wondered if he had just got off the boat.

"A hundred will do," I replied, and felt a little bit foolish. It is always a shock for a cynical, down-to-earth reporter to discover that people do use recognition signals and code words. It is even more of a shock to be expected to participate in the game.

Nevertheless, it was time to move to a table. I walked all the way to the rear, past Sonken, who apparently was playing solitaire as his little pig eyes watched the room. My waiter had hurried ahead and was pulling out a chair.

At my rear, lights gleamed on the Intracoastal Waterway. Joe was well located between the ocean on the front and a wide expanse of canal at the rear. He even had a dock, and twice during the evening he waddled out to greet customers who arrived by yacht.

The waiter brought me a vodka martini with a lemon twist. I tasted it carefully and found it superb. As a meeting place, the Gold Coast Lounge had certain advantages.

Two couples entered and then three more. The dinner hour was at hand, and soon the joint would be packed.

Now the eager waiter was back. He handed me a huge menu, opening it at the last moment. I accepted it with both hands—and hid behind it. For a moment I had a desire to laugh. This was too melodramatic to be true. On the left, above the seafood entree, was fastened a thick manuscript. A paper clip held it in place.

Using the menu as a shield, I removed the manuscript and laid it on my lap. The drooping tablecloth concealed it there. The waiter was talking, recommending some Italian dish I couldn't pronounce. I nodded in agreement. I'd put on another five pounds tonight, but perhaps it was worth it. Yes, I'd have the wine too. Might as well live it up.

The waiter went away only to return with another martini. I drank it fast. No one was near me. The tables on either side were empty. To hell with caution. I picked up the manuscript and began to read.

I continued to read as my dinner came. The food was good,

and I stopped reading long enough to enjoy it. Best food since the Theatrical Restaurant in Cleveland, Mushy Wexler's joint and social headquarters for the syndicate.

The wine was good too. I read some more. Then I ordered brandy and continued to read. People came and went, but the very recklessness of what I was doing was as intoxicating as the brandy.

This is what I read—the gist of it, anyway.

On March 28, 1963, Bill (the Tapper) Dorn met with Fat Hymie Martin at Martin's home in north Dade.

Fat Hymie, unaware that his house had been bugged, talked freely. He was concerned with the situation in Broward County. It had cost him $100,000 to get the political setup he wanted there, he said, and he wasn't getting his money's worth.

Much of the problem was caused by a key man in the vice squad, whom I shall call Henry (which is not his real name). A former New York City cop, "Henry" came to south Florida in the 1950's and worked as a Dade deputy. In 1962, Martin had moved him to Broward to handle a newly created vice squad.

But "Henry" was not properly cooperative. Martin told Dorn that "Henry" insisted on going into Dania and shaking down the numbers writers there.

As Dorn knew, it had taken a lot of pressure to make the two Dania bolita bosses accept Martin as a banker. Now they were threatening to revolt and all because of "Henry's" greed. Martin wanted Dorn to know he had been reasonable. In an effort to solve the problem he had brought in the Fruit Man— the Miami Beach bagman who had an "in" with the attorney general's anti-bookie squad. The Fruit Man had warned "Henry" to stop harassing the writers, but "Henry" had refused. The trouble continued.

"Henry" was offered a chance to pick up some extra money by concentrating his activity in Fort Lauderdale, where Martin had nothing going for him. Anything he could make there was okay. But again "Henry" had refused.

The only think to do, Dorn agreed, was to remove "Henry." It was no great problem, and a good man was already on hand to take over. He, too, had moved up from the Dade sheriff's office. His name was Jim.

Martin was doubtful. Could "Henry" be removed and replaced by Jim without causing comment? Was Jim properly qualified?

Oh yes, said Dorn. Jim was related to him and was absolutely reliable. There was an easy way to handle the problem. Just announce a reorganization, a reshuffle. Abolish the vice squad. That would save $600 a week in ice. Jim could start at $100 a week and be the chief criminal investigator.

Martin said it sounded like it might work, if Jim was strong enough to keep "Henry" under control. Assured this would be no problem, Fat Hymie said he would issue the orders next day. Would The Tapper like to come along?

Dorn said he would like to come, but unfortunately he had a previous engagement.

Dorn soon departed. Next day, Martin left his ranch-style home near the Golden Glades Interchange, and picked up his bodyguard. They then drove east to A1A and turned north to a shopping center in which a syndicate gambling operation prospered in the guise of a smoke shop. The Feds knocked it off sometime later.

But Martin was not concerned with the gambling joint. He parked near a blue and white Mercury bearing a Broward license tag. Leaving his companion in the car, Fat Hymie got out and walked to the Mercury. The man from Broward was waiting there.

It was 8:04 A.M. when Martin entered the car. Unfortunately, for historians, the conversation was not recorded. The conference lasted thirty-one minutes, after which Martin returned to his car and went south on A1A to a fruit store on Collins Avenue just north of Lincoln Road. The Fruit Man was waiting.

The other man drove north to Fort Lauderdale and parked

near the Governor's Club Hotel. The curious eyes who watched him checked out the license number of his car. The man's name was Emerson Allsworth. Not only was he a state representative, he had been Sheriff Michell's official counsel during the first few months of Michell's term.

Two weeks later, the local newspaper carried news of the reorganization of the sheriff's office. The vice squad was abolished. The man nominated by Dorn and approved by Fat Hymie was given top authority. "Henry" was shoved aside, and thereafter no one bothered Dania numbers writers. Fat Hymie was happy.

Very carefully I opened the briefcase I had carried into Joe Sonken's, and placed the long report in it. Then I had another drink.

The dining room was still crowded, but somehow the customers had changed. Where before there had been family-type groups, complete even with children, there were now hard-bitten Mafia types with well painted dolls, who somehow reminded me of Judy.

At my left a dark-haired man was having words with a tall blonde. Even as I looked, he slapped her. The gesture was quick but I could see the red mark on her suddenly white face. It faded as she stood up, said something low and savage, and rushed from the room.

The man finished his drink, dropped a bill on the table and followed. Halfway to the door, someone stopped him. There was a brief conversation, a bark of hard laughter, and the man was gone.

The incident seemingly created no excitement. Everyone was preoccupied with his own affairs. Well, this respect for privacy had stood me in good stead while I read the report. Why should I knock it now?

The waiter brought the check. His face was expressionless. Briefly I wondered about him. Was he really a waiter first and an undercover agent only by accident? Or was it the other

way around? It was none of my business, of course. He had served me well. The check came to $14.86. Cheap enough, considering the time and liquor I had consumed. I dropped a twenty-dollar bill on his oblong tray. Someone else paid his salary, but he deserved a tip from me.

And abruptly I froze. Two couples were being escorted to a nearby table. One of them towered above the rest, his scarred face unmistakable. Bad Eye, they called him. Better known as State Attorney Richard E. Gerstein of Dade County.

Eight years ago Jack Anderson had called this place a message center for the syndicate. Joe Sonken had operated in Miami before moving to Broward. He had conspired with Fat Hymie and Leo Hart to set up a bolita operation in Broward.

Yet here was Gerstein—here in a place where the Big Man himself, Meyer Lansky, liked to eat. Well, no question about it—the food was good.

I was at the bar and headed for the door when Sonken stopped me. "Sir," he said, "you forgot something."

Here came my waiter on the run, holding out my briefcase as if it was a bomb. And blimp-bellied Joe took it from him, and passed it on to me.

"Thank you very much," I said.

"Don't mention it," said Joe.

I didn't even snicker until I got outside. But by the time they brought my car around, I was able to reflect: What a way to make a living!

I calmed down on the drive home by wrestling with a problem. How would I use the information? There was no point in attempting to write a factual account of the evening—the *Herald's* editors would never believe it.

By the time I got home I was beginning to have some doubts myself.

S I X

I CLIMB A LADDER

AND EAT QUAIL

*

Not for me to sail down the Palmetto Expressway in a boat. I decided to stay loose, with a photographer, so I could move in on the heels of the raiders.

It was the end of November. Weatherwise the "season" had begun, despite the fact that socially speaking it didn't start until January, when the horses moved to Hialeah.

Cool nights, perfect for sleeping, were followed by days just hot enough to be delightful. Only the tourists went swimming in the ocean, but natives were well content to desert the beaches. The big spenders were coming; the time to garner the loot and plan next summer's trip to Europe was near at hand.

And where was Messick on a Sunday afternoon? At home watching a professional football game on television? Oh no. I was sitting in the lobby of an almost deserted restaurant in the northwest section of Dade County. Two waiters were cleaning up from the luncheon crowd, but they had time to keep an eye on me. Was I a cop or a crook? Until they were sure, they weren't going to do anything. Just watch—and mutter.

I was waiting for the telephone to ring. Upon arrival, I had deposited a dime and called the number assigned to me. The FBI was efficient. I half expected to be forgotten in the excitement, but no—the man at the other end of the line had his instructions. The word for me was to wait. He would call me. I gave him the number of the coin telephone.

The photographer was restless. He liked to have his instruc-

tions spelled out in advance. I had no sympathy for him—after all, I was operating on faith. Why couldn't he?

Less than a mile away, cars were rushing at seventy miles per hour—the legal limit—along the Palmetto Expressway, which curves to the west around Miami. I closed my eyes and tried to visualize the scene.

Here comes the big car containing two men dressed in the rough khaki of fishermen. The car is pulling a tarpaulin-covered boat. Abruptly it slows and pulls over and off the pavement. The men get out, raise the hood, stare at the motor. One gets a wrench and seems to be making some sort of adjustment.

Minutes pass. The men glance over the high fence that marks the boundary of the expressway right-of-way. On the other side is a series of buildings, one a warehouse. A narrow street ends just short of the fence. Even as the men look, a car approaches along that dead-end street. It stops in front of a gate leading to the building. John (the Greek) Prokos gets out of the car, unlocks the gate.

The two men by the side of the road give a low signal. The tarpaulin covering the boat is tossed aside. Men, perspiration staining their white shirts, leap out. One carries a small plank. Within seconds they are across the boundary fence and rushing toward Prokos. Before he can close the huge metal gate they are inside. Prokos is seized—a search warrant is read.

Perhaps I was psychic, but as I was revising the sequence of events slightly, the phone jangled. I grabbed it. "Messick here."

"They're inside," said the voice quietly. "You can move in now."

I waved to the photographer who had just ordered a soft drink. The waiters watched—their question was still unanswered. We rushed to the car and headed down the highway. A left turn and then a right and we were on Sixty-third Street. The warehouse was less than a half-mile away.

The gate was open. We drove inside. A special agent

stopped us, then grinned broadly as I got out of the car. "They're back there," he said. "You should get some good pictures."

"Back there" was another building some two hundred feet to the rear. It was built like a barn, with a driveway underneath. Another special agent, also grinning like a victor, was stationed in the driveway. He pointed to an old-fashioned wooden ladder, which led upward to what once had been a hay loft. The ladder was brand new, however.

I climbed it gingerly. My photographer—excited now—paused to take my picture, then scrambled up behind me. The loft was empty, except for a special agent. He stood by what appeared to be a blank wall at the rear.

The photographer came alongside of me. "What is it?" he asked. "Where's the action?"

The special agent smiled and pressed the wall. A huge door swung upward, outward and then inward. A garage-type door that, once out of the way, revealed a large room. It was full of special agents. Two of them were talking on telephones—taking bets on the afternoon's ball games—still collecting evidence.

Here came Wayne Swinney, special agent in charge of the raid. Like his men, he was grinning. He had been one of those in the car that pulled the boat into position.

"Everything went beautifully," said Swinney. "We caught them cold."

Later, after we inspected living quarters that were still under construction in the first building, I was given full details.

Following the publication of my story in September, Prokos moved to an alternate site in Broward County—the "Dade-Broward Music Company." Investigation revealed the site had been held in readiness for more than a year. And with the World Series about to begin, the Greek decided to use it.

The FBI soon learned the location, however, and were pre-

paring a raid when, for no apparent reason, Prokos moved back to temporary quarters in Dade County. Still the special agents found him, but by the time they got sufficient evidence to seek a search warrant, Prokos pulled out again. This time he went into what apparently had been intended as a permanent home. Work was still under way on the buildings, but at first inspection the location seemed impregnable.

To reach the hidden room in the loft, agents would need to drive down the dead-end road. They would have to get through the big outer gate as well as an inner gate, which had not yet been installed. They would then have to climb the ladder and find the entrance to the hidden room. By the time all that transpired, evidence could easily be destroyed. Indeed, a special incinerator half filled with ash was found in the loft.

Given another week to complete construction, Prokos might well have had a fortress. But the experienced men of Swinney's "Hoodlum Squad" found the fatal flaw in the scheme—the expressway. Using it to get close, they had waited until Prokos opened the gates. Even then an elaborate alarm system might have spoiled everything, but the system was incomplete. The wires had not been connected.

Greed had defeated the gambler. In his eagerness not to miss the lucrative Series betting, he had exposed himself before he was ready. The special agents had done a tremendous job. I congratulated Wayne Swinney.

"You deserve some credit," the still-happy man allowed. "Your story got him off balance. If he'd stayed in the Langford Building we might never have reached him."

No doubt Swinney was right, but there wasn't time to think about it. In roughly seventy-five minutes the street edition would go to press, and I was out in the boondocks with an unwritten story.

I called the photographer and we started for the gate. Enroute I was stopped by the first special agent to greet us. He was searching Prokos' car. We paused for a look. The trunk

was filled with pamphlets. I looked at a few of them. Violently anti-Turk they were, defending the Greek position on the island of Cyprus.

I stared at the cars rushing along the divided Palmetto Expressway. Well, every man needed to believe in something. Prokos was a gambler by American standards, a lawbreaker. But no doubt he considered himself something more—a Greek patriot.

In the amoral society of south Florida, the two are usually not incompatible.

The *Herald* gave the Prokos story quite a ride. After all, it was one of the first fruits of the campaign. The fact that federal intervention was necessary only made the point clear. The Greek had operated for years in the heart of Miami without pressure from police. When he moved into the unincorporated areas, the 900-man sheriff's department ignored him too. If he had not made the mistake of accepting bets in interstate commerce, the Feds couldn't have bothered him.

Exactly why the apathy of local law officers needed to be made any clearer, I didn't quite understand. Before me was a file on the so-called "Golden Bracelet Case." The incident made the situation about as clear as the waters off Great Exuma in the Bahamas—and you can't get much clearer than that.

The file told an incredible tale. A home was burglarized, a common enough occurrence in south Florida. Jewels and cash were taken. The loot included a distinctive gold bracelet.

Months passed. The robbery, like so many others of its kind, remained an official mystery.

One day the robbery victims attended Tropical Park Race Track but quickly lost interest in the horses, for on the arm of a woman sitting in front of them was the stolen bracelet.

The woman wearing the bracelet proved to be the wife of Manson Hill, chief of detectives for Sheriff Buchanan.

An uproar followed. The sheriff made an investigation. It

disclosed, Buchanan said, that Hill was given the bracelet by a
family friend, an attorney. The attorney said he got it from
the operator of a notorious Miami Beach bar. The operator
said he found the bracelet on the floor of the bar.

And there the sheriff's probe ended—temporarily. But
Floyd Miner, a private eye, used it in his campaign against
Sheriff Buchanan in 1964. A grand jury investigation followed the publicity. Gerstein led the probe, but as so often
happened, the jury was content to rap Buchanan's knuckles.
It said the sheriff should have conducted a better investigation.

Later Buchanan issued a statement: "After reviewing the
findings of the state attorney, the grand jury and our case file,
I have found no fault in the actions of any person in this
department."

And there the matter ended. No one questioned the decision.

A knock on the door and Dick Basinger interrupted my
thoughts. We got into his car and headed north once more,
but this time it wasn't a feint. Let them follow us if they
wished. We were just going to dinner.

The invitation had been relayed through Dick. It came
from Sam, the independent gambler who seldom ventured far
from the Pink House, his gin, and his mistress. But something
was brewing, and we were told to go to the "catfish house"
Sam owned near Pompano.

Now catfish has never been one of my favorite dishes, but
Sam assured me when I called him that the menu would consist of quail. It seemed that in addition to the restaurant Sam
owned a quail farm. And his special guests were treated to the
plump birds, while the regular customers ate fish or steak. We
were to be special guests.

It was soon apparent that Dick was invited because his
services as a guide were needed. I could never have found the
place alone. The northern part of Broward County, like the
southern part of Dade, is farming country. Migrant labor is

brought in to harvest the lettuce and tomatoes and pack it for shipment to the shivering East Coast. There are roads through the farm land, but only a farmer—or a politician in search of votes—would know his way around.

Basinger had been there before. So had most of the other politicians in Dade County, including, as I was later to discover, Emerson Allsworth. Soon he parked outside the square, boxlike building that housed the restaurant.

The manager and nominal owner greeted us as we entered a large dining room. But for special guests like us, the private room was waiting. He led the way between tables filled with farmers and pushed back a folding wall. There, at the rear, was a room large enough to contain a dice table and three roulette wheels. I wondered briefly if it had ever been used for that purpose. Tonight it contained only a long table with a snowy cloth covering it. Four men sat around the table.

One was Sam. He rose to his feet instantly, performed introductions, and asked what we were drinking. I took advantage of his hospitality to call for a Jack Daniels and water. At least the bar here was better stocked than the kitchen of the Pink House.

But as I ordered, I pondered. One of the other men was my old friend and assistant, the ex-gambler I called Charley. A few weeks before Charley had deserted me to work for the man who sat beside him now, Floyd Miner.

It had been Miner's connection that had interested me earlier in the evening in the Golden Bracelet case. Miner, a huge fat man, had been easily defeated by Buchanan in the 1964 campaign, but had gained sufficient prestige to win a job as special investigator for the current grand jury. In selecting him, the jurors obviously thought they were gaining a measure of independence from State Attorney Gerstein. They didn't realize, apparently, that Miner was a close friend of Bad Eye.

Assigned to investigate my stories of wide-open numbers operations, Miner had pulled a coup. Discovering that Char-

ley had provided me with many of my leads, Miner hired him from me. I couldn't object—after all, the *Herald* had been unwilling to put him on the payroll. And Charley's wife was insisting on some revenue.

Later Sam was to laugh heartily as he told how he and Charley wrote out numbers tickets for Miner to take to the grand jury as proof of wide-open conditions. As Sam explained it, there was no real fraud involved. They told Miner the tickets were bought from writers at certain locations where, in fact, writers sold bet tickets. It was simply easier to manufacture some than go out and buy them, Sam said. After all, Miner never knew the difference.

I remembered all the tickets I had bought, and had to agree it was easier, and it was funny in a rather amoral way.

But on this night in Sam's cat-fish house I turned my attention to the fourth man. A tall, rather handsome figure, his name meant nothing. Then Sam mentioned that he was a member of the Dade County Grand Jury. And I began to wonder what was going on here.

There was some talk of politics as first the drinks and then a huge platter of quail arrived. Forgetting my diet, I ate two birds. They were as delicious as Sam had promised. The sour-mash liquor seemed a perfect complement, and I had yet another drink.

"Bring on the dancing girls," whispered Dick at my right, and I knew what he meant. A man could learn to enjoy this kind of life. And with that realization, I pushed away the platter of quail and called for some black coffee.

It was as if a signal had been given. The table was cleared —except for Miner—and Sam opened the business session. Talking to me as much as to the grand juror, he explained he had a plan for cleaning up Dade County. Mr. Miner, he added, was ready to cooperate and had arranged for the grand juror to be present. I was there as an interested member of the press, but with the understanding that at this point everything was off the record.

I didn't say anything. They could understand what they pleased. I reserved the right to decide for myself what my actions would be.

Miner, still eating, stuffed half a quail into his mouth, washed it down with a beer, wiped his mouth with his hand, and concurred.

We all knew, he said, the sheriff's office was the key to conditions in Dade County. He, Miner, had been fighting for years to get good law enforcement. An opportunity now existed.

I was saddened when Charley chimed in to echo Miner—yeah, an opportunity now existed. Charley, I decided, had a new hero.

Basinger stuck his elbow in my ribs. "Wild, ain't it?" he whispered.

Sam took over. His scarred face twisted with effort as he sought the right words. The situation was this. The grand jury would subpoena Sheriff Buchanan at next Tuesday's session. Miner would arrange it. The jury would also subpoena Sam and O'Nan. They would be there waiting to testify when Buchanan came into the jury chambers. They would tell Buchanan the jig was up—they were going to tell the truth.

Meanwhile—and here Sam turned to the tall juror, who so far had said almost nothing—the jury would ask the sheriff specific questions about a $25,000 political contribution he had received from Sam in 1963. The exchange took place in Sam's home with O'Nan witnessing it.

I interrupted at this point to see clarification. Sam explained that the contribution was the final act in the long conspiracy to name Buchanan sheriff and keep him in office. Ousted Sheriff Kelly had succeeded in changing the sheriff's job to an elective basis, and it had become necessary to elect Buchanan to the post he had received by appointment. An election campaign required money, and Sam furnished it in the belief Buchanan would take Hymie Martin and the syndicate off his back.

"It's the Mob that brings in all this crime—all these jewel thieves and other crap," said Sam. "If they would leave the numbers to the local people we wouldn't have all this s---."

Miner and then Charley nodded solemnly. Sam picked up his plot where he left it.

"Get the picture? Buchanan is in the grand jury room. As soon as he hears the first question, he'll know what's coming. And he's trapped. If he tells the truth, he's finished. If he lies, he knows we are waiting outside to prove him guilty of perjury."

There was a long silence, as we indeed got the picture. It was broken by the juror.

"What do you think he'll do?"

Sam grinned wolfishly. "I think he'll resign. I'm so sure of it, I think we'd better start deciding who we want to replace him. The governor will have to appoint somebody, and it might as well be somebody we trust—somebody who'll clean the crooks out."

All eyes suddenly shifted to Miner, and I began to understand why I was there. Perhaps they wanted to give the session an air of respectability for the grand juror's sake, but that was only part of it. And a small part. Miner's ambitions to be sheriff were well known. With Governor Burns preparing to run for re-election, the *Herald's* choice for sheriff of Dade County might be decisive. These people obviously thought I could determine who that choice would be. And they wanted it to be Miner.

With the knowledge that I was being wined, dined, and flattered for a purpose, came a new idea. I tasted it cautiously, not daring to push it too far even in my mind. This situation had possibilities. They wanted to use me. Why didn't I use them instead?

Again the juror interrupted. "What about Gerstein?" he asked. "How am I going to handle him?"

Miner, as a friend of Gerstein, was the obvious person to answer. "Do him a favor," the special investigator suggested,

"and ask him to step outside before you start to question Buchanan. He'll be glad to leave, and it'll shake up the sheriff even more to see him go."

"That's right," said Charley. "It'll shake him up."

There was more excited chatter. Talk about counting eggs before they hatched, these optimists were looking far into the future. With the sheriff out of the way, they could foresee an end to the KY House and Hymie Martin. They could foresee a loose alliance of independent numbers operators, who would play fair with the suckers and tip off the press every time the syndicate attempted to enter Dade County.

I let them talk awhile as I explored the situation, dredging up what I knew of Governor Haydon Burns and his political allies. Inevitably I thought of his patronage man in Broward County—the man who once met with Fat Hymie in a parking lot off A1A—Emerson Allsworth. And suddenly the still nebulous idea began to take form.

"One question," I said. "What happens if Buchanan calls your bluff? Will you and O'Nan go on in and tell the truth so he can be indicted for perjury?"

The silence seemed shocked. All eyes fastened on me as if somehow I had broken up a children's party with an announcement of bedtime. Quick-witted Sam was first to recover. He spread his hands wide.

"The devil himself couldn't make Roy O'Nan tell the whole story to a grand jury," he said, "so there wouldn't be any point in me talking. But Buchanan is weak; he'll break."

"What happens to your subpoenas if he doesn't?" I persisted.

Sam grinned. "Oh, we'll just be excused for the day and not told to come back, I guess."

"Then it really is all just a bluff?"

The man actually shrugged. "I'm a gambler," he said. "I don't deny it. I've got a gambling stamp. I think the man will break, but if he don't we're no worse off than we were."

Miner nodded ponderously. "It's worth trying."

Charley agreed. "Yeah, whatta we got to lose?"

I stood up and yawned. "Don't let me stop you. If it works it'll be a helluva story."

The grand juror began asking questions. He wanted specific information about the money exchange. Apparently he was going to play his part all right. Briefly I wondered why.

Basinger got up to join me. We strolled to the end of the room. "How well do you know Allsworth?" I asked.

Dick looked puzzled. "I'm a friend of his, I guess. A political friend, anyway. Why?"

"Could you set up an appointment for me? Right away—in the next couple of days?"

"Sure, I suppose so." Dick was still puzzled. "What'll I say when he wants to know what it's all about?"

I grinned. "Tell him I want to discuss Fat Hymie with him," I said softly. "That might arouse his interest."

"Hey, Hank," shouted Sam from the table. "Want another drink before we break up?"

"I don't mind if I do," I replied, and everyone smiled happily.

Emerson Allsworth proved to be a slender, youthful man with a baby face that concealed real intelligence. We met in the Howard Johnson's on Federal Highway in Fort Lauderdale for breakfast coffee. Dick had done a good job in preparing the interview. Allsworth was curious, and more than slightly apprehensive. The mystery that still clung to my background helped, as I spoke in guarded terms of his meetings with Fat Hymie.

The man was smooth, but he was also a realist. While admitting nothing, it was soon apparent that, for the moment, I held all the cards. In less than thirty minutes and two cups of coffee, Allsworth was volunteering to help me clean up south Florida.

I asked as a preliminary step, if he would walk across the street to a motel and meet a mutual friend. He agreed readily enough, apparently determined to prove he trusted me.

"My future and the future of my children are in your hands," he said, as we stood up to go.

Basinger and I had rented two adjoining rooms the night before, and Dick spent an hour connecting a microphone in one room to a tape recorder in the other. A plasterer by profession before he turned politician, Dick's skill with his hands was useful in getting the wire through the walls. We had given the operation a test run and it worked beautifully. Now Dick was waiting in the room with the recorder, while I took Allsworth to the other room where the mike was concealed beneath one of the twin beds.

I opened the door and stepped aside to let my guest precede me. The moment was one I had been anticipating. Sam, his scarred face as grim as he could make it, sat in the one chair in the room. At his side within reach on the bed was his snub-nosed, hammerless revolver. I had wondered all night how the smooth politician would react.

He handled it pretty well.

There was one bad moment as Sam growled, "Howdy, Emerson."

"Why, hello," said the politician. "Nice to see you." He turned to me. "We met at that cat-fish place, I think."

There was some more polite conversation, as I stretched out on "my" bed. Emerson had no choice but to sit on the other one—above the mike.

Briefly, I explained the situation. We were interested in cleaning up south Florida. Sam and Roy O'Nan had been subpoenaed to the Dade County Grand Jury. Sam had decided to tell the truth about his relationship with Sheriff Buchanan. O'Nan was going to talk too. Buchanan would have to admit he took the money or face a perjury charge.

Emerson was sufficiently recovered to look bewildered. How did he fit into the picture? This was Broward County.

Sam began to talk. Emerson had influence with Governor Burns. Buchanan was linked politically with Burns. It would hurt Burns' chances for re-election if Buchanan was indicted. All kinds of things might come to light.

Emerson nodded. I was sure he was far ahead of the slow-spoken gambler. But he waited patiently, looking more bewildered than ever.

The situation was this. Emerson could call Burns, tell him the situation. Burns could either remove Buchanan from office, and thereby gain much political favor—especially with the Miami *Herald*—or he could tell Buchanan to resign and save everybody a lot of trouble.

Very true, agreed Emerson. But would the governor believe all this? He might think it just a bluff.

I concealed my smile. That was the very argument I had used with Sam and O'Nan. We had to have proof, I told them.

Sam now produced the proof—two sheets of paper.

Here, he explained, are affidavits. He had signed one and O'Nan the other. He was giving them to me to hold—as insurance. If anything happened to either him or O'Nan, I was free to use them in the newspaper. They would also prove he was not bluffing.

Very solemnly—and for Sam it was a solemn moment—he handed the papers to me. I studied them as if I had never seen them before. But I had sweated blood before convincing Sam and O'Nan to sign them. No one, I argued, would take the word of a gambler and a bagman. There had to be something on paper. If we could convince Allsworth the deal was going through, it would be to his advantage to warn the governor. And the governor would surely tell Buchanan.

It was bad psychology to let Buchanan be surprised by the situation in the grand jury room, where he would have to do one of two things. If he knew in advance what was coming, there was a third alternative—resignation.

To reinforce the case for the affidavits, I pointed out that there might be a leak anyway. And if there was, the existence of affidavits in my possession would be insurance. It would protect the witnesses.

Sam bought the argument first. O'Nan continued to back

away even after I brought a notary to the ex-counting house at the end of the shady lane I had once photographed.

As I typed up the final draft of the statement Sam dictated, O'Nan was screaming, "It's a trap. You'll end up before a Federal grand jury. Listen to me for God's sake."

But for once Sam didn't listen. His faith in me—and the mysterious forces he thought I represented—was stronger. Sam signed and then Roy, still protesting, put his name on the affidavit I had drawn at his dictation. When the notary affixed her seal, I felt relief sweep through me. But the battle wasn't over. I still had to get possession of the affidavits. Once I had them, I would figure out a way to use them in the *Herald*.

Now, in a motel room in Fort Lauderdale, I had them again. They were short, but to the point. Sam declared he had given Sheriff Buchanan $25,000 in varying denominations on a certain day in 1963, and O'Nan said he witnessed the transaction. Properly used, this would blow the lid off the sheriff's department. It would permit a cleanup that could end organized gambling and prostitution, remove the protection that permitted jewel thieves and abortionists to operate freely.

But there was only a moment to gloat. This hand had to be played out first. I passed the affidavits to Allsworth. He read them quickly but carefully, and returned them to me.

"What do you want me to do?" he asked.

"Call the governor," said Sam. "Tell him about these affidavits. Warn him it's all going before the grand jury next Tuesday—in three days."

"All right," said the politician. He glanced around. "There's no phone here."

He was right. Mentally, I kicked myself. We had picked the motel because it was within walking distance of the restaurant where I was to meet Allsworth.

The baby face was smiling now. "I've an idea," he suggested. "Hank, you come to my office. I'll call him from there."

It was my turn to hesitate. Here I controlled the situation,

knew where the recorder was hidden. In Allsworth's office the situation would be reversed.

"Come on," said Allsworth, "and I'll do something I've never done before. I'll call my good friend Haydon Burns and not tell him you're listening on the extension."

I shrugged. Allsworth knew the right bait for a trap—if it was a trap. After all, it was no crime to eavesdrop on a conversation with the governor if the person calling him gave permission. Or was it? Well, it was too tempting to resist.

Sam said he'd call me later. I abandoned the idea of entering the adjoining room to make sure Dick's recorder had been working. Surely, a technical flaw wouldn't spoil everything now. Not only had I the signed affidavits, I had Sam on tape saying he was giving them to me and repeating for Emerson's benefit the substance of what they contained. Now Sam couldn't deny the affidavits if he should ever be confronted with them. The thing had gone wonderfully well. I was just a little confused as to whom I had double-crossed the most.

We went back to the restaurant parking lot, and I followed Emerson's car downtown. It was the same car, I noted, that he had used two years earlier when he met Hymie Martin. The Mercury with the blue body and white top. When we parked near the Governor's Club Hotel, I casually mentioned the coincidence. Emerson winced.

The law offices of Allsworth were quietly luxurious but not elaborate. No one was around on a Saturday morning but a secretary, and Emerson announced he was out to all callers. He sat me down at a telephone in an adjoining office. When one of the buttons on the phone lighted up, I pushed it and picked up the receiver.

There was a delay. Emerson called the Governor's Mansion at Tallahassee only to be told the governor had left some time earlier to fly to his home in Jacksonville. He placed a call to 398-7265 in Jax, but the governor hadn't arrived.

After a rather futile effort at social conversation Emerson turned to some papers on his desk, and I pulled out a file from

my briefcase. It concerned a very curious episode in 1958, when a group of Dade County deputies, fianced by Dade County gamblers, attempted to overthrow the government of Haiti.

Objective of the invasion, which came within a whisker of succeeding, was to gain control of the casino there. I knew from my previous research that the casino in 1958 was licensed to Cliff Jones of Las Vegas. He had attempted to unload it, being out of favor with the government. Some of Fat Hymie Martin's syndicate bosses—even then preparing to sell their Casino Naçional in Havana and get out before Castro got in—went to Haiti to look over the casino. The American consul in Haiti warned off the Desert Inn boys, explaining that political conditions in the country were unstable. After their experience in Havana, the gamblers knew what that meant and they did withdraw.

"Hank," called Allsworth. "I'm going to try again."

I pulled the phone over and put the file back in my briefcase. However weird the past, the present was equally intriguing. The button lighted up, and I picked up the receiver again.

This time the call went through. Emerson needed only to mention his name, and within seconds I heard Governor Haydon Burns. He had a somewhat nasal quality about his voice like that of a Georgia cracker but softer somehow.

Allsworth wasted little time. Without explaining how he happened to get his facts—and I noticed Burns didn't ask—he outlined the situation facing Sheriff T. A. Buchanan.

"I don't see how they could indict him on the word of gamblers," said the governor. "And I'm not about to remove him unless he's indicted."

Emerson protested that the grand jury might make an exception—the heat was on in Miami.

But Burns was unmoved. "Being indicted and being convicted are two different things."

The futility of continuing the argument was apparent to both of us, but Burns wasn't finished. "Call Buchanan," he

ordered, "and tell him what's going on. Tell him I told you to call."

Well, maybe the bluff would still work. Buchanan, with a long weekend to think about it, might decide to step down and take that long-rumored post as head of the highway patrol. In any case, I'd give Sam a chance to play out his hand. If he failed, I had the affidavits. "The Making of a Sheriff—Dade County," would be one helluva story. Almost as good, in fact, as the Broward County version.

Allsworth looked pale and tired after he hung up and came to the door of his office. Momentarily, I felt a twinge of pity. The guy might be a slick operator as a politician, but he had brains and guts—brains enough to recognize realities and guts enough to do what had to be done. By the code of the Amoral Society, his dealings with Fat Hymie Martin were proper enough—so long as he didn't get caught. He apparently was determined to do everything possible to avoid being caught.

I shook his outstretched hand. "We'll have to get together for dinner sometime soon," he said.

"Yeah," I answered. "When are you going to call Buchanan?"

"Right away," he said. "Do you want to listen?"

Suddenly the game lost its flavor. I had done enough eavesdropping for one day. I could be sure Allsworth would obey the governor. There was no need for me to hang around any longer.

I was not so weary, however, that upon reaching home, I didn't call Dick. Did the recorder work?

"Worked swell," he said. "I got every word. It was beautiful." He paused. "What did Governor Burns say?"

I told him and there was silence. When Basinger finally spoke, his voice was serious.

"Know something, Hank?" he said. "I think somebody's going to get killed before this is over."

For some reason, I had the same feeling.

SEVEN

I LOSE SOME SLEEP

AND LEARN ABOUT A PARTY

*

It held promise of high drama, but the dramatics were to come later in the night.

A private eye who earlier had brought in a "solution" to the McFarland murder—it was the same old story—called about 10 P.M. to say I would soon be receiving another call from a man who wanted to meet me. He wouldn't say why, and I hung up in amused disgust. It had been a hectic week and I was tired. Sweating out the grand jury session had been enough adventure for awhile.

Tuesday the jury met on schedule. O'Nan and Sam had been subpoenaed and were waiting in the outer room when Sheriff Buchanan entered. At this stage of the game there had been hope he might yet quit rather than perjure himself. Naturally he wanted to delay until he saw if the witnesses actually appeared to testify against him. Sam said Buchanan turned white when he spotted him, but said nothing. He was before the jury for more than an hour. What happened? No one was sure. But Buchanan did not resign, and Sam and O'Nan—as planned—were sent home without testifying.

It seemed obvious that Buchanan had called the bluff, relying, perhaps, on Governor Burns' faith that a jury wouldn't indict on the word of gamblers. But Sam was determinedly optimistic. Buchanan was weak, he argued. Before the next jury date on the following Tuesday he would crack. O'Nan and Sam were scheduled to return. The trap was just taking a little longer to spring.

I listened to Sam, but already I had begun the second phase of my campaign. Regardless of what Buchanan did, I suggested, why didn't Sam simply go on in and tell the jury the truth? With O'Nan to back up the story, an indictment could be secured if, and I made a point of stressing the if, the tale about the $25,000 was true.

It was true, Sam assured me repeatedly, but to testify, to squeal, ran counter to his code. Tricking a man into quitting was all right, but to go the route of the square was another matter. I didn't argue too much, but at every opportunity I mentioned how easy and simple it would be. On one occasion, as Sam accepted a new king-size combination of gin and juice, he said I was right.

"But it wouldn't be so much fun that way," he insisted.

As far as I was concerned, the present way wasn't much fun. Nor was I in a mood for new intrigue. And two nights later, when the second call came through as promised, I rejected instantly the request for a meet at midnight.

The caller was reduced to a partial identification. He was a member of the Broward Grand Jury and was fed up with the pap State Attorney Quentin Long had been giving the jurors about crime—or the lack of it. Others felt the same way, but all were handicapped. They didn't have any facts. If I would meet with him, perhaps we could figure out a way to start a fire.

Something about the man's voice finally convinced me, and I reluctantly agreed. The chance was too good to miss. If a grand juror wanted information, it was my duty to give it to him, even if I had to do it informally. The juror suggested a restaurant on West Broward Boulevard not too far from the Fort Lauderdale police station.

The restaurant's name had been changed and I had a problem finding it. When at last I learned the new name, I found it closed. But I waited in my new Volkswagen—the *Herald* had finally balked at my use of rental cars—and ultimately up drove two men and a woman. They too had been confused by

the name change. The woman was introduced as Mrs. Bonnie Wetzler, wife of the juror George Wetzler. The second man was a friend, who later adopted the code name "Pan" after a "meet" at a joint which featured pancakes.

Tonight, however, Pan was along, because he had an office nearby. We drove to the office and, with the doors closed and the blinds drawn, turned on the lights and got acquainted.

Wetzler was a tall, slender man with a shock of blond hair. His wife was dark and rather stocky. Pan was tall, broad, and rangy. I wasn't surprised to learn he had formerly been a cop.

Again Wetzler explained the jurors' problems. Several jurors had jobs, he said, which took them about the county, and they knew the numbers racket, prostitution, and other forms of vice existed. But State Attorney Long had paraded a series of police chiefs and deputies through the grand jury room, getting from each assurance that all was well in the war against crime. Could I help? He needed information in order to persuade enough of his colleagues to demand I be called as a witness.

The man seemed sincere, and there wasn't much to lose, so I outlined the rise of Fat Hymie Martin and his career in Broward County. I told the group that the protection system was much older, going back to the 1930's when Sheriff Walter Clark operated bolita out of his office in the courthouse, and Meyer and Jake Lansky set up the casino operations that ten years later were to be among the most plush in the nation. The Lanskys were frequent visitors to the sheriff's office, and the sheriff developed a profitable sideline of slot machines as well.

"Broward County doesn't have a good record of law enforcement," I said bluntly.

"You could say the same thing about Dade County," interjected Pan.

Something in his tone intrigued me, set me thinking. And suddenly the answer came. Pan had been a cop, all right, and

so had his father before him. The father had been rather notorious. In one of the internal struggles for power, the father
had used gangster friends and almost succeeded in framing
the mayor and city manager of Miami. Two men using their
names had gone to Newport, Kentucky, and let themselves be
arrested outside a brothel. The Newport cops cooperated in
the frame. In my research for the Ford Foundation, I had
found letters to the cops from Pan's father.

I kept my face impassive. Fortunately, Bonnie had taken
advantage of the silence to give her views on something. I
strained my memory for the rest of the story. Ultimately the
police captain lost out, quit the force. He had taken a job in
the Keys. And, yes, in a fight with his son, he had been fatally
shot.

I looked at the son sitting across the room. The father had
been a typically amoral product of the Gold Coast. The son
who killed him was on my side. Life had its interesting
moments.

Bonnie ran out of breath, and I finished my recital. George
was vastly impressed. He would begin campaigning to get the
jury back into session, he said, and would demand it call me.
It would help if I could write some more stories about
Broward County—create a little heat, maybe.

I agreed, and we began the tedious business of disengaging
ourselves. At the last minute Bonnie decided she needed reassurance. Wasn't this kind of dangerous? Wouldn't the syndicate kill if necessary to protect its investment? She wanted
George to go ahead and do his civic duty, understand, but
maybe we ought to be careful.

There was no real danger, I stated bravely. The syndicate
had learned the bribe, or the frame, was as deadly as the
bullet and created far less trouble. There wasn't anything to
worry about. No one was going to shoot anyone.

Exactly three hours later, my telephone awoke me. The low
growl of Sam came across the wire.

"They just tried to hit Roy O'Nan," he said. "Ambushed
him."

I had a little difficulty waking. Sam repeated himself twice before I fully comprehended. Roy apparently had saved himself by diving out of his car as gunmen pumped three shots through his windshield. He was unhurt, but scared witless.

Hanging up, I looked at my watch. It was 4:30 A.M. I had been asleep less than three hours. Well, if I had to work all night, so could some other people. I dialed the *Herald*'s city editor, the man appointed by Managing Editor Beebe to "coordinate" the crime drive.

Pete answered quickly enough, and for once he was decisive. When I suggested routing out a photographer to get a picture of O'Nan's car, he yawned. "The holes will still be there in the morning."

Undoubtedly they would be there. As Pete hung up, I fought back an impulse to return to bed. Instead, I dialed O'Nan's home. Charley answered, his voice charged with excitement.

"You should see him, Hank. O'Nan I mean. He's got a gun, and he's given guns to his two boys. I think the old lady's got one too. The guy's still shaking."

Charley explained that Roy had called Floyd Miner, and Miner was there in his official capacity as a grand jury investigator. There was no doubt someone wanted to silence Roy—one way or another—before the next session of the grand jury.

I finally interrupted and Charley turned the phone over to Roy. The ex-bagman's voice sounded strained. "This was for real, Hank," he blurted. "They were trying to kill me."

Apparently someone had been questioning the authenticity of the episode. Well, there would be time for that later. I asked for the facts.

O'Nan explained he had just closed the liquor store—the one he owned in conjunction with an attorney—and got in his car to go home. It was about 3:45 A.M., and two cars were still in the lot. Since the area was a mixed neighborhood, the danger of a break-in was ever in mind. He circled the block and started back to check the lot. As he approached he no-

ticed a car tailing him. Driving into the lot, he saw the cars
that had been there were gone. He stopped to see what the
"tail" would do. It followed him into the lot, went by him and
made a short arc across his front. A late model car, light blue
in color, it contained at least two men—white men. He had
the door open when he saw the gleam of metal, and he hit the
pavement as three shots rang out. The car roared away, going
east on Northwest 46th Street.

"I was so shook up, Hank," said Roy, "I walked over to the
pay phone at the corner of the lot, and when I put my hand in
my pocket for a dime, I found I had the day's receipts. It was
in the way, so I stuffed the wad on the back of the telephone
box and after I made my call I went off and left it there. I
didn't think of it till I got home."

"Is it still there?" I asked, thinking of picture possibilities.

"Hell no, it ain't. I sent one of the boys back for it."

We talked some more. I got Miner on the phone. As grand
jury investigator he was official, but he didn't want to be
quoted. The shooting was actually in the jurisdiction of
Hialeah police, he explained, and Roy was being guarded by
Miami Springs cops because his home was at 81 South Royal
Poinciana Boulevard.

So much for metropolitan government. I went back to bed.
It was still possible to get three hours of sleep.

No one seemed sleepy when I arrived in the city room.
Conference followed conference. The affair was too incredible. Things like that happened in Chicago or Boston, perhaps,
but not in Dade County. There had to be another explanation. Possibly O'Nan was just trying to get out of testifying
and was using this as an excuse.

I listened in amazement. Were these people afraid of reality? Here was a big story, a dramatic story, and yet they
argued.

The first edition of the Miami *News* was carried into the
city room. It contained no story about the shooting. Doubts

deepened. Something must be wrong or the *News* would have the story.

Eventually a few facts were collected. Two shell casings had been found in the dust of the parking lot. The sheriff's crime laboratory, headed by a man generally conceded to be both honest and intelligent, Charles Zmuda, said they were .22-caliber rim fire magnums and had been discharged by either a rifle or a souped-up pistol.

This caused new speculation. Would anyone seriously attempting to kill O'Nan use such a weapon? Even some Federal agents I called expressed doubt. There had to be more to the story.

The pictures were convincing, however. Pete had been right—the holes were still there. And they were dramatic. Small caliber or no, the bullets had made holes big enough to push one's finger through and had caused the glass to fracture spider-web fashion. Part of a bullet was found buried in the rear deck shelf of the car. The bullet, whatever the caliber, could have killed O'Nan.

Edition after edition came without the story, but investigation revealed the *News* didn't print it for one reason only— they knew nothing of it. This came as no particular surprise. Crime reporting in Miami had long been a limited, haphazard matter. Unless someone phoned in a tip, any story could easily be missed. And on this story, the only people talking were talking only to me.

About forty minutes before deadline, a decision was made to shoot the works and play up the story. It ran under a five-column double banner with a three-column closeup of the shattered windshield. Undoubtedly, one reason for the big play was to wipe the eye of the *News*, but it was, nevertheless, a very dramatic story.

On the way home that afternoon I swung off I–95 to the Pink House. Charley was there along with Floyd. Sam ordered a drink for me and all eyes turned as Nan hastened to obey. Her stylish skirt seemed even tighter and shorter than

usual. She had good hip action for a woman who had been three times a mother. She was also a good cook.

The shooting had left Sam in a good humor but jumpy. The boys must be getting desperate, he said. Buchanan was probably sweating it. We should all be careful. They might try again. Everywhere he went he was tailed.

I nodded. To shake my own tail I had reached the Pink House by a roundabout back way. And coming down a lane, from what ordinarily would have been the wrong direction, I spotted a sheriff's car parked in the bushes. There was no possibility of error—the car had a red light on top and the huge sheriff's star on the side. The man in the car was watching Sam's hideout through field glasses.

Well, that was routine and to be expected, we decided. Main business was to review plans for the following Tuesday. Sam and O'Nan would be called again. And Sam would follow my advice. If Buchanan didn't have sense enough to quit, Sam was going to tell the truth and take the consequences.

One honest witness was not enough, I reminded Sam. Would O'Nan talk as well? He seemed scared to me early that day.

Roy would talk, Sam assured me. Floyd and Charley nodded in solemn agreement. Roy was a coward and hated to be pushed into a situation, but in the end he would do what Sam advised.

It sounded good, and I downed my gin-and-juice in a better frame of mind. But my optimism was premature. When the next Tuesday came around, O'Nan—conspicuously guarded now by sheriff's deputies—was rushed into the grand jury room. He soon emerged, white and shaking. He had taken the Fifth, he said loudly. He had refused to talk.

Gerstein, perhaps seeing little point in continuing, excused Sam without calling him. And this time he failed to continue the subpoena. The incident was apparently to be considered closed.

There was gloom in the city room, but also a strange kind

of relief. Several editors made a point of telling me not to be disappointed—they had known all along that neither Sam or O'Nan would talk. Conferences followed, and when I attempted to get across the idea that I had not really cared whether they talked or not, the *Herald* executives stared at me in amazement.

My purpose throughout the affair, I explained carefully, had been to get a printable story. Merely learning the truth was not enough—I had to have proof. In such a situation, where cash had been involved, the only proof was obviously the word of the witnesses. And playing the game by ear, I had ended with what I had sought—signed statements by the witnesses. The fact that both men failed to talk to the grand jury was immaterial. I had been after a story. I could now write it.

I was ready to write it, but the *Herald* was not ready to publish it. There was great discussion, but no one sided with me. Like Governor Burns, they felt no jury would believe the word of a gambler over an official, and they were convinced a jury would eventually be called upon to settle a libel suit if the story was used.

It was a hopeless battle, I decided, and shortly a new incident confirmed my evaluation. Karl Wickstrom, a young and eager reporter, got a confidential tip from the state attorney's office. Karl formerly covered Gerstein's men and, despite his current preoccupation with the crime series, maintained his relationship. Sy Gelber, Gerstein's chief administrative assistant, was his favorite source.

Sy had a hot tip this time. Karl hung up the phone and ran by me on his way to the city desk. I noticed his face was ashen, so I followed. Sy had told him, he gasped, that the shell casings found at the O'Nan shooting scene, matched shell casings on file from a .22 caliber rifle owned by Sam.

The whole thing was a plot, Karl said, a setup. Sam and O'Nan had arranged it to enable them to back away from testifying. Sam was about to be charged with something—Sy

wasn't too sure what—and the *Herald* was about to have egg on its face.

Instantly the city room was in turmoil. Two top executives were out of the building, attending a civic function at a Miami hotel. Karl, striking a blow for his own position, personally called them out of the meeting and back to the *Herald*. I was told to check with Sam—"He may already be arrested," said Karl—but for some slightly insulting and not fully explained reason, a witness was told to listen on an extension to our conversation.

Sam was not only at liberty, he was in a good humor. His laugh bounced off my eardrums, as I told him the latest.

The gun, he said, had been confiscated two years before, when sheriff's deputies took advantage of a shooting incident —I knew what he meant. Someone had shot Sam in the face and a beautiful mulatto, known to the bolita business as Princess Griffin, took Sam to the hospital. Deputies had been notified and they visited the counting house and confiscated everything they could find. Included was the rifle.

Records at the property room showed, we discovered later, the rifle and some other items were returned to a private eye who worked for Sam. But Sam swore he never got the rifle and the "eye" said that while he signed a receipt, the rifle wasn't returned.

It was one of those stories that on the face of it seemed unlikely, but—when the general state of corruption was considered—was quite possible. Much later I got some added information from Captain Zmuda, chief of central services and an honest man.

The crime lab technician was making a routine comparison of the O'Nan casings with the thousands on file, when another officer came in and suggested time could be saved by looking at Sam's old shells. During the short time Sam's rifle was in official custody, it had been test fired and both shell and bullet filed away for future reference.

The technician followed the suggestion and discovered he

had indeed been saved much trouble. The casings did match. The gun was the same.

At the time, I knew nothing of the incident, but the whole thing smelled. I did know enough about the background of Sam and O'Nan's grand jury adventures to doubt they would find it necessary to go to such extremes to avoid testifying. All they had to do was tell Miner, the special investigator and friend of Gerstein. So what was the score?

Sam supplied the answer that afternoon at the Pink House. His good humor gone, his face was grim and his hand never moved more than six inches from the revolver on the couch beside him.

"It may have been a setup," he said. "The plan might have been to kill Roy and blame it on me. Now all they have to do is stash that gun somewhere on my property and then 'find' it."

The idea made sense as I reviewed the situation. The key was the rifle. Would professional killers use a rifle—any rifle—if they wanted only to kill O'Nan? No. A sawed-off shotgun or machine-pistol would have been far more handy. Would Sam have used a rifle—especially a rifle he knew had once been in the custody of the sheriff's office—if he had simply been faking a murder attempt? No. Especially when you considered Sam had a score of weapons ranging from pistols to automatic shotguns. He was a hunter by hobby and instinct.

Then who would use such a rifle? The answer was inescapable. Only someone who knew it once belonged to Sam and wanted it identified as such. Someone who wanted Sam to be blamed for the shooting.

More pieces fell into place. The bullets had missed, but the same results could be achieved by destroying the *Herald*'s confidence in Sam and Roy—and in me. In some ways this was a better deal. Murder would have been too hard to play down, ignore. But a faked murder that boomeranged would

embarrass the *Herald* and possibly destroy me as a working reporter.

Next day I began to get word from my "ears." The news was going around fast that Messick was finished. The grand jury was going to be asked to indict me as well as O'Nan and Sam for conspiracy—conspiracy to frame Sheriff Buchanan on a false charge.

Fears eased, ironically enough, at the *Herald*, even as my own mounted. The lack of official action by anyone against Sam, caused the editors to decide that perhaps it was just a rumor. But when I suggested we should publish my story, the refusal was firm. The subject was too dangerous.

The decline in excitement over the O'Nan shooting coincided with a rise in interest in the Mossler case which was at last coming to trial. Two weeks had been spent selecting a jury, and the task fully occupied State Attorney Gerstein.

Long before I began my crime series, reporters in Miami and around the country had been excited about the Mossler murder. It had a lot of everything: sex, money, and mystery.

Jacques Mossler was fifty-two years old when he married Candy in 1948, and she was twenty-eight. He was a millionaire, and she operated a modeling agency. The marriage took place in Florida, and logically enough, the Mosslers kept coming back. Miami Beach was home for thousands of rich, middle-aged men of Eastern European ancestry. The plush, almost garish setting, apparently helped satisfy ancient hungers born of ghetto life.

In 1964 the Mosslers were living at Governor's Lodge on Key Biscayne, that island in Biscayne Bay connected to the mainland by the Rickenbacker Causeway. And it was there on the morning of June 30, Mossler was stabbed to death— presumably while his wife and some of her children were visiting a hospital ten miles away. It seemed Candy had a headache.

The case was quite a headache for those persons interested in the truth. But it was also a potential gold mine. Key

Biscayne was not part of the city of Miami and thus was in the jurisdiction of the Dade sheriff's office. Chief of Detectives Manson Hill took personal charge. State Attorney Richard E. Gerstein's men moved in too. The smell of money hung over the case.

On July 4, Melvin Powers, the twenty-four-year-old nephew of Mossler, was taken into custody and held without bond in Houston. It was almost a year before he was brought to Miami for a preliminary hearing. A flock of witnesses also made the jaunt—some of them law-enforcement officers from Texas and Arizona. The hearing lasted three days. It was conducted before a justice of the peace in Coral Gables and provided an opportunity for Defense Attorney Percy Foreman to test his mettle against State Attorney Gerstein and such witnesses as Manson Hill.

The hearing got much coverage, but one story was left for me to break a year later. The man who made it possible was that son of a police captain who used the code name Pan. Shortly after my first meeting with him and the Broward juror, Pan gave me the basic story. He had obtained it from an honest Dade deputy.

The deputy said that on July 11, 1965, he had been assigned to assist in the transportation of witnesses to the preliminary hearing. One of the witnesses—an out-of-town officer—passed the word to the deputy that Major Hill had arranged a party for the visitors at the Biscayne Terrace Hotel in downtown Miami. It was a continuous party and the deputy was invited.

On the next afternoon, the deputy went to room 614 at the hotel. He found the visitors as well as several high-ranking deputies. Call girls arrived. A tall man with red hair and freckles beneath his tan was introduced to the deputy as "Mr. Smith."

Two months later the deputy read of my efforts to buy a brothel and recognized Mr. Smith's picture. In reality, he was Red Vaught, boss of the brothels.

Major Hill soon arrived. Two of the deputies complained

that a blonde assigned to them had provided only "blow jobs" because she had been ordered to save herself for Hill. He liked her from the evening before.

More girls were brought in, and the party progressed until Smith-Vaught decided it was time to go home. He was too drunk to drive, however, and the deputy was assigned to take him in a sheriff's car.

They drove to the Racquet Club where Vaught's $80,000 houseboat was moored. Vaught, who talked all the way home, invited the deputy to come aboard for a drink. He was introduced to Red's wife, Ginger—Miami's leading madam.

When the deputy got back to the Biscayne Terrace, everyone was hungry. A great debate ended with the decision to have dinner at the Racquet Club. So the deputy loaded up some prostitutes and again headed up Biscayne Boulevard to the Seventy-ninth Street Causeway.

Vaught and Ginger joined the group for dinner. The club photographer took pictures of the happy party—all on the house, of course. When one appetite had been satisfied, another reasserted itself, and the girls and officers returned to their rooms at the hotel.

The deputy got new orders, however. He was assigned to nursemaid one of the Dade captains. The visitors complained that on the previous night the captain had become disorderly and interfered with their fun.

The assignment continued until about 3 A.M., when the deputy was told to take one of the call girls home. She lived in north Dade. The deputy obeyed, and carefully noted the address. Upon returning to the hotel, he was accosted by one of the visitors, who said he wanted to make sure the girl was paid. She had explained, he said, that Red promised the girls $100 each for the evening, but the visitor felt she might not get it. To please his guest, the deputy again drove to the prostitute's home with the visitor, who apparently satisfied himself the girl wasn't short-changed. Going back to the hotel again, they discovered the disorderly captain had vanished. A

search of all downtown bars was made, before someone found the captain in the bushes near the hotel.

The sky was streaked with purple and gray, as the sun prepared to rise above the Atlantic, when at last the deputy finished his duties for the day and went home.

Two months later, he said, upon reading my story of Vaught and Bessie Winkle, the high brass of the sheriff's office began a search for the pictures made in the Racquet Club. One man was sent to Arizona to collect any the Mossler case witnesses may have saved as a memento of their Miami visit.

The witnesses had managed, however, to get Powers bound over to a grand jury. A few days later on July 20, the Dade County Grand Jury returned two murder indictments. One named Powers but the other was sealed. The defendant was not in custody, it was explained, and the indictment could not be made public.

Candy Mossler—then a patient in the Mayo Clinic in Rochester, Minnesota—quickly ended any mystery.

"They framed me," she was quoted as saying. "The jury must have listened to dope addicts, winos, and ex-convicts. They are trying to get their filthy, greedy, grimy hands on my banks in Miami."

Now, some six months later, the trial was under way. And Candy was to be proved right in her estimation of some of the witnesses used against her. However, she had omitted one category—corrupt law officers.

The situation as far as I was concerned had become impossible. The *Herald* wouldn't print my story about the campaign contribution. O'Nan and Sam wouldn't tell it to the grand jury. And every day came word that just as soon as the state finished with the Mossler case, I was going to be indicted on a conspiracy charge. Furthermore, the *Herald* would then be sued for two million dollars.

I talked to Sam. Something had to give. He listened carefully and agreed. The bluff had failed, but a bluff had not

been necessary. All that was needed was the truth. His silence played into the hands of his enemies.

We reached an understanding. Sam told Miner to convene the grand jury into special session. He would appear and tell the truth. He would attempt to bring O'Nan, but in any case he would go.

The day came and my telephone rang early. It was Sam. "Come by the Pink House," he asked. "I need to get something straight."

I dressed quickly, shaved carefully, and was in my car before I hesitated. Something about Sam's call had been off key. Was he up to another trick? Well, by God, the time for games had passed.

I returned to my study, unlocked a filing cabinet, and from beneath a pile of newspapers produced a locked steel box. I opened it, took out the two statements. Since that session with Allsworth, they had been my most guarded possession.

No one was at the Pink House. A note fastened to the torn screen door informed me that Sam had gone to O'Nan's home to see if O'Nan was as sick as he claimed. I was supposed to wait.

To hell with it. I drove back to I–95 and from there to the Herald. It was still early but Managing Editor Beebe was in his glassed-in office. I didn't speak to him. This was my decision. The less he knew about it, the better for him and the Herald.

Sam answered when I called the Pink House number. He had just returned. Why didn't I wait? No, Roy wasn't going to talk. He was in bed all right, but how sick he was Sam didn't know. All right—was Sam going to talk? The grand jury was waiting. No, Sam had decided there was no use for him to go in alone. They might get him for trying to frame the sheriff. If Roy wouldn't go, there was nothing to be gained by going alone. Sure, he had promised, but he had changed his mind. Okay, but that was the way it was going to be. Sorry, he'd made up his mind.

I'd also made up my mind. Slowly, still holding the receiver in one hand, I broke the connection, then dialed the number of the grand jury. From where I sat in the almost deserted city room, I could look beyond Beebe as he shuffled papers on his desk to the white castles of Miami Beach in the distance. As always, there was an air of unreality about the scene.

Miner answered. Already he had talked to Sam and was preparing to tell the grand jury he had convened them for nothing. When I told him I would be over in fifteen minutes, he seemed vastly relieved.

I left the blue and gold *Herald* building on the edge of Biscayne Bay and drove to the parking lot near the Court-house. The usual buzzards circling above the tower seemed entirely appropriate. A few minutes later came the tangle with Sy Gelber, as his boss crouched silently at the rear of the room. But the statements of O'Nan and Sam went into the record, and my account of how I came into possession of them was also sworn testimony. Let them frame me now if they could.

A week later—confronted with a *fait accompli*—Gerstein called Sam and O'Nan before the jury. O'Nan, still scared and perhaps still trying to make a deal, again refused to talk and was cited for contempt. He gave notice of appeal. But Sam while accusing me of violating my word—made the best of the situation. His face was grim as he came out of the grand jury chambers. Reporters and photographers crowded around, followed him to the elevator, but he managed to whisper a message—"Meet me at the office."

I met him there. The yard of the ex-counting house, at the end of the shady lane, was full of cars when I arrived. Miner was there, and Charley.

Sam, relaxing now, was beginning to enjoy his revenge. "I told the truth," he kept saying. "I told them how that dumb bastard double-crossed me. By God, I'll bet he's sweating now."

A tremendous clatter interrupted. It sounded like a dozen

motorcycles, but it was coming from above. Three men grabbed guns and rushed into the yard. I followed, wishing I had a weapon. There, just above the tallest mangrove bushes, hung the sheriff's helicopter.

I grabbed Sam's arm as he lifted his gun. The whirly-bird dipped and swayed a few seconds, then lifted up and darted away with amazing speed. Presumably it headed for a highway and the rush-hour traffic report.

The rewrite man at the *Herald* took the item when I phoned it in. "Sounds like something out of a James Bond book," he commented. Perhaps that is why the editors didn't let him use it.

EIGHT

*

A change of pace . . . a change of scene. From the mangrove swamps of north Dade to the plush elegance of Miami Beach's finest—the Fontainebleau.

The season had arrived. The sticky heat of summer and the hurricane-force fears of autumn were forgotten. Frankie was opening a two-week stint at La Ronde Room and everyone who was anyone would be there. The $35 minimum only made the event more desirable.

Someone at the *Herald* had read somewhere that a Sinatra opening was traditionally attended by the Mob. All the big wheels of crime allegedly turned out to give Frankie Boy a good start. Whoever wrote or otherwise started that legend, obviously assumed that all the big wheels in crime were members of La Cosa Nostra. Such legend-makers apparently never heard of Meyer Lansky. I was by no means certain the tradition—if it existed—would be observed at the Fontainebleau, but I was willing to go look.

The *Herald* wanted me to go look. I was supposed to be an expert on crime, wasn't I? Ergo, I should be able to recognize on sight all the top gamblers from Alo to Zarowitz.

Assigned to get me inside was the *Herald*'s entertainment editor, genial George Bourke. George had been around for many years and, while on a friendly, first-name basis with many night people, had retained a capacity for ironic detachment. The link between the underworld and the entertainment world was apparent to George, but he felt no need to

censor or defend. It was as much of a fact as the almost invisible accessories that prevent a stripper's act from becoming illegal.

Nevertheless, I couldn't but wonder if George wouldn't be a bit embarrassed if—after smuggling me into La Ronde Room—I insulted the hospitality of the house by panning Frankie's act. He told me to forget it. The boys needed him, he said, a lot more than he needed them.

The scene at the Fontainebleau that night was confusion. A tremendous traffic jam clogged Collins Avenue for blocks. The local yokels might take a Sinatra opening in stride, but the visitors wanted at least a glimpse. I surrendered my Volkswagen to a uniformed doorman and smiled as he commented on the low mileage. No doubt he thought me an eccentric millionaire. What matter the model so long as it was new?

Inside the vast and curving lobby, the place was packed. A low hum echoed as women kissed in greetings and men shook hands. Diamonds and mink for the women, and for the men formal clothes of every color and cut. A parade of peacocks . . . a self-conscious display of wealth.

Bourke spotted me and hastened over to my side. The excitement of the pomp and splendor had reached him, but he had it under control. Taking me by the arm, he guided me into a long line that began forming outside La Ronde Room. No one got inside until his reservation was checked.

The room proved to be a large theater-restaurant, built on several levels. We had a good seat, high up, but with a view of the stage. I was reminded of the Beverly Hills Club outside Newport. It had been designed in much the same way. If anything, it had been bigger. The place also reminded me, on a smaller scale, of the Theatrical Restaurant on Vincent Street in Cleveland—Mushy Wexler's joint.

Bourke was recognized by a waiter. Despite the overflow crowd—extra tables had been set up in every vacant place— we got fast service. I sipped my martini and looked for familiar faces.

Someone tapped my shoulder—a federal agent I had con-

tacted earlier. "Not many of them here tonight," he whispered in my ear. "We'll be just outside."

He moved away, then returned. "Dusty Peters just came in," he said. "There he goes."

I recognized the heavy-set man, once known as the "Mayor of Vanderbilt Square," as he moved down the steps to a place of honor on the lower level. And the noise, the bustle faded briefly as I recalled another scene.

The Singapore Hotel, up Collins Avenue near Surfside. The card room on the mezzanine. A broad, polished table. A group of men stand around that table as a courier empties a suitcase onto it. Bundle upon bundle of greenbacks tumble out, as the men watch casually.

Four of the men I know: Meyer Lansky, his brother Jake Lansky, Vincent (Jimmy Blue Eyes) Alo, and Dan (Dusty) Peters.

The Singapore is Lansky's current headquarters. Every day he leaves his modest ranch-style home in Golden Isles subdivision off Hallandale Beach Boulevard and is driven in a rented Chevrolet to the Singapore. Sometimes the driver is Phil (the Stick) Kovolick, another graduate of the Prohibition Era. Alo—the man who allegedly replaced Frank Costello as Mafia-Syndicate coordinator—drives down from his huge winter home in nearby Hollywood. His affection for Lansky is an old one, but it still puzzles certain experts who can't understand why a leader of the Mafia enjoys the society of a non-Sicilian.

Peters, who represented Lansky in Havana in the days before Castro, now serves his master at the Lucayan Beach Casino on Grand Bahama Island. He is officially listed as a public relations man, but his real role remains what it always was—courier. He brings out the skim from the casino even as other couriers come in from Las Vegas with untaxed profits.

On this day the courier is from Vegas, and the pile of money is huge. Peters watches as at last the men sit down and begin the job of "cutting up" the loot.

Bourke jostled my arm. "There goes Ben Novack," he said.

I returned to reality. . . . The Singapore episode I had incorporated in a series on Lansky. It had run just before Christmas. Few people noticed it. Crime, to be understood, must be explained in terms of safety on the streets or in the homes. Newspaper readers can understand a brothel boss or a numbers writer—but you lose them when you write of international bankers and interstate couriers. Such things, they think, belong in the movies.

Nowhere would you find Meyer Lansky's name on an official record pertaining to the Singapore. But it was his headquarters. Who really controls the Fontainebleau? This question is now the subject matter of a lawsuit in Miami.

The dinner was good, but hardly worth $35. I was beginning to feel a little bored, when a stir passed through the crowd, a spotlight picked up Frankie, and the show was on. The applause was loud, but—perhaps I was imagining things—it seemed a bit restrained. Yet the table-hopping halted and the audience sat ready to be entertained.

"Come Fly With Me," sang Sinatra, and then, "Everybody's Got a Right to Be Wrong." The largely middle-aged crowd appeared to like it. A sentimental mood began developing and it grew as Frankie sang of "The September of My Years."

Abruptly, almost contemptuously, Sinatra broke the spell. He stopped singing and began wisecracking. The jokes were racially pointed—about Jewish gangsters and swinging Jewish mothers.

The crowd laughed politely, and Sinatra turned again to music. But this time he presented what he called "saloon songs," carefully pointing out to nonhipsters that they concerned "bread and broads."

It was as if Sinatra was somehow angry. I got the feeling that many in the audience sensed his emotions and resented them.

By the time the singer reached the final number, his choice seemed a deliberate challenge: "Chicago—My Kind of Town."

The friend of Mafia boss Moe Giancana was making his feelings clear.

But he was applauded—not wildly, not even enthusiastically, but because it was the proper thing to do. And Sinatra understood. He returned for a curtain call to coolly introduce such celebrities in the audience as Anthony Quinn, Gene Barry, and Mark Robison. But despite loud calls from the crowd for "Georgie," he ignored George Jessel. And if anyone still had doubts, he again sang of Chicago.

I was first out the door. Two federal agents—one down from Chicago for the occasion—stood against the wall and watched the crowd pour by them. Aside from Joe Fischetti, last of the three brothers of that name, no high-ranking members of the Mafia appeared.

Of punks there were plenty—young, hard-faced men with diamond rings on their pinkies and painted dolls on their arms. Of spotters for jewel thieves there were several, and they had much to choose from, as portly matrons waddled out where the light could gleam on their diamonds.

Despite the tensions inside I could now sense a satisfaction. These people had attended the most exclusive event of the season. They had seen Sinatra. Like him or not, he was worth seeing. Altogether, it had been an evening of profit.

But not for me. The *Herald* decided my short article on a clash of cultures was a little too subtle. Since I couldn't list any top hoods, it was better to ignore the event and let Bourke handle it in his usual manner.

I didn't object—not even a few nights later when Sinatra and Novack had a fight, and Sinatra canceled his engagement.

From Ben Novack to my old pal Vic was quite a transition, but not necessarily a comedown. It had been weeks since I had heard from the all-right boy. My association with Basinger annoyed him, and he apparently decided I'd have to fumble along as best I could alone.

But his news was too good to keep, so he called. Remember Bessie? Yeah, the madam. Well, she's operating in Holly-

wood. All right? But guess who her neighbor is. This is really
hot, I tell you. You won't believe it. No you won't. She's
living next door to Woody Malphurs. Yeah, the acting chief
of police. Some story, huh?

It was sort of funny at that. And Malphurs knew his neighbor. Vic was sure of it. In fact, he called Malphurs to tip him
that Bessie was going to set up shop in Hollywood and Malphurs replied, "I know. She's living next door to me."

Vic, somewhat astonished, drove out to check. Sure
enough, Bessie's white cadillac was parked in the circular
driveway. The house was large and well located on a corner
that permitted a lookout to watch both ways. It even had a
huge pool.

Was Bessie operating, I asked. Sure she was. Vic had
staked out the place with the help of a Hollywood cop he
trusted. She had at least three girls in the joint, and they went
out on assignment as well as entertaining guests at home.

What was Chief Malphurs going to do about it, was my
next question. Here Vic became typically mysterious. There
was a possibility the whole thing was a plot—arranged by the
syndicate or someone to prevent Malphurs' job as acting chief
being made permanent. On the other hand, maybe there was a
payoff to Malphurs. So many rumors were around it was hard
to be sure.

Realizing that while Vic was good at locating a Bessie
Winkle, he was constitutionally unable to reject a rumor if it
hinted at sinister doings, I decided I'd better have a talk with
Malphurs. He was a veteran Hollywood officer—and that was
not necessarily a point in his favor. Hollywood became a
haven for top mobsters back in the 1930's when Tom Dewey
first applied heat in New York City. At one time or another
almost every hood of note owned a home in Hollywood.
Many—such as Jimmy Blue Eyes, the Stick, and Jake Lansky
—still lived there. The big boy, Meyer Lansky, had moved a
few miles south to Hallandale, where he could keep a better

eye on Gulfstream Park. His home was located just to the east of the race track.

Malphurs, as far as I knew, had never been identified with the Mob, but along with others of the official family, he had tolerated the hoods. Just recently Kovolick had been picked up in a New York hangout where he was conferring with some of the Mafia boys. He had pointed out rather bitterly that, back in Hollywood, no one bothered him, while in his old home town he couldn't have a friendly cup of coffee.

The acting chief proved to be a short, stocky man of middle age. He seemed a little frightened, until I convinced him I wasn't a cop-hater who enjoyed embarrassing people unnecessarily. Once that point was established, he relaxed, ordered a sergeant to bring in some coffee, and told me the story of his neighbor. Even he had to laugh as the irony of it struck home.

He had been away on a hunting trip, he said, when Bessie moved into the house. The house had been vacant for some time, and he was glad upon his return to find it was now occupied. A paved alley ran behind the houses, he explained, and of late it had been developing into a lover's lane.

Shortly after his return, he spotted a woman in the yard next door, went up to the fence dividing the property, and called "Hi, neighbor." The woman came over and they introduced themselves. The name Bessie Winkle meant nothing to Malphurs, he said, although later, when Vic called, he did remember the story of my efforts to buy the brothel.

Bessie inquired, the acting chief continued, what his business was, and he told her, modestly, that he worked at city hall. She pressed for a more specific job description, and he finally told her his title. She didn't seem disturbed, he said, and he pointed out that a police sergeant lived just across the street.

"You'll be well protected," he told her.

We both laughed, but I made a mental reservation. Was it possible that as canny a professional as Bessie Winkle would

buy an expensive house without first finding out about the neighbors? It seemed unlikely. To assume Malphurs had never heard of Bessie was one thing—to assume Bessie had never heard of Malphurs was something else.

Apparently something of my doubt must have shown, for Malphurs quickly asked what I was going to do? I countered —what was he going to do? He was going to raid the place just as soon as he had sufficient evidence, he said. After all, even a madam has a right to privacy, if she isn't breaking the law. So far, a stakeout had produced grounds for suspicion, but nothing on which to base a search warrant.

Ultimately, after considerable discussion, I agreed to hold up on a story. I would give Malphurs time to act properly. He seemed sincerely grateful and confided I wasn't the son-of-a-bitch a certain sheriff said I was.

We talked briefly of the old days. He told me how in 1947 New York officials were looking for Andy Sheridan in connection with a waterfront murder. They discovered Sheridan was sunning himself in Hollywood, and they dispatched a telegram to Hollywood police asking that he be picked up for them. According to Malphurs, a high-ranking officer took the telegram to Jimmy Blue Eyes Alo and asked for instructions. Alo told the cop to "forget it." Police obeyed, but the New York cops raised so much hell it was finally necessary to arrest Sheridan. They nabbed him at the airport. Apparently he missed the plane that would have taken him—and the Hollywood cops—off the hook, so he had only himself to blame when some months later they strapped him in the electric chair. No doubt, being a realist, that was why he could wisecrack about how at long last he was going to cure his piles.

I knew a little more of the story. The New York officials did more checking and learned the fugitive spent some time in Meyer Lansky's Hollywood home while in hiding. A check of toll calls from Lansky's phone showed someone had been in daily communication with Frank Costello in New York,

Lucky Luciano in Havana, and Bugsy Siegel in Hollywood, California.

Malphurs made no apologies for the attitude of the Hollywood cops, but he implied that things had changed. He also mentioned that in some respects it had been an advantage to have the big boys in town. On occasion, he said, when the cops wanted to locate a punk, all they had to do was call Jake Lansky and pass the word. The punk would soon surrender.

I shook hands with Malphurs and left the police building feeling that, as acting chief, Woody would be at least an improvement over the past. He promised to call me when time for Bessie had come.

Vic worried me for several days. Why didn't I write the story? Had I sold out too? Bessie was doing a swinging business now. Lot of jewel thieves were dropping in. The house was probably headquarters for burglars as well as prostitutes.

I managed to stall him on the pretext that we had to discover whether Malphurs was being set up by a rival or was on the take. He was eager to find out, and I paid the penalty—an hour-long telephone report each evening that added up to indecision. Vic just couldn't decide which alternative was most attractive.

Meanwhile, I wrote out a rather long feature about Malphurs and his neighbor and turned it in to the *Herald* with instructions to hold. The raid—if it came—would be at night and near deadline. The actual news story might have to be brief. But the long sidebar could be in type waiting.

And that's the way it happened. I got a call from Detective-Sergeant Fred Rohloff to come to the police station at 7 P.M. I managed to get a photographer assigned and broke away from an afternoon-long editorial conference at the *Herald* in time to get to Hollywood. In order to make it, I had to skip dinner. Late that night I'd stuff myself before going to bed and thus add more pounds to my growing mid-section.

The full-scale briefing was underway when I arrived. A couple of honest Broward deputies had been borrowed—such

men as Frank Troy—and about fifteen of Hollywood's finest had been mobilized. It looked like a lot of effort to catch one madam, but I said nothing. The men were to keep in touch by walkie-talkies, and they were to be stationed in houses all around Bessie's place. The home of the sergeant across the street was command headquarters. A signal would be given when an undercover man was admitted to the house. A search warrant had been secured, but arrests would be made even if there was no action. In recent weeks the undercover boys had gained sufficient evidence to swear out arrest warrants charging Bessie and her three girls with prostitution.

The raid went off as scheduled. I waited in the darkened house across the street and followed the first men in the door when the signal came. And once inside, I doubled up with laughter.

There, on a thick rug before an open fire, sat one of the prostitutes. She was playing with twin babies who were kicking and cooing as the heat warmed their toes. Bessie, clad in sweater and slacks, sat in a lounge chair sipping a highball, as an officer read the search warrant.

Not a man was in the joint. The undercover agent assigned to get in had failed, and the cops—armed with their arrest warrants—proceeded without the icing on the cake they hoped to obtain.

I made a quick survey. The place was plush. A long hall was flanked with bedrooms. We found nine phones in the house, and from one in Bessie's bedroom I called the *Herald* to confirm the raid was on schedule. The house boasted a large patio and pool area at the rear. An intercom system made communications easy.

Returning to the living room, I asked Bessie if she had yet sold the brothel. She glanced at me curiously. "You're Messick," she said. "No, I haven't sold the place yet. Thanks to you." Her voice was without rancor, but suddenly she became sullen. When I asked why she moved in next door to the acting police chief, she put her head in her hands and said

nothing. The beehive wig she wore made her head seem top-heavy.

Malphurs came bustling in, eager to again meet his neighbor. He wore a smile and walked as if relieved of a heavy burden. For the first time I realized what a burden it must have been. With the city council likely to decide any day on making his appointment permanent, he was in no position to have a scandal.

I called the *Herald* on the direct line to Miami that Bessie had installed for the convenience of old customers. It was the same number she had used in Dade County, I noticed. The rewrite man was ready, so I dictated a brief story to run on the front. Details were already in the sidebar I had prepared earlier. As I finished the story, a still smiling Malphurs walked past me. I grabbed his arm.

"Got any last word for the *Herald?*" I asked.

"Yes," he said. "Just say I appreciate the fine cooperation of The Miami *Herald* and Hank Messick."

The rewrite man laughed as I repeated the message. Then a cop yanked the phone out by the roots, and that was that. I went home and raided the refrigerator. Shortly thereafter my phone rang. It was Vic. "Have you heard the latest? They just raided Bessie Winkle."

The Hollywood raid seemed to illustrate how the pendulum had swung back to Broward County. In Dade, O'Nan was still appealing a court order requiring him to talk. Gerstein apparently was content to let the matter drag on indefinitely. After all, the grand jury's life ended in May. Meanwhile, George Wetzler, the vice-foreman of the Broward County Grand Jury, was becoming eager. He had won over a couple of jurors to the point where they would be willing to listen to anything I might care to say.

I decided to feed the fire by preparing a series on Broward County. Writing the stories was easy—I had the information —but getting them published was another matter.

Back in December, *Herald* executives, without any great display of pleasure, agreed to a six-month extension of my contract. It marked the second extension I had received. Obviously the period for winning Pulitzers expired with the old year, but there was some feeling I should be available for a few more months to wrap up loose ends.

The book I counted on to be published in January had been delayed by legal problems, and I was glad to gain even six months of security. I had signed, knowing full well the *Herald* didn't want me to open new fronts in the war against crime. I was supposed to utilize the period to find a new job while polishing off what had been a so far unproductive crusade. I still insisted that if the newspaper published some of my stories about Buchanan, they would get results—but I might have spared myself the trouble.

The four articles I put together about Broward were solid ones. I traced the rise of Fat Hymie Martin in some detail and the career of Sheriff Allen B. Michell. The final article I devoted to the Fort Lauderdale police department and the methods it used to keep the city clean.

But the editors weren't impressed. I decided they were not so much afraid of the series as indifferent. Despite the connections between Dade and Broward crime, there was no real interest in the city room. After all, the *Herald* maintained a Broward bureau to take care of things north of Gulfstream Park.

Foiled again, I looked elsewhere for a spark that might start a fire inside the grand jury. Again Vic came to the rescue. I couldn't quite believe it, however. He was wearing the black vestments and Roman collar of a clergyman. From a long chain around his neck dangled a huge cross, conspicuous in blue enamel. He was now an ordained minister in the Calvary Grace Christian Church of Faith, he said. Sooner or later he would have a church of his own. All right? Meanwhile, his mission was to help the unfortunate. He had found such a person and, by God, Hank, it was a helluva story.

When I restored him to the proper demeanor, I asked for

details. Long ago I learned not to discount anything Vic said. Somewhere, if you could find it, was always a grain of gold. In the case of Bessie, it had been a nugget.

There was this woman, see. All right? She lives in the same subdivision as Meyer Lansky. And her house is out of this world—a marble palace. Cost $250,000 unfurnished. He had seen the papers. A millionaire built it for her.

Anyway, everything was jake until last spring. These two hoods came in and robbed her. She managed to hide a valuable diamond ring in the bed clothes. What? Oh, she was in bed when the hoods came in. They tied her up and left her there. Tied up the maid too. All right? Well, anyway, she got loose and called the cops. They came and naturally they found the ring and stole it. She had done everything to get justice. State Attorney Quentin Long wouldn't lift a finger. The police wouldn't do anything either. So she had turned to him as a minister for assistance.

"What happened to the millionaire? Why didn't he help?"

Vic grinned, displaying crooked teeth. That was the most ironic part of all. The stories about the robbery all identified Virginia (this is not her real name) as the millionaire's wife. All right? Well, he was involved as a partner in various huge real estate ventures. And in Florida a wife—or even a common-law wife—automatically shares his estate. He had signed papers saying he had no wife, that no one had a legal claim on him. If Virginia could establish such a claim he could lose millions.

It sounded wild, but somehow memory was stirred. The *Herald* had received literally hundreds of tips following my first stories. The staff had been snowed under, unable to do much more than write memos and file them away. I seemed to recall some such story. Staffer Clarence Jones had handled it, although the woman had asked to see me.

I called Clarence. Yes, he remembered the tale. The woman seemed a little hysterical. But he had written out a full account of it.

Vic, his clerical duty done, said he was glad to turn the

matter over to me. His manner implied he had much more weighty things awaiting him. But he still had a sense of humor.

"I dressed up the other day," he said, "and went over to the jail. Told them I was there to counsel the prisoners. The stupid jailers didn't know what to do, so they called Sheriff Michell. The old man made me prove I was an ordained minister, and then he told them to frisk me. Get the picture. Frisk a man of the cloth? I objected. Michell said he would let it pass if I assured him I was unarmed. I said, 'Sheriff, I am armed.' He looked sorta surprised, but told me to hand over my weapon and I could go in. I handed over my Bible. 'That's my weapon, sheriff,' I said."

It was funny—at least to me. I recalled Michell asking if I knew what happened to Jake Lingle, and I whooped. Vic joined in, laughing until the tears streamed down his face.

Virginia proved no laughing matter. She had red hair and a well-preserved figure, but when she nervously plucked at the scarf around her neck you could see where the beauty treatment ended. The face was smooth and white—the neck was that of an older woman. Actually, she had a son in college.

It was easy to see why Clarence considered her hysterical. She talked too fast, as if she was afraid her audience might leave. And her thoughts were hard to follow, shooting in every direction. But if you listened long enough, you could find a pattern. You could also conclude that here was a frightened woman, who for too long had been talking to herself.

Her home was proof—overpowering proof—of her sanity. Such a palace I had never seen or dreamed about before. Imported furniture and art objects from Rome and Paris seemed entirely in place against the Georgian marble of which the interior was constructed. The sunken dining room contained a waterfall. Outside was a huge patio and pool, and just beyond a canal led into the Intercoastal Waterway. A Donzi—a speed boat available only to the very rich—was moored at a dock beside the canal.

"He was generous," she said in what was surely an understatement. "He gave me a free hand."

Upstairs, on the wide bed, she demonstrated how she sucked her diamond ring from her finger as the holdup men walked in unmasked, and later managed to spit it out in the bedclothes. The cop who investigated, she said, searched the bedclothes. Later, when she told him one of the bandits had looked inside her black patent leather pocketbook, the cop calmly wiped off the finger prints.

The story sounded incredible—but not impossible. And weeks later I was to find it was true. Under tremendous pressure from newspaper-generated heat, the officer confessed that he had made a career of stealing valuables off dead bodies and receiving stolen property. His conduct at Virginia's house was to seem quite innocent by comparison. The statement, however, was not made public. The officer, still publicly maintaining his innocence, was permitted to resign and accept another police job in a smaller town. More weeks passed before Broward bureau reporter Bill Baynes—with only a little help from me—got a copy of the statement. Even then, I had to raise hell at the *Herald* before they published it.

But when I first talked to Virginia I knew only that the grand jury should hear this story. Essentially, aside from the question of conventional morality, Virginia deserved a hearing if for no other reason than she had been unable to get one. Part of the problem, I could believe, resulted from her millionaire friend, who had exercised his considerable influence to keep her quiet and her name out of the public's eye. So far he had succeeded.

A conspiracy began. I arranged certain things with Wetzler. The grand jury was going to meet soon. A couple of murders and a rape case required routine attention. It would give us an opportunity.

On the day assigned, Virginia—dressed in sober black—was brought to the Broward County Courthouse by her

pastor, the Reverend James Killoran. He seemed to be a sincere as well as sensible young minister, and we talked briefly
during the noon recess. Reporter Jim Savage was there, fully
briefed. Other reporters, who sensed something was up, had
collected. Virginia was going to have full coverage for her
act.

She behaved beautifully. Planting herself in front of the
door to the grand jury room—with the minister beside her—
she asked each juror returning from lunch for permission to
testify. Wetzler, standing tall above the redhead, winked at
me and promised for the benefit of other reporters to make a
motion to hear her.

Last to arrive was State Attorney Quentin Long. For once
his smooth composure fell aside. He lost his cool, as Savage
put it, when Virginia deliberately blocked the door and demanded to be heard. Flashbulbs flickered as the photographers took advantage of the dramatic confrontation. Even a
television camera recorded the action. Oddly enough, events
in Broward were sometimes better covered than in Dade—
perhaps because there weren't so many of them.

Long managed to edge his way around Virginia to the
door. She was still pleading loudly for justice when he escaped
inside. Now what? Most of the reporters—suddenly sympa-
thetic—bet Quentin would win. But they didn't know about
my Trojan Horse—vice-foreman Wetzler.

Sure enough, after some fifteen minutes, Long appeared. If
Virginia wanted to wait until routine business was completed,
the jury would hear her. It might take several hours, however.

"I'll wait all night if necessary," said Virginia sweetly, and
Long retreated. He had lost another round. Making a lady
wait for hours was an unnecessary discourtesy, and the assembled reporters knew it.

Three hours passed before she was admitted. To make sure
her story was heard, she had prepared a two-page history of
the robbery. Dick Basinger had made copies for the press as

well as the jurors. She was to give each a copy, so if Quentin
shut her up, they could still read.

She also had another assignment—to suggest the jury
should take advantage of my presence and hear me. Wetzler
was scheduled to follow up the suggestion with a motion.
Then, if I got inside, I had to find the right formula to keep
the jury in session.

An hour passed before the woman came back. She looked
tired but happy. Getting someone in authority to listen was
for her a victory in and of itself. And here came Long. The
jury would like to hear me, if I didn't mind, but there wasn't
time today. Could I come back tomorrow?

When I said I would be happy to return, his face fell. Obviously he still hoped the whole thing was an unplanned episode. Now it began to look as if someone had been plotting.

The jurors filed out shortly after Long gave them my acceptance. Wetzler winked again as he walked by me. I'd be
hearing from him later in the evening. Long came out last,
walking slowly, but carrying a bundle of papers.

We discovered he had collected all copies of Virginia's
statement from the jurors—to "save" for them.

Very considerate of him, the press corps agreed.

Reporter Savage, for whom I was developing much respect,
met me in the parking lot on the New River side of the courthouse next morning. As we strolled toward the modernistic
building, I explained the plot for the day.

Without telling him Wetzler had briefed me, I said I expected trouble with the jury. That was an understatement.
Long had convinced some of the jurors that I was nothing less
than a Communist agent sent to Florida to discredit local law
enforcement. The several John Birch Society members on the
jury had no trouble swallowing that argument.

In any case, I did not intend to testify in front of Long. I
couldn't tell what happened inside the jury room, but there
was nothing to prevent Jim from quoting me as to what I was

going to do when I got inside. Then, if certain things happened, he would have the key.

The jury assembled. It was composed of several older men, a few women, and some youngish business types. Long swore me to secrecy, then explained that some members of the jury—and he looked at Wetzler who grinned cheerfully—felt it might be wise to see if I had any information about crime in Broward County. He felt personally, and had so assured the jury, that local law-enforcement officers were doing a good job, but if I had any information, he would be glad to hear it and so would the jury.

Unfortunately, I am unable to report what I replied. But, in brief, I did what I had told Jim I would do. I demanded Long and his assistant Hugh Glickstein leave the room.

A long row followed. An old man sitting on my left promptly called me a Communist. He had full faith in Mr. Long, by God, and he didn't like my implications.

Wetzler rose to my defense. He was joined by some half-hearted allies, who may have been curious as to what secrets I possessed. Or perhaps they just welcomed an opportunity to needle Long.

At one point I was asked to leave the room. Reporters were waiting outside, but of course I couldn't talk. Jim nodded. Alone of all of them, he had some idea what was happening.

Five minutes passed, and Long came out. He walked down the hall. The reporters rushed after him. But he couldn't talk either. They came back to me. We waited. I was none too hopeful.

Ten minutes passed, and we were called back in. The jury had a question. Why didn't I want to talk in front of Mr. Long?

In the rear of the room George shook his head as if to indicate the cause was hopeless. Well, maybe it was. But perhaps I could give these apathetic citizens something to think about.

Briefly I outlined the scope of corruption in Broward

County, drawing heavily upon my unpublished series. But where officials were concerned I gave no specifics, explaining that would have to wait. Some members of the jury were intrigued. A few asked questions. But the old man on the left, the Communist-fighter, interrupted. All this was very interesting, but where was my proof? He wanted facts, not hearsay. What were my sources?

I thought back to that evening at the Gold Coast Lounge, and the report I had received there—the tale of Hymie Martin and his reorganization of the sheriff's department. I also remembered other confidential files and faces. I had promised on more than one occasion to go to jail if necessary to protect my sources. Well, perhaps it would now be necessary.

Long was asked if I had a right to refuse to answer a juror's question. He said I did not. I must answer. The jurors looked at me expectantly. I temporized. Long was wrong. I had to answer only if ordered to do so by a judge in open court.

"Bring in the judge," snapped the old man.

Long hesitated. He wanted to give me another chance. Obviously, he didn't want the open court session. But I was stubborn. This was a matter of principle. I had promised not to reveal my sources, but of course if ordered to do so by a judge, I would have no choice.

The grand jury door was opened. The reporters, somewhat bewildered at being invited into a grand jury session, came in nevertheless. Savage looked worried. I managed to give him a small smile.

Judge O. Edgar Williams, a rather youthful-looking jurist despite his black robes, entered. I stood in the witness box, as he rapped his gavel. Long explained the jury wanted him to instruct me to answer its questions. I interrupted to point out that even in such states as Kentucky, reporters were protected by law from revealing sources. Did not the same apply here?

It did not, said the judge. I had to answer. A reporter had no more rights than anyone else in such matters.

Long thanked the judge hurriedly, but I threw in another

question. "Am I required to testify about the conduct of a specific official when that official is present?"

The reporters all looked at each other. For most of them the events of the morning began to make sense for the first time. Obviously, I didn't want to talk in front of Long.

The state attorney's face darkened. The cat was out of the bag, and there was nothing he could do about it. This was open court.

The judge said I had to answer regardless of who was present, if the grand jury so ruled. He closed the court. We stood up as the room was cleared. Then I sat down again.

Would I now answer? Long demanded. I had been ordered to do so. If I didn't, I could be jailed for contempt.

"Go ahead," I said. My voice shook just a little. Well, let them think it was anger. And suddenly I was shaking with rage.

"Go ahead and put me in jail," I yelled. "It would be in line with everything else that has happened here. Leave the crooks alone, but put the people who want to do something about them in jail."

Long yelled back. Savage said later that our voices were plainly audible in the hall. The press thought we were about to fight.

The old man and several of his pals were willing to take me at my word. But Wetzler rose to his feet and yelled back at them. And I managed to get across the idea that I was merely a reporter invited there to give information. It was Long's job to give evidence.

I doubt if I convinced everyone, but abruptly Long sided with me. If I didn't want to talk, all right. Frankly, after thinking about it, he believed I might have a point. On appeal, a higher court might rule a reporter did have a relationship similar to that of an attorney and client.

Ironically, Long's assistant, young Mr. Glickstein, started citing precedents to prove his boss wrong. But he got the message and stopped in mid-sentence.

Slowly the shouting ceased. I was told to consider myself excused. The jury would discuss the matter with Mr. Long. If it decided to hear me on my own terms, I would be notified.

Savage was a little disappointed as we walked back to the car. But I was philosophical. I told him I doubted that this jury would do anything. The thing to do was wait. Ultimately, a good jury would come along. Then we could act. Meanwhile, I had planted some seeds, and he had a good story that might cause some of Broward's complacent citizens to start thinking.

Jim agreed, but he was still disappointed. "It's too bad," he said, "but I guess you're right. There's no use trying anything with Quentin in there."

But we were very wrong. The big story was just ahead.

NINE

I PULL SOME STRINGS

AND OUTWIT A FOX

*

The Broward County Grand Jury was becoming restless. Not much would be needed to get them off and running.

Such was the word relayed by vice-foreman Wetzler. The jury had not met in a body since my struggle with Quentin Long, but some of the jurors had attended informal sessions at the home of a juror. Such meetings usually came about when a suddenly bold citizen visited a juror in his community to tell of his problems in getting justice. Apparently there were a lot of frustrated citizens in Broward County.

"That picture of Virginia blocking the door helped more than anything," George said. "It gave folks some ideas. The jurors didn't like it either. After all, she had a right to be heard."

"What do the jurors think of me?" I asked.

George grinned and ran his finger through his long blonde hair. "Some of them still think you're the devil himself, but I've won over a couple and got some more undecided."

The vice-foreman disclosed that his wife, as energetic as she was attractive, had followed up a suggestion of mine and contacted the Dade County Grand Jury Association. The purpose was to secure a copy of the association's handbook for jurors.

Broward County had neither a handbook for jurors nor a grand jury association to advise them. Twice each year a group of citizens was convened, given a minimum of instruction by a circuit judge, and placed in the hands of the state

attorney. He largely determined how often the jury met during its six-month term, what evidence it could hear, and what indictments were justified by that evidence. Individual jurors seldom had enough facts or enough insight to question either the adequacy of the evidence or the validity of the indictment Long drew at their request. Many jurors in the past assumed the jury was but an extension of the state attorney's office and powerless to bring up any subject not specifically recommended by the boss.

A powerful man was the state attorney of Broward County, even though he did not have the authority of his counterpart in Dade County where the office of state attorney and county solicitor had been combined. Perhaps for that reason, the Broward state attorney devoted only half time to his official duties. Long was able to carry on a private law practice from an office in Hollywood. Routine investigations were left to his chief investigator, a former deputy who served in Dade County before moving to Broward just after Fat Hymie Martin arrived.

The chief investigator still had great influence in the sheriff's department, where Ed Clode consulted with him frequently. Clode had taken him along on a jaunt to California in connection with the alleged investigation of the McFarland murder.

Last fall, following my inconclusive grand jury appearance on the last day of its session, Long announced a big probe of organized crime. He hired as a special undercover agent none other than my sometimes assistant, Vic.

Excited as a boy with a new toy, Vic didn't realize that he was hired only because he had convinced Long he knew everything I was doing. He was supposed to keep an eye on me and report back to the state attorney's office if I got anything hot. That was my theory, anyway, and it seemed confirmed after Vic came to me with the story of his new job.

Just to see what would happen, I planted a small item in the *Herald* about the new undercover man. It pleased Vic

immensely to get his name in the paper, but when his boss heard about the news item, he blew up and fired Vic after only thirty-six hours on the job.

Now, however, according to George, the information Bonnie obtained about the powers of grand jurors was causing resentment to build against Long. While there might be some difference in details between the two county systems, the Dade handbook made it apparent the Broward jurors had not been given any understanding of their basic rights and responsibilities. Some of the jurors were planning another informal session to discuss a protest to the presiding judge. There was growing sentiment for a special session to discuss some of the complaints individual jurors had received in recent days. The pot was boiling.

When Wetzler left, I sat down at my typewriter, stared hard at the pix of Ann (Mrs. Trigger Mike) Coppola I have framed above my desk, and wrote a long memo to the editors of the *Herald* explaining the situation.

The memo concluded with these words: "There could be no better time to run my Broward series than right now."

The series had been ready almost a month. The attorneys had found no major problem and the editors could give no reason for the delay. It was just one of those things—a "lack of communication" within the city room. I personally thought "lack of interest" better described it, so I mentioned that any activity by a grand jury in Broward might cause reaction in Dade. Suppose, I suggested, the Broward jurors indicted their sheriff. That might put Gerstein on the spot and cause him to quit stalling around with O'Nan.

The editors all smiled pleasantly at my optimism. One of them even announced he had bet with a colleague that O'Nan would never talk. That interested me—if anyone on the staff was willing to quit playing devil's advocate and accept a bet on O'Nan, I wanted to meet him. But my investigation disclosed it had been the odds offered rather than any faith in the triumph of justice that had caused him to put his money on the line.

Nevertheless, while assuring me the situation was hopeless, the editors did decide to run the Broward series. After all, it contained some interesting stuff. One last minute hitch developed when the attorneys objected to my identifying one of Hymie's friends as "the Tapper." (I never even thought of using his name.) But we straightened it out by changing "the Tapper" to "the Bug." Why it made the lawyers happier, I didn't bother to inquire. I only wished the guy—whatever he was called—would do a more professional job of tapping my home phone. Half the time I couldn't call out on it because of the electronic interference.

How much good the articles did when at last they appeared, I could never know. Presumably they increased the heat, but by then the temperature around the Broward Courthouse was considerably hotter than hell in midsummer. And this was February.

Wetzler, as vice-foreman, asked State Attorney Long to call the jury into session. When nothing happened, a group of jurors met and drew up a petition calling for an official meeting on February 23.

"We feel this action is necessary in order to fulfill our oath of office to the citizens of Broward County," the petition declared.

Eleven of sixteen jurors signed the petition. A delegation led by Wetzler took it to the office of Circuit Judge Williams only to discover Long had beaten them to the punch. Apparently tipped by some of his friends on the jury—I thought of the Communist fighter—Long had filed a motion to recall the jury on March 2.

Judge Williams told reporters that while the jury had a legal right to recall itself, he had decided to honor Long's motion because the grand jurors gave "no real reason for the special session."

Angrily the jurors went home to wait for the public's reaction. The spectacle of a grand jury trying to call itself into session to investigate crime and corruption, should interest even the blasé citizens of Broward, the jurors decided.

I was personally delighted. We had dramatized the difficulties ordinary citizens such as Virginia encountered in getting past the state attorney to the grand jury room. Now the jury itself was confronted with the same obstacle.

But if the anger of the jurors was hot on the day their petition was rejected, it became a blue flame a few days later when they learned that, contrary to their assumption, their term would end on March 7—a Monday. This gave them only four working days to conduct an investigation and write a final report. The jurors had been led to believe their term expired in April.

I wasn't surprised—remembering the last-day probe the state attorney permitted the previous grand jury to conduct. It was the Big Stall all over again, and it seemed it might work.

Wetzler and his friends—united now in anger as they had never been in civic concern—held a hasty meeting and decided to hire private counsel. One juror, John W. Warren, nominated Ellis Rubin of Miami Beach, and when the others were unable to agree on anyone else, Warren got his way. Rubin, a young and aggressive attorney, was later to win the Republican nomination for attorney general and run a respectable race against incumbent Earl Faircloth.

Six jurors and Rubin met at the courthouse. The press had been tipped, and the jurors held an impromptu press conference in the marble and glass lobby. But again, upon entering Judge Williams' chambers, they discovered Long had been there ahead of them. He had presented a new motion recalling the jury on Monday, February 28, and the judge signed it.

This represented a gain of two days for the jurors—a limited victory. They went home still angry but nourishing the small satisfaction that at least they weren't being entirely ignored. Long, meanwhile, held a press conference to complain that certain members of the press were treating him unfairly. No one told him, he said, that the jury wanted to meet. He would have been happy to have called the session earlier had he known the jurors wanted to go to work.

Jim Savage reported privately that while the press corps dutifully noted Long's comment, few of its members believed it. The reporters on the courthouse beat were beginning to open their eyes at last, he said.

But now the work began for me. The grand jury had only a week to conduct its probe. Was there a chance of getting Long out and a special counsel appointed? No, on both counts, Wetzler said. Long still possessed a loyal minority on the jury. It would fight to retain Long, who, after all, was a candidate for a new congressional seat that reapportionment had created. His friends weren't about to take any action that would hurt him. On the other hand, Long's own actions were hurting his political image. It now seemed unlikely he would continue on a course of open opposition.

I had my doubts. The jury was still dependent on the state attorney for legal advice no matter what evidence we might present. But, as Sam put it, when there's only one crap game in town you keep playing, no matter what the odds.

The problem now was to get witnesses. A night meeting was held at Wetzler's home in southwest Fort Lauderdale. Bonnie had converted it into a command post, and to the meeting she invited several lawmen, several reporters from other newspapers, and George's closest allies on the jury. With Bonnie manning a typewriter, we drew up a witness list. I was able to supply some of the big names: Jimmy Blue Eyes, Meyer Lansky, Hymie Martin, Abe Cohen, and the like. Irene Steubber, a reporter for a local newspaper and a real crusader, tossed in a few more. We included all the big Dade gamblers, who had operated under Fat Hymie in Broward County—such men as Jack Rainwater, James Christian, Ray McLendon, and Hoke (Bookie Mac) McClellan. Bessie Winkle couldn't be overlooked nor her Dade County boss, Red Vaught. After all, Red had once told me the Broward graft scale was less than the Dade scale. We also named some ex-deputies such as Jim Spears—the man who had gone to the syndicate for help in removing Sheriff Michell's cam-

paign manager. For good measure we added the name of the manager, Leo V. Hart.

All in all it was an impressive list. Wetzler promptly turned it over to Judge Williams, who promised to see that subpoenas were issued. Meanwhile, I retired to my typewriter.

Volunteers could suggest witnesses to Wetzler, but once inside the grand jury room it would be up to him alone to ask the right questions. No help could be expected from Long. Other jurors would have only scanty information on which to base questions. My Broward series would be helpful in supplying a general pattern, but specifics would be essential.

I took the witness list and set to work. First came a long memo outlining possible indictments and procedures. I suggested the jurors seek grounds for a possible conspiracy indictment, linking gamblers and officials. Such a net had been used effectively in Newport and should work in Broward. Individual indictments charging gambling, perjury, attempted bribery, etc., were also possible, I wrote: "If you fail to get them on one thing, try for the other. In addition, if they refuse to talk when given immunity, they can be cited for contempt."

Officials, I added, could also be charged with malfeasance, nonfeasance, or misfeasance.

Under procedure, I suggested that "safe" witnesses be called first to establish that gambling and prostitution existed. Chief Holt of the Fort Lauderdale police department agreed to permit his vice squad men to testify. I thought the jury might be interested to hear them describe how known bolita peddlers stood two feet outside the city limits and thumbed their noses—literally as well as figuratively—at city police.

Even the final report got some attention. I advised the jurors to ask the next grand jury to carry on the investigation and to recommend a new jury be convened as quickly as possible.

I then turned to the witness list. For each witness I prepared a number of questions. Seventeen were on Hymie's list. They included:

1. Do you know Sheriff Allen B. Michell?
2. Did you ever meet with Leo V. Hart?
3. Do you know Joe Sonken?
4. Are you—or have you been—a banker for bolita and numbers operators?

The last question was so worded because of information I had received a short time before. The syndicate had removed Fat Hymie as operating director. Too much heat was the real reason, but officially the operators were told the syndicate was unhappy because Hymie had been unable to fix the Cuban National Lottery. A lot of "hot numbers" had fallen recently, costing the syndicate much money. A deal with Castro had been one of the imperatives when the syndicate moved in. Hymie had sought to get around the problem by establishing play on the Puerto Rican National Lottery, but it, while growing, had not replaced "Cuba" as the main item of business.

Many in law enforcement felt Castro didn't make a deal with the gamblers primarily because he already had rigged the lottery for the benefit of the revolution. Months ago Charley explained to me how Castro could tip his agents in south Florida to the number that would fall, and they, by betting discreetly, could win thousands of dollars each week. Yet no effective action had been taken to wipe out a racket controlled by a Communist dictator.

If Fat Hymie could be persuaded to talk, perhaps the jury might ask his opinion of Castro's methods. But I rather felt the veteran gangster would honor the underworld code and remain silent. At the bottom of the list of questions I added: (Note—Hymie will probably take the Fifth. Try giving him immunity and holding him in contempt.)

When the questions were finished, I was still unsatisfied. Something more was needed—something dramatic at the beginning to convert the anger of the jurors into a determination to learn the truth for themselves. If once they understood

what a farce law enforcement had become in Broward
County, they might have the patience to dig hard. A good
witness was needed, someone who could tell the story from
personal knowledge.

Charley came at my bidding. We talked for an hour, and I
took him to the Wetzler home. There plans were made. Charley would be on hand next morning when the jury convened.
Wetzler would tell the jurors he had a mystery witness, who
had to be heard first. He would personally come out and
beckon to Charley. Thus no one would be forewarned, no one
would know the identity of the witness until he was safely in
the grand jury room.

One final chore remained. I called Emerson Allsworth and
made a request. After all, Emerson had volunteered to help.
A few hours later he called back to say he had spent some
time with Judge Williams, and they had found a way of continuing the jury if more time should be needed. The jury
would be called into session first thing Monday, Emerson
said, and the judge would give the necessary assurance.

After thanking Emerson, I called Reporter Savage and told
him what to expect next day. He seemed a little dubious but
didn't argue. I was glad he didn't. It had been a long weekend.

The grand jury session opened with a laugh. Word spread
around the corridors that Madam Bessie Winkle had not been
served with a subpoena. The state attorney's office had somehow missed all the publicity about Bessie living next door to
Chief Malphurs in Hollywood, and had sent the subpoena to
Dade County for service at Bessie's old address.

Some of the reporters seemed to think the mistake a rather
pointed commentary on the state of law enforcement in
Broward.

Another sidebar developed out of the attempt to subpoena
Leo Hart. Deputies arrived at Hart's Fort Lauderdale home
—he had returned to Broward after his mishap in Mexico
City—to discover the witness had moved two hours before.

Not only had he disappeared, but he had taken his furniture with him.

Other big-name witnesses, such as Jimmy Blue Eyes and Meyer Lansky, left home hurriedly and were not served. But the boys located a few hostile witnesses, among them Hymie Martin and Joe Sonken.

The hall was crowded as I got off the elevator. I recognized Joe Sonken immediately—by the blimp-belly and the cigar. Joe glared at me as I walked by. Alone at the end of the hall was a mountain of a man. His belly was as big as Sonken's, but an extra foot of height prevented it from being a blimp. He wore a dark suit, which fitted well despite his size, and dark glasses. Years ago he had been known as "Pittsburgh Hymie," a sharp dresser and a lean and hungry hood.

I stopped in front of him, feeling strangely small in the presence of his overwhelming bulk. He looked down at me, but I could read nothing on his face. His lips were thick—wet, somehow—and they shaped themselves into a half smile.

"How are things with the syndicate?" I asked.

The smile grew just a little, but he didn't speak. I stared again into the dark glasses, shrugged, and walked away.

Charley was waiting around a corner. Well dressed, he looked the part of a prosperous gambler. The jury didn't need to know he bought his suit back in the days when he enjoyed Red Rainwater's favor. Savage—young, excited, and striving to appear bored—joined us. I introduced Charley as "Mr. X," and told him to cherish his scoop. Jim agreed. After hearing the judge a few minutes earlier instruct the jury as I had predicted the night before, Savage was ready to acknowledge I knew the score.

We watched the crowd grow. Interestingly enough, the best dressed men were the lowest paid—cops from Hallandale and Broward deputies, some of whom wore tailored suits, alligator shoes, and sported diamond rings. I marveled again at their mentality. Years before in Newport I had watched crooked cops flaunt their wealth in the face of grand jurors. Was it

arrogance or just stupidity? You'd think they'd have sense enough to leave the rings off for once.

Suddenly I realized I was nervous. Always, it seemed, in a time of crisis I thought back to those heroic days in Newport. The situations were very much the same—but there victory was an accomplished fact to rely upon. Here I had to depend on others—Charley and Savage and, inside the grand jury room, Wetzler.

Well, I had attempted to serve as state attorney by remote control. The rest was up to the man in the room.

And here he came—peeping out a crack in the door, looking hastily around for his mystery witness. I caught his eye. He nodded. I slapped Charley on the shoulder. He walked slowly, almost casually, as if but stretching his legs. When he neared the door, his step quickened, and he was inside before anyone in the hall suspected a thing.

Instantly we were surrounded by reporters demanding to know the identity of the witness. I declined to answer. Jim had a big grin on his face. Later, when the afternoon papers came out, I grinned also. Charley was identified by common consent as an IRS agent. Why, I never knew.

There was little time for smiling after that, for now our forces were divided. Had we been dishonest, had we even assumed the means justified the end, life would have been simpler. But under the law I could not know what went on inside the grand jury room. Wetzler could not report either the testimony or the mood of the grand jury. Yet it was essential I have some inkling of the problems as they developed, of the questions that had not been asked as well as those that had not been answered.

My allies—and I had quite a few—helped some in keeping slightly ahead of the witnesses. Thus we learned a powerful counterattack had been launched, and some ex-deputies we had counted on for aid were now telling others they planned to change their testimony or withhold certain facts. Other deputies, who had talked big before the showdown, now felt it wise to play safe and say as little as possible.

The big problem was an air of defeatism. No one believed there was a chance anything but a rap on the wrist would result. Years before, it had been learned that for eighteen months Broward deputies had not been properly bonded. When the matter was brought up, the sheriff tried to cover by obtaining new bonds and backdating them. But the grand jury, under the leadership of Quentin Long, failed to take any action, despite a serious legal question as to the validity of all arrests made during the unbonded period.

Grounds for pessimism existed, I had to agree.

Actually, my nightly conferences with Wetzler proved very helpful. While he steadfastly refused to discuss anything that happened inside the grand jury room, his demeanor provided a barometer by which I could gauge events. When he was discouraged and dejected, his feelings were so apparent I could guess the witnesses who had testified that day had not delivered the goods. If, on the other hand, he seemed happy, I could feel progress had been made.

There was, of course, no single objective. We weren't out to get Sheriff Michell or Quentin Long. We did want to clean up Broward County and end Fat Hymie's influence. The exact method was up to the grand jury.

I had another motive as well. Pressure in Dade would result from action in Broward—and the Dade arena remained my principal battleground. It was Dade County the *Herald* wanted cleaned up now.

Crisis after crisis arose as the days began to blur. The jury sat for ten or more hours each day, as individual jurors abandoned their normal business and social life in an effort to utilize all remaining time. Quentin Long, still smooth and affable, was on hand each day and managed to convince some of the less-informed reporters he was running the show.

An ex-deputy brought word that Jim Spears had defected. He was going to restrict his testimony. If asked, he was going to say he had destroyed his famous report to Sheriff Michell. I had returned the report to him after making a copy and locking it in a filing cabinet in Miami. The day after Spears testi-

fied—he came out looking rather deflated—I drove to Miami and made a copy of the copy. Shortly after the jury session began next morning, I was standing outside the door with the second copy in my briefcase. The door opened. Wetzler called me inside. I handed over the copy, noted the smile on George's face, and returned to the hall.

Instantly, the press corps swarmed around. Why had I been called? Why was I inside for such a short time? What was in that briefcase?

I shrugged it off, and somebody wisecracked "He's probably got Bessie Winkle in that briefcase."

It drew a laugh, and I added to it with a rather pointed reference to the state attorney's failure to locate her. What followed was even funnier. Subpoenaed Dade deputy Dave Helman dashed down the hall to the state attorney's office. A minute later he returned and collared a young reporter. He pulled the reporter down the hall and came back for another. By the time he returned for a third one, the first had escaped to report I was going to be sued for slander. They were trying to get witnesses to testify about my wisecrack. But for some strange reason none of the reporters queried had heard me make it. One of them managed to get a free lunch out of the deputy, however, but even after a couple of drinks his memory remained bad.

On Thursday came the first climax. Fat Hymie, who had stood patiently for three days, was called into the grand jury room. With him had waited a little man with a white goatee, Harold Ungerleider. I wondered if he was related to any of the Cleveland Ungerleider's, whose brokerage business once numbered President Harding as a client. Months later in Miami, as we waited outside another grand jury room, the elderly attorney confirmed my guess. He had known Hymie since those rum-running days on Lake Erie.

Would Hymie talk? There were those who thought he would. Yet these optimists were the same people who had doubted Fat Hymie existed. I still felt he would't talk. And I was right.

Late in the afternoon, the judge was called. We crowded into an open court session. Hymie, still wearing his half-smile stood big and silent on the left beside his tiny attorney. I looked at him and shivered, remembering how close I had come to the same spot only a few weeks before. Quentin Long, aware the public's eye was upon him, stood at the right, very much the man of the moment.

Judge Williams, still youthful in his robe, rapped for order. Court was in session. Mr. Martin, according to Long, had refused to answer certain questions put to him by the grand jury. Would the judge order him to answer? Immunity had been granted Mr. Martin.

Ungerleider argued briefly the immunity offered was not broad enough to protect his client from federal prosecution. Williams listened, then ordered Martin to answer. A five minute recess was granted to permit Ungerleider and Martin to confer. During the recess reporters rushed to Long's desk to look at the specific questions Martin had refused to answer. I was also curious.

Five questions were listed—they were the first five questions I had drafted for the jury to ask Martin. I laughed out loud and met the broad grin of George Wetzler. He bowed slightly as I saluted. Turning back to the table, I produced my Minox. But assistant state attorney Glickstein interfered. You can't take pictures in a courtroom, he insisted. I didn't protest, but I was to remember the incident.

Martin and Ungerleider were back. Court resumed. The witness stood on his constitutional rights and refused to answer the questions, the attorney said. A gasp went around the room. I heard a reporter whisper, "Just who the hell is he protecting?"

Williams could be decisive enough on occasion. He ruled Martin in contempt of court and ordered him to jail. Ungerleider protested and asked that bond be set. The motion was denied. An elderly bailiff took Fat Hymie by the arm, as the gavel signaled the end of the court session. Cameramen, who had left their equipment outside in order to witness the drama,

broke for the door. When the bailiff—looking like a child beside his huge prisoner—emerged, a dazzling display of lights struck them. Television cameras ground away as spotlights contributed to the heat and glare.

The little smile was still in place as the ex-boss of the numbers racket was taken to the elevator and upstairs to jail. And as he vanished, fatigue struck me like a blow. If nothing else, we had at last convinced many people that Fat Hymie was for real.

On the next day came a break. Months before, assistant managing editor Larry Jinks had agreed to bring me to Gainesville and a journalism seminar at the University of Florida. He still considered it vital I attend, so I left Wetzler and the others to shift for themselves. We flew to Jacksonville, rented a car and drove across country to the college town. It was my first visit, but I found myself too keyed up to enjoy it. Larry left me at a dormitory to rest, while he visisted friends. I stretched out in gratitude, happy to be away from it all for a little while. Just as I drifted off to sleep, the telephone rang. Basinger was calling from Fort Lauderdale. A crisis had arisen, and he felt it his duty to tell me. How he found me neither he nor I could be quite sure.

I told him what I thought they should do, and went back to the pillow. But the illusion of isolation had been lost. I kept expecting the phone to ring again. When at last Larry appeared to take me to dinner and the seminar, I was almost glad to have company.

Jinks was able to use the newspaper headlines to show what the *Herald* had achieved. The first one on September 5, 1965, had read, MEET HYMIE: SOUTH FLORIDA'S RACKET BOSS.

And the very latest *Herald* headline—for March 4, 1966—said, FAT HYMIE GOES BEHIND BARS.

It was all very tidy and I felt I deserved some credit for arranging things. Unfortunately, I had no time to prepare a speech, so I rambled around a bit and then asked for questions. I think Larry was surprised to see the excited reaction,

and even I was astonished to learn how many coeds wanted to come to the *Herald* and help me investigate the prostitution racket.

All in all, it was a satisfactory show, as Larry agreed on the long drive back through the night to Jacksonville. I caught a plane back to Broward, while he took off on an extended recruiting tour of the better journalism schools. I wondered how many idealistic young reporters would be induced by those headlines to sign up with the crusading Miami *Herald*. And briefly I felt a little guilty.

Years ago I had been a journalism teacher. I quit to learn something about the subject. Learning how it was actually practiced, I had been unable to return to teaching. Other reporters constantly suffered the same disillusionment, which was why even a metropolitan newspaper such as the Miami *Herald* had to conduct recruiting programs to keep a staff. The turnover was tremendous, and in my opinion the editors and publishers had only themselves to blame. The quality of newspaper performance dropped year by year, but as the business became less competitive, quality became secondary.

It was 4 A.M. when I arrived home—time enough to get some sleep and be on hand when the grand jury resumed its session Saturday morning. Basinger greeted me in relief. Things had threatened to get out of hand in my absence. Even now he had a feeling the jury was ready to quit.

Savage confirmed that everything since Hymie had been a bit anticlimactic. Sheriff Michell had come out of a long jury session looking a bit grim, but there had been little open action. Apparently the jurors were worn out and didn't plan to ask for an extension. They would draft their report on Sunday and present it Monday. The show would be over.

Confirmation of a sort came from Wetzler. He, for once, had nothing to ask of me. Nor did he want to talk. The heat was on within the jury, he indicated, and any slip would be blamed on him.

Still other hints came from a Broward deputy, who in-

formed me that Chief Clode and some of his friends had flown to the Bahamas for a long weekend. They were confident the worst was over.

I listened to everyone and waited. The excursion to Gainesville had been a break, but it contributed to the general fatigue. I could well understand why the jurors were ready to quit. They had met for six straight days, sometimes sitting for as much as twelve hours. This was the kind of investigation that should have been spread over six months.

Early Sunday I got the call I had been expecting. Emerson wanted me to be the first to know—there would be no indictments. The jury would return a blistering report, call for continued investigation, and leave it at that.

The muscles in my stomach tightened as I asked Emerson the source of his information. He tried to stall, but quickly made up his mind as I pressed the point. His dope came from Glickstein, the assistant state attorney who had rebuked me for producing a camera in court during a recess.

Glickstein was a nice young man, Emerson assured me. In passing on the jury's decision, he was but doing a friend a favor. In any case, Emerson wanted me to know, we had done our best. I shouldn't feel too badly. After all, getting Hymie to jail for twenty-four hours—he had been released on a writ of habeas corpus during my trip—was quite an accomplishment.

I thanked Allsworth and broke the connection. But I didn't hang up the receiver.

Glickstein, according to my information, had been called on to advise the jury as to the law. Apparently, acting upon his advice and with the approval of Long, jurors had decided there was insufficient evidence under the law to indict. And Glickstein was Emerson's friend. As patronage boss for Governor Burns, Emerson had a lot of friends among young and ambitious attorneys. But if Emerson could use his pipeline into the grand jury room to get information, could he not also use it to issue orders?

I picked the phone out of my lap and dialed Wetzler's number. Bonnie answered. She didn't want to bother George—he was getting ready to attend a committee meeting at Long's office. But when I insisted, she called her husband. Briefly, succinctly, I told him what the jury was going to do. I asked no questions, sought no confirmation. The leak to Emerson, I explained, was Glickstein.

George forgot his reserve. "This ought to shake up some of them bastards," he exclaimed. He told me of the committee meeting. It had originally been called to draft a final report. Now it might do something else. Would I come down and talk to the jurors if they wanted me? Fine, he would call.

Again I broke the connection and dialed again. Jim's beautiful young bride answered. She didn't hesitate when I asked for her husband. Jim—by now ready to believe anything I told him—said he would get down to the courthouse immediately.

I went to my typewriter and knocked out a story. Sufficiently veiled and in guarded language, it made clear a leak had occurred from the grand jury to a politician who had met several times with Hymie Martin. I called the *Herald*'s attorney in Miami, argued with him over the wording, and arrived at an acceptable compromise. After rewriting the story and reading it again to the attorney, I telephoned the city room and dictated it to a rewrite man. It would go on the front page.

Jim called to report the jury meeting came off as scheduled. Five jurors attended as well as Long and Glickstein. More details came a few minutes later from Wetzler. Glickstein had admitted leaking the information to Allsworth. My testimony had not been needed, but it might be useful next day before the full jury. Would I, under the circumstances, consent to testify in front of Long? George could guarantee he would not interfere.

I agreed—and early next morning arrived outside the grand jury room. The crowd was gone. Only reporters were

on hand for the final drama. But rumors were flying. My story was being widely discussed. I heard one TV reporter interviewing Long about the alleged leak. The state attorney, still bland and smooth, brushed it aside as "newspaper talk." The TV reporter was happy to accept the explanation. Long, after all, was something of a master at dividing his enemies, and between television and newspaper reporters it was easy to drive a wedge of lies.

Some of the reporters were a little worried, remembering my last session, when I was handed a subpoena and taken inside the grand jury room. But all went smoothly. Long, in his best form, gave me my head. I outlined Hymie Martin's conquest of Broward and gave some unpublished details. When I brought history up to the previous morning, my testimony was interrupted. Long asked me to step outside, while he briefed the jury on a related matter. Wetzler winked as I walked out.

The wait was brief. Even the old man looked at me with respect as I re-entered the room. It was obvious that Glickstein's admission had cast my testimony in a new light. Suddenly, I was worthy of belief. More than that, my entire story had to be credited.

When at last I finished, both Long and the foreman thanked me. Several jurors arose and shook my hand as I walked out. The contrast with my previous appearance caused me to emerge smiling. Only Jim could guess why I was amused.

The day dragged on. I went home, got some sleep, and received a report about dinner time. Long and County solicitor Bob Adams spent ninety minutes in the law library. It was obvious an indictment was being prepared.

About 8 P.M. I returned to the courthouse. Word had spread and crowds were gathering. The jury, tired and now bored, was attempting to get a last-minute report drafted. About 9 P.M. news came that all was ready. The judge was

standing by. But there was another delay. Wetzler tore out of the grand jury room and rushed to Long's office, where a stenographer had been typing the report. Later, I learned George discovered Long had left out a recommendation the next jury continue the probe. Stubbornly, despite opposition from some of his own weary allies, he insisted the report be retyped, and the missing paragraph included. He got his way.

When at last we were assembled in open court, the final report was anticlimactic. It contained little. No one would have paid any attention, however, if it had been a masterpiece of literature. For buried at the end of the report was this paragraph:

"Your Grand Jury returned an indictment against one public official, charging him with a common law crime of misfeasance, nonfeasance and malfeasance in office."

But the indictment was sealed and would remain sealed until the official was in custody.

The wait began. The long deserted marble halls resounded with rumor, as reporters dashed from one vantage point to another. Jim called city desk only to learn that, however certain we might be, the *Herald* could take no chances on naming the accused official. He dictated a story for the early editions. Only a sentence naming the official would be required to complete the day's work.

I thought of other long vigils in other cities, other times. This one was different. It had little suspense. The only question—would the official surrender in time to meet our final deadline.

I put myself in a position where I could watch either door opening into the lobby, and settled down. It was almost midnight when I saw shadows move outside the glass door. I dialed the city room and stood waiting as the shadows came into the lighted lobby and assumed substance. I recognized the well-dressed man who led the way.

"It's the sheriff," I told the reporter in Miami. I could hear

him echo my words, "It's the sheriff," in a shout that must have carried across the city room.

The little procession brushed past me. Sheriff Michell's eyes met mine. He said nothing. I wondered if he remembered his remark to me about Jake Lingle.

TEN

I JAB WITH MY LEFT
AND LAND A RIGHT

*

The Dade County Grand Jury came alive and issued an interim blast at local conditions. Reports indicated State Attorney Gerstein was feeling some mild heat. Various individuals were wondering why witnesses such as Fat Hymie couldn't be called and indictments returned. If it could be done in Broward, why not in Dade?

Herald executives were pleased. The Broward adventure seemed to prove, they reasoned, that the newspaper wasn't after Dade Sheriff Buchanan alone, and at the same time it put new pressure on Sheriff Buchanan. All of which was fine, but meanwhile, when could I get back to work in Dade?

A few chores delayed me. Unexpectedly, the role of king-maker was mine. As patronage boss, Emerson Allsworth would have most to say in the selection of an interim sheriff to serve until Michell was acquitted or convicted. And Emerson, as my eager ally, wanted me to be satisfied. Or so he said.

Discreet checking brought word that the Fort Lauderdale police department would be able to confide in, and work with, Larry Lang, a private eye who had once been a member of that department. I was introduced to Lang one night by a mutual friend. A tall, heavy-set man with dark hair, Lang was eager for the job and assured me he would clean up the department. I was disappointed to discover he had no real knowledge of conditions within the sheriff's office or within the county, but the man surely had the best of recommendations from people whose judgment I trusted.

I passed Emerson the name and got a promise of favorable consideration. But suddenly the agile patronage boss dropped out of sight. No one could reach him for twenty-four hours. Before he emerged, Governor Burns announced he had selected Tom Walker, a Fort Lauderdale insurance executive, to be interim sheriff. Walker had business connections with the publisher of a local newspaper—a fact annoying to some of the *Herald*'s people. I knew nothing about the man, but I couldn't believe an insurance executive was best quailfied to take the action needed in Broward County.

For the only time in my career, I called Allsworth, and got him as he was leaving his office. In no uncertain terms I told him I considered the appointment of Walker a double cross. All my deals with him were off, I said, and when the federal grand jury met I intended to testify. Then I hung up the phone.

Immediately the phone rang again. I decided not to answer it. The ringing continued for several minutes before the caller gave up the effort.

Fifteen minutes later I answered another call. Basinger said Emerson had telephoned and left word with his wife that it was "urgent" Dick talk to him. I told Dick to forget it.

In the middle of dinner, the phone rang again. The voice identified itself as Larry Lang. He wanted to come out and talk to me. I told him I was eating and to wait thirty minutes. He repeated my message to someone and agreed.

With Lang when he arrived was an attorney, who just happened to be Chief Holt's attorney as well. And Emerson was there, supple as ever. He revealed that following my call to him he had located Lang and offered him the number-two job with full power. Walker would be sheriff in name only, he said.

"This is all very interesting," I replied, "but shouldn't you be talking to Walker? I'm flattered to be consulted, but I'm simply a reporter."

Lang looked ill at ease, but the two attorneys smiled

broadly and departed. I called Jim Savage and told him to check with Walker about Lang. Jim soon called back to say Walker knew nothing of Lang and had no intentions of offering him the job. Jim was a bit puzzled—what was going on? I told him he would be the first to know.

Two hours later I got another call from Lang. He was still worried. As yet he had not talked to Walker, but a meeting had now been set for 5 P.M. next day—Sunday. Personally, he expected Walker to balk at the scheme, and for that matter, so did Emerson. If he balked, Emerson promised to make Walker resign and get the job for Lang.

I thanked Lang for the information and went to bed. Whose side was I on, I sometimes wondered. I couldn't always believe I was on my own side, for personal interest would have caused me to seek friends instead of foes. It seemed a little self-righteous to tell myself that my guiding star had to be Truth, but in the troubled waters of Broward County there were no other navigational points of reference. Not for the first time, I wished I could be an Organization Man and leave the deep thinking to the Team. And then I remembered the Team at the *Herald*, and shuddered.

I was taking a nap on the screen porch next afternoon, recouping from the strain of the past week, when a car pulled into the drive. I recognized the driver as Francis Buckley, Democratic candidate for a newly created congressional seat. Joe Varon, who once represented Meyer Lansky, and State Attorney Long were also seeking the Democratic nomination. Buckley was something of a dark horse, but welcome to those who had no desire to choose between Varon and Long. He had been introduced to me by a professor at Broward Junior College.

With Buckley was a stranger, a short, somewhat stout man in his late forties. He had a round, friendly face and a cheerful manner. I wasn't too surprised to learn he was the new sheriff.

Buckley explained the situation. A committee of citizens (all friendly to the newspaper publisher) had drafted Walker

and assured him, among other things, he would have the professional help of the Fort Lauderdale police. Now he had discovered this was not necessarily true. Furthermore, Allsworth was pressuring Walker to appoint Larry Lang as number-two man. Walker was suspicious—he didn't trust Emerson.

Score one for your side, I thought. I didn't trust him either.

Walker, speaking in a slow, deep voice, confirmed Buckley's estimate. We discussed the general situation. While recognizing the man had even less knowledge of conditions than Lang, I was impressed with his intelligence and integrity. Possibly he could be led astray, I thought, but at least he's sincere.

It was apparent that Walker knew his limitations and wanted professional help. He had nothing against Lang it developed, except the fact that Emerson seemed to be sponsoring him. I explained how that happened, and why. Would Walker accept Holt's help via Lang? After all, if the police chief was going to put his prestige on the line, it was logical he should want to work through someone he knew and trusted. Walker agreed.

We parted with words of assurance. Walker got my promise of cooperation. In return, he said he would do his best to reorganize the sheriff's department and give Broward County efficient law enforcement.

About 8 P.M., I received two calls some fifteen minutes apart—Lang and Walker. They had met, talked, and reached an understanding. Each thanked me again. I passed the word to Jim—another scoop. If this continued, he said modestly, the *Herald* might move him to Miami and a job on the city side. I told him to stall them. I needed him to keep an eye on Broward.

For Dade County was claiming my attention. I wrote a transition story about the role of the state attorney's office:

Other agencies can be corrupt or incompetent without necessarily creating a condition of lawlessness, but the

State Attorney has great influence in keeping a county
clean or dirty as he desires. His weapon is the grand jury.
To keep the county clean he must act to make the grand
jury act, and what it does is usually dependent upon what
he does. To allow the county to go to the dogs, the State
Attorney needs to do nothing. But he must do nothing
so convincingly the grand jury will do nothing as well.

The article went on to detail the role of the state attorney
in recent Broward history. It concluded with this sentence:
"Meanwhile, in Dade County . . . "

"Dick Gerstein is my next target."
That was the word I put out at every opportunity—over
my tapped telephone line, in "confidential conversations"
with double agents, and in city-room gossip sessions with fellow reporters.

Making no effort at concealment, I began a probe of the
liquor empire once owned by Jay Weiss. That led to the
strange stock promotions of L. F. Popell. And ultimately the
trail brought me to the plush Lincoln Road, Miami Beach,
offices of young attorney Alvin I. Malnik.

The Weiss case was important in that much of recent
events in Dade could be traced to it. The affair began in 1960
when a striptease dancer, who lived with a deputy sheriff,
became jealous and started checking up on him. The stripper
—a bright girl named Kay—learned, among other things,
that her boyfriend actually took orders from Roy O'Nan,
chief bagman. O'Nan used the deputy as muscle to put the
arm on individual bars and girlie joints that in those days
infested Miami.

Becoming aware the girl was checking up, Roy decided she
would have to go and arranged to have her arrested on
trumped-up charges. When the deputy went along with the
frame, and personally surrendered her after a final fling at a
plush resort—the girl lost her temper. She went to Dan Sullivan, veteran director of the Greater Miami Crime Commis-

sion. Sullivan made a tape of the stripper's story, which contained names, dates, and places. O'Nan had been wise to be worried. Kay had picked up details of his entire operation.

Some of the remarks concerned Gerstein's office so Sullivan —planning ahead—made a new tape and edited out the unflattering references to Gerstein. He then called the state attorney, played the tape, and suggested it be presented to the grand jury foreman.

According to Sullivan, Gerstein objected that to do so would be premature, because the foreman might feel obligated to tell the entire jury about it. And Gerstein wanted to investigate first.

The upshot was that Kay was convicted and ordered by a cooperative judge to leave the state. The deputy was also told to get lost and given $1,000 with which to do it. Years later the ex-deputy told me the story, complaining bitterly that while he was supposed to get $100 a week while in exile, he received only one payment. More impressive than his indignation was his speech. He managed to use a certain four-letter word, or one of its derivatives, three times in a nine-word sentence. For good measure he used the finger of one hand and the fist of the other to illustrate its meaning.

Nothing came of the investigation by Gerstein, but Sheriff Tom Kelly became uncooperative and bagman O'Nan—in cooperation with Sam—decided to replace him with someone more plastic. The long conspiracy that resulted in Tal Buchanan's appointment followed.

Sullivan, meanwhile, got a federal-state probe going into the liquor business. The role of Jay Weiss, a friend of Gerstein, became the central theme of the investigations and led ultimately to a compromise, whereby Weiss and his associates acknowledge certain law violations. They paid small fines and disposed of much of their holdings.

Weiss became involved with Popell in a major stock promotion which made millions before the bottom fell out and the firm went bankrupt. Gerstein, as a friend of both Weiss

and Popell, made many thousands of dollars by buying—and selling—at the right time.

Malnik's name appeared in the closing phases of the Popell stock promotion. He too reaped a tidy profit and went on with Weiss to greater things. My probe of Malnik became more and more complicated.

Later I was to write, "From his base on Lincoln Road, the thirty-two-year-old attorney has been involved with international gangsters, mysterious Swiss bankers, hoodlum elements of organized labor, and top syndicate gamblers."

Among the gangsters, I discovered, was Jimmy Blue Eyes, who had been in the background of Malnik's latest venture involving a combination juke box-motion picture device designed for use in better bars and taverns.

Time Magazine dubbed the young attorney a wizard for his part in the multimillion-dollar deal, but I soon discovered much of the credit belonged to Alo. Basically, it had been another stock promotion with the device known as Scopitone serving as the gimmick. Sharing in the profits, as usual, I found, were both Weiss and Gerstein.

As the picture developed, I was somewhat amazed. The sophisticated executives of organized crime could use this as a pattern for the future. Instead of pay-offs, simply cut a public official in for some crumbs—the droppings from the financial money tree. Give him a timely tip or two and let him help himself. Perfectly legitimate, you know.

I thought I had the rest of the picture when I discovered that early in his career—shortly after graduating from law school—Malnik had been the subject of many complaints to Gerstein's office. The citizens were complaining of certain second mortgages the state attorney's office declined to investigate.

There was much more information, and I put together what I considered to be a four-part series of dramatic impact. It utilized facts, I felt, that no other reporter could have secured. It was dynamite.

The editors of the *Herald* agreed, and so did their attorneys. We argued for days but I couldn't move them. The series was just too hot to handle.

Weeks later, after a New York newspaper published much of the inside story of the Scopitone promotion—a New York federal grand jury was investigating and had subpoenaed half the nation's top hoods—the attorneys permitted the first two articles to run. They cut out references to Gerstein, however. The two stories may have privately caused Gerstein some worry, but they did nothing to mar his public image.

Four months later, after a Securities and Exchange Commission report on the Popell Company—and federal indictments in a bank case involving Weiss and others—the *Herald* ran the third and fourth stories. Gerstein was mentioned, but the real impact of the series had been lost. Besides, as in Broward, I had already gained my objective in another way.

My goal had been, bluntly, to put sufficient pressure on the state attorney to make him do his duty. Perhaps the threat of the unpublished articles, hanging over him like a sword, did the trick anyway. I couldn't be sure. But in any case, on March 29, O'Nan quit stalling and testified before the grand jury.

The editor who bet he would never talk, paid off but remained determinedly pessimistic. "They'll never indict," he insisted. I noticed he didn't offer to bet again.

Meanwhile, success in Broward brought an unexpected dividend. Larry Lang, who had been prowling about the sheriff's offices and finding everything from cash to bolita evidence stored away and forgotten, discovered the "Messick file." He explained that Chief Deputy Clode—who was still hanging on—said the file was evidence of my low character.

I found the contents evidence of something else—a joint effort by the Dade and Broward sheriff's departments to smear me. Reports were included from both departments and proved conclusively that a search had been made from Happy

Valley in the Blue Ridge to Fort Collins in the Rocky Mountains—a search for dirt.

Louisville, where I had lived for eight years before coming to south Florida, was also covered. I was amused to discover the investigating officer—in Louisville for a seminar at the Southern Police Institute—ignored his instructors, who knew me well, and went to a local bookie for data. He was rewarded with wild tales about my "frequent arrests for intoxication," and my efforts to "smear police that had led to my indictment."

The entire report was put into perspective by this paragraph: "It was learned that Messick put a lot of pressure on a bookmaker by the name of Gil Beckley. Mr. Beckley would be a good source of further information on Messick."

I put pressure on Beckley in Newport in 1961. I had also put pressure on him in Miami in 1965. Indeed, Gil (the Brain) Beckley was the subject of one of my first *Herald* stories, in which I described his national lay-off betting empire, which he ruled from a plush apartment in the Blair House at Surfside north of Miami Beach. Following my story, the FBI raided Beckley, using a Negro agent dressed as a chauffeur and carrying on his shoulder a box of expensive Scotch. Two "bodyguards" accompanied the chauffeur and successfully passed the lookouts and other spooks at the Blair House, who protected both Beckley and Jimmy Hoffa when the Teamster boss was in town. Beckley, peeping out of his one-way glass eye-hole, saw the case of liquor and opened the door. The three agents swept in. Wildly dressed in a Chinese robe. Beckley tried to destroy his records, which he had been working on when the bell sounded. The books were in code but later—after the code was broken—Beckley and his men about the country were indicted by a federal grand jury and even now were awaiting trial.

Yet this was the man the sheriff's office thought might have information on me.

In the file were reports on the rental Mustangs I had used

for awhile—apparently they did confuse the boys. There were surveillance reports, including one that detailed how Clode and Mazur searched a bar where they thought I was meeting another officer.

Other reports attempted to trace my life history and succeeded only in so confusing the issue they made no sense. For example—I was said to be still receiving $25,000 a year from the Ford Foundation. Some outfit called McMillion Publishers was allegedly paying me $15,000. The *Herald* didn't list me as an employee, the report continued, but obviously I was working for them and getting paid.

Some of this financial information was given a publisher of a local scandal sheet. He printed it and aroused the interests of a local Internal Revenue agent who soon notified me of an audit of my tax returns, an audit which resulted in my getting a whopping refund.

In the file were the pictures made of me by the Broward sheriff's photographer last fall, when I was subpoenaed before the grand jury. The photographer had already confirmed the assignment, and apologized.

Upon going through the file I learned that—in a last effort to convince Lang and Walker—a deputy told them I framed George Ratterman in Newport back in 1961. Walker, who knew Ratterman, called him long distance. George, who had been drugged in a Cincinnati bar while Gil Beckley watched, then taken to Newport and put to bed with a stripper, was happy to tell Walker the truth—that I had helped prove his innocence. Clode resigned two minutes later.

The discovery of the file coincided with a report from Starr Horton, a Miami businessman who happened to be the current president of the Miami Crime Commission. Horton, without disclosing his sources, said he had learned of a plot to frame me in Dade County. A few weeks later, when Horton disclosed he was a part owner of a soon-to-open Las Vegas casino, we figured his sources were pretty good.

George Beebe ordered me to stay out of Dade County,

while Clarence Jones wrote a full-length "profile" of me. Clarence did a good, if flattering story attributing to me the abilities of a professional con man. It ran on the second front under an eight-column banner: WHO IS THIS REPORTER HANK MESSICK?

With the story ran my picture, the first time I had consented to its use since I had indisputable evidence that the boys already had the pics made in Broward County. On the editorial page Don Shoemaker also contributed a few flattering paragraphs, describing me as having the appearance of an unmade bed.

The publicity, the editors felt, would protect me. I hoped they were right, but I continued to avoid bars and nightclubs and curtailed my social life even more. The pressure continued to build, however, and my nocturnal raids on the refrigerator became my only assurance of easy sleep. My trousers were becoming tight.

Things were moving fast now. Miami Mayor Robert King High—a candidate for the Democratic gubernatorial nomination but not given much chance against incumbent Haydon Burns—decided to join the fight against crime. I was called to his office in a skyscraper overlooking Biscayne Bay, and offered the job of heading a crime probe. Under the city charter, High explained, the City Commission could turn itself into a Crime Commission and hold hearings. Years ago the Kefauver Committee had done much to alert the community. Perhaps a small scale model could do some good today. But a chief investigator was needed.

High was short, redheaded, and sincere. A liberal mayor, he had made a career of championing the underdog. Several years ago he had gone out on the streets to buy bolita tickets, thus proving to the public and the police how wide open things were. But Chief Walter Headly was entrenched—and protected by civil service. High had been unable to achieve any real reform.

I didn't doubt his motives were at least partly political, but

I was tempted. Remembering how public hearings in Kentucky had contributed to the reform campaign, I thought High's idea a good one. Yet I knew the *Herald* wouldn't want me to undertake the task. Editorially, the newspaper was pro-Burns. Most of the reporters were for High, but of course that made no difference.

When I declined the job, High asked me to nominate someone. Instantly I thought of Dick Wallace, even then preparing to retire as senior supervisor of the Miami Intelligence Division of the IRS. An able man was Dick—and one who had no illusions about local conditions. He would be ideal if he could be persuaded.

High knew Wallace and immediately called him. After thirty years of federal service, Dick was looking forward to a private law practice and was reluctant, but ultimately he was persuaded to take the job. The *News* and *Herald* bannered his appointment as an "Untouchable." He worked for weeks, lost twenty pounds he could ill afford—I marvelled at the injustice of it—and came up with only one hearing. The key witness was a mystery man beneath a silk hood. Only a few of us knew at the time it was my old buddy, Charley—at last paying off some of his debt to Red Rainwater.

The hearing caused a sensation, but when the county commissioners refused to give the City Commission county-wide subpoena powers, Wallace had little choice but to let his two-month contract with the city expire. Months later, an inspired Dade County Grand Jury was to make excellent use of the many leads provided by the Wallace crime files. At the time, however, all the hoods he wanted to question were remaining outside the city limits, where he couldn't reach them. Thus, despite heroic efforts by Wallace and his little band of Untouchables—Bert Anderson, retired IRS inspector; George Vilas, retired IRS special agent; and Norman Anderson, a young Miami police officer of impeccable reputation—their investigation faltered for lack of jurisdiction. High, by then deeply embroiled in last minute political struggles, let the crime probe die with Wallace's final report to the City Com-

mission. Yet his wisdom in selecting Wallace—a nephew of the fabled Elmer Irey who "got" Al Capone and Waxey Gordon—was to have immediate and unexpected consequences.

For suddenly Dade County needed a sheriff. The Dade County Grand Jury, running out of time and confronted with action in Broward County, indicted Tal Buchanan on five counts of election fraud and two counts of perjury.

The perjury charge—one was dropped as identical—alleged that Buchanan lied when he said he didn't receive $25,000 from Gambler Charles Robertson in 1963.

Election fraud charges grew out of the fact that various persons listed as "contributors" to Buchanan's campaign, denied giving him any money. The names had been pulled out of thin air in an effort to account for funds received.

Rumors had been flying for days, but *Herald* editors managed to discount them. Buchanan was out of the state when the jury reported, apparently thinking the storm had blown over. With Karl Wickstrom, I waited outside the grand jury door all afternoon. The recent Broward experience was all too fresh for me to achieve much excitement. Because of Buchanan's absence the indictment was returned sealed. Everyone knew who the person named must be—but no one could be quoted officially.

We drove to the shores of Biscayne Bay and entered the blue and gold building housing the *Herald*. The city room was calm. Everyone was typing, goofing off, or chatting. Yet we had phoned thirty minutes earlier with the news.

It developed that *Herald* executives—who never really believed it would happen—still weren't sure it had happened. And if it had, who knew if perhaps it wasn't a plot? Gerstein was tricky, you know.

Conferences followed. The street edition had gone to press, but a decision had to be made on how to handle the story in upcoming editions. I said very little—feeling that familiar sense of anticlimax.

Someone turned on a television set. Channel Four's Ralph

Renick led his 6 P.M. newscast with the flat statement—
"Sheriff Buchanan was indicted today. . . ." He explained that
while the indictment was still sealed, there could be no other
answer.

We looked at the managing editor expectantly. He
squirmed—then made his decision. The lead would say that
"according to Ralph Renick," Sheriff Buchanan had been indicted.

I left the conference room feeling just a little sick.

A few minutes later one of the editors hurried by—on his
way home. He looked more than a little sick. "I'm worried,"
he said, as he walked past my chair.

Glancing around the city room, I could see no one free
with whom I cared to celebrate. Those reporters who had
been most closely associated with me were busy trying to put
together an acceptable story—the indictment of Buchanan
story would not carry my byline. To hell with it. I went down
to the visitor's parking lot—where I was permitted to keep my
car—and drove home to Fort Lauderdale.

It was a long evening, broken only by calls from Sam and
Charley. They were happy anyway.

Buchanan flew home next day, held a press conference and
gave me hell. It was all my fault, he said. Meanwhile, his
political friend Governor Burns was forced to suspend Buchanan and name an iterim sheriff. I pressed hard here. If a
good man could be given the job, we could achieve victory.
He could clean out the crooks, raid the gamblers, and take the
heat off the witnesses.

Don Shoemaker, editor of the newspaper, was consulted by
Burns. I felt the political support of the *Herald* was sufficiently important to Burns, that he would honor Shoemaker's
request. Checking with my more responsible sources, I came
up with a list of five names who would do the job. But I soon
learned that—as far as Shoemaker was concerned—the political campaign took precedent over the crime campaign. My
nominees were of no political importance. Burns wanted a

man who could match Dick Wallace as an "untouchable," and at the same time, satisfy the political factions.

Ultimately Robert Floyd, a former Miami mayor and judge, got the nod and agreed to serve thirty days. That was long enough—it would carry past the primary.

My fears proved well founded. Floyd, a man of great reputation, served his allotted time and did absolutely nothing to correct conditions within the department. Operations continued as before—and the pressure began to mount on Sam and O'Nan. They were feeling the strain—Nan confided one afternoon that Sam was suffering from all kinds of nervous problems including hives on "his privates."

I protested in vain to Shoemaker, but he was too interested in the gubernatorial campaign to care. The *Herald* blandly endorsed Burns, annoying a lot of Miami readers in the process, and the paper's political pundits proudly prophesied Burns would win in the first primary. Since a third candidate was running, some folks thought a second primary might be necessary, but the *Herald* had no such fears. High was very much the underdog. The "Burns Blitz" would take care of him.

It didn't.

High finished second to Burns, but the governor lacked a majority and a second primary was necessary. In a short but hectic campaign, Burns became rattled and threw punches wildly and carelessly. Most of them boomeranged. Perhaps the most bizarre stunt was the appearance at Miami International Airport of Congressman Adam Clayton Powell. He flew down from Washington, stayed just long enough to hold an informal press conference in which he declared his support of Mayor High, and flew back to Washington. High forces denounced the "endorsement" as a Burns trick. In any case, it failed to work.

When the votes in the second primary were tallied, the little redhead won easily. And in a state that had not seen a Republican governor since Reconstruction, the road ahead seemed

smooth. Claude Kirk, a businessman from Jacksonville, had the Republican nomination and was making brave sounds, but few people listened. Enough to live with was the wonder of a lame-duck governor.

January was a long way off, but I could remember my conversation with High and feel encouraged. Ultimately, we might get something done. In Florida the governor is chief law-enforcement officer. He has authority to act when local officials fail. High would act, I believed.

Meanwhile, the Miami *Herald* won Sigma Delta Chi's public service award. It wasn't quite the Pulitzer but it was the next best thing.

With startling suddenness the pendulum swung back to Broward County. There Judge Louis Weissing acted on routine motions to quash charges which had been filed on the basis of the Michell indictment. But his actions were not routine—he granted the motion.

No one got very excited at first. Twenty days were permitted for a new "information" to be filed. It was assumed Solicitor Bob Adams should logically have encountered problems with the hastily drawn indictment he had helped State Attorney Long prepare. He now had time to correct the errors.

But Jim Savage called. He had been obeying my orders to keep an eye on things, and his reporter's instinct was in fine form. Apologizing for disturbing me at home on Saturday evening, Jim said he was convinced that Adams had decided not to refile the charges and would so announce on Monday.

I thought enough of Savage's instincts to call Interim Sheriff Walker out of a party at Pompano. He returned to his insurance office and we conferred. The sheriff still found the political realities a bit unbelievable. Repeatedly he expressed confidence Adams would file new charges. Only recently, at the solicitor's request, he assigned men to dig into the files,

and already they had uncovered much useful information. The probe was continuing. Why would Adams quit now?

I thought I knew who had the answer. Adams was an appointee of Burns, on recommendation of Allsworth. He owed his job to Emerson and it was a job he was proud to get. The way had been cleared for him when the former solicitor, a veteran, inexplicably stepped down to the lesser paying post of public defender.

Emerson was as eager to cooperate as always. He promised to meet next morning in Walker's office. The editor of the Fort Lauderdale *News* also attended the session, and a joint newspaper campaign was planned. Walker was to issue a long statement to both papers, stressing conditions he had found within the department and warning of a plot to restore Michell to office without a trial.

Savage got the scoop as usual for the *Herald*, and we agreed to meet again Monday morning in the sheriff's department. I arrived early and was listening to Walker again express confidence Adams would carry on the fight, when word came the solicitor had sent a telegram to Governor Burns. The meeting adjourned to Adams' office, where Emerson joined us. The youthful solicitor, his eyes red and his face pale, was obviously under a tremendous strain. He read a prepared statement declaring that he could not in good conscience file new charges. He had uncovered no evidence to support the indictment.

(Since the indictment was a misdemeanor, prosecution fell within the jurisdiction of the solicitor. The state attorney turned over only the printed indictment. Incredibly, all grand jury testimony and evidence that had led to the indictment was covered by the secrecy rules and not available. Adams, who was expected to prosecute, had been forced to build his case from scratch. Only in the past few days had he sought investigative aid from Walker. I could understand why his evidence might be incomplete—but he had another ten days in which to dig.)

Despite questioning by Lang and Walker, the solicitor refused to reconsider. He had already sent a telegram to the governor, he said. He couldn't turn back now.

Emerson said he would call the governor and ask him not to reinstate Michell until the question was settled. He left the room. I looked at Walker and read my question on his face. We could be sure the governor would hear from his patronage boss—but what would he hear? I began to sense wheels within wheels.

The debate made good newspaper copy. Adams' action coming on the heels of the big story written the night before, shook the county. No one knew what was going on, but it was obvious strings were being pulled. Something unorthodox was happening.

Perhaps Emerson won a delay—or suggested it for reasons of policy. Burns waited exactly twenty-four hours and announced the reinstatement of Michell.

"I am very pleased with the result," said the sheriff. "I've been vindicated."

Several of us decided that was a matter of opinion, and next day when the new Broward Grand Jury met in special session, it appeared we might not be alone in our sentiments. However, the threat of the first and much earlier than usual hurricane of the season caused the jurors to break off early and go home for the day. Reporters speculated as to whether the hurricane was the only reason for their grim expressions.

Savage was busy trying to keep up with events, as personnel changes developed or were rumored. Lang was first to be fired, and he went down fighting. Michell announced to a wondering press conference that all the reforms instituted by Walker had, in fact, been planned by him. But Jim would not be diverted from a special story. He had seen some of the reports in Michell's files, so he asked about the investigation of me. Walker admitted the investigation and explained:

"When he (Messick) first came here and started writing about gangsters, we thought we should find out where he lived

in case somebody should shoot him—so we'd know what house to go to."

It added a little amusement to an otherwise tense press conference. But I was glad Jim took advantage of the opportunity—it was to be the only chance he had. For exactly twenty-four hours after Michell returned to his desk, the grand jury reindicted him.

This time the effort by Long was a little more specific. Exact places and dates were spelled out.

Four hundred miles away in Tallahassee, Governor Burns resuspended the sheriff. Walker, after some delay, was reappointed interim sheriff, and within hours Lang and others who had been fired were back on the job. Missing, however, were several Michell deputies, comprising what had been known as the "Dade County faction." Walker originally hesitated to fire them without evidence—even when most of them refused to take lie detector tests, which their condition of employment made mandatory if requested. But now they were not returned.

Also sporting an empty desk was the solicitor's office. Adams, still fighting a lonely battle in his soul, announced he was resigning "To ensure public confidence in the prosecution of the new Michell charge." Appointed interim solicitor was a local attorney, Al Skaf. Allsworth announced, however, that the patronage committee would soon meet to consider a successor to Adams on a full-time basis.

Skaf, a brisk and energetic lawyer, quashed any doubts that he wouldn't follow through on the new indictment. Not only did he follow through, but he very speedily detected a possible fatal flaw and corrected it after conferring with the attorney general's office. Those of us who knew the inside story were not surprised. Exactly why Long encouraged the grand jury to return the second indictment, we didn't understand. But few people were ready to assume the jury could have acted so decisively on its own.

I happened to be in Miami when the indictment was re-

turned. George Beebe wondered out loud when he heard the news: "How did that happen?"

Larry Jinks, his capable "no-man," replied with a look at me, "Perhaps we'd better not ask."

I said nothing.

A growing confidence could be detected around the city room these days. It was reflected in the new eighteen-month contract I persuaded them to sign. Securitywise, I was now set through the end of 1967. But for some reason I never felt more lonely. The paper had refused to give me a staff job.

In an amoral society, the appearance is more important than the reality. Right now, the crime campaign appeared to be a success. What would happen if the powerful forces, struggling just beneath the surface to regain their grip on the Gold Coast, had a streak of good luck?

Somehow, without willing it, I was way out on a limb by myself.

Well, anyway, Broward County was back in shape for the moment. Once again it was time to turn to Dade. The Buchanan case was beginning to heat up again.

ELEVEN

I PLAY WITH BUGS

AND FACE DISASTER

*

I parked off Twelfth Avenue and walked back to the station. A burly attendant, his uniform spotted with grease, lounged in the doorway. No, the boss wasn't around. Probably find him over in the market somewhere.

I thanked the man, turned as if leaving, then swung back. Red Rainwater been by yet? Yes, hours ago. How about the Tapper? Yeah, he was in earlier. What about Judge Turner? No, not today. He stopped by yesterday.

I muttered something about being late and crossed the street. The Farmer's Market, an institution in the northwest part of Miami, sprawled before me. Long rows of sheds, each containing scores of stalls. Vegetables dominated—tomatoes from Homestead, beans, lettuce.

Everyone knew the man I was seeking and pointed me. Shortly I found him, an elderly, thin-faced fellow with a hat and few teeth. He was polite enough when I introduced myself. Sure he knew of Hank Messick. Why didn't we go over to a restaurant for coffee?

The restaurant was across Twelfth Avenue. Formerly it had been called by another name. As we walked, I asked who had operated it then. He named a gambler, famous in the days of the S & G Syndicate.

Clean and almost empty was the little restaurant. We found a booth and ordered coffee. The waitress winked as she served it. Later, she would watch the post-conference activity and report to me. Given time, I reflected, I could develop a spy system.

199

"What can I do for you, Mr. Messick?" inquired the old man. I noticed his hand trembled as he stirred his coffee.

"Tell me something first," I said. "Why do they call you the 'Mayor of the Market'? Is it an official title?"

The man chuckled, pleased in spite of himself. "No, sir, there's nothing official about it. I've just been here on this corner for so long I know all the farmers. They listen to me and when I tell them what political signs to put on their trucks, they usually do it. The politicians figure I got influence so they come to me for support."

"Who did you support in the primary?"

"Burns," said the toothless man. "I thought he was a shoo-in."

It figured. I asked other questions. Yes, the mayor of the market was a friend of Sheriff Buchanan. In fact, the sheriff had sent him an honorary deputy's badge after the last election. He was also a friend of Dick Gerstein, he said, and he had known Judge Turner since Jack was a boy.

The man was on the defensive—but he was also curious. What was I driving at? He hadn't decided, but he was willing to submit without protest to my cross-examination in order to find out.

I continued to list officials, but I also threw in some gamblers—Rainwater, McLendon, Bookie Mac, Foots Stallings. The "mayor" knew them all. In fact, the officials and the gamblers bought gasoline from him. They came by at least once a week.

The admission made me smile. I recalled some surveillance reports I had seen. The city of Miami once staked out the "mayor's" place and noted the strange assortment of customers who dropped in regularly. But the investigation was called off when a high-ranking police official showed up and spotted the detectives.

"You might say, Mr. Messick, that I know just about everybody in this town that is anybody," the old man said. "After all, I've been around a long time." He paused and

studied my face. "Now just what is it you are leading up to?"

"Only this," I said. "I have information the gamblers are planning to fix Sheriff Buchanan's case and you're the go-between. I thought I should check it out with you before I wrote anything."

The mayor's coffee cup sloshed over and the brown stain crept across the table top. I watched it balloon toward me, wondering incuriously if it would reach the edge of the table. It stopped two inches short.

"Why, that's crazy," said the old man. "I wouldn't do anything like that."

I grinned cheerfully. "You'll have to admit it has possibilities," I told him. "The gamblers stop by your place regularly. You'd be a perfect middle man."

"That don't mean nothing," he retorted. "They got to buy gas somewhere."

Casually, I pulled out a notebook, plucked a black "U.S. Government" pen I had borrowed for the occasion from my pocket, and prepared to take notes.

"I'll be happy to quote you," I said. "Just what is your comment?"

"It's a lie," said the mayor. "Just say it's a lie."

I wrote it down, carefully and conspicuously. "Thank you, sir." I reached for some change, but he grabbed my arm. "I'll get it." The waitress winked again, as I went by her to the door.

From the market I drove to the *Herald* and placed a call to Judge Jack Turner. His secretary said he was tied up now. Would I like to leave a message? I left word for the judge to call me at his earliest convenience. With that out of the way I went back to the "the room without windows," as the office of Editor Shoemaker is called. It is a plush and spacious room, richly paneled and lushly carpeted, but it could be in Detroit or Charlotte as far as the view of Biscayne Bay was concerned.

Shoemaker, who was editor of an Asheville, North Carolina, daily, while I worked twenty miles away on a semiweekly, was glad enough to see me. Relations between the news and editorial departments were usually strained. As an independent contractor I could go where staff reporters and news editors feared to tread. On several occasions I had prodded Shoemaker into action, but the needed coordinated campaign, utilizing all the power of both news and editorial departments, was only a dream. Yet, since no one else would, I tried again.

The situation, I explained, was becoming critical. Neither Interim Sheriff Floyd nor his successor, George Leppig, had taken any action to clean up the sheriff's department. Buchanan was officially out, but his men still held key positions, and nothing basically had changed. The pressure on witnesses had increased, if anything. Sam had buckled and fled to Georgia, where he owned a huge farm outside Atlanta. I had my doubts if he would return for trial. The man was convinced the whole thing was rigged.

Couldn't Sam be forced to return? Shoemaker was puzzled. Wasn't the man under subpoena? No, I said. Despite Sam's clear warning to Gerstein that he would testify only if subpoenaed, the state attorney hadn't bothered. He had left the door open, and the sheriff's people—under Floyd and then Leppig—had kept up the pressure. Georgia was one of two states where a witness could find sanctuary. There was no way to bring him back if he didn't want to come.

While checking the basis for Sam's fears, I continued, I received information that a $20,000 assessment had been collected from gamblers—a defense fund, it was called. In just a few days Judge Jack Turner would rule on a state motion for a continuance—a motion made necessary by Sam's absence. If the judge desired, he could toss the whole case out the window. Already, he had quashed the fraud charges. Only the perjury count remained.

Shoemaker assured me Judge Turner wouldn't be a party to such a scheme. The Editor had Spoken. Call Turner back, he ordered, and tell his secretary you are calling at my request. He'll answer. I promised to try, but meanwhile, couldn't the *Herald* editorially ask for a special prosecutor? Sam might return if he felt he had a chance.

"I'll write the editorials," said Shoemaker. "You stick to reporting."

I left the room without windows and put in the call to Turner. The secretary was friendly, but no reply came from the judge. Other word was coming in, however. I discovered that when I was well away from the restaurant that morning, the mayor took off too. He went down the avenue to the Justice Building—that modernistic temple in the Civic Center —and talked to both Judge Turner and Gerstein.

Ripples spread around the building and out into the street. Major Manson Hill, the sheriff's chief of detectives, was notified. By now the only question being asked in certain quarters was, "How did Messick find out?" Hill searched his office and thought he found the answer—an electronic "bug."

The device was no longer working, but there was no way to know when it stopped. How much else had Messick heard?

Reports reaching me that afternoon and evening told of near panic in the upper ranks of the invisible government. If I could bug the chief of detectives, I could bug anyone. All the sheriff's technical people, as well as some private facilities, were mobilized and "sweeps" were make of key offices. No other devices were found, but that didn't mean there hadn't been some in the past or wouldn't be some in the future. More and more the question boiled down to "Who?" Who helped Messick plant the bug?

The confusion was rather amusing, and I fed the flames at every opportunity. But there was little time to enjoy it. Sam, by long distance from Georgia, refused to return. If, he said, a delay could be gained, he would be back later. Right now he

was too busy trying to sell his two hundred acres to some Georgia real estate promoters.

I could understand Sam's reluctance. With Judge Turner on the bench and Gerstein prosecuting, there was room for pessimism. The obvious answer was to secure a special prosecutor and get a change of venue. I argued with Shoemaker that no official should be tried by the system of which he was a part. But the editor's confidence remained high, despite the fact that Turner had not returned my call.

The day came for the hearing on the motion for continuance. I attended as an observer, leaving the reporting routine to a staff writer. Assistant State Attorney Al Sepe represented Gerstein. Buchanan was represented by Harry Prebish, a small, dark man with a reputation of being one of the leading criminal attorneys in Miami. Sepe went through the motions, explaining his key witness was ill in Georgia. Asked the nature of the illness, Sepe replied, "Hives." I remembered Nan's comment, and wondered if the problem was still localized. Before I could smile, Judge Turner hit the ceiling. The request for a delay on such ground was disgraceful.

I thought for a moment that this was the ball game—he was going to dismiss the charges. But Turner—also a dark, slender man—recovered. He apologized to the defendant, Sheriff Buchanan, and to his attorney. Reluctantly, he said, he was going to grant the motion. But if the witness set foot in Miami, he wanted him put in jail as a material witness. He was not going to let a gambler thumb his nose at a public official.

There was much more of this before the judge changed the subject. There was another matter, he said, that had come to his attention. He had learned that a certain reporter had been investigating reports of a "fix"—reports that he, Judge Turner, had been offered a bribe to throw out the charges.

There was silence in the tiny courtroom, and although my name had not been mentioned, all eyes turned toward me.

The activity by the reporter, continued the judge—his

voice shaking—bordered on contempt. In fact, he was ordering the state attorney to investigate and report back to him if contempt proceedings should be started.

The gavel banged. Court was adjourned. Reporters pressed around the judge, seeking additional information. I heard my name. He was leaving no doubt about whom he was talking.

In the hall outside, a crowd had gathered. Alerted by the grapevine that is standard in every courthouse, attorneys, deputies, and other officials had gathered for the fireworks. I stood chatting with reporter Wickstrom when Major Hill walked up. It was the first time I had met the man I had heard so much about, and I held out my hand. He took it automatically, then dropped it hurriedly.

Hill was handsome, I decided. Seemingly slender, I recognized he was really big in a supple way. His features were regular, and his white teeth shone. But there were dark patches under his eyes—and his eyes were cold. This was the most-feared man in Miami.

He hit fast and hard. What had I told the mayor of the market about him? Had I said he was involved in a bribe? Exactly what did I say he had said? And so on, ad infinitum.

As far as I could remember, my only mention of Hill had been to determine if the old man knew him. Obviously Hill was trying to confirm that my information had been obtained via the bug in his office. So I counterattacked.

"What's this about a bug in your office, Major?"

For a moment I thought he would strike, as his cheeks flushed, and the hand he held about waist high formed a fist. But then he grinned.

"You paid somebody to put it in there, didn't you?" he said. "We're looking into it."

"Keep looking," I said and turned away. "Come on, Karl. Let's go see Sepe."

Gerstein joined us in Sepe's office. Everything was sweetly reasonable. Of course I had a right to ask questions. The judge was wrong. But he had ordered an investigation, and

one had to be made. I could give a statement now or come back later with an attorney.

I promised to return later. Major Hill was waiting in the outer office as I left. "You can go in now," I told him.

Unreason ruled at the *Herald*. Only garbled reports had been received, and the editors were in a panic. They bundled me off to the law offices of their attorneys for a full-scale conference. The lawyers seemed a little puzzled as to what they were expected to advise, but one editor finally clarified the situation by asking:

"What are the dangers?"

The only danger anyone could think of was that I might be held in contempt. But the *Herald* was not involved in that. When I assured the gathering there wasn't the slightest chance I would be held in contempt, there was disbelief. Judge Turner's alleged remarks were quoted to me.

"This entire deal was designed for one thing only," I said. "They want to find out where I got my information."

The attorneys agreed I might be right. On the other hand, I might be wrong. As far as they could see, there wasn't much we could do about it. We would have to play it by ear.

Those weren't the exact words used, but that's what it amounted to. The ride back to the office was a little strained. The three editors apparently were unable to decide just what the conference had accomplished. I had other things to think about at the time.

Two days later I presented myself to Sepe, accepted a subpoena, and dictated a statement. In it I gave everything but the name of my source. Sepe tried bluster, then flattery. Finally, he dismissed the court reporter and we talked "off the record and man to man." He was a little worried about the Buchanan case, he said. In fact, he would like to get rid of it. If I could provide an excuse, he would ask Gerstein to relieve him. Perhaps we could get a special counsel appointed.

I soon understood the new approach and waxed chummy. We had a long discussion of personal problems. I told him

again I would be glad to give the source of my information to the grand jury. But after all—I lowered my voice—if there was any leak, it might cause somebody to get killed. And it would surely cause my source to lose his job. I couldn't afford to have that happen. God knows, it was hard enough to get information out of the sheriff's department as it was.

Sepe said he understood how I felt, but he could hardly restrain his smile of triumph. The friendly approach had worked—I had tipped my hand without realizing it.

I concealed my smile until I was out of the office. Someone was going to catch hell unjustly—that I knew. But my real source was protected. He was on the inside, all right, but he didn't wear a badge.

A week later I achieved my goal—an appearance before my third Dade County Grand Jury. This one had been in session for more than six weeks, and as yet had made no moves. The foreman, however, was—in Shoemaker's words —a white man, and could be expected to have a mind of his own. An ex-reporter, now a public relations man, was also on the jury and had promised to push for a real probe.

Gerstein was in the room as usual, but the questioning was handled by Sy Gelber. I was asked to explain the incident Judge Turner wanted investigated. Again I told the tale, still not mentioning the name of the source. Gelber interrupted with a specific question. I promised to name the source at the end of my testimony if the jury still wanted it. Meanwhile, I asked them to ponder what might happen to the man if his name were leaked. Grand jury leaks had occurred in the past.

The foreman took over the questioning and was joined by my friend on the floor. The topic became Sam and why he had not returned to testify. I answered frankly—the man was afraid. Gerstein glowered at me as I swung for a four-bagger. Rightly or wrongly, I said, many potential witnesses didn't trust the state attorney and wouldn't work with him. There was justification for this attitude. Certainly, in nine years Gerstein had done nothing to curb organized crime and vice in

Dade County. If anything was to be done, either in the Buchanan trial or in additional investigations, a special counsel would be necessary.

There was a sudden silence in the room. Even Gerstein was quiet. I had struck a nerve, perhaps.

The foreman broke the silence by asking me to step outside for a moment. The jury was not supposed to deliberate in front of witnesses. I went through the double doors and took a seat in the waiting room. A minute later Gelber and Gerstein came out. They turned from me and vanished into an office. Perhaps five minutes passed, and the foreman invited me back into the jury room. Broad grins greeted me. The air felt strangely cleaner.

The foreman bent over from his seat at the bench and addressed the pretty court reporter. She was to take down the testimony but she was not to transcribe it. Her notes were to be locked up and not given to anyone unless she received written orders from the foreman or vice-foreman. Did she understand? She did, and looked up at me with a smile. I decided it might be an omen.

"Now tell us about Dick Gerstein," came the order.

More than ninety minutes later I walked stiffly from the grand jury room. No reporters waited outside. It was a bit like my appearance in January, when the Mossler case was drawing all attention. A lot had happened since that day, since that semihostile grand jury. As I emerged into the glare of midsummer, I looked up at the top of the courthouse. The buzzards were gone.

And only then did I realize no one had returned to the subject of my mysterious source. The question I had promised to answer had not again been asked. The jury had not pushed the matter. So much for Judge Turner. The episode had served its purpose well.

From a frightened fink, Roy O'Nan changed suddenly into a chirping canary. Not since the days of Kid Twist and Mur-

der, Inc., had such a complete about-face occurred. The bagman decided to babble.

Many people later questioned O'Nan's willingness to talk so
freely. Unable to believe he had reformed, they went to the
other extreme and assumed some sinister plot was involved.
The truth was somewhere in between.

O'Nan frustrated me for months. I listened to his lies, his
evasions, his loudly expressed fears, and gradually achieved
some understanding of the man. I could distinguish truth from
fiction.

He delayed testifying as long as possible, thinking that Gerstein would relent. But the state attorney was also under pressure. When at last he did talk—as we were to discover later—
he said as little as possible in the presence of Gerstein. On
some matters he lied. I could understand why. What crook
would not have lied under the circumstances?

But even with the Buchanan case coming to trial, he persisted in believing a deal could be arranged to let the sheriff
resign in return for a dismissal of charges. He allowed me to
listen to some taped telephone conversations with friends of
Buchanan that gave substance to his hopes. Meanwhile, however, the underworld was squeezing O'Nan. He apparently
was classed as an outlaw, and his under-the-table interests in
various businesses, ranging from hospitals to a liquor store,
were up for grabs. One by one they took his hard-won profits
from him, not realizing, apparently, that even a worm will
turn.

A "White Paper" on organized crime, planned by a national television network, gave me an opportunity to take advantage of the increasing economic pinch on O'Nan. I had
not even considered asking the *Herald* for money, but when a
television crew came to Miami and retained me as a "consult-
ant," I saw a way to serve all our ends.

How much the network paid O'Nan, I never found out. He
was a hard bargainer, demanding $50,000 as a starter. Ulti-
mately, however, they reached agreement, and in an hour-

long interview O'Nan told all. His story went on tape and color film in the gardens of Vizcaya, that splendid monument to the glories of the Old World and the wealth of the New. The thought of O'Nan, sitting in that marble palace and talking of corruption, delighted my imagination.

Ultimately, the network used only a fraction of what he told them. Plans were changed at the last minute as the section on south Florida was junked and some old film of Joe Valachi substituted. But for my purposes, O'Nan was now past the point of no return.

The *Herald* stolidly refused to take advantage of the opportunity, but O'Nan—realizing he had committed himself and life itself hung in the balance—became my ally. Thus when a representative of the grand jury foreman came to me for advice, I consulted O'Nan.

The jury and Gerstein had agreed on a compromise. If a suitable person could be found, the jury would hire him as special counsel, and Gerstein would name him to prosecute the Buchanan case.

I was rather unhappy about the scheme. Obviously Gerstein had agreed rather than risk an open break with the jury. And the jurors apparently felt that Gerstein's promise to name their man special prosecutor could be obtained in no other way. The problem was to find a man acceptable to Gerstein, who at the same time would do an adequate job. The state attorney still had veto power over any name submitted.

The first names I suggested—former federal investigators and prosecutors—were rejected. I managed to kill two names advanced by Gerstein. A stalemate threatened the entire program. It was broken, ironically enough, by O'Nan. He consulted his sources and passed on the name of Lucius Cushman.

I knew nothing about Cushman except he was a veteran attorney, an older man. But the representative of the foreman was delighted. "Why didn't I think of Lucius?" he asked. "It's the perfect choice."

The man's excitement served only to increase my doubts, but it was too late. Within hours Cushman had accepted the challenge—a decision worthy of admiration—and had met with a committee of jurors. The word came back that all was settled.

The new counsel-prosecutor proved to be a peppery little man with a penchant for white suits. Soon O'Nan, who was quite happy to have nominated the new public figure, labeled him "Snow White," and the nickname stuck. My editors, alarmed at last by the continuing absence of Sam, authorized me to work with Cushman if he officially requested my aid in writing. He promptly wrote such a glowing letter, they asked him to rewrite it.

There was time for only one expedition before special grand jury counsel Cushman had to concentrate on being special prosecutor. I brought him to Fort Lauderdale and a secret meeting with two Dade deputies and a secretary. Among other things, Cushman obtained that night sworn testimony about the sheriff's office party for Mossler case witnesses—the party that featured brothel boss Red Vaught as cohost.

But my friends were a little uneasy at Cushman's reactions when they told of other things involving amoral activity. The little attorney brushed it aside rather brusquely. Later, we were to learn why. In his youth the attorney had made a mistake. It received little attention at the time, but it did become a matter of record. And with the Buchanan case about to begin, certain parties learned of that record and started a smear campaign. Not so veiled hints were printed in certain columns, and threats were heard that, if necessary, the full story would be published. Blackmail was the word for it.

I was told the truth by Cushman—who could only groan, "It was thirty years ago, Hank. Can't a man live down the past?"

Sympathy was possible, but I couldn't help wondering if a knowledge of the facts on record had been a factor in the

acceptance of Snow White as special prosecutor. It had seemed too easy at the time.

Once again, there was nothing to be done, and admiration replaced sympathy as I watched Cushman buckle down to his job. Judge Turner denied a motion for a new delay despite the fact that Cushman had only a few days to prepare. The trial would go on as scheduled. Its outcome was a foregone conclusion unless Sam returned.

A frantic period followed, as far away in Georgia Sam squirmed. When I reviewed the past, remembered the time when Sam was eager and O'Nan reluctant, the present reversal was almost comical. I put into motion certain things I felt might work when I learned Cushman had authorized the private eye who served as special grand jury investigator to go to Atlanta and persuade Sam to return. I objected strenuously —Sam knew the guy was a friend of Gerstein. He would discount all my stories of Cushman's independence and remember only the "handle" they had on the special prosecutor.

Indeed, I began to wonder if perhaps Sam wasn't right to stay away. And when my editors declined to intervene, I abandoned hope. My personal position was becoming impossible. I had the responsibility, it seemed, but not the authority. And there was a limit to what bluff could achieve. For months my relations with *Herald* executives had been getting worse as the situation grew more and more complex. The editors had expected nothing like this when they hired me. They didn't know how to handle the campaign, and they were unwilling to delegate power to me. My perch at the end of the limb became more lonely by the minute. The battle could still be won, if proper leadership was exercised. But how was I to lead the fight if no one heeded my advice?

Sam remained in Georgia and the trial opened. Cushman determined to go ahead with one key witness only. There was a possibility, he felt that sufficient additional testimony could be obtained to prevent a directed verdict. If the defense was

forced to put Buchanan on the stand, cross-examination might yet salvage the situation.

It seemed a forlorn hope, but I presented myself to the city room to be available if needed. A call came, but it was the defense who wanted me. Months ago the defense had subpoenaed me for the first trial date. Cushman assured me that a new subpoena was necessary and none had been forthcoming. Now a spokesman for the defense was claiming the first subpoena was valid.

The *Herald*'s attorneys were consulted and finally ruled I had better present myself. Upon arriving, I was ushered before Judge Turner, who put me under oath and ordered me to remain available. When I asked about the validity of the subpoena, the judge frowned. It was his custom for one subpoena to hold over to future dates. In any case, I was now under the rule of the court.

Angry and more than a little scared, I took a seat in the hall. It was the beginning of three days of ordeal. If a friendly face appeared, I dared not speak. For at my heels were spooks, watching, listening, and occasionally making remarks to anger me. The high brass of the sheriff's department wandered in and out, sneering, insulting. All the while defense witnesses talked to each other constantly, despite the court's orders. Even some of Cushman's witnesses made a point of discussing the case in front of me.

O'Nan waited his turn, immaculately dressed, determinedly confident. I couldn't help but admire the man. He had guts at least, fighting it out even though he knew as well as I the battle was hopeless. On the second day, he testified—for hours. The cross-examination was rough, I gathered, but from my seat in the hall I could get little information. *Herald* reporters assigned to the case were bending over backward to be fair—to Buchanan. I was treated almost as an outsider. They were afraid to talk to me outside the courtroom or even back at the *Herald*.

Nevertheless, Cushman managed to get a lot into the

record. He presented Buchanan's grand jury testimony, which contained some damaging admissions: a relationship with O'Nan and Sam; the fact he had lived at the Purple Manor; and certain problems with campaign contributions.

Other witnesses added additional evidence that, while circumstantial, would have tightened the rope around the sheriff if Sam had been present to supply the key testimony about the exchange of money. Roy's word was not enough.

On the third day Cushman decided to put me on the stand. I didn't quite understand his reasoning—something to do with the fact I had heard O'Nan tell the story of the $25,000. This, presumably, would give weight to his words. But before he could question me, defense attorney Harry Prebish interrupted and won the right from Judge Turner to ask me about something else. Brutally, insultingly, he set the stage with preliminary questions about possible tape recorders I might have concealed, and then swung his haymaker. Hadn't I been talking to O'Nan out in the hall awhile ago—in defiance of the court's instructions?

O'Nan, wrung dry by both sides, had not been excused. And on this the third day—tired, angry, and bored—I had spoken to him. We didn't discuss the case, and we soon were joined by a friendly private eye. I said little during the three-way conversation, and most of my words were directed at the third man. Some spook had reported us.

The attorney disregarded my statement that defense witnesses had been talking for three days. He bored in. What had I discussed with O'Nan?

Cushman stood by helplessly. Judge Turner glowered down from the bench. The press corps waited eagerly, anticipating my downfall. I spluttered angrily—for this inquisition, coming as a climax to weeks of strain and days of insult—had brought me to the edge. I couldn't take much more. Realizing it dimly, I decided to play safe. Who knew what the spooks might have overheard? Who knew what they might have recorded on concealed devices?

I searched my mind and listed everything, every subject I could remember having discussed with anyone during my three days in the hall. It ranged from speculation about Sam's absence to the weather. Prebish kept demanding more, and I kept talking until I could think of nothing else. Let him make something of that if he could.

He could. I was quickly dismissed—but not excused—after Turner ruled I couldn't answer Cushman's questions. O'Nan was brought in next. I learned later he was asked what he had discussed with Messick. Roy decided to play safe too—he denied saying anything.

It was a gambit that vastly impressed *Herald* reporters. Obviously, either O'Nan or Messick lied under oath. The inclination was to assume that I had told the truth. This made O'Nan a perjurer—and cast doubt on everything he had testified about previously.

The entire affair had taken place outside the jury's presence, and thus could have no bearing on their thoughts. But Turner used it, nevertheless, to sustain the motion for a directed verdict. He waxed indignant in denouncing the case against the sheriff—it had rested, he said, on the word of an admitted gambler and the lies of an obvious perjurer.

I was still sitting outside when the verdict was entered. A private eye once employed by the *Herald*, brought the word to Mrs. Buchanan. She yawned prettily, smiled at me, and got up to give her husband the traditional kiss of vindication. I wondered what she thought of his admissions about the Purple Manor.

Under the strange rules that seemed to apply in Turner's court, I didn't dare leave until Cushman came out and excused me. The judge, he said, had decided not to cite either O'Nan or me for contempt. Damned noble of him, I thought.

Cushman looked tired in his white suit, a little unreal. He belonged to a more flamboyant age, when morality was more a matter of blacks and whites. His had been an impossible assignment in the absence of Sam—but had he done his best?

I wasn't too sure. Considering the threat of smear hanging over him, however, it was remarkable he had even appeared.

I stood up to leave, only to recognize a familiar face. It was the juror who months ago had met at Sam's place near Pompano and enjoyed a quail dinner. I had not seen him since my grand jury appearance shortly thereafter.

The man, tall and lanky, leaned toward me. "I've got just one comment," he said. "Shit."

Under the circumstances, it seemed rather appropriate.

The *Herald* quit.

There was no other word for it.

Buchanan called a press conference next day, declared he was going to sue Messick and the *Herald* for countless millions. He had been vindicated and now the people responsible would pay.

I was called to the *Herald* and told to begin no more investigations, to cooperate no more with Cushman in his capacity as special counsel to the grand jury. From now on, until my contract expired, I was to concentrate on getting material to defend against the expected suit.

Wearily, I protested. The suit was still only a threat. Buchanan had nothing to gain by it and everything to lose. Meanwhile, we still had Cushman and the grand jury. We also had Buchanan's damaging grand jury testimony in the record. There was still grounds for hope if we would but fight back. On the November ballot was a charter amendment to abolish the office of elected sheriff. It might easily carry despite the directed verdict.

No use. I went home to find a call from New York. The network had been notified that Buchanan had been acquitted, O'Nan had been indicted for perjury, and I had been sued for two million. What was the story?

I calmed them down but they still had one question: What was the *Herald* going to do? If it would continue the fight, the network would go ahead with the south Florida portion of the White Paper. If not . . .

There was nothing to do but admit the truth—the *Herald* had quit. The voice in far away New York said it was sorry. Well, I was sorry too.

Next morning I was more than sorry—I was sick at my stomach. I read a tiny editorial, which commented on the directed verdict and the immediate reinstatement of Buchanan by Governor Burns. It was all inevitable, the editorial said. No one could have done otherwise.

I remembered something I had learned just before the trial —Judge Turner visited the room without windows on Friday before the trial began. Had he been assured something perhaps—something that explained his brutal treatment of me?

After vomiting twice, I wrote out a statement, dressed, and drove to Miami. Lee Hills, now executive editor of all the Knight Newspapers was in town. He had been managing editors in the days of the Kefauver Committee. Under his leadership, the *Herald* won a Pulitzer. I wanted to see him.

The meeting was a stormy one. Hills brought in two top executives. I spoke my mind—frankly, bitterly. The battle could yet be won, I said, but the *Herald* had quit. It was now ready to return to the policy of see no evil, hear no evil, know no evil, that had existed before I came. Well, let it. I was through. As soon as I could find a new job, I was quitting. Meanwhile, I wanted my statement printed. The *Herald* could quake all it pleased—I intended to go down fighting.

Hills heard me out, asked some intelligent questions, and promised to see that my statement was published. He ordered me to take a vacation—I had not had a day off since the campaign began a year before. When I was rested we would talk again.

The two editors glared at me, but had nothing to say—in my presence, anyway. Hills left to catch a plane to Detroit and the meeting broke up. I went home, packed, and headed south again for the Florida Keys. There was no question about it—I was completely exhausted.

My vacation lasted twenty-four hours. Then came the call.

Buchanan, still feeling vindicated, had fired Colonel George Leppig and Captain Charles Zmuda.

Leppig had served as acting sheriff. Apparently Buchanan decided he had acted the part too well. Well, I couldn't consider him a great loss. But Zmuda was another matter. As chief of central services, he had charge of the crime lab. A man of unquestioned integrity and national reputation, the sheriff's department could ill afford to lose him.

Why had he been fired? It was my fault, the voice said. Buchanan believed Zmuda was my ally, the man I had sought to protect, the man who had bugged Hill's office for me. And Zmuda planned to fight back.

Under the circumstances I again had no choice. If Zmuda was willing to fight, I had to help.

Next morning as I ate breakfast prior to checking out, I was astonished to read a front page editorial in the *Herald*. It blasted Buchanan for firing Zmuda, demanded a new grand jury investigation, and called for the sheriff to resign immediately.

Nothing remotely like it had appeared in all the months I had been working with the *Herald*. I thought of Lee Hills. This was in his style. And suddenly my stomach began to unknot.

In losing a battle, had we perhaps won a war?

TWELVE

I OBSERVE A BUST

AND REMEMBER A PICTURE

*

The campaign entered a new phase. The *Herald*, paralyzed by a Hills-ordered reorganization, was alternately brave and indecisive. Ultimately, when the dust settled, the newspaper would speak with a more consistent voice. Until then, other means would be needed to maintain the pressure.

Ralph Renick, news director of Channel Four, took up the slack. A tall, handsome television pioneer, Renick had taken a few swings at conditions over the years and was ready to try again. Contributing to his decision was the realization that only last-minute fears of New York executives had prevented him from being scooped on the south Florida story. Waiting and eager to help was that nationally-known bagman, Roy O'Nan.

Apparently a little unsure of how far to trust Roy, Renick asked my aid. The *Herald*'s attorneys had just rejected a new series I had prepared. I was annoyed. Television would give me a chance to bring the material to the public and, at the same time, prove how baseless were the attorney's fears. I agreed to appear in person with my new evidence.

The thirty-minute special starring Messick and O'Nan had tremendous impact. It also had unexpected consequences. Suddenly I was a celebrity. After writing scores of articles for months, it was rather humbling to become famous after one TV exposure.

But famous I was—and I celebrated the anniversary of my first story in the *Herald* by appearing on another TV pro-

gram. Local radio stations also sought me, and I was in demand as a civic club speaker.

At first I balked. Speeches, TV shows, etc., required too much time. I had no opportunity to dig for new stories. But as changes continued at a snail's pace at the _Herald,_ and the editorial voice of the newspaper remained largely silent, I decided I was lucky to be in demand. Things needed saying. If I couldn't write them, I would speak them.

We formed a strictly unofficial brain-trust. In addition to Renick, there was Charles Zmuda and his attorney, Shelby Highsmith. Shelby had been one of the names I originally submitted for Cushman's job. Also joining us was Bill Reed, youthful director of the University of Miami Law Center. Bill had learned the ropes in a cleanup of Kansas City.

A close working relationship was maintained with Cushman. Snow White was digging now and getting results. Even the grand jurors realized a showdown was at hand. If the vote to abolish the office of elected sheriff failed, Buchanan would be almost untouchable. Indictments would be futile as the System acted to take care of its own. But if the vote carried, the sheriff was finished. It was that simple.

We persuaded Cushman to turn to the Wackenhut Corporation for special investigators. Formed ten years earlier by ex-FBI special agent George Wackenhut, the corporation boasted of its staff of ex-FBI agents. It was now international in scope.

Renick, meanwhile, kept up the pressure. Waving the banner the _Herald_ had dropped, he nightly presented shocking facts, topped with lucid hard-hitting editorials. Rival TV commentators began to scream—and to fire back with pro-Buchanan editorials. Even the late night radio "talk" shows got into the battle. Most were anti-Messick, anti-Renick. Buchanan was live on one or the other almost every night. The exception was the Lee Vogel Show, which featured such sterling characters as Zmuda, Renick, and Messick.

Climax of the radio war was the action one night of a pro-

Buchanan commentator in reading my grand jury testimony —given in January—over the radio. We raised hell immediately and drew from Judge Turner the admission that he turned over all grand jury testimony in the Buchanan case to the sheriff's attorney, Harry Prebish, without imposing any restrictions on its use. The attorney had given my testimony to the radio commentator.

Judge Henry Balaban, the jurist guiding the succeeding grand jury, denounced the release of testimony in strong terms, but Gerstein and his assistant, Gelber, promptly appeared on the same radio program to assure the listeners the reading of my testimony was proper.

I got a chance to fire back in a speech before a record crowd at the Tiger Bay Political Club. Gelber appeared the week before and had great fun making light of the crime campaign. I answered him in my speech, point by point, and blasted Turner and Buchanan as well. The applause at the end left no doubt I had won. After that Gelber made no more speeches. I, on the other hand, was in greater demand than ever.

Crime at last became an issue—not only locally but in the gubernatorial campaign. Republican Claude Kirk took advantage of the heat to blame his Democratic opponent, Miami Mayor Robert King High, for conditions in the city. High was caught in a crossfire as Republican Kirk blandly ignored the fact that Dade County as a whole stood second in major crimes in the county, and Broward County to the north was sixth.

High complained the attack was unfair. I wondered why he didn't take the offensive, pointing out how with limited powers he had fought gambling interests in Miami. His failure to react puzzled me, but one night I got the answer.

A call came from a Miami cop. He was unusually mysterious, saying only he had to see me right away on a matter of life or death. Would I meet him at "the tall one's place on Miami Avenue?"

I finally deduced that the "tall one" was Renick, and his place was the television station. Such a setting for a meet inspired confidence. I drove to Miami. At the studio I found Mayor High. He asked me to wait for an aide and in the interval became engrossed in a TV drama. It was a western triangle—a son, attracted by the glamour of a retired fast-gun artist, broke with his father. So fascinating was the story, High asked for a conference room containing a television set. In the middle of our discussion of organized crime, he stopped to watch the climax—the son put aside the gun with which he had been practicing and settled things with his fists. The father was vindicated, and High was a little disgusted with the corny solution to what had appeared to be a sophisticated problem.

With the problems of the old frontier settled, we turned to the new. I warned High he was making a mistake in attempting to evade the crime issue. Too many people were fed up in Dade County. High agreed that people were sore but he insisted his position was clear—the citizens knew how he stood on the subject and needed no reassurance. In any case, the experts were convinced he would win easily—so why worry? The reason for our meeting was to plan for the future.

I sighed and shut up. The little redhead outlined his program. Come January, he wanted to launch a campaign against crime. As governor he would have the powers he had lacked as mayor. Would I be interested in a job—a state job as chief investigator for a new State Crime Commission. My assignment would be simple: drive the Mob out of Florida. He would give me a free hand and almost unlimited resources.

The idea staggered me, but I recovered enough to wonder if High really understood what he was proposing. A proposal originally recommended by Dick Wallace in his final report to the City Commission.

Of course he understood. He was aware of the entrenched interests, the sensitive toes, the relation of crime to politics and politics to business. But I should understand something—

he had won this chance to be governor by a fluke. No one had a claim on him because no one had thought he could win. He was free to act.

Who could refuse such a challenge? Not I. We shook hands on the deal and went back to our respective campaigns. More than ever I thought them related.

Things continued to break for the good guys—unexpected things like the recapture of Georges Lemay in Las Vegas.

Lemay gained international fame a year before, when his picture was flashed on local television screens via a communications satellite. He was wanted in Canada for the theft of hundreds of thousands. Someone in Fort Lauderdale recognized the picture, and Lemay was arrested. Shortly thereafter he bought his way out of the new, "escape-proof" Dade County Jail and vanished. Some guards were charged with accepting bribes, but the sheriff's probe was generally considered a formality. Now, when Buchanan could least afford it, Lemay was recaptured, and the old scandal was back in the headlines.

Other headlines came with the first indictment—my pal Red Vaught. The brothel boss was indicted on prostitution charges in connection with that famous party for Mossler case witnesses.

And co-host Major Hill resigned rather than waive immunity before the grand jury. I wrote the story—and was proud it carried my byline. Hill was allegedly the brains of the sheriff's department, and he was out now.

Everyone chuckled when the former detective chief announced he was moving his family to Georgia. I wondered what Sam would say if they met up there.

The grand jury was sitting almost daily now, hearing gamblers, bagmen, and finally Fat Hymie Martin in his first appearance before a Dade Grand Jury.

In Broward County, still tossed about in legal limbo, were two contempt citations for Hymie, but he had spent only a day in jail. With him now was his bantam attorney, Harold

Ungerleider. The same arguments were made with the same results. Martin refused to talk and was ordered to jail. He stayed there five days before a kindly federal judge ordered him released on bond.

Red Rainwater, for many years the principal bagman in Miami, was given the same choice. He decided to talk. Others followed his example. Dave Schifrin, the man O'Nan called the "Chinese Jew," talked but apparently denied he had replaced O'Nan as county bagman. The jury indicted him on perjury charges.

Buchanan fought back fiercely. He was on the radio every night and anti-Renick television announcers gave him free space. In public speeches he assailed Messick first and Renick second. It was all a Communist conspiracy, he repeated, designed to deprive the little man of his right to vote.

The drama of the grand jury was beginning to grip the citizens of Dade as dramatic developments followed each other like a soap-opera serial. But Charles Zmuda and attorney Highsmith temporarily stole the show. Hearings were held on the charges Buchanan had reluctantly filed to back up his impulsive action in firing Zmuda. They lasted two nights. Buchanan even put his wife on the stand in a last minute effort to prove his charges.

I sat beside Zmuda's ailing wife, helping him by comforting her, as my mind went back to 1961 in Newport. There, in a crowded courtroom, attorney Henry Cook had torn apart the frame of George Ratterman, reform candidate for sheriff. History was repeating itself here tonight, and I, for one, had no doubt of the outcome.

Coolly, almost too quietly, Highsmith mounted his defense. He proved the allegations against his client to be not only false but completely without foundation. Buchanan didn't wait to hear the verdict of "not guilty." And the spotlight shifted back to Cushman.

Not much time remained. By a coincidence, which some pro-Buchanan commentators thought was a conspiracy, the

life of the grand jury officially ended on November 8—
election day. And the gubernatorial campaign was heating
up fast. High was beginning to worry. Kirk played it smooth,
evading the issues, talking at length about the virtues of a
"pro-business, antitax program," and returning always to the
problem of Miami crime. Again I warned the mayor that
crime had become a "gut issue," but he refused to change his
plans.

On October 19 the grand jury dropped a bomb. Five men
were named in indictments: ex-major Manson Hill; Lieutenant Colonel Leslie Van Buskirk; Sergeant David Helman;
Sergeant Peter Panos; and a well known burglar, Joseph
(Chicken) Cacciatore.

And this time the charges were dynamite—burglary, grand
larceny, and prostitution.

For weeks, in a dozen speeches, I had been repeating:
"There is a relationship between crimes of vice and crimes of
violence. An official can no more be half corrupt than a
woman can be half pregnant. A cop who will take with
one hand from a gambler, will take with the other from a
jewel thief."

The indictments seemed to confirm my theory.

I was proud of the *Herald* that day. It played the story
beautifully, and for once, carried the extra sidebars that gave
meaning and background. For impact, the front page
matched Renick's TV presentation.

Resignations competed with indictments as such top
officers as Captain Richard Gladwell and Lieutenant Richard
Wright quit the department. But Buchanan kept fighting—
proving once again that Sam's estimate of him as "weak" was
wrong. The indictments, he thundered, were false. There was
no crime in Dade County to speak of, he said. The whole
affair was a plot to undermine law enforcement, to deprive
citizens of the right to vote that their sons were dying in Viet
Nam to preserve.

And his allies on radio, television, and some elements of

the press, printed his propaganda and repeated his lies. For some years a bitter battle had raged in Dade County over metropolitan government, and Buchanan appealed to every prejudice the struggle had aroused. The unhappy truth seemed to be that while many people didn't trust the sheriff, they distrusted even more the political establishment. Remembering that the establishment once let Buchanan be appointed sheriff, I could see why the feeling of mistrust existed. In fact, I shared it.

The *Herald*, finally annoyed at having its thunder stolen by Renick, sought a quick way to make a contribution. I was asked to once more go out into the wilds of the central Negro district and check the numbers racket. The assignment seemed superfluous to me—only a few days earlier I had covered the arrest of one of Hymie Martin's principal lieutenants, as he left a counting house on Miami Beach. Special agents of the Internal Revenue Service had tailed him about Dade County for weeks, as he picked up thousands of bolita tickets. It was obvious action continued unhampered.

My old guide Charley consented to accompany me, and we made a sentimental journey of it. In one afternoon we revisited locations we had touched fourteen months before. Most of the old writers were still at their stations. The turmoil that had engulfed the county in the intervening months seemed to have passed almost unnoticed.

One thing had changed, however. The old sense of adventure, of discovery, was gone. I was getting old, I decided, and the act of retracing my steps had no appeal. It was a bit like covering the Kentucky Derby, I told Charley. The first assignment was fun, the second a bore. Charley grinned but disagreed. With an insight that surprised me, he delivered a theory.

"It ain't a gamble any more," he began. "Last year, it was all a big question mark. You didn't know if you could buy tickets. You didn't know if there was a syndicate, or if there was, what it would do. You couldn't even be sure the paper

would print your stories if you could get them. Today, you got all the answers so it ain't no fun."

The ex-gambler lighted a cigarette. "That ain't all," he continued, groping for words. "I figure you've changed a little. Last year you weren't a do-gooder exactly, but you had some idea of reforming us crooks. I don't get that feeling any more. You're not so sure now it makes any difference."

I managed to laugh, but Charley's words cut deep. Was he right? I didn't really know. When you get off the high road and fight with crooks on their own ground, you're likely to get a bit dirty. But I took the assignment without any illusions. After my experiences in Newport, I had known what would happen. So how could I be disillusioned?

Was it, instead, merely a question of realities? The world was changing. Old values, old frames of reference, were being discarded before new ones were ready. Perhaps the Gold Coast was ahead of the rest of the country in reaching a moral limbo. With an economy based largely on an overabundance of wealth—tourists and retired millionaires—this was possible. And in such an amoral society, would not citizens rely on the techniques of the gambler—the bluff and the bribe?

Ultimately, as man adjusts to the material wealth science is creating, new standards will evolve. A generation that looks to the stars will surely cherish and pass along the ideals that brought man out of the jungle. Meanwhile, however, the old order crumbles and confusion reigns.

Perhaps my adventures in south Florida had brought not disillusion, but understanding. And with understanding would naturally come a certain impatience with old methods. This is why our numbers-buying expedition had to seem dull and pointless. Risk existed still. If recognized by unfriendly deputies, arrest was possible on a charge of possession of bolita tickets. But risk without purpose provides little challenge, little justification.

We had bought ten tickets at as many locations. It was

nearing dinnertime. Charley planned to attend a football game in the Orange Bowl, and I was ready to go home.

The Herald played the story well and no doubt its editors convinced themselves it meant something.

Meanwhile, the grand jury met for the last time before turning in its final report on election day. Most observers were pessimistic. Surely little more could be expected. The jury had waited too long to get down to work with Cushman. But Snow White—as the special counsel was now known—still had a few surprises.

I rejected another long vigil outside the grand jury door and went home. The six o'clock news program on Channel Four merely noted the jury was still in session. I kept the set on, however, and about two hours later the first bulletin was read.

Five officers including Helman, Hill, and Van Buskirk had been indicted on new grand larceny counts.

Some thirty minutes later came the second bulletin—Sheriff Buchanan and Dave Schifrin had been indicted on charges of conspiring to accept bribes from gamblers and brothel operators.

Snow White had done his duty.

Three days later the citizens of Dade County put their seal of approval on the work of the grand jury. By a comfortable margin they voted to abolish the office of sheriff.

The full extent of the victory became apparent when the grand jury's final report—released too late to influence the voters—was published. Under a section entitled "Most Shocking Disclosures," the jury report stated:

> There was evidence of burglaries, thefts and similar crimes being planned and carried into effect with the knowledge of deputies.
>
> There was testimony that burglars and thieves were required to report the amount of their hauls and to divide with officers of the law.

There was evidence of a well organized system of "fences" through which the proceeds of burglaries, robberies or thefts were disposed of with knowledge of officers of the law.

The section dealing with vice concluded with these words:

The jury finds that during the past 10 or 15 years, gambling, prostitution and other forms of vice have flourished in Dade County with the obvious knowledge and active cooperation or tacit acquiescence of many local law-enforcement agencies.

There was much more—a rap at judges, a call for continued investigation. And Judge Henry Balaban, the man who had charged the outgoing grand jury, told the new one that it must continue the probe to "crush an invisible government with incredible powers."

More than a year before, on August 23, 1965, in my first memo to the editor, I had written:

There is in South Florida a second government. Invisible to many citizens, it is nonetheless real. It exists side by side with legally constituted agencies of government on all levels except the federal. Many legally elected or appointed officials hold high rank in this second government and use their constitutional authority to advance the aims of their real masters.

This was the time to quit. My job was done.

Becoming disengaged was not so easy. There was first a decision on what to do next. And this had become complicated. For with victory came defeat. Robert King High had been badly beaten by Republican Kirk, as around the country a flood of dissatisfaction swept Democrats from office. Even

in Dade County, High failed to get the large vote he had counted on—and I thought I knew why.

But with his defeat went the job he had offered—a chance to clean up the state. In a way, I wasn't unhappy. After fifteen years as a crime reporter, I was tired. My old dream of a Caribbean Island retreat was more attractive than ever.

That time of year was at hand—when the air is cool and the sun is hot. A time to rest and regain strength. A time to dream and a time to plan.

There was much to remember as I swung gently in a rope hammock in my own back yard. I stared up at the leaves of a mango tree and turned back the pages.

There was the night in Washington, D.C., last spring. Called to testify before the Long Committee, I had dashed off without packing. And in getting out of a cab, I heard a terrible sound—my trousers splitting.

Robert Peloquin, a friend in the Organized Crime Section of the Justice Department, came to my aid. Henceforth he would be known as "the Needle." He stitched the seam and laughed. Next day I sat before the Long Committee with much on my mind. Senator Long wanted me to blast the IRS and its wire-tapping practices. The IRS wanted me to say as little as possible. A television crew wanted me to blast Senator Long. And I hoped to put some heat on sheriff's deputies back in Florida who had tapped my phone, trailed me about, and smeared me from coast to coast.

But the big question worrying me was more basic—would Peloquin's stitches hold?

Another scene—the coast of Cuba looming rapidly from the blue-green waters of the Caribbean. And off that coast, a ship flying the red flag of the Soviet Union. Lieutenant Richard E. Jaffe, United States Coast Guard Reserve—in civilian life a talented Treasury agent—leaned through the open hatch and shot pictures. My story of that patrol and Jaffe's color picture of the red freighter made page one of the *Herald*. As an amusing sidelight, I later heard "feedback" from the underworld indicating that my presence aboard the Coast

Guard aircraft confirmed their belief that I was a "Fed" in disguise.

My mind skipped to another adventure. While guiding the television crew about Miami, we stopped to take a picture of the home of Morris Kleinman, charter member of the Cleveland Syndicate. A Bay Harbor Island cop interfered. We would have to have Mr. Kleinman's permission.

Walter Sheridan, Don Silverman, and I walked to the outer door of the patio. The old rum-runner, his white hair flying, met us in person. Sheridan introduced himself. Kleinman talked willingly—he knew damned well this was another of Messick's tricks.

As former head of Bobby Kennedy's top-priority "Get Hoffa Squad," Sheridan could handle a witness. He soon drew the admission that Messick had been right about Kleinman transferring a large sum from Las Vegas at a time when Fat Hymie Martin was expanding into Broward County. Kleinman denied it went to Hymie, however. When Silverman asked what happened to it, the gambler gaped in amazement.

"Do you think I'd tell you?" he said.

We prepared to leave. Kleinman followed us through the door, waved to the cameramen grinding away on the street, and shook hands all around. I was last in line, and he held on for a minute. "Are you Messick?" he demanded.

"Do you think I'd tell you?" I replied.

My thoughts turned to another house on the east side of Biscayne Bay—the home of Miami Beach Mayor Elliott Roosevelt. I sat in the huge living room beneath paintings of Elliott's parents, and wished my father could see me. President Roosevelt had been his beau ideal.

Elliott was big and tall, with the same wide grin, but it was his wife, Patti, who did most of the talking. She conceived a daring plan to clean up Miami Beach. With her help we could trap the Fruit Man, that friend of Hymie Martin. She would offer to sell out Elliott, and with a concealed mike record the evidence.

Mayor Roosevelt seemed unwilling to go along with the

plan, but when he left the room for a moment Patti told me she would try it without his knowledge if I could arrange things. I declined. Shortly thereafter I learned *Herald* columnist Charles Whited had signed to co-author Patti's life story. I agreed it should be interesting.

Another interesting story came to mind—the death of Petey Arnold. A Chicago boy, Pete was born Arnstein. As a man he was unfortunate in his publicity. Pete got no notices even when he moved to Miami in the 1940's and became president of Mother Kelly's Night Club. His partners—blimp-bellied Joe Sonken and Irving (Nig) Devine—got the headlines.

Perhaps the crowning blow came when Louis (Little New York) Campagna died on Pete's boat, the "Ollie A." Reporters overlooked Pete in their eagerness to describe others in the party—men like Joe Fischetti, Tony Ricci, and Paul (The Waiter) DeLucia.

Pete died of a heart attack in the bed of his mistress. The woman called a jewel thief who lived down the hall and together they pulled Pete out to his car. Local police cooperated and reported he died in the car. I got the story from the best sources but—for no apparent reason—the *Herald* denied Pete in death the publicity that had escaped in life. Nevertheless, I cherished the memory. Somehow, it seemed to fit into the pattern of an amoral society.

There were other things to remember, as I pulled the hammock out of the shade and peeled an orange from a nearby tree:

The incident only nights ago when police officers charged into the house with drawn guns as the kids dived beneath the nearest table. The officers explained they had seen a light flicker in the back yard, and the children crawled out in unanimous agreement that life was more fun than television. Not for the first time did I thank the honest cops of the Fort Lauderdale police department who continued an around-the-clock vigil until the afternoon of election day.

Christmas Eve and the calls from worried *Herald* execu-

tives who had just received anonymous warnings that a syndicate contract had been let for me. Allegedly, their imported enforcer was already in town. I discounted the story, but my back felt naked as I stood in front of a window carving the Christmas turkey.

The standing ovation given me by the congregation of Temple Israel after a determined effort had been made to brand me as antisemitic because of references to such men as Bugsy Siegel, Meyer Lansky, and—in another class—Richard Gerstein.

A handshake from a Negro policeman on the streets of Miami. The cop stopped me in broad daylight to tell me to keep fighting. "We're with you," he said.

The traffic ticket I got from a Dade deputy after making an illegal left turn to escape another deputy who was tailing me from the Pink House. You can't win, I told myself at the time.

And speaking of the Pink House, the face of Nan as she sought assurance that True Love is Most Important of All even if Sam wouldn't divorce his wife and marry her.

Much to remember and little time. For wheels set in motion were still turning. I could not stop them no matter how tired of battle I might become.

In Broward County, the trial of suspended Sheriff Michell was suddenly at hand. A miracle had been required to get the man indicted. Another miracle had brought him to trial. A third would be needed to get a conviction. And I was fresh out of miracles.

Since 1948, nine sheriffs had been elected along the Gold Coast—Dade, Broward, and Palm Beach Counties. Of those nine, six had been suspended or fired. Not one of those six had been convicted. The System protected its own.

While attention was focused on Dade, things had been happening in Broward. The third judge now sat in the case and the third solicitor was preparing to prosecute. The defense was ready for trial.

More as a gesture than anything, I appeared before the

fledgling Broward Crime Commission and warned that a directed verdict was now inevitable. The judge was on record as having said "a thousand men in the sheriff's department couldn't wipe out bolita." The prosecutor—a young assistant solicitor—had little experience and no real understanding of the case. Worse—although of this I said nothing—Emerson Allsworth had been defeated in the Republican sweep and was no longer interested in "assisting" me.

Once more I proved a prophet as the Michell trial became a replay of the Buchanan farce. Again I was pulled in as a witness and harrassed. This time, however, Judge Douglas Lambeth undertook to question me.

Lambeth, perhaps remembering the mistakes I had made in the Buchanan trial, tried to make me lose my temper. When I persisted in smiling—I, too, had learned a lesson—he lost his own temper and in an amazing display of malice ordered me taken into custody by the bailiff. A call to Attorney Highsmith resulted in my release, but I had not heard the last of Lambeth.

The trial ended exactly as I had predicted—in a directed verdict. Lame-duck Governor Burns reinstated Michell within the hour, and on the surface, at least, things were back where they had been eight months before.

But I knew differently. Broward County had enjoyed a period of good law enforcement for the first time in its history. Ironically, as if aware that time was running out, deputies on the eve of Michell's acquittal staged the biggest bolita raid in the history of the county. The Dania operation centering around the Paradise Club was the target, and the men Fat Hymie had courted years before were arrested.

The lesson of Dade County was plain—lasting reform could be achieved only at the ballot box. And I felt sure that when election day rolled around once more, the people of Broward would vote for reform.

I had another reason for confidence. A call came from George Wackenhut. He wanted to see me right away.

We sat in his Coral Gables office and I looked at a small bust of J. Edgar Hoover as he talked. A dedicated ex-FBI agent was George. Well, that was all right with me. I numbered others of that description among my friends.

Sitting straight and tall, George put it to me bluntly. He was planning—had been planning for years—a new section on organized crime. He was now ready to go ahead with it and was looking for a man to put in charge. The job was mine if I wanted it.

I thought of the sunlight on the Caribbean, of the clean air and the white sand. But Wackenhut wasn't finished.

Already we had our first customer, he said. Governor-elect Kirk had already retained the Wackenhut Corporation. His eyes on the 1968 Republican Vice-Presidential nomination, Kirk intended to do something about crime. He had turned to Wackenhut as an old friend, someone he could trust. The state of Florida—not just Miami or Dade County—would be the battlefield.

"It'll be your responsibility as head of the Organized Crime Section," said Wackenhut quietly. "You'll be in command."

I thought of the *Herald* and the confusion of good intentions still existing there. I brooded for a moment on the choices open to moral men in an amoral society. I recalled the gangsters who waited, confident in the assurance that an alliance for good was an unnatural arrangement. And last of all I thought of the nameless ones who had risked much to fight beside me.

Faint and far away, but unmistakable, the bugles sounded. As we shook hands, I wondered where I would put my autographed picture of Bobby Kennedy.

EPILOGUE

I TAKE A BACK SEAT

AND ENJOY THE RIDE

*

It is an unhappy fact that reform movements often begin to disintegrate in the moment of victory. Citizens seize upon any excuse to quit crusading. After all, civic virtue is a rather unnatural value in an amoral society, and excesses in pursuit of virtue can become embarrassing.

On the face of things, the citizens of Florida seemed to have excuse enough as 1967 began. E. Wilson Purdy, a professional law officer of highest caliber, was brought in to fill Tal Buchanan's shoes. And George Wackenhut was named "General" of Governor Kirk's "War on Crime." Nevertheless, the gangsters noticed a lessening of pressure and confidently expected the worst was over. The hurricane of public indignation had passed. Let Wackenhut and Purdy finish the job.

Purdy, for one, was not so optimistic as the citizens. He took charge of a department still riddled with corruption and protected by civil service. Many officers in key positions sought to hamper their new boss. Purdy was forced to move slowly, replacing men as opportunities developed. Both he and his new men had much to learn about the jungle that was Dade County. He was vulnerable in that he held his job by appointment. One slip and he could be removed, even as Sheriff Tom Kelly had been fired to make way for Buchanan.

Among those waiting for him to make a mistake was my old friend Sam, a bit disgruntled that after all his efforts he

236

still didn't control a sheriff. While waiting for Purdy to stumble, Sam sold the Pink House and took the ever-faithful Nan to a new hideout.

The "War on Crime" so loudly proclaimed by Kirk proved to be even less of an immediate threat. It was soon apparent to me that both Kirk and Wackenhut were more concerned with appearance than reality. They talked a good fight but achieved little.

The governor had begun campaigning for the Republican Vice-Presidential nomination within seconds of his election. The crime war was a propaganda tool in the new effort. Wackenhut also profited by the vast amount of publicity. He held daily press conferences as the stock in his company climbed from about six to twenty points per share. Meanwhile, a few retired ex-FBI agents were hired to fight crime. They knew little about the subject and had no great desire to learn. Wackenhut, who knew even less, finally gave me the authority he had promised. I exercised it for about ten days and managed to bring some order out of the complete confusion that existed behind the scenes. Among other things, I brought in my friend Shelby Highsmith as legal advisor—a move that was to have important consequences—and began probes aimed at Meyer Lansky and Jimmy Blue Eyes. Both men lived in Broward County. My period of authority came to an abrupt stop when I was told to halt all Broward probes until Judge Douglas Lambeth finished with me.

Back in November Lambeth had promised to cite me for contempt because of my prediction that the Michell trial would end in a directed verdict. I heard no more from him until my job with Wackenhut was made public late in December. On December 30, I was served with an order to show cause why I shouldn't be held in contempt. A hearing was set for January 27. Wackenhut assured me at the time there was nothing to worry about. After all, as of January 3, I would hold a commission as special investigator for the governor. Nevertheless, as indications mounted that Lambeth was de-

termined to put me in jail for six months, Wackenhut changed his tune. I was bluntly told that all probes in Broward would have to wait until the case was settled and that, furthermore, neither he nor the governor could intervene to help me.

I retained Shelby Highsmith to represent me, and Lambeth countered by appointing a special prosecutor. And suddenly I could detect the fine hand of Emerson Allsworth. The special prosecutor was the attorney whom Allsworth had brought to my home along with Larry Lang in the days an interim sheriff in Broward was being selected.

Not content with one prosecutor, Lambeth appointed another one in Dade to determine if I had said anything contemptuous down there. The newly appointed Dade prosecutor represented several Mafia extortionists in a case that began when the victim brought his story to me. I passed him to the FBI, which did its usual good job and convicted three of the men.

Other attorneys who had reason to dislike me were cooperating with the judge behind the scenes. Word spread that I was to be given six months in jail. My effectiveness as a reporter and as a special investigator were to be completely destroyed.

Once again I was alone at the end of a limb, but I had been there before. I talked to a few people in key positions. As a direct result, Highsmith was called to Fort Lauderdale by a representative of the judge. If I would make a public apology, the matter would be dropped. Shelby called me at Wackenhut's office for a decision. Loyally, I transferred the call to Wackenhut. I didn't want to apologize, but I did want to investigate Lansky. Shelby presented the situation to our mutual boss as I listened on an extension. Wackenhut told me to apologize.

The climax came in a carefully prepared drama next day in Lambeth's court. On cue, everyone spoke the lines written for him in advance. I almost blew mine. Half through the state-

ment, I became so angry my voice broke. The temptation to tear up the paper I was reading was overwhelming, and Shelby looked up in alarm as I wavered. But I had given my promise. Somehow I finished reading the statement, and the episode was over. I had escaped a jail sentence, but I felt dirty. My emotions weren't soothed any when Wackenhut blandly commented, "That wasn't so bad, was it?" When he casually added that we still should leave Broward County alone, I quit on the spot.

Shelby, who had not enjoyed the court scene either, persuaded me to continue. Things would change eventually, he said. I refused any more responsibility for the crime war, but I did agree to stay on as a collector of intelligence. I couldn't be sure anyone would read the memos I dictated, but it no longer seeemed to matter.

New disillusionment came quickly. Back in December I had written a long story for the *Herald* about the relation of syndicate gamblers in the Bahamas to such Bahamian officials as Sir Stafford Sands. A year before, I had exposed Lansky's connections with gambling there. Other writers for the *Wall Street Journal* had joined in and won a Pulitzer Prize in the process. Largely as a result, the voters tossed Sands and his "Bay Street Boys" out of office in January—an upset as unexpected as Kirk's victory. Now, suddenly, I saw a unique opportunity to justify the use of a private detective agency to fight crime. Already we were allegedly fighting Lansky in Florida. If the new government of the Bahamas could be persuaded to hire us to probe Lansky there, we could do what no official agency could do: work both sides of the Gulf Stream. I took the idea to Wackenhut. It was a good idea, he agreed, but unfortunately Sands was his client. In fact, Sands' daughter was working for Wackenhut in Miami. She didn't need to work, he added, but it was an easy way to keep an eye on her for Sir Stafford.

It was the final straw. I wanted nothing more to do with Wackenhut. George called it a "black day" when I resigned.

Just for fun I offered to stay on if he would let me go after Lansky. He declined.

I had thrown away a year's contract with the *Herald* to join Wackenhut. When I walked out after seven weeks, the underworld was sure I was up to something. It was another Messick trick. Apparently in an effort to learn more, the "spooks" began watching my house again. It seemed like old times.

Meanwhile, Wackenhut's alleged war dragged on for nine months. Very little was achieved, and for what was accomplished Shelby Highsmith deserved most of the credit. He managed to gain Kirk's confidence and took unofficial charge of the investigations. Recognizing the limitations of Wackenhut's staff, he turned the effort into a battle against local corruption rather than crime. A few successes gave Kirk something to brag about.

It soon became apparent to everyone but Wackenhut that any effective war on crime would require new legislation. A long fight between Kirk and the Florida Legislature followed, but in the end a Bureau of Law Enforcement was created, with statewide powers and ample financing. It took over on October 1, 1967, and Wackenhut's role as "General" was ended.

Appointed to head the new agency was my old friend Bill Reed. He could thank Highsmith for persuading Kirk to name him. A former cop turned law professor, Bill was young and aggressive. In fact, back when I was planning a crime war for Bob High—before his startling defeat—I had asked Reed to serve as my executive officer. He could now put to use for Kirk the elaborate plans we had prepared. Somehow, it seemed rather funny.

I'm sure Bob High would have appreciated the irony of Reed's appointment, the more so since Kirk had poked fun during the campaign at High's plans for fighting crime. But the red-headed Mayor of Miami—still recovering from the shock of his defeat—had suffered a heart attack in midsummer and died within hours.

In the weeks that followed my resignation from the crime war, I experienced moments of frustration. But gradually I began to enjoy the role of observer. If south Florida was to be cleaned up, more than one man was needed.

The Miami *Herald* made one effort to continue the campaign I had begun. Jim Savage and Clarence Jones dug into the ownership of Miami Beach hotels and were startled to learn that all I had told them was correct. Two of their three articles were published before a ten-million-dollar libel suit was filed against the newspaper. That brought the campaign to a screeching halt. After all the fears of *Herald* editors and attorneys over my stories, I found it interesting that the long-awaited suit should come only after I had left the paper. And suddenly I was popular again—the paper asked me to help them fight the suit.

Meanwhile, some of the indictments returned the previous year reached the courtroom. All went well at first. Constable Ray Bradley, who sometimes collected graft for Red Rainwater, was convicted. Dave Schifrin, the man who succeeded Roy O'Nan as county bagman in 1963, was next to be found guilty. And a new grand jury indicted Rainwater on perjury charges.

The "feds" scored as well. Gil (the Brain) Beckley was given ten years in prison. John (the Greek) Prokos was convicted in federal and state courts.

Apparently frightened by the willingness of trial juries to convict, attorneys for the remaining defendants changed their tactics. Their chance came when the U. S. Supreme Court ruled in the "Garrity Case" that a public official's testimony cannot be used against him if he was "coerced" into waiving his immunity for fear of losing his job. Tal Buchanan promptly claimed he was so coerced. A few days later, judges tossed out his indictment along with those of Manson Hill, Leslie Van Buskirk, George Busby, Ernest Ferguson, and David Helman.

Cushman filed an appeal against what he called "the retro-

active application" of the Garrity decision, but meanwhile, a case against a high-ranking Miami police officer was tossed out on the same grounds. In August a judge dismissed a Broward indictment against bolita boss Fred Chapman on the grounds that Cushman had promised him complete immunity.

Harry Prebish won another victory when the case against brothel boss Red Vaught collapsed. Testimony at the trial had established that the party was held, that Vaught and such deputies as Hill were present, and that prostitutes provided entertainment. Even the pictures of Red and the officers were introduced. But the key to the case was evidence Red actually paid the girls cash for their services. Two Texas officers had testified to the grand jury that he did, but the officers now refused to return to Miami for the trial. In their absence, Prebish admitted all the details but the essential one and offered no defense. Once again, Prosecutor Al Sepe lost another case.

The reaction continued and reached a climax when Judge Carling Stedman, a former aide of Gerstein, ruled that the grand jury that had followed the one advised by Cushman was illegally constituted. More indictments went down the drain, and again an appeal was filed. If nothing else, the appeals sufficed to keep the ex-deputies from demanding their old jobs back.

Another deputy was lost when two masked men tried to pull an eighteen-thousand-dollar stickup. One of the masked men was killed by deputies waiting on the scene. The other surrendered—and proved to be an off-duty deputy. Former Dade Sheriff's Captain Richard Gladwell also got into trouble. He was one of fourteen persons indicted in Pennsylvania on charges they defrauded an insurance company of $3,408,801.

In Dade, successive grand juries continued the practice of employing independent counsel. One of those selected in 1967 was Joseph Manners, a former special attorney for the Justice Department. I had recommended him the year before

for the post Cushman ultimately was given. When his chance came at last, Manners turned the tide. Working closely with Sheriff Purdy, he supervised a grand jury that began returning conspiracy indictments against scores of bolita figures, from operators down to writers. How many of them would result in convictions only time would tell, but the procedure made numbers suddenly hard to buy.

While all this was going on, a gang war of sorts broke out. Days after Fat Hymie Martin was released from jail after serving five months for contempt, the body of Nate Ehrenberg was found floating in Biscayne Bay. Nate had taken over the numbers racket for the syndicate when Hymie first got hot. Apparently someone was unsatisfied with the way he operated it.

Hymie vanished, reportedly returning to Pittsburgh. And in the power vacuum he left behind, other men began to move. Bombs began going off all along the Gold Coast. More and more bodies were found. Governor Kirk held a press conference and announced there would be no more, but apparently the gangsters weren't listening. The killings continued.

The press was unable to find out what was going on, and I for one didn't try. It seemed safe to assume that eventually— if and when the public returned to apathy—the syndicate would stop the killings, install a new bagman, and return to business. The stage would then be set for a new cycle of reform. In the meantime, I could ponder the FBI's crime report for 1966. During that year of turmoil Dade County had dropped from second to third place in the nation. Broward County had fallen from sixth to fourteenth.

Why did Broward County improve so much more than Dade? My old friend Dick Basinger noted that whereas Tal Buchanan was out of office in Dade for only about five months in 1966, Allen Michell in Broward had been out from March to November.

That observation seemed to sum it up very nicely.

INDEX

Adams, Bob, 176, 194–97
Allsworth, Emerson, 99, 107, 111, 112, 117–18, 174–75, 179–81, 195, 238
Alo, Vincent, 14, 137, 139, 142, 144, 163, 167
Altamura, Tommy, 68
Anderson, Bert, 190
Anderson, Jack, 89, 95
Anderson, Norman, 190
Arnstein, Peter, 89, 232

Balaban, Henry, 221, 229
Barry, Gene, 141
Basinger, Dick, 66–67, 70, 74–75, 81, 86–92, 106–13, 118, 141, 152–53, 172, 173, 180, 243
Batista, Fulgencio, 18
Baynes, Bill, 151
Beckley, Gil, 51, 187, 241
Beebe, George, 7, 8, 123, 134, 198
Blout, Charles, 26–28
Bolita drawings, 24–28, 75–76, 121, 234
Bourke, George, 137–41
Bradley, Ray, 241
Brink, Jimmy, 42
Broward brothel, 29–45
Broward County, Florida: crime rate in, 221; election of sheriffs in, 233
Broward County Grand Jury: 151–57, 158; investigates syndicate, 166–78; special session petition of, 161–62
Broward Crime Commission, 234
Buchanan, T. A., 61, 65, 71, 73, 77, 78, 84–85, 105–106, 179, 184, 191–92, 200, 204, 212–16, 217, 218, 225–26, 228, 236, 241, 243

Buchanan, Mrs. T. A., 215
Buckley, Francis, 181–82
Burns, Haydon, 110, 111, 113, 117–18, 127, 174, 180, 192–94, 196, 197, 217, 234
Busby, George, 241

Cacciatore, Joseph, 225
Calvary Grace Christian Church of Faith, 148
Campagna, Louis, 232
Capone, Al, 88, 191
Capone, Mandy, 88
Carinci, Tito, 51
Castro, Fidel, 13, 18, 23, 139, 165
Chapman, Fred, 76, 242
Cheeseboxes, 46–52
Christian, James, 76, 163
City Commission of Miami, 189, 190–91
Clark, Walter, 87, 94, 121
Cleveland Syndicate, 12–13, 41, 42, 231
Clode, Ed, 67–72, 85, 95, 159, 174, 188
Cook, Henry, 224
Coppola, Mrs. Mike, 160
Cosa Nostra, La, 137
Costello, Frank, 139, 144
Cuban National Lottery, 18, 22, 23, 165
Cushman, Lucius, 210–16, 220, 228, 241–43

Dade County, Florida: crime rate in, 221; election of sheriffs in, 233; government of, 76
Dade County Grand Jury: 2–6, 61–64, 108, 179, 190, 242; crime re-